Child & Adolescent
Psychopathology

This book is dedicated to my children, Luke and Rachel, who always inspire me to be the best; to my mother, Jean, who taught me how to do it; and to Fred, for his continued support and encouragement.

Child & Adolescent Psychopathology

A Casebook

Linda Wilmshurst

SAGE Publications
International Educational and Professional Publisher
Thousand Oaks ▪ London ▪ New Delhi

For information:

 Sage Publications, Inc.
2455 Teller Road
Thousand Oaks, California 91320
E-mail: order@sagepub.com

Sage Publications Ltd.
6 Bonhill Street
London EC2A 4PU
United Kingdom

Sage Publications India Pvt. Ltd.
B-42, Panchsheel Enclave
Post Box 4109
New Delhi 110 017 India

Printed in the United States of America

Library of Congress Cataloging-in-Publication Data
Wilmshurst, Linda.
Child and adolescent psychopathology : a casebook / by Linda Wilmshurst.
   p. cm.
Includes bibliographical references and index.
ISBN 0-7619-2781-6 (paper)
  1. Child psychopathology—Case studies. 2. Adolescent psychopathology—Case studies. I. Title.
RJ499.W46 2003
618.92′89—dc211

                 2003009608

This book is printed on acid-free paper.

03 04 05 06 07 10 9 8 7 6 5 4 3 2 1

Acquisitions Editor:	Jim Brace-Thompson
Editorial Assistant:	Karen Ehrmann
Production Editor:	Julia Parnell
Copy Editor:	Kristin Bergstad
Typesetter:	C&M Digitals (P) Ltd.
Indexer:	Michael Ferreira
Cover Designer:	Janet Foulger

Contents

Preface

Tell me and I'll forget. Show me, and I may not remember. Involve me, and I'll understand.

—Native American Proverb

The major goal of this casebook is to provide the reader with an opportunity to gain deeper insight into the complexities of childhood psychopathology. A case study approach is used to *involve* the reader in the simulated practice of child psychopathology. As problems unfold, a dynamic illustration of a given child's problems can be observed during several different stages of development and from the perspective of different theoretical viewpoints. Within a developmental context, complex problems of child and adolescent adjustment become grounded in the realities of family and school experiences. Case studies presented in this text are especially relevant to the study of child psychopathology, because all cases are based on actual clinical cases. Although the cases have been altered to maintain confidentiality, they continue to represent actual *living files,* and as such, provide a unique opportunity to capture the dynamics of childhood psychopathology in virtual presentations of life as the children develop and unfold before the reader's eyes.

Cases have been selected to include a breadth of childhood and adolescent psychopathology and are representative of the high rates of comorbidity demonstrated in this population. Each case presents an opportunity to practice and develop clinical skills in the assessment, diagnosis, and treatment of childhood disorders from a number of theoretical perspectives and at various levels of interest and expertise. The text is suitable for upper-level undergraduate students in its rich presentation of case materials that demonstrate applications of many of the core concepts in child psychopathology (e.g., how therapists from differing theoretical backgrounds would approach a given case). The text is suitable for graduate students in providing opportunities to practice and hone clinical skills across a breadth of clinical cases with opportunities for in-depth discussion and application in specialty areas of concentration: assessment, diagnosis, and treatment. The text can be a valuable resource for courses in child psychopathology, abnormal child psychology, developmental psychopathology, child psychotherapy, child assessment, and case formulation in child psychopathology.

- *Case studies provide diagnostic information* at two levels. Case studies are presented to illustrate the *dual nature of diagnosis* in its emphasis on *diagnosis as case formulation* (ongoing process of information gathering, problem solving, hypothesis testing) and *diagnosis as the formulation of an outcomes statement* (classification or conclusion).

- *Case studies provide comprehensive assessment information.* Case information is available from a variety of sources (case history, observations, psychometric assessment, raw data, clinical interviews) and developmental contexts (individual child, family, school, peers) to encourage students to develop skills in integrating information from diverse sources.

- *Case studies provide opportunities to develop and practice skills in case formulation.* A semi-structured flexible format for case formulation is presented and demonstrated to emphasize how case formulation can apply to a wide variety of theoretical perspectives and developmental contexts. Each case provides an opportunity to develop case formulations that address developmental issues relative to the case and to evaluate outcomes relative to expectations.

- *Case studies provide information on current research findings and conceptual issues.* Questions posed at the end of each case will challenge the reader to integrate information concerning conceptual issues and/or research findings with material presented in each case.

- *Case studies provide information concerning Evidence Based Treatments (EBTs).* Each case is accompanied by a discussion of current *Issues in Treatment.* However, advanced students can also have the challenging opportunity of forging new directions in integrating information from effectiveness studies in the development of individual intervention plans and a "case-based" pragmatic approach to treatment (Fishman, 2000).

- *Case studies provide opportunities to discuss issues in classification from a variety of conceptual frameworks and different systems of service delivery.*

■ *Case studies demonstrate unique issues in the classification of childhood disorders.*

Research has demonstrated that insecure attachment and social skills deficits can have a profound impact on a child's mental health; however, for purposes of classification, neither of these maladaptive patterns is recognized by *DSM* (*Diagnostic and Statistical Manual of Mental Disorders*) as a disorder. Other issues in classification include: variations between classification systems (categorical, dimensional, developmental) and unique classification features within different systems of service delivery (mental health vs. education).

Although the case study can be seen to provide the materials necessary to develop and enhance clinical skills in all the areas listed above, the reader should not lose sight of the fact that, ultimately, each case study in this text is a story about a lost child. In these "living files," the children have lost the path to normal development. Based on clues provided in the story, the reader's goals are to determine a child's current path relative to normal adjustment and redirect the child's course in the right direction. With these goals in mind, read their stories and develop your expertise so that you can be better prepared to help the next child who may find you.

About the Author

Linda Wilmshurst, Ph.D., ABBP, received her doctorate from the University of Toronto and has had extensive international involvement with children and adolescents in academic, clinical, and school settings. As a university professor, she has taught in the Clinical and School Psychology programs at Texas Women's University, University of Houston, Victoria, and the University of Western Ontario. As a practitioner, she has provided school psychological services in Ontario and Florida, and has held clinical positions as the Senior Psychologist at Madame Vanier Children's Services (a children's outpatient and residential mental health center); Psychologist at a Provincial Residential School for Severely Learning Disabled Youth; and as a consultant to Thames Valley Children's Center (a rehabilitative center for children and youth with neuromuscular disorders), and the Provincial School for the Deaf. Her research expertise centers on high-risk youth with a focus on enhancing social skills through community recreation and an evaluation of community-based treatment alternatives for youth with severe conduct disorder. She is a Diplomate in Clinical Psychology, American Board of Professional Psychology, and is a licensed clinical and school psychologist. Her combination of professional practitioner experience and university teaching/research, internationally, gives her a perfect background for constructing this casebook. In her course work and in supervising interns, she has come to appreciate how a case study approach is the best way to develop skills in case formulation that inherently link treatment objectives to empirically based interventions.

List of Tables

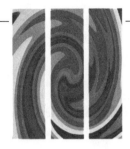

PART I

Child and Adolescent Psychopathology and Case Formulation

UNDERSTANDING THE COMPLEXITIES OF CHILD AND ADOLESCENT PSYCHOPATHOLOGY

A fundamental challenge inherent in the study of child and adolescent psychopathology is that the task of distinguishing normal from atypical behavior is a complex endeavor. There are several reasons for the complexity involved in making this distinction in childhood and adolescence.

Ten Reasons Why Child and Adolescent Psychopathology Can Be Complex: The Many Faces of Childhood

Determining "normal" from "abnormal" behavior requires an ability to determine whether the *degree* to which the behavior is demonstrated (intensity, duration, and frequency) is *atypical,* and requires:

1. Knowledge of what is *normal or atypical within a developmental stage:* for example, knowledge that at 3 years of age temper tantrums are often a common occurrence, whereas frequent acts of interpersonal aggression are not typical behaviors for a 3-year-old.

2. Knowledge of what is *normal or atypical between or across developmental stages:* for example, knowledge that frequent tantrum behavior is common at 3 years of age, but atypical behavior for a 10-year-old.

The ability to recognize the signs and manifestations of maladaptive behavior requires:

3. Knowledge of *how child psychopathology is manifested at various developmental levels:* for example, the many faces of childhood depression, which may appear as "failure to thrive" in infancy; acting-out in preschoolers; or substance abuse in adolescents.

4. Knowledge that *adult disorders may present differently in childhood:* for example, the "depressed/sad" features of adult depression may appear as "irritable mood" in a child.

Recognition of high rates of overlapping and comorbid symptoms requires:

5. Knowledge of common *comorbid internalizing disorders* such as depression and anxiety, which may appear undifferentiated as "negative affectivity" prior to adolescence.

6. Knowledge of common *comorbid externalizing disorders* such as attention-deficit/hyperactivity disorder (ADHD), oppositional defiant disorder (ODD), and conduct disorder (CD).

7. Knowledge of the tendency for specific disorders, like ADHD, to co-occur often with several other *externalizing* (oppositional defiant disorder and conduct disorder) *and internalizing* (anxiety, depression) *disorders* and learning disabilities.

Recognition of the importance of situational or contextual variables in understanding the underlying dynamics of problem behaviors:

8. Knowledge that *situational or contextual variables* also play a significant role in the evaluation of child and adolescent problems and solutions and that behaviors may be more evident in one environment (home) than another (school) or pervasive across situations.

Risks and protective factors can also serve a preventative function in early detection of signs associated with maladjustment.

9. Knowledge of risks and protective factors can alert to warning signs and assist in the development of preventative measures.

There is an understanding that there are several possible pathways that may produce the same outcome—*equifinality*—and that similar risks may produce different outcomes—*multifinality* (Cicchetti & Rogosch, 1996).

10. The importance of including the developmental context in child and adolescent evaluations is crucial to a thorough understanding of not only a child's present level of distress or dysfunction, but of how the difficulties came to be *(developmental pathway)*. An understanding of the underlying processes that trigger and maintain maladaptive behaviors can serve to enhance our ability to produce case formulations (Shirk & Russell, 1996) that focus on developmentally appropriate treatment planning.

Finally, a comment regarding the nature of the referring source, itself, which is an additional complicating factor. Whereas adults often self-refer, referrals for childhood problems mostly result from adult concerns. However, behaviors that may be concerning to parents (nightmares, aggression, overactivity) are often frequently reported in "normal" children. In addition, there may be wide variations evident in parent responsiveness to a child's given problems, based on extraneous and intervening circumstances at the time (tolerance level, awareness, environmental or family stressors).

OVERVIEW OF THE CASEBOOK

The casebook is designed to involve the child clinician in the process of developing case formulations for children and adolescents who demonstrate a wide variety of maladaptive thoughts, behaviors, and feelings. Using "A Case Called Jeremy" as a guide, Part 1 of the text outlines the three stages of case formulation (problem identification, problem explanation, and treatment solutions) and identifies important areas of knowledge and expertise required to optimize understanding and success in achieving the goals at each stage. "A Case Called Jeremy" involves the reader in the ongoing process of case formulation as new information is added and as hypotheses are generated and reformulated from a variety of theoretical perspectives.

In Part 2 of the text the reader is provided with opportunities to apply knowledge and practice skills in developing case formulations for 14 cases representing a wide variety of child and adolescent problems. Cases provide an in-depth look at the multiple pathways that can lead to maladaptive behaviors and how children can be buffered from harm or become increasingly more vulnerable based on individual and environmental (family, school, peers) influences. Each case is followed by a discussion of empirically based treatments and post-case questions that challenge the reader to apply theory and research to case-based practice.

Last, but certainly not least, supplemental information provided in Appendixes A through C contributes a wealth of additional information for advanced areas of study. In Appendix A, students in assessment will find the raw data provided for four of the cases especially appealing and are encouraged to use this additional information in case formulation and report writing exercises. A sample report and exercise in differential diagnoses is also provided for the Case of Colby. "A Clinician's Guide to Educational Classification," available in Appendix B, provides an in-depth view of the educational classification of four primary childhood disorders—a must for advising parents and for integrating assessment results within a school-based setting. Information regarding specific assessment instruments and resources referred to in the case studies is available in Appendix C.

BUILDING A CASE FOR CASE FORMULATION

It has been estimated that 4 million youth (11% of all youth) in the United States suffer from significant mental illness resulting in seriously impaired functioning at home, school and in their relationships with peers (Shaffer et al., 1996). The most frequent reason that parents seek clinical support for their children is for disruptive behavior, including defiance, temper tantrums and aggression (Offord, Adler, & Boyle, 1986; Quay, 1986).

INTRODUCING . . . A CASE CALLED JEREMY

Segment One: The Intake

Jeremy is a 6-year-old Caucasian boy who was referred for psychological assessment by his pediatrician. Jeremy lives with his mother and maternal grandmother. Jeremy takes Adderol twice daily (morning and noon) and Resperdol three times daily (morning, noon, and evening). Jeremy has been taking Adderol for 2 years and Resperdol for the past year. Medications were prescribed to assist in controlling Jeremy's behavior, which has been described as hyperactive, impulsive, and noncompliant. Despite suspicions of his family and pediatrician that Jeremy is a very bright boy, this year Jeremy is repeating the kindergarten program, since he was considered "too immature" to progress to Grade 1.

Jeremy's mother provided the following background information. Jeremy weighed 7 pounds, 6 ounces at birth. The pregnancy, labor, and delivery were all described as normal. However, Jeremy was severely jaundiced at birth and remained in the hospital for 5 days while he was placed under special lights called bili-lights, which alleviated the jaundice. It was determined that neonatal jaundice was the result of G6PD Deficiency (an inherited human enzyme deficiency). The G6PD condition results in an allergic reaction to fava beans, which can induce a severe anemic response. A similar response could develop if Jeremy developed viral hepatitis or pneumonia. Due to a vulnerability to developing allergic responses, he is monitored by his pediatrician, and all medication trials have been closely supervised. Jeremy has had no adverse reactions to the Adderol or the Resperdol.

According to his mother, Jeremy's milestones were achieved ahead of schedule: walking at 8 months and speaking in simple phrases at 7 months. Despite this remarkably early language development, Jeremy experienced articulation problems in his first years, which his mother attributes to constant bouts of recurring ear infections. However, by 2½ years, his vocabulary development continued to escalate. According to his mother, Jeremy was using words such as *humiliation* and *victimization* in his conversation and would also engage in long conversations about experiments he was conducting in his "laboratory." Currently, Jeremy is receiving assistance for articulation from the speech pathologist at the school.

Shortly after his second birthday, Jeremy began using *No* as a retort for everything and, according to his mother and grandmother, power struggles have been going on ever since. According to grandmother, "Jeremy is as stubborn as a mule!" However, as much as Jeremy will say "No" or "I *amn't* gonna do it," he can be relentless when he is given the same treatment. In these circumstances, "Jeremy just won't take *No* for an answer." Jeremy coined the word *amn't* as a short version of "am not" when he was about 2 years of age, and his mother and grandmother continue to find it very amusing and have repeatedly taunted him with it, saying they "amn't gonna do it either."

According to mother and grandmother, Jeremy can argue about anything and everything and will "throw a fit" if he does not win the argument and get his way. Although he likes to be challenged by doing difficult tasks, like puzzles, he is very quickly frustrated and easily upset when he can't solve something. His mother believes that these behaviors have caused problems with the other children at school as well, because Jeremy can be very stubborn and always wants to be the first in line or the first to do anything. Jeremy will push others out of the way in order to be first, and many of the other children do not want to play with him.

Jeremy was described as a very active and curious toddler. He was generally a good sleeper (mother said that he just wore himself out) and had a good appetite. According to mother, Jeremy has always had his "good days and bad days." He can be fun and playful, but then again, he can be very difficult and demanding. There were some difficulties with "potty training" and once again, parents suggested this might be due to Jeremy's stubborn nature.

Grandmother said that eventually he was trained by 3 years of age; however, she attributes successful training to monetary rewards. At one point, grandmother was rewarding successful potty episodes at $5.00 each.

When asked about any health issues, mother stated that Jeremy has been in good health. He has not had an ear infection in the past 2 years. He is vulnerable to skin rashes and seasonal allergies. They believe that Jeremy inherited both of these conditions from his grandmother, who has significant bouts of psoriasis and allergies to pollens and grasses.

Reportedly Jeremy loves to go to school, but he has had considerable difficulty adjusting to formal school routines and expectations. There have been problems with the other children due to Jeremy's impulsive and willful behaviors, as well as his tendencies to carry boisterous and loud activities from the schoolyard into the classroom, resulting in frequent classroom disruptions. It was the consensus (home and school) that Jeremy should be retained in kindergarten due to issues of immaturity, problems relating to peers, and lack of productivity regarding academic schoolwork. His teacher was unable to estimate Jeremy's current levels of functioning due to issues of noncompliance and failure to complete assigned work.

When asked why they were concerned enough at this point to have Jeremy assessed, the reply initially was that it was the pediatrician's recommendation. When pressed further, mother and grandmother stated that they were very interested in knowing what Jeremy's IQ was.

Question

Does Jeremy suffer from a significant mental illness? According to Shaffer and colleagues (1996), chances are approximately 1:10 that he does. If Jeremy has a disruptive behavior disorder, how typical is he of the host of other children referred for behavior disorders? What information does the clinician require to determine whether or not Jeremy's difficulties fall within this clinical range? And how does the clinician determine the unique features of Jeremy's problem relative to other clinically referred children? What are the essential questions that need to be addressed?

Kronenberger and Meyer (2001) present a framework for diagnosis, assessment, and treatment based upon three essential questions that must be answered by the child clinician. The authors suggest that regardless of the presenting problem or the theoretical background of the therapist, the child clinician is usually faced with providing answers to three primary questions:

1. What are the primary characteristics of the child's problem?

2. How does the clinician conduct an in-depth evaluation of the problem?

3. How does the clinician decide which interventions are appropriate?

The authors suggest that each of the questions addresses a specific issue or aspect of child psychopathology. Clinicians respond to the first question when they choose to characterize a child's problem through the use of a *diagnostic category,* or provide a *provisional diagnosis* or *a case formulation* based upon presenting information of symptoms and features. The second question involves the in-depth evaluation or assessment process and requires knowledge of appropriate *interview and observational techniques, as well as broad assessment strategies* (e.g., cognitive, behavioral emotional functioning), and *syndrome-specific tests* (e.g., instruments to detect anxiety, depression, etc.) to assist in confirming or ruling out potential diagnoses. The final question requires knowledge of evidence-based treatment methods (EBTs) that can be applied to modify the problem (Kronenberger & Meyer, 2001, pp. 1-2).

Although the questions can be answered by the majority of theoretical viewpoints, Held (1996) suggests that there is a greater need for therapists to spend more time reconsidering the nature and composition of the theoretical system that guides their practice in what she calls the *three predetermined components* of therapy:

1. what constitutes problems or impediments to solutions

2. what causes those problems or impediments to occur

3. what methods can help clients to solve their problems, overcome their impediments and obtain their goals. (p. 37)

Since responses to all three components can be highly influenced by theoretical background, it is very important that clinicians are aware of their own theoretical biases in forming their opinions. Looking at a case through a set of theoretically colored glasses can affect all aspects of information processing, including: hypothesis testing, problem formulation, problem selection, observation, assessment, interpretation, and treatment. The influence of theory on practice will become increasingly clear as case formulations are constructed from various theoretical viewpoints and applied to the case study of Jeremy.

In addition to theoretical framework, another influence that can impact on the formulation of clinical impressions and questions is the role of previous experience. According to Fishman (2000), *experts* and *novices* approach case formulation in different ways. Experts assess cases guided by theoretical assumptions, relevant research, and previous recollections of similar cases (an internal database). With these tools in hand, experts can then adapt information to apply to the unique features of the new case. However, novices, lacking experience and an internal database, often follow rules and procedures in a cookbook fashion, without attending to the unique features of the individual case. With this in mind, case studies presented in this text have been designed to assist the developing practitioner in acquiring a range of case-based information and providing opportunities to apply theory to practice through the process of developing diverse case formulations.

CASE FORMULATION AND CHILD AND ADOLESCENT PSYCHOPATHOLOGY

Regardless of theoretical orientation, increased emphasis has been placed on the role of *case formulations* in linking empirical research to practice initiatives and treatment planning. In recent years, several books and articles have addressed the importance of *case formulation* (Eells, 1997; McWilliams, 1999; Shirk & Russell, 1996), *case conceptualization* (Berman, 1997; Stevens & Morris, 1995), and *problem-solving strategies* (Mash & Terdal, 1997) in the identification of individual and situational determinants of maladaptive behavior. Case formulation has been explored by proponents of the majority of theoretical perspectives, including: *psychodynamic* (Eells, 1997; McWilliams, 1999; Shirk & Russell, 1996), *behavioral* (Barlow, 1986; Kazdin, 1983; Mash & Terdal, 1997; Turkat, 1985), *cognitive-behavioral* (Bruch & Bond, 1999; Persons, 1989), and *family systems* perspectives (Berman, 1997). Within the realm of child psychopathology, research linking child outcomes to *parenting styles* (Baumrind, 1991; Patterson, DeBaryshe, & Ramsay, 1989; Sroufe & Fleeson, 1986), and *attachment patterns* (Ainsworth, Blehar, Waters, & Wall, 1978); Belsky, 1988; Sroufe, 1983) suggests that these areas could also provide rich materials for weaving into the fabric of case formulations.

Weerasekera (1996) defines *case formulation* as a process conducted to provide a "hypothesis of how an individual comes to present with a certain disorder or circumstance at a particular point in time" (p. 5). Therefore, the case formulation can provide a guiding framework for assessing and organizing information in a manner that allows for movement beyond a diagnosis based upon symptom description. The goal of the case formulation is to develop treatment plans based on information regarding not only whether the behavior, thought, or emotion is deviant, but hypotheses concerning how this behavior/thought/emotion developed and why it is being maintained. Although the concept of case formulation has its origins in the psychodynamic approach, the organizational framework inherent in this approach is readily adaptable to a variety of theoretical approaches. The usefulness of the case formulation approach is gaining increased recognition across a wide variety of theoretical perspectives regarding adult as well as child populations (Hersen & Porzelius, 2002; Shirk & Russell, 1996).

Shirk and Russell (1996) have adapted the case formulation approach to accommodate a developmental psychopathology framework. Within this paradigm, the authors suggest the need for therapies to uncover and target for change *those underlying processes* that serve to precipitate and maintain the disorder. Based on the concept of developmental pathways, the authors argue that treating the disorder without knowing the underlying processes is risky business. For example, if Jeremy is diagnosed with oppositional defiant disorder (ODD), and the clinician treats Jeremy like a generic ODD case and applies a "brand name" treatment, there is a risk that the clinician may not be targeting the true processes that are instrumental in causing and maintaining the disorder in Jeremy's specific case. Knowledge of *developmental pathways* and *equifinality* (Cicchetti & Rogosch, 1996) suggests that there are several different ways that ODD might be caused, and an important facet of developing a treatment plan for Jeremy would be to isolate those *underlying processes* or unique features responsible for causing and maintaining Jeremy's behaviors. McWilliams (1999), another strong proponent of the case formulation approach, also emphasizes the need for individual case-based treatments and cautions that the recent fervor over EBTs (empirically based treatments) and manualized treatments is de-emphasizing the importance of focusing on the clinically unique features of each case.

Although Shirk and Russell (1996) apply case formulation to several theoretical perspectives (psychodynamic, humanistic, and cognitive), they do so from a perspective of change processes directed at changing "internal" representations only. In their discussion of the Shirk and Russell model, Wenar and Kerig (2000) demonstrate how case formulations can be adapted to target changes in the environment as well, thereby adding behavioral and systemic theories to the mix.

The case formulation approach is a good match for child psychopathology because it supports an understanding of underlying processes (cognitive, behavioral, and emotional) that can be applied to an ecological systems model (Bronfenbrenner, 1979, 1989) and provides an opportunity to address how risks and protective factors can impede or assist treatment. The approach also provides a unique opportunity to guide therapeutic interventions in a way that melds research findings within the context of ecological validity. The framework is pliable enough to accommodate information from most theoretical frameworks.

The *case formulation* approach is particularly well suited to clinical/developmental child concerns, because the approach

1. is applicable to child, adolescent, and adult populations;

2. supports an understanding of underlying processes (cognitive, behavioral, and emotional);

3. supports an ecological systems model (Bronfenbrenner, 1979, 1989) and readily allows for consideration of the impact of personal and environmental factors on past and present functioning at several levels: *individual, immediate, social & economic,* and *culture*;

4. provides an opportunity to address how risks and protective factors can impede or assist treatment;

5. provides a unique opportunity to guide therapeutic interventions in a way that melds research findings within an ecologically valid context;

6. is particularly compatible with behavioral therapy, which has demonstrated positive research outcomes for children in a number of areas (Weisz, Weiss, Han, Granger, & Morton, 1995);

7. can also accommodate cognitive behavioral training programs such as those that have been demonstrated to reduce anxiety (Kendall et al., 1992) and depression (Stark, Reynolds, & Kaslow, 1987);

8. is compatible with parent training programs in behavioral methods that have been suggested as one of the most effective treatment methods of treating disruptive disorders (Spaccarelli, Cotler, & Penman, 1992);

9. is pliable and can accommodate multimodal programs, such as programs designed for children with attention deficit hyperactivity disorder (ADHD), that combine parent education, psychosocial treatment (behavior and contingency management), and pharmacology (Barkley, 1997).

Three Stages in Case Formulation: A Conceptual Model

As a construct, case formulation conforms to the set of *three essential questions* suggested by Kronenberger and Meyer (2001) and the *three predetermined components* of therapy identified by Held (1996). The model of case formulation presented in Table 1.1 has been developed as means-end heuristic to assist the *novice clinician* in identifying sources of knowledge and competencies that may assist in answering the necessary questions at each stage of the process.

Table 1.1   Three Stages of Case Formulation: Goals, Process, and Influences

Stage	Goals (What)	Process (How)	Success in Achieving Goals:	
			Knowledge	Competencies
1. Problem Identification/ Clarification	Determine nature of child's problem Focus: **Pinpoint** the problem	Differential diagnoses	Etiology of disorders Child development Developmental contexts Classification systems Abnormal child Risk and protective factors Research Assessment	Convergent thinking Attention to detail Data analysis Decision making
2. Problem Interpretation/ Understanding	Clinical impression of precipitating & maintaining variables Focus: **Magnify** the problem	Generate Hypotheses re: dynamics of problem	Theoretical assumptions: • Psychodynamic • BioMedical • Behavioral • Cognitive • Family systems • Attachment/ Parenting Empirical findings	Divergent thinking Flexible thinking Contextualize problem Pattern recognition Application of theories to practice & research to practice Integration of information from diverse sources Analysis & synthesis
3. Treatment Formulation	Develop an effective treatment plan	Linking problems to solutions Monitoring treatment effectiveness	Efficacy treatments Effectiveness treatments (EBTs)	Synthesis of information Contextualize solution Evaluation & monitoring

Stage 1: Problem Identification

The degree to which the clinician is successful in identifying the problem can be influenced by several factors, including: knowledge of normative expectations, awareness of the etiology of disorders, and familiarity with empirical research. The range of assessment methods employed (observation, interview, psychological tests, rating scales, projectives) and nature of information generated can all impact on isolating a problem for further investigation.

In some multiple-problem cases, differential diagnoses may be complex and there may be a need to prioritize among problem areas based on urgency and/or severity of problems. At this stage, emphasis is often placed on the acquisition of information using a wide variety of assessment techniques and sampling information across various ecological contexts (home and school).

One outcome of a comprehensive assessment might be that what was originally thought to be "the main problem" is actually secondary to another problem identified by the assessment. As a process, case formulation is subject to revision and reformulation. Decision-making skills, convergent thinking processes, attention to detail, and the ability to see consistent patterns in a child's behavior are all competencies that will help to clarify the nature of the problem.

Stage 2: Problem Interpretation/Understanding

While the goal at Stage 1 is to narrow the focus and pinpoint the problem, once the problem is identified the next step is to place the problem under a microscope and magnify with a lens to discover how the problem developed and how it is being maintained. At this stage, divergent thinking is required to generate hypotheses regarding a number of possible pathways that may have led to the problem. Historical data can provide important information regarding possible genetic (family pathology) or event-based causes (family or school history, traumatic events, etc.). Knowledge of risks and protective factors may assist in better understanding possible factors that might exacerbate or moderate the problem.

At this stage, theoretical assumptions can have a profound impact on generating hypotheses to explain how the problem developed. It becomes increasingly important to be aware of theoretical biases and to substantiate hypotheses with empirical support. Success at this level is increased by the ability to apply research findings to the unique contextual features of the case. At the beginning of Stage 2, emphasis is placed on generating a number of possible hypotheses to explain the problem. Toward the end of this stage, decision making is required to select potential working hypotheses in order to develop a treatment plan. The ability to integrate information from diverse sources provides a deeper understanding of the nature of the problem, the dynamics surrounding the problem, and how the problem is embedded in context. The degree of success in achieving the goal of Stage 2, *determining what is precipitating and maintaining the problem*, will ultimately determine the success of Stage 3, *intervention,* or *problem solution.*

Stage 3: Treatment Formulation

In the third and final stage of case formulation, the focus is on finding solutions to the problem(s) identified in Stage 1 and interpreted in Stage 2. Ultimately, knowledge of evidence-based treatments (EBTs) and the ability to select from available treatments those methods that best apply to the unique needs of the case are required. Competencies in monitoring and evaluating treatment effectiveness are also significant at this stage in order to validate the effectiveness of the treatment.

Case Formulation: A Work in Progress and a Work in Process. Conceptually, the model of case formulation presented suggests a three-stage process. It is important to emphasize, however, that case formulation is a fluid and dynamic process that has a built-in capacity for flexible thinking and hypothesis revision at all stages. In this way, case formulation can become case *reformulation*, allowing for increased refinement and evaluation of problem areas and treatment plans.

Case Formulation: A Case Called Jeremy. The goal of the first stage in case formulation is to *identify the problem.* With this goal in mind, the reader is directed to return to "A Case Called Jeremy, Segment One: The Intake," review the information available in Segment One, and provide answers to the following questions:

1. What are Jeremy's main problems?

2. What is Jeremy's primary problem?

3. What other information would be helpful in answering the above questions?

Stage 1: The Goal of Case Formulation

The initial goal of developing a case formulation (Stage 1) is to *define the problem* or *determine the nature of the problem.* Given the information provided thus far, pinpointing the problem is not an easy task. With respect to the reason for referral, the pediatrician is vague, stating that medication has been prescribed for *impulsive, hyperactive, and noncompliant behaviors*. At this point, there is a lack of formal assessment information that might help clarify the extent to which these behaviors are currently demonstrated or have been in the past. When the caregiver is questioned regarding the primary reason for assessment, the response, interestingly enough, has nothing to do with problem behavior and instead is articulated as a desire to obtain Jeremy's IQ.

In order to understand a problem, it is necessary to decide which information is most relevant to the potential solution and then direct attention to that portion of the information (Matlin, 2002). In Jeremy's case, however, finding the problem becomes the first hurdle. Although there is considerable literature devoted to *problem solving*, there is very little attention to the task of *problem finding* (Brown & Walter, 1990; Hennessey, 1994; Matlin, 2002). In fact, the art of problem finding has been so poorly researched that it has been speculated that the act of problem finding might actually be discouraged by educators (Brown & Walter, 1990). Rather than venture on a problem-finding mission, a more productive task might be to highlight several reasons why it may not be possible to determine the problem at this juncture, and what types of information could assist the process at this stage.

Box 1.1

THINKING OUT LOUD

Sections titled "Thinking Out Loud" will provide opportunities to consolidate information, identify areas for further exploration, and assist in working through the process of case formulation.

The fact that Jeremy is repeating kindergarten is an indication that Jeremy has not developed some of the necessary skills that would predict successful school adjustment. However, at this point, more information is needed to determine whether lack of success in school is a function of *a lack of ability (comprehension) or a lack of performance (production)*. Despite a relatively good amount of detailed information available from the "virtual intake session" in Segment One, the information is not helpful in determining whether problems cited are significantly deviant from the norm. The informal manner of their description and the anecdotal comments do not assist in answering important questions regarding the *intensity, frequency, and duration of the behaviors* relative to normative expectations.

Stage 1: Areas of Knowledge

Several areas of knowledge can assist the clinician in defining and refining the characteristics of the problem, such as knowledge of: normal development, developmental contexts, abnormal child psychology, differing systems of classification, assessment instruments and familiarity with various assessment techniques, and recent research concerning child psychopathology (Table 1.1).

Knowledge of Normal Development. One important area of knowledge that can assist in the evaluation of child characteristics is knowledge of normal development. Placing the intake information within a developmental framework provides information regarding Jeremy's behaviors relative to normative expectations. One major developmental task required for successful adaptation is the development of *self-control,* or the child's ability to evaluate alternative responses to situations or events. Self-control can determine the degree to which the child is able to inhibit undesirable responses and engage in appropriate responses (Kendall & Braswell, 1993). Historically, *lack of self-control* is a behavioral deficit that has been associated with a number of different psychopathologies (Wenar & Kerig, 2000). At approximately 2 years of age, toddlers begin to *internalize standards of appropriate behavior* and develop increasing ability for *self-control or self-regulation* and decreased need for being controlled by others (Power & Manire, 1992). Children begin to internalize parental standards verbally, in modeling increasingly complex rules to guide their behaviors (Kochanska, Murray, Jacques, Koenig, & Vandgeest, 1996). This self-verbalization has also been suggested as an essential link in assisting children in delaying responses and inhibiting impulsive responding (Barkley, 1997). Therefore, in pinpointing problem behaviors for Jeremy, lack of self-control may be one behavioral deficit worth considering.

Other areas of developmental concern that can impact negatively on adjustment include: poor ability to modulate emotional expressions (*emotion regulation), low frustration tolerance,* and *low task persistence*, especially for low interest tasks (Bridges & Grolnick, 1995). Jeremy's loud and boisterous behaviors in the classroom also suggest poor mastery of *ego resiliency* (Block & Block, 1980), which requires an understanding that certain behaviors or expressions are acceptable in some situations and not in others.

Developmentally, the toddler period (approximately 1 to 2½ years) represents a time when children move toward greater autonomy and independence. At this time children often exert their will through open *defiance* ("No!") as a way of exerting their newfound independence and will. However, Jeremy's open defiance of adult authority has persisted well beyond the toddler period, suggesting the need to investigate the extent to which these behaviors are impacting on other areas of development.

This text shares the viewpoint that problems of children and adolescents represent deviations from normal development, or development gone awry (Wenar & Kerig, 2000). Psychopathology as a developmental construct is complex because of the number of interacting forces that impact on the child and adolescent over time and the number of different developmental pathways that these interactions can create (Sroufe, 1997). Although change is inherent in the process of development, there is also an underlying continuity to the process (Thompson, 1999) that is itself stable and predictable and allows for the measurement of observed behavior relative to developmental expectations. Therefore, Jeremy's lack of *self-control, poor emotion regulation, and noncompliance* may be seen as maladaptive behaviors that, if not corrected, have the potential to remain stable and impact on other aspects of development in a negative manner.

Box 1.2

THINKING OUT LOUD: ISSUES OF SELF-CONTROL AND NONCOMPLIANCE

Knowledge of child development has assisted in identifying two potential problems for further investigation: issues of self-control and noncompliance.

Issues of Self-Control. Further investigation regarding the degree of self-control evident across situations and the methods of self-control used by Jeremy will be required to determine the extent to which self-control is a *behavioral skill deficit* (lack of ability to inhibit responses), *production deficit* (lack of motivation to inhibit responses), or *learned response to certain environmental contingencies* (lack of self-control has been reinforced by goal attainment). If self-control is a behavioral deficit, we would expect to see other behaviors, such as impulsivity, inability to follow rules, and poor response to behavioral consequences, across different situational contexts.

Issues of Noncompliance. Although Jeremy evidences a "lack of self-control" in some areas, he seems to be "powerfully in control" in other areas of life. At 2 years of age, Jeremy discovered the power of the word *no* and, *power struggles* and *noncompliance* have continued ever since.

Within a secure environment, through parental use of appropriate limit setting and guided responding, children learn to modulate their requests and gain greater self-reliance. However, if attachments are insecure, caregivers are unavailable, and/or limit setting is inconsistent, self-reliance can be compromised, resulting in perpetuation of power struggles, persistence of angry responses, lack of interest in task mastery, and pervasive emotional detachment (Sroufe, Fox, & Pancake, 1983).

Investigation of Self-Control and Noncompliance Will Require Further Assessment. Although child characteristics are clearly important in defining the nature of Jeremy's problem(s), the role of parenting practices on negative behavioral outcomes in children has also been well documented (Campbell, Pierce, Moore, Marakovitz, & Newby, 1996; Patterson, Capaldi, & Bank, 1991). Therefore, further information is required regarding: family history (including pathology and information regarding early attachment patterns), family rearing patterns, behavioral ratings and descriptions across situations (home and school), normative indices/observational reports of frequency and intensity of behaviors, and estimates of cognitive/intellectual functioning.

Knowledge of Developmental Contexts: Bronfenbrenner and Ecological Psychology. Viewing Jeremy's behaviors from the developmental perspective has added considerable depth to problem definition. However, thus far we have considered Jeremy's behaviors only from the level of *individual characteristics* (Bronfenbrenner, 1989). According to Bronfenbrenner, development is influenced by a series of concentric circles or spheres of influence. The first level, or the *inner circle,* represents the child's individual makeup and includes the biological beginnings, including the DNA code, which makes the individual unique.

However, children by necessity are highly embedded in context. One criticism that has been directed toward child assessment is the fact that the process often focuses exclusively on the child's symptoms to the exclusion of other environmental influences, such as the child's family system or peer network (Kendall, 1993). Questions are often directed toward discovering what the child's problem is, without consideration of these other "spheres of influence." One model that can enhance our understanding of developmental contexts is the ecological approach developed by Uri Bronfenbrenner (1979, 1989).

Bronfenbrenner presents an ecological framework built on the assumption that human development evolves in response to influences at several levels: *individual characteristics* (biological context, such as genetic makeup, temperament, intelligence), *immediate environment* (family, school, peers, community neighborhood), *social and economic factors* (poverty, divorce, family stress), and *cultural context*. According to Bronfenbrenner, influences between spheres have a ripple effect as energy emanates and reverberates from one circle to the next, much like the ripples caused by a pebble thrown into water.

Bronfenbrenner's ecological approach emphasizes the individual's interactions with others in the environment and the interlocking environmental systems that are characterized by differing expectations, roles, and norms. The relationship between the individual and the environment is reciprocal and interactive. Bronfenbrenner believes that we cannot fully understand development without an appreciation of how an individual interacts with each environmental context. Bronfenbrenner proposed four levels of influence beyond the inner circle of the individual: immediate *(microsystem)*, social and economic *(exosystem)*, and cultural context *(macrosystem)*.

A major source for determining developmental progress is the compatibility among the environmental systems. According to Bronfenbrenner, the *mesosystem*, which represents the interaction between two microsystems, predicts the degree to which a system remains healthy, functional, and in balance. For example, if there is a communication breakdown between Jeremy's family and the school (two immediate environmental influences, or microsystems), then the opportunities for successful progress could be compromised. However, if the home and school support a similar agenda (e.g., compliance with rules, respect for authority, motivation to do well), then the likelihood of success would be predicted to increase.

Based on the nature of the environmental forces, these contexts can erect barriers and obstacles to development *(risk factors)* or provide buffers, shielding the child from potential harm *(protective factors)*. The following descriptions will serve to summarize the potential impact that may be evident at different levels of influence:

Immediate Environment (Microsystem). The impact of family environment on Jeremy's development can be seen in Jeremy's modeling of inappropriate and negative behaviors, such as his shouting matches with his mother. Research has demonstrated that negative parenting practices, such as power assertion and negative discipline, are predictive of later development of aggressive behaviors in children (Loeber & Disshion, 1983). In coercive exchanges between the parent and child, ineffective parenting often results in escalating conflicts and perpetuation of noncompliant behaviors (Patterson, Capaldi, & Bank, 1991).

Social and Financial Context (Exosystem). Although the child is not immediately impacted by employment conditions, inflation rates, or community development, the resulting influence on parenting and home conditions can have a profound impact on the developing child. Jeremy's mother is a student and his grandmother is on a small disability pension. They are also living far from their state of origin and have severed ties with the paternal grandfather's side of the family. Mother is under stress physically, resulting from a car wreck several months ago.

Cultural Context (Macrosystem). Research has demonstrated that children who suffer from low socioeconomic status are more likely to encounter problems of conduct, academics, and social relationships, regardless of ethnic minority status (Patterson, Kupersmidt, & Vaden, 1990). Because low income is often associated with single-parent families and ethnic minorities, many studies have confounded the influence of these factors. However, when children are both impoverished and members of an ethnic minority, the long-term implications of living in poverty increase dramatically (Wilson & Aponte, 1985).

The ecological system is particularly useful for addressing issues faced by many minority children (Gustavsson & Balgopal, 1990). One such issue might be the need to integrate potentially conflicting belief systems involving family, school, and peer norms or expectations. Children may be challenged by conflicting sets of norms and values, resulting in conflicts of loyalty and a lack of cohesion or congruence between the opposing systems in their life.

In the case study of Shirley, "Worried to Perfection," cultural factors play a prominent part in the lack of resolution regarding Shirley's distress.

Box 1.3

THINKING OUT LOUD: ISSUES IN PARENTING STYLE AND ATTACHMENT HISTORY

Within the family context, the role of *parenting skills* or parenting style can also be viewed from a developmental perspective. If the toddler period is a time of flexing autonomy and gaining greater self-restraint, what are the developmental tasks required of the parent to encourage the development of these skills in the child? Research has isolated several key *patterns of parent-toddler interaction* that can impact on child outcomes. Parents who anticipate when to intervene in *frustrating tasks* often prevent escalation of problems, while parents who intervene at inappropriate times or not at all often produce negative outcomes of increased frustration and reduced task persistence (Spiker, Ferguson, & Brooks-Gunn, 1993). Research has demonstrated that *parents' ability to set limits and provide clear guidelines* in the toddler period has long-term implications for positive child outcomes in the future (Erickson, Egeland, & Sroufe, 1985).

A CASE CALLED JEREMY

Segment Two: Family Context

Family history reveals that there is a history of mental instability in the maternal family. Jeremy's mother and grandmother are currently on medication for depression (Prozac), and Jeremy's mother notes that she has had episodes of depression "on and off" for years. She did not do well in school and also wonders whether she has a learning disability or attentional problems as well. Mother is 25 years of age, is unemployed, and is currently taking one course at the local college. Grandmother is 55 years of age and is on a small disability pension. Grandmother reports that she is a highly anxious individual, as well as depressed, and has problems "worrying" about most things. Jeremy's grandmother said that most people in the family have "some mental problem or another" and added that her sister (Jeremy's great aunt) will not leave the house (agoraphobic) and has panic attacks. Apparently, the maternal grandfather is an alcoholic and is also subject to violent outbursts and depression (bipolar?); his inability to tolerate medication made him "impossible to live with." Shortly after Jeremy's birth, grandmother moved in with her daughter and Jeremy to help with child rearing, since mother suffered an episode of postpartum depression. During this period, mother was not able to care for Jeremy adequately and spent much of her time in bed sleeping. Grandmother was able to perform child-rearing duties during this period (which lasted about 3 months), but admitted that she was "very anxious" about being a mother that late in life, fearing she might do something wrong, since it had been more than 20 years since she had to care for a baby. Mother reports that Jeremy's birth father told her he was "clinically classified as insane" and that he often engaged in reckless, dangerous behaviors and had been in trouble with the law. Jeremy has had no contact with his birth father or grandfather since his birth.

Mother is continuing to recover from a car wreck that she was involved in 9 months previously, when her car was sideswiped by a truck. Although she was not hospitalized, she did sustain major bruising and continues to receive chiropractic treatment twice a week. Mother and grandmother report that the teacher at Jeremy's school showed Jeremy a picture of the car, which had appeared in the newspaper. Jeremy was so upset and fearful when he saw the picture that he did not want to go to school for 6 weeks following the accident because he was afraid of separating from his mother. This was a very difficult time for the family because of the stress of the accident and Jeremy's behaviors. Jeremy's school attendance was sporadic during this period because grandmother didn't have the energy to "drag" Jeremy to school most days and mother was recuperating from her injuries.

As part of the intake information, mother completed the Parenting Stress Index (PSI; Abidin, 1995). Mother rated Jeremy at or above the 99th percentile in areas of distractibility/hyperactivity, inability to adjust to changes in environment, and demandingness.

Elevations on these scales are typical for parents of children with ADHD, with demandingness often the peak scale (Abidin, 1995). With respect to family stresses, mother endorsed only concerns about her health as a significant stressor.

Stage 1: Areas of Knowledge, Continued

Jeremy's family history provides important information regarding Jeremy's vulnerability to certain disorders, based on knowledge of the role of genetic transmission in the etiology of disorders. In addition, the information also raises concern regarding a number of other risk factors that might impact on development (mother and grandmother both suffer from depression; economic stressors; external family supports are minimal; and the likelihood for dysfunctional family patterns is high).

Knowledge of Etiology. Although isolating a definitive genetic link in childhood has been difficult due to confounding variables such as IQ and SES (Yoshikawa, 1994), there are several research findings to suggest that Jeremy's family context places him at considerable risk for developing a mental disorder.

From a *bio-medical perspective* with a focus on brain (neurotransmitter) and body, genetic transmission of temperamental factors such as Jeremy's high activity level (Goldsmith, 1983; Plomin, 1989) suggest that Jeremy may have inherited a genetic predisposition toward defiant, noncompliant, and hostile behavior. Mother reports that the biological father engaged in risky and antisocial behavior. Epidemiological studies have linked childhood disruptive behaviors to antisocial biological fathers, even when the children were adopted (Mednick & Hutchings, 1978). Some possible biological causes of aggressive behaviors in adults have been attributed to elevated levels of the male hormone testosterone (Dabbs & Morris, 1990). Low levels of DBH, responsible for converting dopamine to noradrenaline, have also been implicated in risky and impulsive behaviors due to the possible effects of producing higher thresholds for fear and sensation seeking in some children (Quay, 1986). First-degree relatives of children with ADHD also demonstrate greater likelihood of ADHD, depression, alcoholism, conduct problems, and antisocial disorders (Biederman, 1991; Biederman, Faraone, Keenan, Knee, & Tsuang, 1990).

In addition to a vulnerability for developing externalizing disorders, Jeremy's family history is also positive for internalizing disorders such as mood disorders (mother and grandmother are both depressed, grandfather may be bipolar) and anxiety (grandmother may have generalized anxiety disorder, a maternal aunt has panic attacks with agoraphobia). Research shows that children of depressed parents are three times more likely to experience a major depressive episode (Beardslee, Bemporad, Keller, & Klerman, 1983) and are more vulnerable to disorders of depression and/or anxiety (Eley & Stevenson, 2000; Kovacs, 1997).

Knowledge of Risks and Protective Factors. Although isolated risk factors may show little prediction of disorder prevalence, the overall potential for negative outcomes increases rapidly as the risk factors increase (Rutter, 1979; Sameroff, Seifer, Barocas, Zax, & Greenspan, 1987). Several risk factors are evident for Jeremy at all contextual levels. At an *individual level (child characteristics)*, Jeremy has likely inherited a predisposition for developing comorbid internalizing and externalizing disorders. Although average intellectual potential is normally considered a protective factor (Luthar & Zigler, 1992), Jeremy may use his intellectual capacity to "outwit and outsmart" his parents by developing manipulative strategies and power struggles. At the *immediate level (family and school) and economic/social levels*, additional risk factors are evident, including: insecure attachment (Rutter, 1995; Sroufe, 1983), poverty (Duncan, Brooks-Gunn & Klebanov, 1994; McLoyd, 1990), parental psychopathology (Cicchetti & Toth, 1998), poor school adjustment, and lack of peer relationships (Blum et al., 2000).

Box 1.4

**THINKING OUT LOUD: FAMILY
HISTORY AND THE BIOMEDICAL APPROACH**

Given the family history, research regarding possible genetic transmission of abnormal dopamine levels in ADHD populations, and reported problems in areas of emotion regulation and self-control, indications are that Jeremy is at risk for developing a behavioral disorder and/or an emotional disorder. Studies have also shown that children with ADHD experience neurological abnormalities in the frontal lobes (decreased activity) and parts of the limbic system (Barkley, 1997, 1998) that contribute to lack of planning ability and low impulse control.

The psychologist will require more information to assist in better defining the characteristics of the problem. At this point, although his mother and grandmother have provided a good deal of information regarding Jeremy's background and behaviors, Jeremy still remains little more than a cardboard character.

Direction: At this point, the psychologist requires some first-hand observational information to bring young Jeremy to life.

A CASE CALLED JEREMY

Segment Three: Action—Enter Jeremy

Jeremy literally exploded into the clinician's office, abruptly letting go of his mother's hand and immediately trying to pry open the WISC-III test kit on the table. The psychologist was able to halt further efforts to dismantle the test kit with a firm, "Not yet, Jeremy," while providing drawing paper and markers for his immediate attention. Despite his whirlwind arrival, his mother did confirm that Jeremy had taken his medication prior to coming. Mother left immediately after introducing Jeremy to the psychologist, and Jeremy evidenced no noticeable reaction to being left with a stranger or to his mother's departure. Although the psychologist attempted to engage Jeremy in conversation, Jeremy's poor articulation skills made conversation difficult. Jeremy was also far more interested in getting to the manipulatives, which were undoubtedly the "good stuff" of the assessment for him, in all respects. Test behaviors and learning style were highly notable. Jeremy presented as an extremely active youngster who was very fidgety and restless throughout the assessment sessions. Although he was responsive, he did have some difficulty staying on task when required and in complying with specific requests. Jeremy often shifted his position throughout the assessment sessions: sitting, standing, kneeling, rocking, and walking around the room. Attention span and compliance with task demands varied considerably across tasks. Tasks requiring manipulation of materials and hands-on activity were responded to with far more enthusiasm and focus than verbal tasks. Questions that required oral responses and provided minimal visual input were responded to poorly, if at all. During the vocabulary test, rather than provide oral answers in response to word definitions, Jeremy delighted in giving clues to the psychologist in visual form in a game-playing type of format. When asked to spell the word *cat* on the test protocol, Jeremy jumped out of his chair and drew a large picture of a cat on the blackboard. When asked to describe what a "clock" was, Jeremy made an arrow on the blackboard in the room pointing to the clock above it. When asked for a definition for the word *hat,* Jeremy again ran to the blackboard and added a hat to his drawing of the cat.

On tasks that were maximally engaging (blocks, puzzles, picture arrangement), it was often necessary to curb Jeremy's enthusiasm. On these tasks, Jeremy often attempted to grab test materials before they were introduced and ignored instructions to wait until materials were presented. Throughout the assessment sessions, Jeremy was very intent on his own agenda, and there were frequent compliance issues. Redirection to task was also required on a frequent basis throughout the assessment. Due to difficulties with sustaining attention and redirection to task, assessment was conducted over two 35-minute sessions. At the completion of the first session, Jeremy heard the elevator and immediately ran out of the room and down the hall toward the top of a long staircase. The psychologist noted concerns regarding safety issues, since Jeremy could easily have fallen down the stairs. Mother and grandmother took the opportunity to scold Jeremy for his behavior and told Jeremy that as a consequence they were no longer going to stop at a restaurant on the way home.

Over the course of the two assessment sessions, when engaged in a task he enjoyed doing, Jeremy was able to attend to the stimulus materials adequately and problem solve without impulsive responding. He did evidence frustration on occasion, when he was unable to obtain an adequate solution and appeared fatigued after working unsuccessfully on a puzzle for 1½ minutes. However, he was able to regroup and was more successful on the next two puzzles attempted. Jeremy was often difficult to understand due to speech sound substitution errors such as "wabbit" for "rabbit" and "ewebwoddy" for "everybody" and cluttering of words resulting in indistinct utterances. However, Jeremy readily repeated phrases when asked for clarification.

Box 1.5

**THINKING OUT LOUD:
OBSERVATIONAL INFORMATION**

Based on the psychologist's observations regarding Jeremy's behavior in the clinic office and during the assessment, the probability that Jeremy exhibits a behavioral disorder, such as attention-deficit/hyperactivity disorder (ADHD), is gaining increased support. However, the psychologist has reservations about venturing a diagnosis at this point since there are some inconsistencies in Jeremy's behaviors. When motivated, Jeremy seems to be able to curb some of his impulsive responding. Compliance issues noted by his mother were also demonstrated during the assessment sessions, although Jeremy did attempt to provide responses in spite of his lack of compliance. It was almost as if the lack of compliance was a habitual response and Jeremy was trying to navigate around it. Questions of Jeremy's manipulation of his environment to meet his own ends may be an issue here. Also, at times Jeremy's behaviors verged on "game playing," perhaps to see how much he could get away with. Jeremy seemed to have a repertoire of rather sophisticated manipulative strategies.

Questions and Direction. The psychologist reviewed the *DSM* checklist responses, which Jeremy's mother completed for the intern during the intake interview, with the intention of determining the frequency and duration of problem behaviors, such as impulsivity, hyperactivity, and noncompliance. However, whether behaviors represent significant deviations from the norm may depend to a large extent on the type of classification system (categorical or dimensional) the rating scales were derived from.

A CASE CALLED JEREMY

Segment Four: *DSM* Rating Scales

During the clinical intake interview, Jeremy's mother responded to several checklists derived from criteria outlined in the *Diagnostic and Statistical Manual of Mental Disorders* (*DSM-IV-TR;* American Psychiatric Association [APA], 2000). A sufficient number of items were endorsed for the attention-deficit/hyperactivity disorder (ADHD) scale to suggest significant difficulties with Inattention (7 of 9 items) and Hyperactive/Impulsive Behavior (9 of 9) in the home. In addition, mother also endorsed six of a possible nine items from the scale for oppositional defiant disorder (ODD).

Stage 1: Problem Classification and Diagnosis

According to the *Diagnostic and Statistical Manual of Mental Disorders* (*DSM-IV*), a diagnosis of ADHD requires endorsement of six symptoms of Inattention, or six symptoms of Hyperactive/Impulsive behaviors. Jeremy's mother has endorsed sufficient symptoms to suggest a diagnosis of

ADHD-Combined Type, since Jeremy meets criteria for both aspects of ADHD, providing other criteria are satisfied. The remaining criteria involve sufficient frequency (often), duration (prior to 7 years of age) and intensity (pervasive across situations) of symptom presentation. In addition, since only four symptoms are required for a diagnosis of ODD, symptom endorsement is also positive for the presence of ODD based on Jeremy's frequent negativistic, defiant, argumentative, hostile, and noncompliant behaviors in the home. Since the *DSM* notes that ODD behaviors are primarily evident in the home environment and with familiar adults and peers, noncompliant behaviors may not be self-evident during an assessment or in the school environment (APA, 2000, p. 100). Therefore, Jeremy's mother has endorsed sufficient criteria to suggest a diagnosis of both ADHD and ODD, based on *DSM* defining criteria. Further support for the presence of ADHD and ODD can be found in research literature that has found high rates of comorbidity for these two disorders. Research suggests prevalence rates from 35% to 60% for co-occurrence rates for ODD and ADHD in clinically referred children by the time they are 7 years of age (Kuhne, Schachar, & Tannock, 1997).

Box 1.6

**THINKING OUT LOUD:
CONTROVERSIES IN THE CLASSIFICATION
OF CHILD AND ADOLESCENT DISORDERS**

A classification system can provide an important tool for clinical decision making by defining major categories or dimensions of pathology and answering questions regarding the nature and severity of the problem. However, whether one uses the categorical system (*DSM*), dimensional system (Behavioral Rating Scales, e.g., Achenbach System of Empirically Based Assessment [ASEBA], Achenbach & Rescorla, 2001; Behavior Assessment System for Children [BASC], Reynolds & Kamphaus, 1992), or normative development as the blueprint for defining pathology may impact significantly on how the problem is conceptualized.

Whereas the categorical system considers a disorder as present or absent, the dimensional system conceptualizes maladaptive behavior as the negative end of an adaptive-to-maladaptive continuum. Both systems have been criticized regarding the appropriateness of their use with child and adolescent populations. While the *categorical system (DSM)* has been criticized for its all-or-nothing approach to diagnosis (Achenbach, 1995), primarily adult orientation, and lack of developmental perspective (Wenar & Kerig, 2000), criticisms surrounding the *dimensional system* (rating scales) have focused on the reliability of scales that are dependent upon a rater's perception (subject itself to variations in mood states, biases, etc.) and inconsistencies in rater agreements across contexts (Achenbach, McConaughy, & Howell, 1987), informant groups, and problem areas. Another criticism of the *DSM* categorical approach has been that behaviors that do not qualify as "mental disorders" may still cause significant impairment. For example, peer relationship difficulties, although not considered a "mental disorder," are predictive of long-term outcomes of maladjustment in areas of school dropout, criminal behaviors, and delinquency (Blum et al., 2000; Parker & Asher, 1987).

Direction: The Need for a Comprehensive Assessment

Given reservations regarding the exclusive use of the *DSM* classification system for children and adolescents, inclusion of rating scales from the dimensional systems will provide additional information.

Evaluation of cognitive functioning (intellectual assessment) may assist in answering questions regarding skill versus production deficits and to determine how thought processes might be impacting on behavioral concerns.

In order to obtain a more in-depth analysis of a definitive impression of Jeremy's cognitive, emotional, and behavioral status relative to normal developmental expectations, the psychologist obtains *further information based on norm-referenced assessment measures.*

A CASE CALLED JEREMY

Segment Five: Formal Psychological Assessment

Responses to the Wechsler Intelligence Test for Children (WISC-III) revealed that Jeremy's Verbal Intelligence Score was within the Average to High Average range at approximately the 66th percentile (Verbal IQ Range 99-112). Jeremy's Performance Intelligence Score was within the Superior range, at approximately the 98th percentile (Performance IQ 121-137). There was a 26-point discrepancy between his Verbal Intelligence score and his Performance Intelligence score, which is highly significant and occurs in less than 10% of the population. Given the magnitude of this discrepancy, calculation of the Full Scale Intellectual Score would be meaningless, since it would merely represent the numerical average of two very discrepant scores (Kaufman & Lichtenberger, 2000). Caution should be used in interpretation of the Verbal Intelligence score as a valid indicator of Jeremy's verbal skills, since Jeremy's motivation and cooperation were both suspect during the administration of the verbal segment of the WISC-III.

Scores for visual reasoning were more consistent and revealed very strong performance overall. Relative strengths were noted in visual acuity (noting missing details in pictures), visual motor speed, and modeling of block designs, which were all at the 98th percentile. Jeremy did evidence a significant weakness in a mazes completion task, suggesting weak planning ability and problems with impulse control (see Barkley, 1997).

Academically, segments of the Wide Range Achievement Test (WRAT-3) revealed inconclusive information, since Jeremy completed only those questions he wanted to try. When asked to draw a boy, Jeremy stated that he would draw a man, instead. The drawing was very immature in areas of line juncture and body proportion.

Jeremy's mother completed the Conners Parent Rating Scale (CPRS-R:L) and the Child Behavior Checklist (CBCL). According to ratings on the CPRS-R:L, Jeremy demonstrates clinically significant symptoms of attention-deficit/hyperactivity disorder, predominantly of the impulsive/hyperactive type. In addition, oppositional behaviors and perfectionistic tendencies were also in the clinical range. Responses also noted that Jeremy complains of physical symptoms more than the average child and that he can be prone to anxiety. Ratings on the CBCL noted that Jeremy can be distracted by his thoughts and tends to perseverate on ideas.

Jeremy's teacher completed the Conners Teacher Rating Scale (CTRS-R:L) and the Teacher Report Form (TRF: Achenbach). Although the teacher ratings were less elevated than Jeremy's mother's ratings in all areas, his teacher did also note some concerns regarding perfectionistic tendencies. According to the TRF, Hyperactive-Impulsive Behaviors were at the 95th percentile, indicating significant difficulties in this area. In addition, thought persistence was also noted as an area of difficulty.

Jeremy participated in providing responses to the Joseph Pre-School and Primary Self-Concept Screening Test. Jeremy's responses indicated that his Global Self-Esteem was within the High Positive range.

Box 1.7

THINKING OUT LOUD: ASSESSMENT INFORMATION FOR LATER CONSIDERATION

Although above-average intelligence is usually thought of as a protective factor (Luthar & Zigler, 1992), it is possible that at this point in time superior intellectual ability may place Jeremy at greater risk for maladaptive behavior. Jeremy has developed a strong repertoire of manipulative strategies that may be more resistant to correction than if he were not so high functioning. Another way in which his superior intelligence may be a risk factor is that Jeremy's lack of success academically may be even more frustrating for him. The significant discrepancy between Verbal and Performance IQ may also indicate a specific learning disability, which might complicate academic progress. Certainly at this point, Jeremy's academic skill levels are virtually nonexistent. Whether academic difficulties result from a specific learning disability or an inability to apply himself remains to be seen.

At this point, the psychologist will also want to contact the pediatrician to determine whether Jeremy's dosage of medication might be altered, since there is considerable room for improvement in the inhibition of behaviors (impulsivity) and in emotion regulation.

Stage 1: Problem Definition: A Summation

Based on assessment results, intake information, and clinical observations, the psychologist produced the following preliminary summary and diagnostic impression:

Summary of Jeremy's Formal Assessment. Jeremy is a 6-year-old boy who is currently repeating kindergarten at JJB Elementary School. Jeremy is a bright and engaging child; however, he is experiencing difficulties at home and at school as a result of hyperactive and impulsive behaviors. Although Jeremy scored in the Superior range on tasks of visual reasoning, his scores on verbal reasoning tasks were less impressive due to several factors. Jeremy was not as interested in complying with verbal tasks that were less able to sustain his interest and attention. Therefore, his performance on verbal tasks likely reflected this lack of task engagement rather than a true index of his learning potential. Despite his excellent reasoning ability, Jeremy may continue to experience difficulties due to poor ability to regulate activity levels relative to task demands. Difficulty with regulation of his activity level was noted when Jeremy was either *understimulated* (task was not interesting to him) or *overstimulated* (task was very exciting). In the former case, Jeremy revealed poor attention span and distractibility, while in the latter case he showed poor restraint and impulsivity. Problems with compliance were also noted throughout, suggesting that Jeremy also experiences difficulties in situations where he is not in control and where he is expected to follow directions that may or may not be to his liking.

Stage 1: Diagnostic Impression/Formulation

Jeremy presents with several symptoms of attention-deficit/hyperactivity disorder, predominantly impulsive-hyperactive type (ADHD), and meets the criteria of consistently matching at least six of the *DSM* symptoms from this category: often fidgets and squirms; often leaves his seat when he should be seated; often runs excessively; is often on the go; talks excessively; and has difficulty waiting his turn. These behaviors were endorsed in the home, at school, and were evident during his assessment. In addition, Jeremy also meets the *DSM* criteria for oppositional defiant disorder (ODD), matching at least four of the following symptoms: easily angered and annoyed with others and presents with negativistic and defiant behaviors resulting in issues of noncompliance, temper outbursts, arguments with adults, and refusals to comply with parental requests. Behaviors of noncompliance (ODD) are manifested primarily in the home situation, which is consistent with *DSM* diagnostic features (APA, 2000, p. 102).

Box 1.8

**THINKING OUT LOUD: LINKING
STAGE 1 TO STAGE 2 CASE FORMULATION**

The goal of Stage 2 in case formulation is to conduct an in-depth analysis of the problem to determine the underlying causes to be targeted for treatment/intervention. Jeremy's problems have been narrowed down to two broad areas for consideration:

1. problems of self-regulation/lack of self-control

2. problems of noncompliance

Issues in Self-Control. Based on the results of the comprehensive assessment and on available knowledge regarding the etiology of ADHD, it is the clinician's impression that the underlying cause for Jeremy's problems in self-regulation has its basis in a biomedical/genetic origin, and that lack of self-control represents a behavioral deficit for Jeremy. Support for this hypothesis is based on direct observation and norm-referenced rating instruments, suggesting that behaviors are pervasive across situations and are accompanied by associated features of impulsivity, problems following rules, and poor response to behavioral consequences.

Directions in Self-Control. Although the exact causes of ADHD are not yet known, there is increasing research evidence suggesting abnormal levels of dopamine in this population (Waldman et al., 1998), which might be genetically transmitted (Biederman et al., 1993). Given the medical nature of the disorder, it is not surprising that the most widely successful treatment for ADHD is the use of stimulant medication. Although Jeremy is currently taking Adderol for the ADHD, further dialogue with the pediatrician is necessary to determine if altering the dosage or type of medication might be more successful in achieving better regulation of behavioral control.

Noncompliant Behaviors. Jeremy's noncompliant behaviors are evident in negativistic, defiant, argumentative, and hostile responses to requests, and although evident to a degree across situations, are evident primarily within the home environment. Since research has implicated negative and controlling parent practices in the development and maintenance of noncompliant behaviors (Beauchaine, Strassberg, Kees, & Drabick, 2002), assessment at this stage will focus on further elaboration of parenting practices regarding noncompliant behaviors.

Stage 2: Problem Explanation/Formulation

Goal: To develop a greater understanding of precipitating and maintaining influences regarding Jeremy's noncompliant behaviors.

Stage 2: Knowledge and Competencies

At Stage 2 in the case formulation process, the task is to *interpret* information generated in Stage 1 and to isolate potential pathways that might account for how the problem developed and is being maintained. Important sources of knowledge at this stage include an awareness of the *differing theoretical positions* regarding the etiology of behavior disorders and the available *empirical support* for these assumptions (see Table 1.1). Due to the high volume of child and adolescent referrals to clinics for behavior disorders, considerable research has been generated and models proposed to explain the development of behavior disorders in children (Quay, 1986).

At this stage, several key skills can be beneficial in achieving the goals. Initial focus on generating a number of hypotheses can be assisted by a divergent thinking style and a flexible approach to problem solving, which can transcend theoretical biases. Ultimately, application of theory and research to practice will require the ability to integrate information from diverse sources.

Box 1.9

THINKING OUT LOUD: DEVELOPING HYPOTHESES REGARDING NONCOMPLIANCE

Further assessment of parenting practices will be conducted to determine how Jeremy's noncompliant behaviors are manifested in the home environment and to obtain specific descriptions regarding how the parents respond to Jeremy's noncompliant behaviors.

1. How did Jeremy develop noncompliant behaviors (cause)?

2. What is maintaining noncompliant behaviors (maintenance)?

A CASE CALLED JEREMY

Segment Six: Meet the Parents

The psychologist met again with Jeremy's parents (mother and grandmother) to fulfill several goals:

1. provide the family with feedback regarding his assessment results (Intelligence Test, Behavior Rating Scales, Observed Behaviors)

2. develop a better understanding of Jeremy's behavior from the family's point of view

3. develop a hypothesis regarding the underlying dynamics concerning Jeremy's noncompliant behaviors

During this session, mother and grandmother were very interested in finding out about Jeremy's intelligence scores. They listened intently to information regarding Jeremy's strengths; however, they minimized any comments regarding difficulties that Jeremy encountered in complying with some of the test demands. Jeremy's mother came to his defense regarding his relatively low vocabulary score, suggesting that the test was beneath him and reasoning that he would have been more cooperative if the task had been more challenging. Although it was demonstrated that Jeremy's academic skill levels were basically at a pre-kindergarten level, his parents were adamant that Jeremy's poor school performance resulted from Jeremy's teachers not challenging him enough at school. Grandmother once again drew attention to Jeremy's excellent skills in taking apart small appliances and using the word *victimization* at 2 years to substantiate their claims of high intelligence.

In an attempt to understand better how Jeremy's noncompliant behaviors were being expressed and managed within the home, the psychologist administered the Home Situations Questionnaire (Barkley, 1997). The questionnaire was used to obtain more specific information regarding behaviors in the home; in addition, the instrument was also used as a method to generate dialogue and provide information concerning mother's and grandmother's parenting styles, methods of disciplining, and the parents' abilities to work as a cohesive team in child rearing. Questions were also directed toward previous history to obtain additional information regarding possible secure versus insecure attachment patterns noted in the past.

The Home Situations Questionnaire is helpful in isolating compliance problems in three areas within the home: compliance with instructions, commands, or rules. Four situations surfaced as being the greatest areas of difficulty for the family regarding Jeremy's noncompliant behaviors: when parents are talking on the telephone; when parents are watching television; when Jeremy is asked to do chores (cleaning the room); and when Jeremy is asked to do homework.

Problem areas were discussed at length. Parents were also asked to role-play how they would interact with Jeremy under problem conditions, and then to role-play how the other parent would respond to Jeremy given the same condition. Based on the dialogue and role play, the following information was obtained regarding specific responses to issues of noncompliance. Two areas of compliance difficulty were selected for further investigation. The parents selected Problems with Chores and Talking on the Telephone as the two problems areas of most concern:

Problems With Chores (specifically, when Jeremy is asked to clean up his room, pick up his toys, etc.)

Mother and grandmother provided the following information regarding their responses to Jeremy's lack of compliance concerning requests to clean his room.

Grandmother and mother agreed that when asked to clean his room, Jeremy typically engages in argumentative behaviors (why he shouldn't have to do it), delaying tactics (says he will do it later), manipulations (asks for help), or refusals (says he can't or won't do it). There was also agreement in the methods used by each parent, saying that they had figured out the "good cop, bad cop" routine would finally confuse him. Mother said her initial response was to count to three. However, Jeremy had pretty well figured out that most times there wasn't going to be anything happening after the three count, so this was not very effective. Mom said that when Jeremy won't clean his room, she usually then resorts to yelling and screaming. She proudly related a scenario that had recently happened. According to mother, during one of the screaming sessions, Jeremy yelled back at her "as loud as possible." In order to prove a point, mother screamed as loud as she could, just to show him that she could scream louder. He tried but he couldn't do it, so she said he has learned his lesson that she screams the loudest. While mother screams, grandmother basically gives in and will clean the room for him to avoid any further problems.

Talking on the Telephone (specifically, Jeremy stands in your face and talks so you can't hear the telephone; he won't wait until the call is finished)

Mother's typical response to the above problem was to take the phone outside (if the weather was nice) or to yell at Jeremy. Grandmother reported getting very upset with him and hanging up the phone as a result.

Box 1.10

**THINKING OUT LOUD:
LINKING THEORY TO RESEARCH**

The psychologist has continued to obtain information regarding how Jeremy's noncompliant behaviors are managed or mismanaged in the home. However, the way in which these interactions are interpreted will depend upon the theoretical assumptions that are applied to explain how or why these interactions have developed. In order to emphasize the breadth of interpretations available and to encourage the use of divergent and flexible thinking skills (see Table 1.1), the following section is devoted to a better understanding of how different theoretical approaches might explain the dynamics in Jeremy's case.

Stage 3: Applying Theoretical Assumptions to Case Dynamics

Case Formulation and Treatment Implications From Five Different Perspectives

The following section is devoted to case formulations developed from five different theoretical frameworks: psychodynamic, attachment and parenting, cognitive (social cognitive), behavioral, and family systems.

Case Formulation From a Psychodynamic Perspective. From a traditional psychoanalytic perspective, Jeremy's impulsive, aggressive, and excessively demanding behaviors would represent the external manifestations of unconscious conflicts resulting from an imbalance in the underlying personality structure. In Jeremy's case, noncompliant behaviors may be explained by the strength of the *id,* relative to ego and superego development, and the id's influence in driving these behaviors. When Jeremy was an infant, his mother's depression and grandmother's anxious parenting style may have resulted in the development of feelings of insecurity and anxiety regarding gratification of his *oral* needs. As a toddler, struggles with toilet training may have set the stage for conflicts due to unresolved issues of autonomy and rebellion against parental controls. Reframing Jeremy's behavior within an Ericksonian perspective, noncompliance might imply unresolved mastery of developmental tasks related to trust versus mistrust and/or autonomy versus dependence.

From the vantage point of ego psychology, Jeremy's controlling behaviors represent lack of resolution of the "rapprochement phase" in the separation-individuation process occurring in the second year of life when the toddler is faced with awareness of separation, separation anxiety, and conflicting desires to stay close to the mother. During this stage, the goal of the child is to gradually replace the sense of omnipotence found in the close (symbiotic) parent bond, with feelings of autonomy resulting from a strengthened sense of self (Mahler, Pine, & Bergman, 1975). Normally, the process of gaining greater independence and self-identity is facilitated by the parent, who performs the dual role of remaining emotionally available while gently encouraging the push toward greater independence (Settlage, 1977). Jeremy's unresolved conflicts, at this stage, become evident in the resurgence of anxious feelings surrounding the threat of separation following his mother's car accident. Jeremy developed severe symptoms of separation anxiety for 6 months, not wanting to let her out of his sight. Theory would predict that conflicts between autonomy and dependence would be repeated throughout development, especially in vulnerable times, such as periods of loss or illness (Kramer & Akhtar, 1989). According to Mahler, successful resolution of the conflict at this stage is achieved through the development of an internal representation or model of the parent-child relationship that can sustain separation due to the securely developed ego. Although ego psychologists, like attachment theorists, also talk about an internal representation, according to Fonagy (1999) there is a fundamental difference in emphasis on the role of how the relationship is perceived by both schools of thought. While attachment theorists see the relationship as the primary source of development, ego psychologists focus on consolidation of the ego as the primary task and relegate the attachment relationship to a secondary influence in assisting to facilitate or impede this goal.

Therapeutic Implications. Based on the underlying processes that operate to drive Jeremy's negativistic (noncompliant, hostile, argumentative) behaviors, there are several possible avenues for intervention. Depending on the psychodynamic therapist's orientation, the therapeutic process might focus on the individual child (working through internal conflicts in play therapy), the parent (helping a parent resolve his or her own childhood conflicts and traumas) or parent-child dyad (conjoint play therapy). Psychodynamic developmental therapy for children (PDTC) is a relatively recent advancement in psychodynamic therapy for children developed by Fonagy and Target (1996). Although the approach is psychodynamic in origin, the authors draw on principles of social information processing (social cognition) in developing techniques to assist children in linking thoughts to feelings and behaviors (*reflective processes*). A PDTC therapist might provide *corrective experiences* through play therapy and the use of metaphor to assist Jeremy in replacing negative externally controlling behaviors with greater understanding of emotion and internal controls.

Box 1.11

THINKING OUT LOUD: THE PSYCHODYNAMIC CASE FORMULATION

The foundations of psychodynamic theory are rooted in uncovering the internal and often unconscious processes that drive an individual's behaviors and the maladaptive internal working models responsible for a weakened sense of ego development. As such, the psychodynamic approach is not an easy fit with empirical research, and controversy has ensued regarding what has been called the "efficacy versus effectiveness research debate." According to Fishman (2000), the debate basically pits experimental controls versus contextual relevance, which he suggests can be remedied by developing research guidelines for case-based research. Messer (2000) emphasizes the need for translating empirical findings into practical or pragmatic psychology, which he argues can be achieved through the development of databases of case-based research to support context-sensitive case studies. Recently, Fonagy and colleagues (Fonagy, Target, Cottrell, Phillips, & Kurtz, 2002) provided increased recommendations to assist in incorporating empirical findings in evidence-based practice. The success of the PDTC approach (Fonagy & Target, 1996) has been documented in research for a wide variety of childhood disorders (Fonagy & Target, 1994). However, this approach has been far more successful for children with internalizing disorders (85% success rate for depression and anxiety), than for children like Jeremy who have ODD (30% success rate for ODD).

Case Formulation Based on Theories of Attachment and Parenting. Embedding attachment theory in an ecological-developmental framework, Greenberg (1999) explains psychopathology resulting from the interplay of maladaptive factors evident in the child, parent, and environmental context. Drawing on principles of *equifinality* (different pathways may lead to the same disorder) and *multifinality* (similar disorders may produce multiple outcomes, based on other extraneous factors such as timing and number of other stressors), Greenberg builds his model based on four underlying processes suggested in theoretical models of attachment: internal working models, neurophysiology of emotion regulation, observed behaviors, and functional-motivational processes.

Internal Working Models. Attachment theorists believe that the security or insecurity evident in primary attachment relationships set the stage for a child's expectations (*internal working models*) regarding how a caregiver will respond; their own role in producing these responses and the degree of security/insecurity ultimately serve as a template for projecting the dynamics of all other future relationships (Ainsworth et al., 1978; Belsky, 1988; Bowlby, 1969/1982). A secure attachment may serve as a protective factor buffering the child from the development of pathology in the future, while insecure attachments may place the child at greater risk for the development of behavioral and emotional problems

(Fonagy, 1999; Greenberg, 1999). Placing Jeremy's disruptive behaviors within the context of his early attachment relationships would predict the development of internal working models (IWMs) based on a high-risk insecure attachment pattern, evident in the *avoidant attachment pattern*, or *the disorganized/disoriented attachment*. Early history reveals that Jeremy's mother suffered postpartum depression shortly after his birth. At times, mother is withdrawn and emotionally unavailable; at other times, mother can be harsh, emotionally charged, and highly punitive (yelling, spanking) in her attempts to control his behaviors. The *authoritarian parenting style* inherent in this highly punitive and harsh parenting style is predictive of the development of an *avoidant attachment pattern* (Rubin, Hymel, Mills, & Rose-Krasnor, 1991). Within this context, Jeremy's IWM or cognitive-affective schema for relating would be based upon hostile and aggressive behaviors that developed in response to a parent who is rejecting and emotionally unavailable. However, a maternal history of psychopathology continues to be prevalent throughout the formative years. Emotional instability and parental tendencies to vacillate between being unresponsive (rejecting) and being overreactive (and possibly frightening) could set the stage for a highly unpredictable and frightening schema (Carlson, Cicchetti, Barnett, & Braunwald, 1989; Main & Hesse, 1990), resulting in Jeremy's becoming disoriented/disorganized in his responses and unable to construct an organized schema. In the absence of a secure and trusting bond, Jeremy is at risk for developing an internal working model or schema of relationships based on anxiety, anger, mistrust, and fear (Main, 1995). Main and Hesse (1990) speculate that controlling and bossy behaviors seen in preschool children with disorganized patterns of attachment may represent a mix of unresolved dependency needs and anger manifested in attempts to take control of the relationship in the absence of structure. The disorganized attachment response seems to be the most severe, with implications for the development of psychopathology across the lifespan (Cassidy & Mohr, 2001). Jeremy's grandmother's parenting style represents an anxious and passive response that most closely resembles the *permissive-indulgent style* (Baumrind, 1991): low on structure and predictive of negative child outcomes, including failure to develop a sense of responsibility and lack of self-control (Baumrind, 1991).

Observable patterns in this family suggest considerable disorganization in the family schema, evident in the manner in which they relate to each other and the chaotic nature of how chronic stressors continue to impact on their development, individually and as a unit. Cassidy and Mohr (2001) contend that disorganization in the infant and adult suggests a "profound sense of helplessness" (p. 284), since facing a frightening or challenging situation with no apparent strategy can lead to the use of desperate (e.g., dependent and child-like behaviors; aggression and rage reactions; attempts to withdraw) and futile strategies (Solomon & George, 1999). Within this framework, the parent-child dyads are often imbalanced and thrust into a hostile/helpless pattern with one member of the dyad being the hostile aggressor and the other member being the passive, helpless, and overwhelmed recipient (Lyons-Ruth, Bronfman & Atwood, 1999). It is highly probable that mother was herself a victim of physical abuse, since her father was subject to violent rage episodes, especially when drinking. It has been shown that mothers with a history of physical abuse often assume the aggressor role in these dyads (Lyons-Ruth & Jacobvitz, 1999). Within this context, the grandmother-mother and grandmother-Jeremy dyads also fit the hostile/helpless pattern, with grandmother assuming the passive role in both dyads.

Neurophysiology of Emotion Regulation. Neurological findings suggest that humans require positive experiences of resolving fearful situations to allow for a build-up of brain structures that help to regulate responses to anxiety and fear-producing situations (Siegel, 1999). In dysfunctional attachment relationships, such as the disorganized attachment, caregivers are not a source of assistance in the regulation of emotion, such as fear, but become the fear-causing agent. Therefore, lack of help in regulation of emotion may result in an inability to self-soothe when upset, lack of skill development for effective coping, and complex approach-avoidance impulses in the presence of the frightening caregiver (Main & Hesse, 1990).

Observed Behaviors. Disruptive behaviors may serve an instrumental role in the attachment process by acting to control and regulate caregiver proximity and attentiveness. Through the use of negative attention-seeking behaviors, such as noncompliance, the child can "lock in" attachment figures based on the use of negative attachment behaviors. It has been suggested that these maladaptive behaviors may fit with the overall schema of family dysfunction (Marvin & Stewart, 1990).

Motivational Processes. Maladaptive attachment patterns can also impact on the child's development of a social orientation and subsequent prosocial competencies. Jeremy's lack of social reciprocity and "me first" attitude preclude strong social motivation at this point in his life. Furthermore, his understanding of relatedness is of a hostile and power-based framework that will likely translate into negative behaviors in social situations due to bossiness, bullying, and aggression. Research has linked early secure attachment to enhanced sociability, compliance, and emotion regulation (Ainsworth et al., 1978; Greenberg, 1999). Jeremy's difficulty with issues of compliance and emotion regulation are self-evident, and his lack of a secure attachment would predict outcomes of poor sociability, and difficulties with self-control and anger management (Carlson & Sroufe, 1995; Thompson, 1994).

The interactive nature of the child-and-caregiver influence (Bowlby's concept of *reciprocal determinism*) can account for variations in security/insecurity of attachment determined more by child characteristics (e.g., difficult temperament, high activity level) in some cases, and immediate environmental characteristics (parenting style) in other cases (Belsky, 1999). In Jeremy's case there is strong evidence to suggest that both factors are highly interrelated. Greenberg, Speltz, DeKlyen, and Endriga (1993) propose a risk factor model for behavioral disorders that incorporates *insecure attachment* as one of the four domains of influence, including: *atypical child characteristics, ineffective parenting, and family environment.*

The fact that Jeremy's mother did not see him as a "difficult child" does not rule out risks for insecure attachment. In addition, based on family history, mother may have a far greater threshold for conceptualizing what constitutes "difficult behaviors" in children compared to a parent exposed to more normative models. While the quality of the attachment relationship can be seen as a risk or protective factor in its own right, research has also demonstrated that within the context of multiple risk factors (low SES, family stress, parent maladjustment, etc.), the likelihood of developing an insecure attachment also increases (Belsky, 1996).

Therapeutic Implications. Although there is significant research linking insecure attachment in infancy and toddlerhood with disruptive behavior disorders in later childhood (Goldberg, 1997; Greenberg, DeKlyen, Speltz, & Endriga, 1997), far less attention has been directed toward the application of attachment theory to clinical treatment, especially concerning treatment of disorganized individuals (Cassidy & Mohr, 2001). Research focusing on avoidant and anxious attachment patterns has remained largely rooted in a psychodynamic approach and has focused primarily on infant-parent psychotherapy (see Lieberman & Zeanah, 1999, for review). The goal of these programs is to assist the child to become more securely attached to the parent(s). Many of the programs are lengthy due to the emphasis on building a therapeutic working alliance with the intervener and the need for extensive ongoing assessments of child-parent or child-caregiver (foster care) interactions and family circumstances. Observations of joint play and discussions provide opportunities for insight-oriented dialogue designed to assist parents in developing more appropriate perceptions of their child and interactional patterns based on building greater empathic attunement with the child's needs. Based on the belief that obstacles to attachment can occur on several levels (infant, parent, environment), therapeutic goals in these programs are to determine the nature of the obstacles blocking attachment (individual differences) and to design treatment to address these specific areas (Zeanah et al., 1997).

One intervention program developed to assist families of behavior disordered children that melds attachment theory with a cognitive-behavioral approach to parent training is the Seattle Program developed by Speltz and colleagues (Greenberg & Speltz, 1988; Speltz, 1990). The program focuses on the absence of "negotiation skills" in the family, and sees the communication breakdown in the parent-child dyad as a primary obstacle to forming a cooperative partnership. The four-phase intervention program is designed to: educate parents regarding underlying developmental processes inherent in struggles between autonomy and control adjusting parental expectations accordingly; reframe the child's behaviors within a developmental framework; focus on limit setting and problem prioritizing; and communication/negotiation skills.

Box 1.12

THINKING OUT LOUD: ATTACHMENT THEORY AND CASE FORMULATION

In two studies of clinic-referred children with ODD, researchers found that up to 80% of the children demonstrated insecure attachments, and that the majority of attachment patterns were of the controlling type (DeKlyen, Speltz, & Greenberg, 1996; Greenberg, Speltz, DeKlyen, & Endriga, 1991). Children who demonstrated the controlling pattern exhibited hostile, punitive, or rejecting behaviors toward their caregiver upon reunion (Greenberg, 1999). Research has also suggested the possibility of trans-generation effects, since mothers of insecurely attached boys with ODD were also found to have backgrounds rooted in insecure attachment (DeKlyen, 1996).

The link between attachment and emotional understanding has also been investigated and results suggest that secure attachment fostered understanding rather than avoidance of negative emotions (Laible & Thompson, 1998). The inability to deal effectively with negative emotions or negative information has been demonstrated repeatedly in the case study of Jeremy, both by Jeremy himself, and by his mother and grandmother. Thompson (1999) suggests that "lessons learned" in attachment relationships may be instrumental in defining expectations in such areas as how others react when the child is experiencing difficulties coping with stress, anxiety, or fears.

Although the Speltz (1990) program has considerable promise, especially for use with children beyond the zero-to-3 population targeted by most attachment programs, at this point in time there is no current empirical support for the program. Interventions linking attachment theory and cognitive behavioral approaches continue to be a viable area for future research.

Case Formulation Based on Social Cognitive Theories. Research concerning children's understanding of social relationships has also been applied to the development of social skills and problem solving in social situations (Coie, 1985; Coie & Dodge, 1983; Schwartz, Dodge, & Coie, 1993; Spivak & Shure, 1982). Studies have demonstrated how children's faulty reasoning about their social relationships can influence inappropriate behavior, whereas cooperative problem solving can serve to enhance more positive social exchanges (Hartup & Laursen, 1993). By the end of the preschool period, children have developed consistent expectations about their social worlds, and act accordingly (Main, 1995; Main & Hesse, 1990). For Jeremy, however, witnessing patterns of parent behavior that are inconsistent or negative may result in problems developing a consistent set of beliefs.

The child's cognitive belief system can be reinforced by adult responses to child behavior patterns. Research has demonstrated that adults respond with less than positive reactions to children who present as "difficult" to manage (Bugental, Blue, & Lewis, 1990). These adult responses can set the stage for further extension of the child's belief system.

Teachers often react to impulsive children with increased control, while at the same time providing nurturance typical for a much younger child. Since expectations for self-control and compliance are minimized, children are not encouraged to develop skills in increasing self-management. The result is a self-fulfilling prophecy, since caregiver behaviors serve to reinforce and strengthen the existing negative belief system (White & Kistner, 1992). The longer the belief systems are allowed to continue and are reinforced, the more difficult the possibility of reframing becomes (Erickson et al., 1985). Jeremy's immature behaviors have resulted in his repeating the kindergarten program, which will serve to reduce the overall expectations that he behave at an age-appropriate level. At home, Jeremy's behaviors are out of control and controlling. Socially, Jeremy has few children who will play with him on a regular basis.

Jeremy's behaviors are at risk for social rejection; studies have revealed that children rejected by peers are often aggressive, argumentative, and retaliatory toward others (Dodge, Bates, & Pettit, 1990). Furthermore, research has demonstrated that these negative behaviors often resulted from tendencies to misinterpret ambivalent social situations as hostile, or what has come to be known as the *hostile attribution bias*.

Although child characteristics undoubtedly influence the emergence of disruptive behaviors, including aggressive, hostile, and defiant responses, the influence of coercive and negative parenting practices on the development and maintenance of these behaviors is well documented (Campbell et al., 1996; Patterson et al., 1991; Snyder, Schrepferman, & St. Peter, 1997). The coercion model has been hypothesized to describe the processes involved in the parent-child exchange that serve to precipitate and maintain aggressive and defiant behaviors (Patterson et al., 1991; Patterson et al., 1989; Snyder et al., 1997). In this model, parent-child interactions are seen to escalate hostile behaviors in a pattern of increasing arousal (Snyder, Edwards, McGraw, Kilgore, & Holton, 1994), which becomes negatively reinforced. Observational studies of parent-child attempts at conflict resolution have determined that while mothers of nonaggressive boys are successful in decreasing conflict, mothers of aggressive boys tend to escalate conflict (Snyder et al., 1994).

In describing her attempts to control Jeremy's behaviors, mother describes how she can "out yell" and "out stomp" Jeremy. The pattern of escalating behaviors matches the coercive pattern described in the literature. The battles are ongoing, and even though his mother might win the occasional battle, Jeremy's noncompliance will continue to prevail.

From a social cognitive perspective, one reason parents of aggressive children are unsuccessful in de-escalating conflict may be due to a *negative attribution bias* regarding their aggressive children. Especially in ambivalent situations, or when compliance is not immediately forthcoming, parents of aggressive children may anticipate more defiance and resistance and act accordingly (Bargh, Lombardi, & Higgins, 1988). Research also suggests that this negative bias may be accompanied by an external locus of control with parents of aggressive children blaming the behavior on stable personality trait, which is beyond the parent's control; for example, "Jeremy's as stubborn as a mule" (Dix & Lochman, 1990; Strassberg, 1995). Within this paradigm, parents' negative schema drive coercive parenting practices that serve to further escalate aggressive child responses. This pattern of negative expectations is clearly articulated by both mother and grandmother, who anticipate that Jeremy will argue about "everything and anything" and wear them down with his persistence and stubborn personality. An interesting comment about this family is that even though negative comments are made regarding Jeremy's behaviors, comments are often couched in humor or sarcasm and on occasion even boasted about.

Research also suggests that parents of aggressive children generate fewer cognitive strategies for child noncompliance when compared to parents of nonaggressive children (Azar, Robinson, Hekimian, & Twentyman, 1984). Recently, Beauchaine and colleagues (2002) found that parents of aggressive children were especially deficient in providing solutions to child noncompliance when required to do so under pressured conditions and that solutions for noncompliance deteriorated over the course of several trials. The authors recommend the need for treatment plans to target the underlying processes of negative attribution bias and affect regulation, which they suggest are the pivotal factors that drive coercive parenting patterns.

Therapeutic Implications. The cognitive behavioral approach seeks to understand the link between thinking and behaving. Therefore, the cognitive behavioral therapist would focus on how Jeremy's faulty belief system might contribute to aggressive behavior. Social cognitive treatment might involve role-play in areas of social cue awareness and the underlying processes that contribute to the development of prosocial behavior, such as secure attachment, social perspective taking, empathy, and self-control.

Parent training using cognitive behavioral methods would focus on negative attributions, emotion regulation, and, ultimately, on increasing effective strategies for behavior management.

Box 1.13

THINKING OUT LOUD: SOCIAL COGNITIVE THEORY AND CASE FORMULATION

In their investigation of maternal responses to child noncompliance, Beauchaine and colleagues (2002) investigated whether parents using ineffective and harsh methods of discipline fail to generate alternative solutions due to an *availability deficit* (limited repertoire) or an *accessibility deficit* (processing deficit during times of stress). The authors contend that research support for the accessibility bias has important implications for parent training programs devoted to teaching parents alternate methods of child management, since parent attributions may undermine successful use of the skills taught. The authors emphasize the need to address negative attributions and adding an affect-regulation component to parent training programs in order to enhance treatment efficacy (Webster-Stratton, 1994).

Case Formulation Based on Behavioral Theories. Mash and Terdal (1997) advocate the "functional/utilitarian approach" to the assessment of children and families that is inherent in the behavioral-systems assessment (BSA) of child and family disorders. According to the authors, behavioral assessment would more closely adhere to the broader meaning of diagnosis, which "considers diagnosis to be an analytic information-gathering process directed at understanding the nature of a problem, its *possible causes*, treatment options and outcomes" (p. 12; emphasis added).

Within this system, "*possible causes*" are often defined within the context of other *overt* situational variables, context variables, structural organizations, and functional relationships. The authors' comment that "BSA is more often concerned with behaviors, cognitions and affects as *direct samples of the domains of interest than as signs of some underlying or remote causes*" (p. 11; emphasis added) clearly distinguishes the behavioral approach to case formulation from other theoretical approaches that have targeted underlying processes as integral to understanding the problem.

Emphasis on integrating diagnosis and classification with BSA strategies (Barlow, 1986; Kazdin, 1983) and the use of behavioral analysis in the decision-making process (La Greca & Lemanek, 1996) have increased the focus on current behavioral assessment practices. With the recent emphasis on conducting functional behavioral assessments in the schools, behavioral intervention planning has been pursued with renewed vigor. It has been debated by some that a functional behavioral assessment is a better approach to intervention planning than classification of disorders by either the dimensional or categorical approaches (Cone, 1997; Haynes & O'Brien, 1990).

Proponents of the behavioral assessment approach argue that the problem-solving strategy inherent in this approach provides a flexible system of hypothesis testing for conducting assessments of children and families for several purposes, including diagnosis, prognosis, treatment design, and treatment efficacy/evaluation (Mash & Terdal, 1997). The continuity between conducting the behavioral assessment and developing the behavioral intervention are emphasized throughout by proponents of the behavioral assessment approach (Mash & Terdal, 1997; Wielkiewicz, 1995). Once the assessment is completed,

Table 1.2   Functional Behavioral Assessment of Jeremy's Noncompliant Behaviors

Precipitating Conditions	Behaviors	Consequences	Results (Reward)
Requests to: Clean room Pick up paper on floor Put away toys	Says it's not fair Says he will "do it later" Asks for help (manipulation) Refuses	Engagement in conflict Repeated requests Assistance provided Power struggle & conflict escalation, or Abandon request	**Rewards** Negative attention Escape/avoid task **Punishment** Physical or verbal aggression

a behavior management program can be developed based on the prevailing assessment information. The behavioral framework consists, at its basis, of a four-stage process designed to: *identify the problem, analyze the problem, implement a plan,* and *evaluate the plan.*

Within the behaviorist tradition, it is possible to identify Jeremy's noncompliant behavior as a *behavioral deficit* (low levels of obedience) or a *behavioral excess* (high levels of noncompliance). Placing Jeremy's behaviors within a functional behavior assessment (FBA) paradigm (see Table 1.2), the goal is to identify the problem as it relates to Precipitating Conditions, Consequences, and Results. One of his parents' presenting complaints is Jeremy's lack of compliance when asked to clean his room. In this case, the *precipitating conditions* would represent the requests initiated by the parents that would begin the behavioral sequence of events. When faced with these requests, Jeremy demonstrates the following repertoire of *behaviors (argues, delays, manipulates, refuses)*. When faced with these behaviors, parents respond with a number of reactions or consequences ranging from doing the task themselves (in whole or part) to escalating battles that may end in either abandoning the request or in harsh punishment.

In developing a behavioral plan, it is preferable to concentrate on increasing a deficit behavior than on reducing an excessive behavior. In this case, it is preferable to increase obedient behavior than to attempt to reduce noncompliant behavior, since increasing a positive behavior can be positively rewarding in itself. At this point in time, the positive reinforcement that Jeremy is receiving due to his noncompliance far outweighs the occasional and inconsistent punishment he may receive. The behavior plan would be to shift the positive reinforcement to obedience rather than reduce noncompliance.

Principles of operant conditioning predict that there are two options available for increasing or maintaining obedient behavior: *positive reinforcement or negative reinforcement.* Reinforcements are acts that have a positive outcome and, as such, will be rewarding, thereby increasing the likelihood that a behavior will be repeated. *Positive reinforcement* involves the addition of a reward (e.g., clean your room and you will get a sticker book). *Positive reinforcement,* however, is not always what it appears to be, and in Jeremy's case his parents unknowingly reinforce many of his negative behaviors in various ways: humor (suggesting acceptance), boasting (suggesting pride), and providing increased attention. In this case, Jeremy is rewarded by *negative attention,* which to Jeremy might be better than no attention at all. *Negative reinforcement,* not to be confused with punishment, is also rewarding because it involves the removal of a negative (e.g., if you clean your room, you will not have to take out the trash). Negative reinforcement has sometimes been called *escape* because it allows one to escape a negative consequence. Jeremy's argumentativeness and noncompliance are often negatively reinforcing because they allow him to escape having to do a task. Principles of learning also provide a set of assumptions for reducing or eliminating behavior: *punishment* that involves adding a negative consequence and/or *penalty,* removing a positive. Complete withholding of any reinforcement will eventually result in elimination of the behavior, or what the behaviorists refer to as *extinction.*

Although coercion theory from a cognitive framework attended to the underlying processes of negative attribution and emotion regulation, a behaviorist might use the theory to describe the antecedents and consequences of noncompliance. Parents who eventually yield to a child's escalating and demanding behaviors serve to *positively reinforce the child's misbehavior* (child eventually gets what child wants) and at the same time give *negative reinforcement for their own compliance* (cessation of whining and complaining). Therefore, the parent learns that giving in will stop the demands, while the child learns that increased demands result in parent compliance. Since positive and negative reinforcement serve to strengthen behaviors, parent and child become "locked in" to an escalating and never-ending battle.

Another powerful source of learning is observation. Bandura's (1977) understanding of the social aspects of learning has been instrumental in increasing our awareness of the possible implications of observing the behavior of others. Children's observation and subsequent modeling of adult behavior can have positive (nurturing and empathic caring behaviors) or negative (aggressive responses, e.g., witness of domestic violence) consequences. These responses can be immediately observable or can be evident in a delayed response. Bandura's studies of the impact of observed aggression on modeling behavior have gained increased appreciation in contemporary investigations regarding children who witness domestic violence. In considering our example of the child demonstrating aggression at school, the social behaviorist may seek to confirm or rule out whether the child may be imitating behaviors observed in the home.

Barkley (1997) suggests a four-factor model, which can be used to explain factors that can maintain and increase noncompliant behavior. According to this model, predisposing characteristics include the following:

1. the temperament of the child (temperamental, high emotional reactivity, impulsive, active, inattentive);

2. temperament of the parents (immature, temperamental, and impulsive);

3. child management patterns (inconsistent, harsh, indiscriminate and coercive parenting, and poor monitoring of child activities); and

4. distressed family environment (financial, health, and personal stressors).

The model is well suited as a framework for a case formulation that can integrate information from across theoretical models.

When evaluating Jeremy's temperament, consideration would be given to the frequency and intensity of behaviors demonstrated across contexts, while attention to attachment concerns would focus specifically on the quality and effectiveness of the parent-child relationship. Jeremy's temperament has historically demonstrated problems in areas of adaptation to change, and being emotionally reactive, evidencing difficulties with emotion regulation (Bridges & Grolnick, 1995).

The family dynamics also note additional risk factors, such as a history of family pathology and the underlying dynamics inherent in this mother-grandmother parented family that often seems to shift roles as to who is the parent and who is the child. Jeremy's high level of intelligence is an additional contributing factor in his ability to manipulate his environment and escape/avoid compliance requests.

Research has repeatedly demonstrated that the nature of parent-child interactions is a strong predictor of childhood noncompliant, defiant, and aggressive behavior patterns. Poor management practices due to ineffective, inconsistent, and indiscriminate parental controls often result in overly harsh but inconsistent discipline and inadequate monitoring of activities. As a result, child noncompliance becomes an effective means of avoidance or escape from doing undesirable tasks such as picking up toys or cleaning a bedroom. Mother and grandmother are often at odds over setting limits and often present Jeremy with contradictory messages. Grandmother is particularly reinforcing of Jeremy's manipulations and often gives in, allowing his successful escape or avoidance of unpleasant tasks. Jeremy's mother often responds with escalating and coercive responses ("screaming as loud as possible"), likely due to their occasional success ("he couldn't scream as loud, even though he tried, so I won that time"). In this context, Jeremy has learned how to successfully avoid unpleasant tasks on the one hand, and learned to model negative behaviors on the other.

Therapeutic Implications. The effectiveness of positive reinforcement, time-out, and behavioral contracting as components of child management programs have been well documented for use with punitive families (Cohn & Daro, 1987; Forehand & McMahon, 1981). Based on the FBA, the therapist might determine that Jeremy's noncompliant behavior is being rewarded by escape/avoidance of tasks and by parental attention. A behavioral plan to increase compliant behavior might involve a reward program for positive responses to requests. Through the use of behavioral tools such as knowledge of schedules of reinforcement and objective observation techniques, behavior intervention plans can be developed, monitored and modified to assist with behavioral change. Rewarding obedience with attention and praise, issuing demands that are clear and age appropriate, and providing consistent follow through would strengthen Jeremy's compliant behaviors. One method of increasing obedience that has empirical support is the use of a hierarchy of tasks from high compliance (Jeremy has least resistance to compliance) to low compliance (Jeremy consistently resists the task). Building on earlier successes has proven to be a source of motivation in increasing compliance with more difficult tasks later on (Ducharme & Popynick, 1993).

Box 1.14

THINKING OUT LOUD:
BEHAVIORAL THEORY AND CASE FORMULATION

Although Mash and Terdal (1997) argue against narrowly contrasting behavioral assessment with more traditional assessment approaches, they do suggest some fundamental conceptual differences between the two approaches. According to the authors, the behavioral systems assessment (BSA) approach tends to focus on state (situation-specific patterns of behavior) versus trait (underlying personality dynamics) characteristics, ideographic versus nomothetic comparisons, and places emphasis on stability and discontinuity over time versus consistency and stability of underlying causes.

It is important to note, however, that despite the current emphasis on conducting behavioral assessments in the schools, behavioral analysis should involve a multisituational analysis, which requires gathering information concerning the child's behavior, cognitions, and affects as they present across multiple situations, as seen by various informants. Despite the undisputed importance of attention to situational variables in conducting behavioral assessments, giving situational factors their due importance has often been neglected in child assessment (Mash & Terdal, 1997). Furthermore, behavioral intervention plans implemented within the home often fail due to lack of consideration of the feasibility of family follow through in situations that may pre-empt participation due to a high level of stressors (Emery, 2001).

The importance of developing early treatment interventions to reduce noncompliant behaviors is evident in the repeated associations of defiant behavior and later maladjustment in adolescence and adulthood. A recent meta analysis of psychosocial treatments for children and youth with ODD and conduct disorder revealed behavioral parent training programs to be a successful method for reducing deviant behavior in young children (Brestan & Eyberg, 1998).

Home-based, parent-delivered interventions often are the result of programs directed toward parent management training (PMT), and research has demonstrated that between one third and two thirds of children show clinically significant improvement (Barkley, 1997; Kazdin, 1996). The rationale for PMT is based on the premise that coercive parent-child interchanges and environmental contingencies are predisposing factors in the development and maintenance of oppositional, defiant, and noncompliant behaviors. Given the dynamics involved in this family and the issues of compliance, the goal would be to develop a home-based behavioral intervention plan.

Case Formulation From a Family Systems Theoretical Perspective. Family systems theory is represented by a variety of approaches that emphasize the family unit as the focus of assessment and intervention. This theoretical framework acknowledges the family system, itself, as a unit made up of many subsystems: parent-child, marriage partners, siblings, extended family, and so on. Within families, behaviors are often directed toward maintaining or changing *"boundaries," "alignment,"* and *"power."* Often a family's degree of dysfunction can be defined by boundaries that are poorly or inconsistently defined, or those that are too extreme (too loose or too rigid).

Salvador Minuchin (1974), a proponent of structural family therapy, described several family patterns that can contribute to dysfunction. In *enmeshed families,* boundaries between family members are often vague and members of the family are overly involved in each other's lives. Jeremy's family is an enmeshed family of three. The boundaries between mother and daughter and child are often blurred and role reversals are common. Jeremy is often privy to information that is inappropriate, given his age. According to Minuchin, *enmeshed families* (lacking in boundaries) may see a child's need to individuate as a threat to the family unit. Therefore, Jeremy's bids for independence may be undermined by his parents in order to promote dependence on the family. However, the family is also *conflictive,* evidenced by poor problem-solving abilities, tendencies to abdicate power to Jeremy, and tendencies to minimize or deny problems. Attempts at problem solving are short lived and grandmother and mother do not support each other or agree on child-rearing practices. Grandmother's tendency is to be overindulgent, give in to Jeremy, and then withdraw. Mother attempts to discipline but is inconsistent and too harsh. Other clusters that cause family problems include triangular relationships, which undermine the importance of the primary parent partnership. Triangular relationships that serve to shift the balance of power include: *the parent-child coalition* (grandmother and Jeremy vs. mother), *triangulation* (Jeremy caught between his grandmother and mother), and *detouring* (maintaining Jeremy as focus of the problem to avoid acknowledging their own issues or problems). Given the number of problems evident in the lives of the mother and grandmother, identifying Jeremy as the problem can serve the important function of distracting attention from their own difficulties and dysfunction. Given Jeremy's superior intelligence, it is likely that Jeremy will use these triangular relationships to his advantage. Within a family of little structure, Jeremy can readily manipulate his parents, set up his own rule system, and increase his position of power and control.

Communication problems in the family are evident in the use of vague generalities, rather than specifics; tendencies to digress away from important issues; lack of organization; chaotic thought processes; tendencies to minimize; and misplaced and inappropriate humor. With respect to commands, mother issues primarily *beta commands,* which are vague and are often intercepted by other commands, as opposed to *alpha commands,* which are clear and concise. Beta commands are often associated with noncompliance because the commands are difficult to follow (ambiguous) or because other commands are issued simultaneously (Forehand, 1977).

Treatment Implications. Within the family systems approach, the family therapist would create an alliance with the family by joining the family and observing family interactional patterns from the inside out.

Once the problem has been formulated, the therapist works with the family to restructure the family interactions toward positive growth and change. In Jeremy's case, the therapist would likely focus on repositioning the balance of power and on improved problem solving and communication.

Case Formulations and Theoretical Positions: A Summation

Viewing Jeremy's case from five different theoretical perspectives is an important exercise in demonstrating how different theoretical viewpoints conceptualize the same behavioral disorder; in this case, Jeremy's noncompliant behaviors. A summary of each of these case formulations is presented in Table 1.3.

As is readily apparent in Table 1.3 and the previous discussions, treatment methods can also vary widely, based on the case formulation generated. At a metacognitive level, theoretical assumptions can be seen to demonstrate *equifinality,* since many theoretical pathways can be developed to explain the emergence of the same problem behavior (noncompliance) or mental disorder (ODD).

Given the wide range of theoretical viewpoints available, it becomes increasingly clear that clinicians may view any given behavioral response from a variety of different angles. It is also evident that although some theories tend to overlap (cognitive/behavioral/social), features of other theories may be more difficult to integrate (biomedical or psychodynamic). In many cases, theory influences the direction of the investigator's focus on determining the causes for a behavior: for example, internal/external forces, past/present influences, and individual/interpersonal characteristics.

Although emphasis in Part 1 has been on the unique contributions of each theoretical framework to assist in clarity of presentation, there is an increased awareness of the need to integrate information in a trans-theoretical effort. Recent research has increased our awareness of the complexity of childhood disorders (Kazdin, 1997; Kazdin & Kagan, 1994) and, as a result, emphasis has shifted from single-factor to multiple-factor and interactive explanations for childhood disorders (Mash & Wolfe, 2002). As a result, contemporary

Table 1.3   Case Formulation From Five Theoretical Perspectives: Jeremy's Noncompliant Behaviors

Theoretical Model	Case Formulation		
	Problem Identification	Problem Dynamics (Factors That Precipitate & Maintain the Problem)	Treatment
Psychodynamic	Internal & unconscious conflict: Needs & anxiety Weak ego development	Id vs. ego, superego Autonomy vs. dependence Rapprochement: Separation-individuation & anxiety Internal working model & weak ego	Play therapy Parent therapy Conjoint play therapy
Attachment & Parenting	Insecure attachment: Avoidant or disorganized Obstacles to attachment	Maladaptive internal working models -> Relationships as hostile, angry, anxious, fearful) Emotion regulation (high arousal) Demands and control Parenting styles: Permissive-indulgent Authoritarian Inconsistent Trans-generational attachment issues	Working alliance Insight oriented Independence as positive development Increase security of relationship
Cognitive	Maladaptive thought processes Negative attributions Faulty beliefs	Coercion model & negative attributions: **Parents**: Negative attribution bias & poor emotion regulation **Child**: Hostile attribution bias + poor emotion regulation	CBT for parents and Jeremy to change faulty belief systems, increase emotion regulation, effective strategies for behavior management
Behavioral	Identify contingencies that positively reward behavior	Coercion model & positive reinforcement Conflict rewarded by negative attention Delays and manipulation rewarded by task avoidance	Functional behavioral assessment Identify contingencies and alter behavior Positive rewards for obedience
Family Systems	Identify boundaries, triangular relationships, & communication styles	Imbalance in power: Parent child coalition: Grandma + Jeremy vs. mom Triangulation: Jeremy vs. Mom + Grandma Hostile/helpless dyads: Jeremy + Mom vs. Grandma Beta Commands and lack of structure	Working alliance with family Restore balance of power Reposition boundaries Improve communication style

clinicians often integrate assumptions from several theoretical frameworks in an effort to assess the many factors that may serve to predispose, initiate, and maintain disordered behaviors, with the ultimate goal of developing treatment plans based on a better understanding of what will work best, under which conditions, for which populations, experiencing which presenting problems.

Case Formulation and Post-Case Questions

At the end of each of the case studies presented, the reader will find a list of *Post-Case Questions* that have been developed to challenge the reader to apply information from theory and research to the case in question. As a beginning exercise, the following questions address the case of Jeremy:

1. Based on the case formulations presented for Jeremy, develop a treatment plan that uses information from at least three of the theoretical frameworks presented.

2. Which of the theoretical frameworks would you use to best describe the role of the grandmother in Jeremy's life? How would you incorporate grandmother in the therapeutic plan? What are the possible risks and what are the possible protective factors that grandmother would bring to the treatment focus?

3. According to Bronfenbrenner, the *mesosystem* predicts the degree to which a system remains healthy, functional, and in balance. Given the information you know about Jeremy's family and the school system, describe what you believe the current status to be and how you would attempt to maximize the *mesosystem* between these two environmental contexts.

4. Using coercion theory as the overarching dimension, describe power struggles in the family from the viewpoint of cognitive, behavioral, and family systems theories.

REFERENCES

Abidin, R. R. (1995). *Parenting Stress Index* (3rd ed.). Odessa, FL: Psychological Assessment Resources.

Achenbach, T. M. (1995). Diagnosis, assessment and comorbidity in psychosocial treatment research. *Journal of Abnormal Child Psychology, 23,* 45-65.

Achenbach, T. M., McConaughy, S. H., & Howell, C. T. (1987). Child/adolescent behavioral and emotional problems: Implications of cross-informant correlations for situational specificity. *Psychological Bulletin, 101,* 213-232.

Achenbach, T. M., & Rescorla, L. A. (2001). *Manual for the ASEBA School-Age Forms & Profiles.* Burlington, VT: ASEBA.

Ainsworth, M. D. S., Blehar, M. C., Waters, E., & Wall, S. (1978). *Patterns of attachment.* Hillsdale. NJ: Lawrence Erlbaum.

American Psychiatric Association (APA). (2000). *Diagnostic and statistical manual of mental disorders* (4th ed., text revision). Washington, DC: Author.

Azar, S. T., Robinson, D., Hekimian, D., & Twentyman, C. T. (1984). Unrealistic expectations and problem-solving ability in maltreating and comparison mothers. *Journal of Consulting and Clinical Psychology, 52,* 687-691.

Bandura, A. (1977). *Social learning theory.* Englewood Cliffs, NJ: Prentice Hall.

Bargh, J. A., Lombardi, W. J., & Higgins, E. T. (1988). Automaticity of chronically accessible constructs in person by situation effects on person perception: It's just a matter of time. *Journal of Personality and Social Psychology, 55,* 599-605.

Barkley, R. A. (1997). *Attention Deficit Hyperactivity Disorder.* New York: Guilford.

Barkley, R. A. (1998). *Attention-deficit/hyperactivity disorder: A handbook for diagnosis and treatment* (2nd ed.). New York: Guilford.

Barlow, D. H. (1986). In defense of panic disorder with agoraphobia in the behavioral treatment of panic: A comment on Kleiner. *The Behavior Therapist, 9,* 99-100.

Baumrind, D. (1991). The influences of parenting style on adolescent competence and substance use. *Journal of Early Adolescence, 11,* 56-95.

Beardslee, W. R., Bemporad, J., Keller, M. B., & Klerman (1983). Children of parents with major affective disorder: A review. *American Journal of Psychiatry, 140,* 825-832.

Beauchaine, T. P., Strassberg, Z., Kees, M. R., & Drabick, D. A. G. (2002). Cognitive response repertoires to child noncompliance by mothers of aggressive boys. *Journal of Abnormal Child Psychology, 30,* 89-101.

Belsky, J. (1988). Child maltreatment and the emergent family system. In K. Browne, C. Davies, & P. Strattan (Eds.), *Early prediction and prevention of child abuse* (pp. 291-302). New York: John Wiley.

Biederman, J. (1991). Attention deficit hyperactivity disorder (ADHD). *Annals of Clinical Psychiatry, 3,* 9-22.

Biederman, J., Faraone, S. V., Keenan, K., Knee, D., & Tsuang, M. T. (1990). Family-genetic and psychosocial risk factors in DSM-III attention deficit disorder. *Journal of the American Academy of Child and Adolescent Psychiatry, 29,* 526-533.

Biederman, J., Rosenbaum, J., Bolduc-Murphy, D., Farone, S., Chalfoff, J., Hirshfeld, D., & Kagan, J. (1993). A three year follow-up of children with and without behavioral inhibition. *Journal of the American Academy of Child and Adolescent Psychiatry, 32,* 814-821.

Berman, P. S. (1997). *Case conceptualization and treatment planning: Exercises for integrating theory and clinical practice.* Thousand Oaks, CA: Sage.

Block, J. H., & Block, J. (1980). The role of ego-control and ego-resiliency in the organization of behavior. In W. A. Collins (Ed.), *Minnesota Symposia on Child Psychology* (Vol. 13). Hillsdale, NJ: Lawrence Erlbaum.

Blum, R. W., Beuhring, T., Shew, M. L., Bearinger, L. H., Sieving, R. E., & Resnick, M. D. (2000). The effects of race/ethnicity, income and family structure on adolescent risk behaviors. *American Journal of Public Health, 90,* 1885-1891.

Bowlby, J. (1982). *Attachment and loss: Vol. 1. Attachment* (2nd ed.). New York: Basic Books. (Original work published 1969)

Brestan, E. V., & Eyberg, S. M. (1998). Effective psychosocial treatments of conduct disordered children and adolescents: 29 years, 82 studies, and 5, 272 kids. *Journal of Clinical Child Psychology, 27,* 180-189.

Bridges, L., & Grolnick, W. (1995). The development of emotional self-regulation in infancy and early childhood. In N. Eisenberg (Ed.), *Social development: Review of child development research* (pp. 185-211). Thousand Oaks, CA: Sage.

Bronfenbrenner, U. (1979). *The ecology of human development.* Cambridge, MA: Harvard University Press.

Bronfenbrenner, U. (1989). Ecological systems theory. *Annals of Child Development, 6,* 187-249.

Brown, S. I., & Walter, M. I. (1990). *The art of problem posing* (2nd ed.). Hillsdale, NJ: Lawrence Erlbaum.

Bruch, M., & Bond, F. W. (1999). *Beyond diagnosis: Case formulation approaches in CBT.* New York: John Wiley.

Bugental, D. B., Blue, J., & Lewis, J. (1990). Caregiver beliefs and dysphoric affect directed to difficult children. *Developmental Psychology, 26,* 631-638.

Campbell, S. B., Pierce, E. W., Moore, G., Marakovitz, S., & Newby, K. (1996). Boys' externalizing problems at elementary school: Pathways from early behavior problems, maternal control, and family stress. *Development and Psychopathology, 8,* 836-851.

Carlson, E. A., & Sroufe, L. A. (1995). Contributions of attachment theory to developmental psychopathology. In D. Cicchetti & D. J. Cohen (Eds.), *Developmental psychopathology* (Vol. 1, pp. 581-617). New York: John Wiley.

Carlson, V., Cicchetti, D., Barnett, D., & Braunwald, K. (1989). Disorganized/disoriented attachment relationships in maltreated infants. *Developmental Psychology, 25,* 525-531.

Cassidy, J., & Mohr, J. J. (2001). Unsolvable fear, trauma, and psychopathology: Theory, research, and clinical considerations related to disorganized attachment across the life span. *Clinical Psychology: Science and Practice, 8,* 275-298.

Cicchetti, D., & Rogosch, F. A. (1996). Editorial: Equifinality and multifinality in developmental psychopathology. *Developmental Psychopathology, 8,* 597-600.

Cicchetti, D., & Toth, S. L. (1995). Developmental psychopathology and disorders of affect. In D. Cicchetti & D. J. Cohen (Eds.), *Developmental psychopathology: Vol. 2. Risk, disorder and adaptation* (pp. 369-420). New York: John Wiley.

Cicchetti, D., & Toth, S. L. (1998). The development of depression in children and adolescents. *American Psychologist, 53,* 221-241.

Cohn, A. H., & Daro, D. (1987). Is treatment too late?: What ten years of evaluative research tells us. *Child Abuse and Neglect, 11,* 433-442.

Coie, J.D. (1985). Fitting social skills interventions to the target group. In B. Schneider, K. Rubin, & J. Ledingham (Eds.), *Peer relationships and social skills in childhood* (Vol. II). New York: Springer.

Coie, J. D., & Dodge, K. A. (1983). Continuity of children's social status: A five-year longitudinal study. *Merrill-Palmer Quarterly, 29,* 261-282.

Cone, J. D. (1997). Issues in functional analysis in behavioral assessment. *Behavior Research and Therapy, 35,* 259-275.

Dabbs, J., & Morris, R. (1990). Testosterone, social class and antisocial behavior in a sample of 4,462 men. *Psychological Science, 1,* 209-211.

DeKlyen, M. (1996). Disruptive behavior disorders and inter-generational attachment patterns: A comparison of normal and clinic-referred preschoolers and their mothers. *Journal of Consulting and Clinical Psychology, 64,* 357-365.

DeKlyen, M., Speltz, M. L., & Greenberg, M. T. (1996, January). *Predicting early starting behavior disorders: A clinical sample of preschool oppositional defiant boys.* Paper presented at the International Society for Research in Child and Adolescent Psychopathology, Santa Monica, CA.

Dix, T., & Lochman, J. E. (1990). Social cognition and negative reactions to children: A comparison of mothers of aggressive and nonaggressive boys. *Journal of Social and Clinical Psychology, 9,* 418-438.

Dodge, K., Bates, J., & Pettit, G. (1990). Mechanisms in the cycle of violence. *Science, 250,* 1678-1683.

Ducharme, J. M., & Popynick, M. (1993). Errorless compliance to parental requests: Treatment effects and generalization. *Behavior Therapy, 24,* 209-226.

Duncan, G. J., Brooks-Gunn, J. & Klebanov, P. K. (1994). Economic deprivation and early childhood development. *Child Development, 65,* 296-318.

Eells, D. (Ed.). (1997). *Handbook of psychotherapy case formulation.* New York: Guilford.

Eley, T. C., & Stevenson, J. (2000). Specific life events and chronic experiences differentially associated with depression and anxiety in young twins. *Journal of Abnormal Child Psychology, 28,* 383-394.

Emery, R. E. (2001). Behavioral family intervention: Less "behavior" and more "family." In A. Booth, A. C. Crouter, & M. Clements (Eds.), *Couples in conflict* (pp. 241-249). Mahwah, NJ: Lawrence Erlbaum.

Erickson, M., Egeland, B., & Sroufe, L. A. (1985). The relationship between quality of attachment and behavior problems in preschool in a high risk sample. In I. Bretherton & E. Waters (Eds.), Growing points in attachment theory and research. *Monographs of the Society for Research in Child Development, 50*(1-2, Series No. 209), 147-186.

Fishman, D. B. (2000, May 3). Transcending the efficacy versus effectiveness research debate: Proposal for a new, electronic "Journal of Pragmatic Case Studies." *Prevention & Treatment, 3,* Article 8. Retrieved December 1, 2002, from http://journals.apa.org/ prevention/volume3/pre00300008a.html

Fonagy, P. (1999). Psychoanalytic theory from the viewpoint of attachment theory and research. In J. Cassidy & P. Shaver (Eds.), *Handbook of attachment: Theory, research and clinical applications* (pp. 595-624). New York: Guilford.

Fonagy, P., & Target, M. (1994). The efficacy of psychoanalysis for children with disruptive disorders. *Journal of the American Academy of Child and Adolescent Psychiatry, 33,* 45-55.

Fonagy, P., & Target, M. (1996). A contemporary psychoanalytical perspective: Psychodynamic developmental therapy. In E. D. Hibbs & P. S. Jensen (Eds.), *Psychosocial treatments for child and adolescent disorders: Empirically based strategies from clinical practice* (pp. 619-638). Washington, DC: American Psychological Association.

Fonagy, P., Target, M., Cottrell, D., Phillips, J., & Kurtz, Z. (2002). *What works for whom? A critical review of treatments for children and adolescents.* New York: Guilford.

Forehand, R. L. (1977). Child noncompliance to parental requests: Behavioral analysis and treatment. In M. Hersen, R. M. Eisler, & P. M. Miller (Eds.), *Progress in behavior modification* (Vol. 5, pp. 111-148). New York: Academic Press.

Forehand, R. L., & McMahon, R. J. (1981). *Helping the noncompliant child. A clinician's guide to parent training.* New York: Guilford.

Goldberg, S. (1997). Attachment and childhood behavior problems in normal, at-risk, and clinical samples. In L. Atkinson & K. J. Zucker (Eds.), *Attachment and psychopathology* (pp. 171-195). New York: Guilford.

Goldsmith, H. (1983). Genetic influences on personality from infancy to adulthood. *Child Development, 54,* 331-355.

Greenberg, M. T. (1999). Attachment and psychopathology in childhood. In J. Cassidy & P. Shaver (Eds.), *Handbook of attachment: Theory, research and clinical applications* (pp. 469-496). New York: Guilford.

Greenberg, M. T., DeKlyen, M., Speltz, M. L., & Endriga, M. C. (1997). The role of attachment processes in externalizing psychopathology in young children. In L. Atkinson & K. J. Zucker (Eds.), *Attachment and psychopathology* (pp. 196-222). New York: Guilford.

Greenberg, M. T., & Speltz, M. L. (1988). Contributions of attachment theory to the understanding of conduct problems during the preschool years. In J. Belsky & T. Nezworski (Eds.), *Clinical implications of attachment* (pp. 177-218). Hillsdale, NJ: Lawrence Erlbaum.

Greenberg, M. T., Speltz, M. L., DeKlyen, M., & Endriga, M. C. (1991). Attachment security in preschoolers with and without externalizing problems: A replication. *Development and Psychopathology, 3,* 413-430.

Greenberg, M. T., Speltz, M. L., DeKlyen, M., & Endriga, M. C. (1993). The role of attachment in early development of disruptive behavior problems. *Development and Psychopathology, 5,* 191-213.

Gustavsson, N. S., & Balgopal, P. R. (1990). Violence and minority youth: An ecological perspective. In A. R. Stiffman & L. E. Davis (Eds.), *Ethnic issues in adolescent mental health.* Thousand Oaks, CA: Sage.

Hartup, W., & Laursen, B. (1993). Conflict and context in peer relations. In C. Hart (Ed.), *Children on playgrounds: Research perspectives and applications*. Ithaca: State University of New York Press.

Haynes, S. N., & O'Brien, W. H. (1990). Functional analysis in behavior therapy. *Clinical Psychology Review, 10,* 649-668.

Held, B. (1996). Solution-focused therapy and the postmodern. In S. D. Miller, M. R. Hubble, & B. Duncan (Eds.), *Handbook of solution-focused brief therapy* (pp. 27-43). San Francisco: Jossey-Bass.

Hennessey, B. A. (1994). Finding (and solving?) the problem. [Review of Problem finding, problem solving and creativity]. *Contemporary Psychology, 40,* 971-972.

Hersen, M., & Porzelius, L. K. (Eds.) (2002). *Diagnosis, conceptualization and treatment planning for adults: A step-by-step guide*. Mahwah, NJ: Lawrence Erlbaum.

Kaufman, A. S., & Lichtenberger, E. (2000). *Essentials of WISC-III & WPPSI-R assessment*. New York: John Wiley.

Kazdin, A. E. (1983). Psychiatric diagnosis, dimensions of dysfunction and child behavior therapy. *Behavior Therapy, 14,* 73-99.

Kazdin, A. E. (1996). Problem solving and parent management in treating aggressive and antisocial behavior. In E. D. Hibbs & P. S. Jensen (Eds.), *Psychosocial treatments for child and adolescent disorders* (pp. 377-408). Washington, DC: American Psychological Association.

Kazdin, A. E. (1997). A model for developing effective treatments: Progression and interplay of theory, research and practice. *Journal of Clinical Child Psychology, 26,* 114-129.

Kazdin, A. E., & Kagan, J. (1994). Models of dysfunction in developmental psychopathology. *Clinical Psychology: Science and Practice, 1,* 35-52.

Kendall, P. C. (1993). Cognitive behavioral therapies for youth: Guiding theory, current status and emerging developments. *Journal of Consulting and Clinical Psychology, 61,* 235-247.

Kendall, P. C., & Braswell, L. (1993). *Cognitive-behavioral therapy for impulsive children* (2nd ed.). New York: Guilford.

Kendall, P. C., Chansky, T. E., Kane, M., Kim, R., Kortlander, E., Roana, K., Sessa, F., & Siqueland, L. (1992). *Anxiety disorders in youth: Cognitive-behavioral interventions*. Needham Heights, MA: Allyn & Bacon.

Kochanska, G., Murray, K., Jacques, T. Y., Koenig, A. L., & Vandgeest, K. A. (1996). Inhibitory control in young children and its role in emerging internalization. *Child Development, 67,* 490-507.

Kovacs, M. (1997). Psychiatric disorders in youths with IDDM: Rates and risk factors. *Diabetes Care, 20,* 36-44.

Kramer, S., & Akhtar, S. (1989). The developmental context of internalized preoedipal object relations: Clinical applications of Mahler's theory of symbiosis and separations-individuation. *Psychoanalytic Quarterly, 57,* 547-576.

Kronenberger, W. G., & Meyer, R. G. (2001). *The child clinician's handbook* (2nd ed.). Needham Heights, MA: Allyn & Bacon.

Kuhne, M., Schachar, R., & Tannock, R. (1997). Impact of comorbid oppositional or conduct problems on attention-deficit hyperactivity disorder. *Journal of the American Academy of Child and Adolescent Psychiatry, 36,* 1715-1725.

La Greca, A. M., & Lemanek, K. L. (1996). Editorial: Assessment as a process in pediatric psychology. *Journal of Pediatric Psychology, 21,* 137-151.

Laible, D. J., & Thompson R. A. (1998). Attachment and emotional understanding in preschool children. *Developmental Psychology, 34,* 1038-1045.

Lieberman, A. F., & Zeanah, C. H. (1999). Contributions of attachment theory to infant-parent psychotherapy and other interventions with infants and young children. In J. Cassidy & P. Shaver (Eds.), *Handbook of attachment: Theory, research and clinical applications,* (pp. 555-574). New York: Guilford.

Loeber, R., & Disshion, T. J. (1983). Early predictors of male adolescent delinquency: A review. *Psychological Bulletin, 94,* 68-99.

Luthar, S. S., & Zigler, E. (1992). Intelligence and social competence among high-risk adolescents. *Development and Psychopathology, 4,* 287-299.

Lyons-Ruth, K., Bronfman, E., & Atwood, G. (1999). A relational diathesis model of hostile-helpless states of mind: Expressions in mother-infant interaction. In J. Solomon & C. George (Eds.). *Attachment disorganization* (pp. 33-70). New York: Guilford.

Lyons-Ruth, K., & Jacobvitz, D. (1999). Attachment disorganization: Unresolved loss, relational violence, and lapses in behavioral and attentional strategies. In J. Cassidy & P. R. Shaver (Eds.), *Handbook of attachment: Theory, research, and clinical applications* (pp. 520-554). New York: Guilford.

Mahler, M. S., Pine, F., & Bergman, A. (1975). *The psychological birth of the human infant: Symbiosis and individuation.* New York: Basic Books.

Main, M. (1995). Recent studies in attachment: Overview, with selected implications for clinical work. In S. Goldberg, R. Muir, & J. Kerr (Eds.), *Attachment theory: Social, developmental and clinical perspectives* (pp. 407-474). Hillsdale, NJ: Analytic Press.

Main, M., & Hesse, E. (1990). Parents' unresolved traumatic experiences are related to infant disorganized attachment status: Is frightened and/or frightening parental behavior the linking mechanism? In M. T. Greenberg, D. Cicchetti, & E. M. Cummings (Eds.), *Attachment in the preschool years: Theory, research, and intervention* (pp. 161-184). Chicago: University of Chicago Press.

Marvin, R. S., & Stewart, R. B. (1990). A family systems framework for the study of attachment. In M. T. Greenberg, D. Cicchetti, & E. M. Cummings (Eds.), *Attachment in the preschool years: Theory, research, and intervention* (pp. 51-86). Chicago: University of Chicago Press.

Mash, E. J., & Terdal, L. G. (1997). *Assessment of childhood disorders* (3rd ed.). New York: Guilford.

Mash, E. J., & Wolfe, D. A. (2002). *Abnormal child psychology* (2nd ed.). Belmont, CA: Wadsworth.

Matlin, M. W. (1998). *Cognition* (4th ed.). New York: Harcourt Brace.

Matlin, M. (2002). *Cognition* (5th ed.). Fort Worth, TX: Harcourt College.

McLoyd, V. (1990). The impact of economic hardship on black families and children: Psychosocial distress, parenting and socioemotional development. *Child Development, 61,* 311-346.

McWilliams, N. (1999). *Psychoanalytic case formulation.* New York: Guilford.

Mednick, S. A., & Hutchings, B. (1978). Genetic and psychophysiological factors in asocial behavior. In R. D. Hare & D. Schalling (Eds.), *Psychopathic behavior: Approaches to research.* Chichester, UK: Wiley.

Messer, S. B. (2000). A psychodynamic clinician responds to Fishman's case study proposal. *Prevention & Treatment, Volume 3, Article 9.* Available on the World Wide Web at http://journals.apa.org/prevention/volume3/pre00300009c.html

Minuchin, S. (1974). *Families and family therapy.* Cambridge, MA: Harvard University Press.

Offord, D. R., Adler, R. J., & Boyle, M. H. (1986). Prevalence and sociodemographic correlates of conduct disorder. *The American Journal of Social Psychiatry, 4,* 272-278.

Parker, J., & Asher, S. R. (1987). Peer relations and later personal adjustment: Are low-accepted children at risk? *Psychological Bulletin, 102,* 357-389.

Patterson, G. R., Capaldi, D., & Bank, L. (1991). An early starter model for predicting delinquency. In D. Pepler & K. H. Rubin (Eds.), *The development and treatment of childhood aggression* (pp. 139-168). Hillsdale, NJ: Lawrence Erlbaum.

Patterson, G. R., DeBaryshe, B. D., & Ramsey, E. (1989). A developmental perspective on antisocial behavior. *American Psychologist, 44,* 329-335.

Patterson, C. J., Kupersmidt, J. B., & Vaden, N. A. (1990). Income level, gender, ethnicity, and household composition as predictors of children's school-based competence. *Child Development, 62,* 485-494.

Persons, J. B. (1989). *Cognitive therapy in practice: A case formulation approach.* New York: W. W. Norton.

Plomin, R. (1989). Environment and genes: Determinants of behavior. *American Psychologist, 44,* 105-111.

Porzelius, K. (2002). Case conceptualization: An overview. In M. Hersen & K. Porzelius (Eds.), *Diagnosis, conceptualization and treatment planning for adults: A step-by-step guide.* Mahwah, NJ: Lawrence Erlbaum.

Power, T., & Manire, S. (1992). Child rearing and internalization: A developmental perspective. In J. Janssen & J. Gerris (Eds.), *Influences on child rearing and moral prosocial development.* Amsterdam: Swets and Zeitlinger.

Quay, H. C. (1986). Conduct disorders. In H. C. Quay & J. S. Werry (Eds.), *Psychopathological disorders of childhood* (3rd ed., pp. 1-34). New York: John Wiley.

Reynolds C. R., & Kamphaus, R. W. (1992). *Behavior Assessment System for Children (BASC).* Circle Pines, MN: American Guidance Services.

Rubin, K. H., Hymel, S., Mills, S. L., & Rose-Krasnor, L. (1991). Conceptualizing different developmental pathways to and from social isolation in children. In D. Cicchetti & S. L. Toth (Eds.), *Rochester Symposium on Developmental Psychopathology: Vol. 2. Internalizing and externalizing expressions of dysfunction* (pp. 91-122). Hillsdale, NJ: Lawrence Erlbaum.

Rutter, M. (1979). Protective factors in children's responses to stress and disadvantage. In M. W. Kent & J. E. Rolf (Eds.), *Primary prevention of psychopathology: Social competency in children* (pp. 49-74). Hanover, NH: University Press of New England.

Rutter, M. (1995). Clinical implications of attachment concepts: Retrospect and prospect. *Journal of Child Psychology and Psychiatry, 36,* 549-571.

Sameroff, A., Seifer, R., Barocas, R., Zax, M., & Greenspan, S. (1987). Intelligence quotient scores of 4-year old children: Social-environmental risk factors. *Pediatrics, 79,* 343-350.

Schwartz, D., Dodge, K., & Coie, J. (1993). The emergence of chronic peer victimization in boys' play groups. *Child Development, 64,* 1755-1772.

Settlage, C. F. (1977). The psychodynamic understanding of narcissistic and borderline personality disorders. Advances in developmental theory. *Journal of the American Psychoanalytic Association, 25,* 805-833.

Shaffer, D., Fisher, P., Dulcan, M. K., Davies, M., Piacentini, J., Schwab-Stone, M. E., Lahey, B. B., Bourdon, D., Jensen, P.S., Bird, H. R., Canino, G., & Regier, D. A. (1996). The NIMH Diagnostic Interview Schedule for Children Version 2.3 (DISC-2.3): Description, acceptability, prevalence rates and performance in the MECA study. Methods for the Epidemiology of Child and Adolescent Mental Disorders Study. *Journal of the American Academy of Child and Adolescent Psychiatry, 35,* 865-877.

Shirk, S. R., & Russell, R. L. (1996). *Change processes in child psychotherapy.* New York: Guilford.

Siegel, D. (1999). *The developing mind: Toward a neurobiology of interpersonal experience.* New York: Guilford.

Snyder, J., Edwards, P., McGraw, K., Kilgore, K., & Holton, A. (1994). Escalation and reinforcement in mother-child conflict: Social processes associated with the development of physical aggression. *Development and Psychopathology, 6,* 305-321.

Snyder, J., Schrepferman, L., & St. Peter, C. (1997). Origins of antisocial behavior: Negative reinforcement and affect dysregulation of behavior as socialization mechanisms in family interaction. *Behavior Modification, 21,* 187-215.

Solomon, J., & George, C. (1999). The place of disorganization in attachment theory: Linking classic observations with contemporary findings. In J. Solomon & C. George (Eds.), *Attachment disorganization* (pp. 3-32). New York: Guilford.

Spaccarelli, S., Cotler, S., & Penman, D. (1992). Problem-solving skills training as a supplement to behavioral parent training. *Cognitive Therapy and Research, 27,* 171-186.

Speltz, M. (1990). The treatment of preschool conduct problems: An integration of behavioral and attachment concepts. In M. T. Greenberg, D. Cicchetti, & M. Cummings (Eds.), *Attachment in the preschool years: Theory, research, and intervention* (pp. 399-426). Chicago: University of Chicago Press.

Spiker, D., Ferguson, J., & Brooks-Gunn, J. (1993). Enhancing maternal interactive behavior and child social competence in low birth weight, premature infants. *Developmental Psychology, 64,* 754-768.

Spivak, G., & Shure, M. B. (1982). The cognition of social adjustment: Interpersonal cognitive problem-solving thinking. In B. B. Lahey & A. E. Kazdin (Eds.), *Advances in clinical child psychology* (Vol. 5, pp. 323-372). New York: Plenum.

Sroufe, L. A. (1983). Infant-caregiving attachment and patterns of adaptation and competence. In M. Perlmutter (Ed.), *Minnesota Symposium on Child Psychology* (Vol. 16). Hillsdale, NJ: Lawrence Erlbaum.

Sroufe, L. A. (1997). Psychopathology as an outcome of development. *Development and Psychopathology, 9,* 251-268.

Sroufe, L. A., & Fleeson, J. (1986). Attachment and the construction of relationships. In W. Hartup & K. Rubin (Eds.), *Relationships and development.* Hillsdale, NJ: Lawrence Erlbaum.

Sroufe, L. A., Fox, N., & Pancake, V. (1983). Attachment and dependency in developmental perspective. *Child Development, 54,* 1615-1627.

Stark, K., Reynolds, W., & Kaslow, N. (1987). A comparison of the relative efficacy of self-control therapy and behavioral problem-solving therapy for depression in children. *Journal of Abnormal Child Psychology, 15,* 91-113.

Stevens, M. J., & Morris, S. J. (1995). A format for case conceptualization. *Counselor Education and Supervision, 35,* 82-94.

Strassberg, Z. (1995). Social information processing in compliance situations by mothers of behavior-problem boys. *Child Development, 66,* 376-389.

Thompson, R. A. (1994). Emotion regulation: A theme in search of definition. In N. A. Fox (Ed.), The development of emotion regulation, biological and behavioral considerations. *Monographs of the Society for Research in Child Development, 59,* 25-52.

Thompson, R. A. (1999). Early attachment and later development. In J. Cassidy & P. Shaver (Eds.), *Handbook of attachment: Theory, research and clinical applications* (pp. 265-286). New York: Guilford.

Turkat, I. D. (1985). *Behavioral case formulation.* New York: Kluwer Academic/Plenum.

Waldman, I. D., Rowe, D. C., Abramowitz, A., Kozel, S. T., Mohr, J. H., Sherman, S. L., Cleveland, H. H., Sanders, M. L., Gard, J. M., & Stever, C. (1998). Association and linkage of the dopamine transporter gene and attention-deficit disorder in children: Heterogeneity owing to diagnostic subtype and severity. *American Journal of Human Genetics, 63,* 1767-1776.

Webster-Stratton, C. (1994). Advancing videotape parent training: A comparison study. *Journal of Consulting and Clinical Psychology, 62,* 583-593.

Weerasekera, P. (1996). *Multi-perspective case formulation: A step towards treatment integration.* Malabar, FL: Krieger Publishing.

Weisz, J. R., Weiss, B. B., Han, S. S., Granger, D. A., & Morton, E. (1995). Effects of psychotherapy with children and adolescents revisited: A meta-analysis of treatment outcome studies. *Psychological Bulletin, 117,* 450-468.

Wenar, C., & Kerig, P. (2000). *Developmental psychopathology: From infancy through adolescence* (4th ed.). New York: McGraw-Hill.

White, K., & Kistner, J. (1992). The influence of teacher feedback on young children's peer preferences and perceptions. *Developmental Psychology, 28,* 933-940.

Wielkiewicz, R. M. (1995). *Behavior management in the schools: Principles and procedures* (2nd ed.). Needham Heights, MA: Allyn & Bacon.

Wilson, W. J., & Aponte, R. (1985). Urban poverty. *Annual Review of Sociology, 11,* 231-258.

Yoshikawa, H. (1994). Prevention as cumulative protection: Effects of early family support and education on chronic delinquency and its risks. *Psychological Bulletin, 115,* 28-54.

Zeanah, C., Boris, N. W., Heller, S. S., Hinshaw-Fuselier, S., Larrieu, J., Lewis, M., Palomino, R., Rovaris, M., & Valliere, J. (1997). Relationship assessment in infant mental health. *Infant Mental Health Journal, 18,* 182-197.

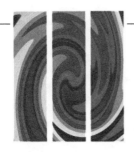

PART II

Case Studies

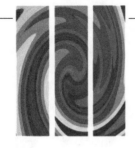

Case 1: Colby Tyler

Attentional Problems or Distracted by Life?

Colby, a 14-year-old teenager in the ninth grade, came to the clinic accompanied by his mother, Tina. The appointment had finally been booked after Tina found Colby's midterm report card crumpled in the garbage can. Not only was he failing one course, he was performing miserably across all subjects. When confronted, Colby lashed out at her, saying it was her fault, and ran out of the house. Tina admitted to running down the street after him, yelling like a "maniac." It was at this point that she realized that things had gotten out of control and that she needed help with Colby. His academic performance and temper outbursts were getting worse and worse. Tina explained that she also felt less able to cope with circumstances lately, due to her recent separation from her husband, Josh. Colby and his 7-year-old sister, Susy, continued to visit with their father every Wednesday and every second weekend. Colby's parents both have university degrees. Tina works as an advertising account executive and Josh is an entrepreneur.

DEVELOPMENTAL HISTORY/FAMILY BACKGROUND

Despite a normal and full-term pregnancy, Tina stated that the labor was lengthy (12 hours) and ended with a forceps delivery. Tina reported that she was under a lot of stress during her pregnancy due to marital conflicts, and admitted to smoking and having an occasional drink during the pregnancy.

Colby weighed 6 pounds, 2 ounces, and although somewhat underweight, he seemed to be in good health at birth. The first 3 months were very difficult for Tina and Colby due to Colby's sensitive digestive system. After eating, Colby would often have bouts of projectile vomiting, diarrhea, and colicky behavior. Although Tina tried to nurse Colby, he was constantly hungry (feeding every 2 hours), and after 6 weeks, the doctor felt that Colby and mom would both be better off if he went on formula. Eventually, Colby settled into a better routine, although digestive problems and poor sleep patterns continue to be areas of difficulty for him, especially when under stress. On occasion, Colby will complain of stomachaches and ask to stay home from school. He also has difficulty both falling asleep and staying asleep. On many nights, Colby is still awake when Tina goes to bed, which is around midnight.

Developmental milestones were achieved within normative expectations, with the exception that Colby started to read spontaneously at 2 years of age. His first sight word was "Sears"; he pointed to the catalogue after seeing a commercial on TV. After that, he started recognizing labels and logos on billboards and on the television. He was able to read printed words on paper by about 2½ years of age. Language skills also developed rapidly, and Colby's conversational skills were very well advanced by the time he entered nursery school.

Although Colby's health has been generally good, he had a severe outbreak of hives at 5 years of age (source never detected) and was placed on an elimination diet for one month during which time his food was restricted to rice and lamb broth. Colby has never been hospitalized, although he does have a tendency to be accident-prone and has experienced cuts, scrapes, and bruises from falls and bike accidents. Colby's hearing and vision have both been assessed. Hearing is within normal limits, and glasses have been prescribed for distance vision.

When asked about family history, Tina noted that Colby's maternal grandmother has always been an anxious woman who has many fears and who has been on medication for depression. Colby's maternal grandfather was a heavy drinker and often became aggressive and physically abusive to his wife and eldest son. Colby's maternal grandfather also had Parkinson's disease and eventually died after a lengthy battle with Alzheimer's. Tina feels that her mother also likely suffers from post-traumatic stress disorder, due to the violence in the home. Although Tina's parents lived some distance away, Colby has maintained contact with his grandmother through her bi-yearly visits. Tina is herself an anxious woman who was a witness to domestic violence. Colby's paternal grandmother and grandfather are deceased and, according to Tina, there was no known pathology. There is a paternal uncle who has problems with alcohol and is also believed to have some psychotic features (hallucinations and delusions). He is unable to support himself, is currently on assistance and is basically estranged from Tina's husband.

Tina described her marriage of 15 years as very turbulent. There was a previous marital separation due to Josh's infidelities, about 8 years earlier; however, Tina discovered that she was pregnant with Susy and they reconciled the marriage. Tina was never able to re-establish a sense of trust in Josh, and their relationship continued to slide. During the past year, the children had been exposed to many arguments and verbal accusations that centered around Josh's denial of any infidelities. Although Tina and her husband Josh had been living in the same house for the past year, they slept in separate rooms. Six months ago the house finally sold and they moved into separate quarters. Tina has been seeing a counselor for the past year.

REASON FOR REFERRAL

Colby presented as an articulate and well-mannered adolescent. According to Colby, his mother really got very upset and angry when she found his report card. He wasn't eager to share it with her because she got very angry at him after the parent-teacher conference in January. He described the parent-teacher conference as embarrassing and frustrating. First of all, both his mom and dad were present, and were throwing cold stares at each other across the room. All his teachers were in the room at the same time, and he felt like he was on trial. Only one teacher, his English teacher, Mr. Brighton, had anything good to say about him. The other teachers made him angry by saying that he wasn't trying, wasn't motivated, and didn't care about his schoolwork. Mrs. Fischer said that most times Colby wasn't prepared for class and didn't even bring his text with him. All accused him of wasting his potential. After all, Colby had been identified as a "gifted" student as part of the Grade 4 screening for the Gifted Program.

Colby's IQ was 151. However, in spite of all this intelligence, Colby had never really been a shining academic. In elementary school, Colby managed to get by with the little amount of effort he put in. However, Colby began to really slide academically when he entered Grade 9. Currently, Colby's grades are well below what would be expected, and he may not pass Chemistry at all. Colby is up most nights until very late and he can't get up in the morning. He has been late many times, and the school counselor has called Tina often to complain about Colby's tardiness.

Historically, Colby has always had problems sleeping. As a consequence, getting ready for school in the mornings had been problematic, with one exception. One day a week, when Colby attended the Gifted Program, he would have no difficulty getting up or being on time. The Gifted Program was Colby's favorite day of the week and Colby was noticeably distressed upon learning that the gifted program would not extend into the secondary school level.

The level of Colby's intelligence was evident in his articulate conversational style and the depth of his knowledge in areas of interest, like computers. He was an engaging youth who was very captivating. However, as the conversation turned toward academics, Colby's entire demeanor changed, and he became very quiet. Tina addressed the issue of homework, which was a constant source of frustration for both of them. Colby seemed to have tremendous difficulty staying on task; everything was a potential distracter. Little things, like the telephone ringing or a noise outside, would be enough to break Colby's concentration, and once off-task it was very difficulty to get him back on track. However, when Colby was playing computer games, he was riveted to the screen, and it would become very difficult to disengage Colby from the task. Tina could not understand how Colby could be so intensely focused when interested in something and so distractible when interest level was low. Like Colby's teachers, Tina thought it was a question of motivation. Tina described how Colby would begin each academic year all motivated and excited about school: new binders, pencils, and so on. Within a matter of weeks, however, old patterns would return and Colby would begin sleeping in, assignments would remain incomplete, and pencils would be lost or misplaced. According to Tina, Colby was the master of good intentions. Although Colby would often start projects with great enthusiasm, he had considerable difficulty sustaining this effort over the long haul. The Gifted Program was the only place where Colby really seemed to do well.

When asked what was so special about the Gifted Program, Colby said the teacher was fantastic, most of the kids were great, and they did a lot of computer work and mindbender logic games. Tina interjected that she had talked at length with the teacher of the gifted program, who described Colby as a great kid and a wonderfully creative and divergent thinker. The teacher of the gifted program thought that one of Colby's difficulties might be that he had so many ideas that it was very hard for him to put things down on paper. He had, as she described it, "an explosive mind for brainstorming."

When asked about temper outbursts, Tina said that at times Colby seems incredibly patient and she saw this behavior at its best when he was tutoring younger children in a reading program and giving golf lessons. However, at other times, Colby could be highly reactive and respond with a short fuse. At these times, Colby would be more prone to take things personally, be less responsive to logical reasoning, and be in a highly aroused state. When in this aroused stated it is not possible to reason logically with Colby until he settles down, which can take a while.

According to Colby's mother, behavioral outbursts had increased since the marital break-up. Tina stated that Colby has never adapted well to change and that the emotional split and physical move have likely added to the intensity of Colby's reactions. Having to shift between two households was not easy for Colby, especially in light of his problems with losing things and misplacing his notes. Colby now seemed even more disorganized than before. Tina also wondered whether Colby at some level somehow blames himself for the split.

When asked about the separation, Colby said very little. He said that his little sister was upset because he got to choose where he wanted to live and she didn't. He said she doesn't understand. It's awful to have to choose. Colby said his dad asked him why he chose to be with his mom and he said "because she is closer to school." Colby said that his dad called him "shallow." According to Tina, Colby has a tense relationship with his father because Josh tries to compete with Colby instead of supporting him. Tina said she is afraid that unless there are some answers to what is going on with Colby at this stage, Colby may end up having real problems. As it is, he can get very angry and flare up in a second, and this is really beginning to worry her. In response to that comment, Colby just looked at his mother and said, "I have been living in a house that is like the movie "The War of the Roses" . . . and you wonder why I get angry."

ASSESSMENT RESULTS

The actual raw scores for Colby's assessment are presented in Appendix A. The following is a summary of those findings. Note that information regarding specific assessment instruments can be found in Appendix C.

Responses to the Weschler Intelligence Scale for Children (WISC-III) confirmed overall intellectual functioning within the very superior range (Full Scale IQ Range 142-154), with minimal difference noted between Verbal and Performance functioning. However, Colby's score on the Freedom From Distractibility Index (working memory) was significantly below his Verbal Comprehension score, and Processing Speed (visual motor speed) was significantly below all other indices. Slow speed of psychomotor responses noted on paper-and-pencil tasks was accompanied by fatigue, awkward writing style, and ease of distraction. Despite adequate core academic skills (reading, spelling, math calculations), Colby had significant problems organizing his ideas when asked to write a short paragraph. Colby had difficulty getting started on the task, changed his topic many times, and after approximately 10 minutes, ultimately produced a very short but well-written passage of two lines. Colby's mother completed the Conner's Parent Rating Scale (CPRS-R:L) and the Achenbach Child Behavior Checklist (CBCL). Significant elevations were noted on scales of Somatic Complaints, Anxious-Depressed Mood, and Attention Problems. Teacher responses on the Conners (CTPS-R:L) and Teacher Report Form (TRF) also noted significant problems with Inattention. Colby's self-ratings on the Youth Self-Report (YSF), Conners Well Adolescent Self-Report Scale (CASS:L), and Beck Youth Inventories (BYI) revealed significant elevations for Internalizing, Inattentive Behaviors, and Low Self-Concept, and significant elevation of Depressed and Anxious Moods.

POST-CASE QUESTIONS

1. According to Russell Barkley (1997), sustained attention comes in two different forms: *contingency-shaped attention* and *goal-directed persistence*. Factors that can be instrumental in increasing or decreasing contingent attention include: task novelty, intrinsic interest, reinforcing properties inherent in the task, fatigue state of the participant, and presence or absence of adult supervision. According to Barkley, this form of sustained attention is often not problematic for ADHD children. However, goal-directed persistence requires sustained persistence of attention and effort in the absence of highly reinforcing task properties, which is extremely problematic for children with ADHD.

   a. Based on Barkley's descriptions of the two forms of sustained attention prepare a response for Colby's mother that would address her questions regarding why Colby can stay focused for long periods of time playing video games but is extremely distracted while attempting his homework assignments.

   b. Given your understanding of sustained attention, how might Colby's "Gifted" intelligence serve to further exacerbate his problems?

2. Based on the information presented in the case study, would Colby's symptoms match criteria in the *DSM* for attention-deficit/hyperactivity disorder (ADHD)?

3. Develop a case formulation for Colby from two theoretical perspectives. How would these formulations impact on different treatment outcomes?

4. Colby was identified as "gifted" when he was in the fourth grade. Do you believe that Colby's "gifted" label was ultimately a positive factor or a negative factor in his development? Explain.

ISSUES IN TREATMENT

The most widely researched treatment for ADHD is the use of stimulant medication. Four types of medications that are often prescribed include: methylphenidate (Ritalin), dextroamphetamine (Dexedrine), pemoline (Cylert), and a mixture of amphetamine salts (Aderol). Each of these medications has been demonstrated to be effective in reducing the symptoms of ADHD in numerous clinically controlled trials (Greenhill, 1998; Spencer et al., 1995). Although at one time there were concerns about whether pharmacotherapy in children predisposes them to subsequent substance abuse, there is research evidence to the contrary (Greenhill & Setterberg, 1993), and data have actually shown a protective role for stimulant treatment. In recent studies of ADHD and substance abuse, Wilens (2001) found that ADHD youth who took medication had lower rates of substance use (marijuana, cocaine, alcohol) compared with controls. Although medication has been proven effective in reducing symptoms of inattention, impulsivity, and hyperactivity, effects have not been consistently demonstrated to carry over to other areas such as social relationships or academic achievement (Pelham, Wheeler, & Chronis, 1998).

There has been significant controversy regarding the overuse of stimulant medication for children with attention deficit hyperactivity disorder (Diller, 1996). Although research has supported the use of methylphenidate (trade name, Ritalin) as a performance enhancer for children and adults with ADHD, it has been estimated that the use of stimulant medication has increased as much as 300% since 1990 (Hancock, 1996; Robison, Sclar, Skaer, & Galin, 1999). Although a recent study of prevalence rates for primarily inattentive, primarily hyperactive, and combined subtypes of ADHD conducted in Tennessee (Wolraich, Hannah, Pinnock, Baumgaerrel, & Brown, 1996) revealed 4.7%, 3.4%, and 4.4% respectively, as many as 10% to 12% of all boys in the United States are currently taking Ritalin for ADHD (Leutwyler, 1996). Although there has been significant research and theoretical emphasis placed on the primarily hyperactive/impulsive type of ADHD (Barkley, 1997), there is relatively little information concerning the Predominantly Inattentive Type of ADHD, which has been in existence as a separate type of disorder only since the *DSM-III*.

In part, the tendencies to overprescribe medication may result from the fact that the core symptoms of inattention, restlessness, and impulsivity found in attention deficit hyperactivity disorder (ADHD) also occur in other disorders such as anxiety, learning disabilities, and childhood depression. There is also evidence that only one third to one half of children diagnosed as ADHD by their pediatrician have had any type of psychological or educational assessment to support the diagnosis (Leutwyler, 1996).

There is growing evidence of a symptom shift in adolescence (Barkley, 1998). Earlier symptoms of blurting out answers, noisy play, and problems with turn taking that were noted in childhood are replaced by symptoms of impatience and restlessness in adolescence. Barkley has suggested that diagnostic considerations should be given to adolescents who present with a lower number of symptoms than in childhood. In the adolescent years, it is also very likely that weak organizational skills and poor follow-through will have significantly greater impact on school performance due to the increased emphasis on independent work and increased complexity in the environment caused by the use of multiple teachers in multiple classes (Cantwell, 1996). Adolescents with ADHD are at increased risk for school failure, poor social relationships, low self-esteem, car accidents, and substance abuse (Rosenbaum & Kienke, 2001). Therefore, the management of ADHD will often require a multimodal approach, combining psychosocial and medical interventions. Other forms of treatment that have been demonstrated to be effective for children with ADHD include: behavior modification and contingency management in the classroom, cognitive behavior modification (CBM), and parent training (Pelham et al., 1998). However, while contingency programs in the classroom have been demonstrated to improve behavior, results may not transfer to other situations. There are many examples in the research literature of attempts to justify the use of CBM for children with ADHD, in programs designed to increase verbal self-instruction, problem-solving strategies, cognitive modeling, and self-monitoring. The underlying premise in these approaches is that training in problem solving will assist children with ADHD to manage behavioral self-control better (Hinshaw & Erhardt, 1991). However, while initial results of CBM were encouraging, more recent evidence suggests that CBM in isolation does not enhance outcomes for children with ADHD (Pelham et al., 1998).

Most recently, results of an investigation into the use of multimodal treatment methods (MTA) for ADHD sponsored by the National Institute of Mental Health were presented by Dr. Peter Jensen at the 13th Annual Research Conference: A System of Care for Children's Mental Health, 2000. The MTA study (The MTA Cooperative Group, 1999) was a multisite study over a 14-month period that compared the individual and combined treatment effects of stimulant medication, an extensive psychosocial program involving both parent and teacher input and training, and a summer day program. The control groups for the study received their normal community-based services. Results revealed that medication alone was the single best treatment for reducing the core symptoms of ADHD and that psychosocial programming did not enhance the impact of medication alone. However, for children who also demonstrated a comorbid mood disorder or parent/family dysfunction, the combined treatment (medication plus parent and teacher training) was the most effective. The combined treatment was also most effective in reducing non-ADHD behaviors, such as aggression, inappropriate social skills, and poor parent-child interactions.

REFERENCES

Barkley, R. A. (1997). Attention deficit hyperactivity disorder. In E. J. Mash & L. G. Terdal (Eds.), *Assessment of childhood disorders* (pp. 71-129). New York: Guilford.

Barkley, R. A. (1998). *Attention deficit hyperactivity disorder: A handbook for diagnosis and treatment* (2nd ed.). New York: Guilford.

Cantwell, D. P. (1996). Attention deficit disorder: A review of the past 10 years. *Journal of American Academy of Child and Adolescent Psychiatry, 35,* 978-987.

Diller, L. H. (1996). The run on Ritalin: Attention deficit disorder and stimulant treatment in the 1990s. *Hastings Center Report, 26,* 12-18.

Greenhill, L. (1998). Attention-deficit/hyperactivity disorder. In B. T. Walsh (Ed.), *Child psychopharmacology* (pp. 91-109). Washington, DC: American Psychiatric Association.

Greenhill, L. L., & Setterberg, S. (1993). Pharmacotherapy of disorders of adolescents. *Psychiatry in North America, 16,* 793-814.

Hancock, L. N. (1996, March 18). Mother's little helper. *Newsweek,* pp. 51-56.

Hinshaw, S. P., & Erhardt, D. (1991). Attention-deficit hyperactivity disorder. In P. Kendall (Ed.), *Child and adolescent therapy: Cognitive-behavioral procedures* (pp. 98-128). New York: Guilford.

Leutwyler, K. (1996). Paying attention: The controversy over ADHD and the drug Ritalin is obscuring a real look at the disorder and its underpinnings. *Scientific American, 272*(2), 12-13.

The MTA Cooperative Group. (1999) A 14-month randomized clinical trial of treatment strategies for attention-deficit/hyperactivity disorder. The MTA Cooperative Group. Multimodal Treatment Study of children with ADHD. *Archives of General Psychiatry, 11,* 1073-1086.

Pelham, W. E., Jr., Wheeler, T., & Chronis, A. (1998). Empirically supported psychosocial treatments for attention deficit hyperactivity disorder. *Journal of Clinical Child Psychology, 27,* 190-205.

Robison, L. M., Sclar, D. A., Skaer, T. L., & Galin, R. S. (1999). National trends in the prevalence of attention-deficit/hyperactivity disorder and the prescribing of methylphenidate among school children: 1990-1995. *Clinical Pediatrics, 38*(4), 209-217.

Rosenbaum, J., & Kienke, A. (2001, May). Program and abstracts of the 154th Annual Meeting of the American Psychiatric Association, New Orleans.

Spencer, T., Wilens, T., Biderman, J., Faraone, S. V., Ablon, J. S., & Lapey, K. (1995). A double-blind, crossover comparison of methylphenidate and placebo in adults with childhood-onset attention deficit hyperactivity disorder. *Archives of General Psychiatry, 52,* 434-443.

Wilens, T. E. (2001). ADHD and alcohol or drug abuse. Program and abstracts of the 154th annual Meeting of the American Psychiatric Association, New Orleans.

Wolraich, M. L., Hannah, I. N., Pinnock, T. Y., Baumgaerrel A., Brown, J. (1996). Comparison of diagnostic criteria for attention-deficit hyperactivity disorder in a county-wide sample. *Journal of American Academy of Child and Adolescent Psychiatry, 35,* 319-324.

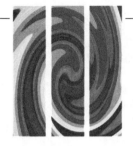

Case 2: Scott Michaels

Boys Will Be Boys?

Scott came to the intake interview accompanied by his mother, Ruth. Scott is 9 years of age and is currently in Grade 4 at Second Street School, which he has attended since his earliest enrollment in kindergarten. According to Ruth, the presenting concerns are twofold: academic problems at school and behavior problems at home.

DEVELOPMENTAL HISTORY/FAMILY BACKGROUND

Ruth described the birth history as uneventful. Scott was born 2 days early and weighed 8 pounds, 4 ounces. Developmental milestones were mildly delayed, and Scott walked at 15 months. Scott was slow to speak and did not use simple phrases at 3 years. Speech problems continued, and Scott received assistance for problems with articulation and speech production in pre-kindergarten and kindergarten.

Scott was described as an active infant who was not content to take long naps. Sleeping was not a problem, however, since he seemed to need his rest after all the activity. There was a problem with bed-wetting until Scott was 6 years of age. The problem was resolved when they stopped allowing Scott to have apple juice before bedtime. As a toddler, Scott seemed to be more demanding than all of Ruth's other children put together. Scott was not content to stay in the playpen like his other siblings. He would often scream and have tantrums until Ruth took him out of the playpen. However, when he was out of the playpen, he seemed to be into everything. Scott was very easily frustrated and difficult to calm down, especially if he couldn't have his way. At first, Ruth said she could distract him by offering something else, but that usually didn't last very long. Ruth added that for Scott the "terrible twos" never went away, but just got worse with each passing year.

Ruth recalled one incident that occurred shortly after Scott's sixth birthday. On this occasion, Ruth had asked Scott to help her pick up some toys that his brother Brian (aged 4) and sister Tia (aged 2) had scattered. All of a sudden, Scott started grabbing toys out of their hands, and throwing them at Tia and Brian. Then he went over to his toy box and dumped the entire toy box all over the floor. The event made such a lasting impression on Ruth that since that time she has not asked Scott to help her with cleaning up.

Scott's academic difficulties became evident early in his schooling, and Ruth was contacted by the teacher diagnostician who recommended that Scott have his vision and hearing tested to rule out any physical reasons for Scott's learning problems. Although Scott's vision was normal, testing of central auditory processing (CAP) revealed a selective attention deficit in the left ear, problems tuning in to auditory information, and likely difficulties with visual tracking. Recommendations from the CAP assessment were to present information to the dominant right ear, cuing prior to presenting information, and assistance in copying information from the board. Ruth stated that she had asked her family physician for a referral to have Scott tested for learning problems; however, when she took Scott to the appointment (about a year ago), she was told that testing was not necessary because Scott did not have any "developmental" problems. Ruth could not elaborate further on the nature of the therapist's expertise.

Ruth outlined the following family history during the course of the intake interview. There is a history of depression (maternal grandmother) and alcohol abuse (maternal grandfather) in Ruth's family. Ruth's father was incarcerated several times for assault resulting from fights in local bars. Ruth's only brother, Jacob, was bright but did poorly in school. Jacob seemed to fall in with the wrong crowd and dropped out in Grade 9. He spent some time in juvenile detention for breaking and entering, but eventually got back on track when he joined the armed forces, where he received training as a mechanic.

Ruth's husband Eric knows very little about his own family history, since he was adopted as an infant. Eric's adoptive parents were killed in a car accident shortly after Ruth and Eric were married. Eric has no known siblings. Ruth liked school and graduated from high school prior to getting married to Eric. Eric did not do well in school, and he did not complete high school. He currently works at a local box-making factory. Ruth worked as a grocery clerk at the local supermarket after graduation, until the birth of her daughter when she was 20 years of age. Ruth has not returned to work since that time. Ruth admitted that they have had financial problems recently, since the money from her husband's inheritance has been exhausted.

Although she was never diagnosed with depression, Ruth does admit to feeling overwhelmed and exhausted much of the time, especially since the birth of Tia. Ruth is considering returning to work now that Tia is in school, but she is afraid of what the consequences will be for Scott's behavior. Ruth recalled recently going to a shower for a neighborhood friend and returning home to find the kitchen an absolute mess. Apparently, Scott had deliberately messed up the kitchen in her absence because he was upset that she was not there to make his lunch. When asked why he had messed up the kitchen, Scott said that it was his mother's fault. If she had been home, it wouldn't have happened. When asked how he would feel about his mom returning to work, Scott said that it would be unfair, and that moms should be home for their kids.

Ruth described Scott's relationship with his siblings in the following way. Scott gets along with his youngest sister, Tia (5 years), the best, while his relationship with his older sister, Christine (11 years), is the most problematic. She added that Scott often responds to Christine in the same way he responds to his mother. When asked to clarify what she meant, Ruth replied that whenever Christine wants Scott to help her with dinner or the dishes, he starts a huge argument. It always ends the same way, with Scott saying that "it's unfair" and that he has to do all the work, or it's not his turn. Finally, Christine ends up just doing it herself, rather than argue with Scott. Scott's relationship with his younger brother Brian (7 years) is less predictable. When Scott wants to play with Brian and Brian goes along with him, they have a great time. However, when Brian does not want to follow Scott's lead, Scott will lose his temper very quickly.

REASON FOR REFERRAL

When asked what brought her and Scott to the clinic at this point in time, Ruth stated that Scott had become progressively more difficult to manage. He walks around with a "chip on his shoulder" and responds to even the smallest requests with an inflated emotional response. The outbursts have increased in frequency and intensity. Ruth admitted that she is beginning to "lose it" more frequently, herself. According to Scott, his mother is always picking on him and asking him to do things, like chores, that his brothers and sisters should be doing. He added that he only gets mad when his mother is "not fair."

Scott's school reports have noted increasing difficulties, especially in reading comprehension. Scott struggles with retaining the sequential order of information, and with problems recalling information he has read. He is slow to copy information from the board and his notes are not only messy, but often incomplete. Scott is receiving approximately 30 minutes daily of resource help to focus on reading, spelling, and written work. His teacher is very supportive of an assessment for Scott to provide specific information to assist with programming. The teacher noted that although behavioral problems are not significant at school, Scott does have some difficulty accepting criticism and waiting his turn. The teacher has also noted, on more than one occasion, that Scott will complain that the teacher has not been fair. Homework assignments are often incomplete or not returned, despite attempts to set up a home-school communication system.

Scott was asked to comment on his feelings about school. Scott said that the kids were alright, but that some of the teachers were not so great. When asked what he liked best about school, Scott rolled his eyes back and said "Recess." Scott became defensive when questioned about academics and said that he could do better if the teacher didn't pick on him. He also said that the teacher is always busy with other students and doesn't have the time to answer his questions. He says he has to sit and wait until the teacher finally gets around to his question and that's why he doesn't get his work done. According to Scott, the resource room teacher is also too busy with other kids to help him. Scott added that if the teacher would explain schoolwork better, he would be able to understand it better. He described his teacher as unfair in the amount of work she expected students to do. Outside of school, Scott said he really likes playing hockey and that he probably would drive racecars, like NASCAR, when he was older. He said he wouldn't go to school if he didn't have to.

Ruth began to describe the current home situation by saying that Scott is a good-natured boy when things are going his way. However, he can be very difficult to manage when asked to comply with any requests that interfere with his own agenda. Ruth has tried various incentive programs (such as using the purchase of a new bike as a reward for completing his homework for a week); however, after receiving his incentive, Scott loses all motivation and things go right back to where they began. She described it as a tug of war to get him to do anything. Attempts to set up a communication system with the school have been undermined by Scott's forgetfulness to bring messages home. At times, when asked to do something, Scott will be very touchy, talk back to her, and begin yelling and complaining that it is unfair and comparing himself to his sister who he says has no responsibilities around the house. At the worst of times, tantrums will escalate into a shouting match that involves throwing things and yelling. During these times, Ruth admits to "losing it," and producing numerous threats and ultimatums. More often than not, these scenarios end with Ruth completing the tasks herself, just to stop the battle. At the best of times, Scott will not be confrontational, though he will still avoid doing tasks by either passively ignoring the requests or trying to buy time, saying he will do it later (when a TV program is finished, or when he finishes what he is working on, etc.). Ruth stated that sometimes it just seems easier to do it herself than to nag and hound Scott.

Scott's relationship with his older sister is very poor, since Scott is often jealous and resentful of any attention that she receives. Yesterday, when Christine asked him to turn down the volume on the television because she was on the telephone, Scott deliberately turned the volume up to the absolutely loudest notch. Ruth seemed notably depressed in her admission that it is getting to the point that everyone at home is afraid to ask Scott to do anything for fear of retaliation.

When asked about her husband Eric's role in the management of Scott's behaviors, Ruth stated that her husband often works the 4:00-11:00 shift and is not home when Scott has his behavioral outbursts. Although Eric tries to be supportive of her, he has said that he thinks that Ruth is making too much out of Scott's behavior. After all, he says, "Boys will be boys." When Eric and Scott do things together, like fishing, there are rarely any outbursts.

Ruth is very hopeful that the assessment will not only provide help for her to manage Scott's behavior at home, but perhaps also help to convince her husband that Scott is in need of some kind of management program. Right now, Eric is of the opinion that Scott will just grow out of it.

At the completion of the intake interview, Ruth admitted in confidence to the psychologist that she was feeling increasingly overwhelmed, distraught, and alone. Her husband seemed to be withdrawing from the family and was coming home from work later and later, often stopping in at the local sports bar before returning home. There were many arguments about money and Ruth's desire to return to work, since her husband was not in favor of her working. Ruth was feeling less and less capable of managing Scott's escalating problems. At Ruth's request, a referral was provided to a therapist for her to obtain supportive therapy.

ASSESSMENT RESULTS

The actual raw scores for Scott's assessment are presented in Appendix A. The following is a summary of those findings. Information regarding specific assessment instruments can be found in the Appendix C.

Examiner comments noted frequent requests for repetition throughout the assessment, word-finding problems and tendencies toward word substitutions (e.g., using "found" instead of "lost"). Overall intellectual functioning on the Weschler Intelligence Scale for Children (WISC-III) was within the Average Range (IQ Range 82-93) with no significant discrepancy between Verbal (Low Average) and Performance (Average) functioning. Academically, Scott was functioning commensurate with his intellectual level in all areas except spelling and reading comprehension, which were approximately one grade below the expected level. Response to parent ratings scales revealed significant elevations on Aggressive Behavior, Attention Problems, Total Externalizing and Internalizing (CBCL); Oppositional, Hyperactive-Impulsive (CPRS-R:L). Teacher ratings noted clinical elevations for Social Problems and Attention Problems, as well as Inattention and Hyperactive-Impulsive Subscales (TRF). Scott endorsed items at the clinical level on the BYI for Disruptive Behaviors and the Anger Inventory.

POST-CASE QUESTIONS

1. Using situational and contextual factors, explain why Scott's behaviors were described as more oppositional at home than at school. Is this a common finding?

2. Barkley (1997a) has developed a theoretical model for ADHD that places *"Behavioral Inhibition"* as the focal point of the model. According to this model, the ability to delay or inhibit a given response allows for the necessary time required for executive information processing to occur. Included within these executive processes are: abilities to manipulate information mentally (working memory); self-regulation (emotional control, motivation/drive); self-reflection (inner speech, problem solving); and reconstitution (analysis and synthesis). Furthermore, the ability to maintain the delay is also required to block possible interference factors (see Barkley, 1997b, for a complete description of this model of hyperactivity and impulsivity).

How might the concept of "behavioral inhibition" be used to help explain Scott's behaviors? At a minimum, Scott demonstrates at least two comorbid disorders. What are the two disorders? How often do they occur together in clinical populations? Using Barkley's model of behavioral inhibition, explain the underlying dynamics in these two comorbid disorders.

3. The role of parenting practices in the maintenance and management of disruptive behavior disorders has been well documented (Barkley, 1997a

Chamberlain & Reid, 1991, 1998; Patterson, Reid, & Dishion, 1992). Various theoretical perspectives have focused on different aspects of parent-child interactions in maintaining maladaptive behaviors—for example, coercion theory (Patterson et al., 1992) and conflicting goals of connectiveness versus individuation (Mahler, Pine & Bergman, 1975). Develop case formulations to explain how Scott's interactions with his family members serve to sustain his disruptive behavior from the following perspectives: biomedical, psychodynamic, behavioral, cognitive, family systems, and parenting style/attachment.

4. The concept of *equifinality* suggests that a disorder may develop from multiple pathways. Scott and Jeremy (the introductory case) both have oppositional defiant disorder and ADHD. How would your treatment programs for Scott and Jeremy differ? How would they remain the same?

ISSUES IN TREATMENT

Oppositional defiant disorder (ODD) is one of the most stable disorders of childhood; the prognosis is therefore often poor (Rey, 1993). The transition from normal behavior demonstrated in what has been called the "terrible twos" to ODD behavior is evident in the frequency and intensity of noncompliant behaviors that continue to persist well beyond the toddler period (Gabel, 1997). Risk factors that have been associated with ODD include: parent depression, substance abuse, and antisocial personality disorder (Billings & Moos, 1983; Griest, Wells, & McMahon, 1980); attachment problems noted in insecure attachment (DeKlyen, 1996) and anxious avoidant attachment patterns (Erickson, Sroufe, & Egeland, 1985); difficult temperament (Rey, 1993); parenting style and level of parental involvement (Frick et al., 1993; Griest et al., 1980).

One of the difficulties in locating evidence-based treatments specifically for ODD is that despite evidence of the existence of ODD and conduct disorder (CD) as two distinct disorders (Frick et al., 1993), treatments are often discussed relative to the broader category of "disruptive behavior disorders," which include both ODD and CD. In a recent meta-analysis, Brestan and Eyberg (1998) reviewed psychosocial treatments for disruptive behavior disorders (ODD or CD) in 82 studies involving more than 5,000 youths. The authors then evaluated the treatment programs relative to criteria suggested by the APA Task Force. Results revealed two models of intervention, both involving parent training, that met with the more stringent criteria established for *Well Established Psychosocial Interventions:*

1. A parent training program involving videotaped modeling (Webster-Stratton, 1984) has been successful in reducing deviant behaviors in children and increasing parent competencies in the management of behavior problems (Spaccarelli, Colter, & Penman, 1992; Webster-Stratton, 1984, 1994). In this model of intervention, parents receive training in therapist-led groups.

2. Behavioral parent training programs (Alexander & Parsons, 1973; Bernal, Klinnert & Shultz, 1980; Firestone, Kelly, & Fike, 1980) based on a manual called *Living With Children,* developed by Patterson and Guillion (1968), have also demonstrated success across several controlled studies. Lessons obtained from the manual *Living With Children* have been successfully incorporated into behavioral treatment programs designed to teach parents how to implement behavioral change by targeting problem behaviors, rewarding incompatible behaviors, and ignoring or punishing undesirable behaviors.

Other treatments for school-aged children that are cited as Probably Efficacious Treatments (Brestan & Eyberg, 1998) include: problem-solving skills training (Kazdin, Esveldt-Dawson, French, & Unis, 1987; Kazdin, Siegel, & Bass, 1992), and anger control therapy (Lochman, Burch, Curry, & Lampron, 1984; Lochman et al., 1989):

Problem Solving Skills Training (PSST: Kazdin, 1996)

A typical problem-solving intervention would teach children how to approach a problem in a logical and predictable fashion, using a six-step procedure (Kazdin et al., 1987; Kendall, 1988).

1. Define the problem

2. Identify the goal

3. Generate options

4. Evaluate options

5. Choose the best option

6. Evaluate the outcome

Children are taught how to apply this approach to social problems in a number of ways, including role playing, social reinforcement, and therapeutic games. The PSST procedure is administered individually over 20 sessions, each lasting approximately 45 minutes.

Coping Power (Larson & Lochman, 2002)

This anger control program has evolved from an original 12-session school-based program called *anger coping* (Lochman, Lampron, Gemmer, & Harris, 1987), to a 33-session program called Coping Power (Lochman & Wells, 1996) with sessions for a parent group recently added. Children develop skills in anger management through in vivo practice sessions (weekly groups of six children) using problem solving techniques to address specific goals and objectives in social situations. Children are also taught to be aware of feelings and physiological states associated with anger arousal.

In their research review, Brestan and Eyberg (1998) found that the majority of interventions involved direct contact with the child and/or the child's parent (usually mother) and usually were based on cognitive behavioral techniques. In their summation, the authors conclude that age may be the overarching variable that determines the effectiveness of the outcome of treatment: parent training programs would be more effective for younger children, while cognitive behavioral methods may be more applicable for older, school-aged populations.

There is evidence to suggest, however, that for some groups (Kazdin et al., 1992), combining PSST and parent training may be more effective than either treatment, alone.

Academic Interventions

An empirical review of specific programming remediation for difficulties in reading and written expression reveals the following information. The importance of developing phonological awareness for reading acquisition and spelling has been demonstrated by several researchers (see Rathvon, 1999, for a review). Therefore, strategies that focus on improving phonics (e.g., Fernald Keller Approach) can be helpful in assisting Scott in developing greater phonetic awareness. Given Scott's learning profile, the following specific strategies may be helpful. A *Repeated Readings* approach (O'Shea & O'Shea, 1988) is suggested to target difficulties in decoding (sight word vocabulary, fluency) and comprehension, and to enhance Scott's attention to task as well as independent work habits. Cognitive approaches to spelling, such as the *12 plus 1* strategies for remediation of misspellings (Montgomery, 1990), would also be very helpful in emphasizing the phonetic as well as rule-based aspects of spelling.

Focus on improving homework submission and reducing home conflict regarding homework completion. A homework management program would be helpful to increase productivity (percentage of homework completed) and accuracy (percentage completed correctly) of homework, using a combination of home-note, self-monitoring, and group contingency approaches based on the Good Behavior Game Plus Merit approach developed by Darveaux (1984).

REFERENCES

Alexander, J. F., & Parsons, B. V. (1973). Short-term behavioral intervention with delinquent families: Impact on family process and recidivism *Journal of Abnormal Psychology, 81,* 219-225.

Barkley, R. A. (1997a). Attention deficit hyperactivity disorder. In E. J. Mash & L. G. Terdal (Eds.), *Assessment of childhood disorders* (pp. 71-129). New York: Guilford.

Barkley, R. A. (1997b). Behavior inhibition, sustained attention and executive function. *Psychological Bulletin, 121,* 65-94.

Bernal, M. E., Klinnert, M. D., & Schultz, L. A. (1980). Outcome evaluation of behavioral parent training and client-centered parent counseling for children with conduct problems. *Journal of Applied Behavior Analysis, 13,* 677-691.

Billings, A. G., & Moos, R. H. (1983). Comparison of children of depressed and nondepressed parents: A social-environmental perspective. *Journal of Abnormal Child Psychology, 11,* 463-486.

Brestan, E. V., & Eyberg, S. M. (1998). Effective psychosocial treatments of conduct disordered children and adolescents: 29 years, 82 studies and 5,272 kids. *Journal of Clinical Child Psychology, 27,* 180-189.

Chamberlain, P., & Reid, J. (1991). Using a specialized foster care community treatment model for children and adolescents leaving the state mental hospital. *Journal of Community Psychology, 19,* 266-276.

Chamberlain, P., & Reid, J. (1998). Comparison of two community alternatives to incarceration for chronic juvenile offenders. *Journal of Consulting and Clinical Psychology, 66,* 624-633.

Darveaux, D. X. (1984). The Good Behavior Game Plus Merit: Controlling disruptive behavior and improving student motivation. *School Psychology Review, 13,* 510-514.

DeKlyen, M. (1996). Disruptive behavior disorder and intergenerational attachment patterns: A comparison of clinic-referred and normally functioning preschoolers and their mothers. *Journal of Consulting and Clinical Psychology, 64,* 357-365.

Erickson, M. F., Sroufe, L. A., & Egeland, B. (1985). The relationship between quality of attachment and behavior problems in preschool in a high-risk sample. In I. Betherton & E. Waters (Eds.), Growing points of attachment theory and research. *Monographs of the Society for Research in Child Development, 50*(1-2, Series No. 209), 147-166.

Firestone, P., Kelly, M. J., & Fike, S. (1980). Are fathers necessary in parent training groups? *Journal of Clinical Child Psychology, 9,* 44-47.

Frick, P. J., Lahey, B. B., Loeber, R., Tannenbaum, L., Van Horn, Y., Christ, M. A., Hart, E. L., & Hanson, K. (1993). Oppositional defiant disorder and conduct disorder: A meta-analytic review of factor analyses and cross-validation in a clinic sample. *Clinical Psychology Review, 13,* 319-340.

Gabel, S. (1997). Oppositional defiant disorder. In J. D. Noshpitz (Ed.), *Child and adolescent psychiatry* (Vol. 2, pp. 351-359). New York: John Wiley.

Griest, D., Wells, K. C., & McMahon, R. J. (1980). An examination of differences between nonclinic and behavior problem clinic referred children and their mothers. *Journal of Abnormal Psychology, 89,* 497-500.

Kazdin, A. E. (1996). Problem solving and parent management in treating aggressive and antisocial behavior. In E. S. Hibbs & P. S. Jensen (Eds.), *Psychosocial treatments for child and adolescent disorders: Empirically based strategies for clinical practice* (pp. 377-408). Washington, DC: American Psychological Association.

Kazdin, A. E., Esveldt-Dawson, K., French, N. H., & Unis, A. S. (1987). Problem-solving skills training and relationship therapy in treatment of antisocial child behavior. *Journal of Consulting and Clinical Psychology, 55,* 76-85.

Kazdin, A. E., Siegel, T. C., & Bass, D. (1992). Cognitive problem-solving skills training and parent management training in the treatment of antisocial behavior in children. *Journal of Consulting and Clinical Psychology, 60,* 733-747.

Kendall, P. C. (1988). *Stop and think workbook* (2nd ed.). Ardmore, PA: Workbook.

Larson, J., & Lochman, J. E. (2002). Helping school children cope with anger: A cognitive-behavioral intervention. New York: Guilford.

Lochman, J. E., Burch, P. R., Curry, J. F., & Lampron, L. B. (1984). Treatment and generalization effects of cognitive-behavioral and goal-setting interventions with aggressive boys. *Journal of Consulting and Clinical Psychology, 52,* 915-916.

Lochman, J. E., Lampron, L. B., Gemmer, T. C., & Harris, S. R. (1987). Teacher consultation and cognitive-behavioral intervention with aggressive boys. *Psychology in the Schools, 26,* 915-916.

Lochman, J. E., Lampron, L. B., Gemmer, T. C., & Harris, S. R. (1989). Teacher consultation and cognitive behavioral interventions with aggressive boys. *Psychology in the Schools, 26,* 179-188.

Lochman, J. E., & Wells, K. C. (1996). A social cognitive intervention with aggressive children: Prevention effects and contextual implementation issues. In R. D. Peters & R. J. McMahon (Eds.), *Preventing childhood disorders, substance abuse and delinquency* (pp. 111-143). Thousand Oaks, CA: Sage.

Mahler, M. S., Pine, F., & Bergman, A. (1975). *The psychological birth of the human infant.* New York: Basic Books.

Montgomery, D. (1990). *Children with learning difficulties.* New York: Nicholas Publishing.

O'Shea, L., & O'Shea, D. (1988). Using Repeated Reading. *Teaching Exceptional Children, 1,* 26-30.

Patterson, G. R., & Gullion, M. E. (1968). *Living with children: New methods for parents and teachers.* Champaign, IL: Research Press.

Patterson, G. R., Reid, J. B., & Dishion, T. J. (1992). *Antisocial boys.* Eugene, OR: Castalia.

Rathvon, N. (1999). Effective school interventions: Strategies for enhancing academic achievement and social competence. New York: Guilford.

Rey, J. M. (1993). Oppositional defiant disorder. *American Journal of Psychiatry, 150,* 1769-1777.

Spaccarelli, S., Cotler, S., & Penman, D. (1992). Problem-solving skills training as a supplement to behavioral parent training. *Cognitive Therapy and Research, 16,* 1-18.

Webster-Stratton, C. (1984). Randomized trial of two parent-training programs for families with conduct-disordered children. *Journal of Consulting and Clinical Psychology, 52,* 666-678.

Webster-Stratton, C. (1994). Advancing videotape parent training: A comparison study. *Journal of Consulting and Clinical Psychology, 62,* 583-593.

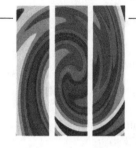

Case 3: Arthur Watson

Won't or Can't:
A Case of Mistaken Identity

Arthur, who was 15 years and 5 months of age, came to the interview accompanied by his mother and father. Mr. and Mrs. Watson were requesting a psychological assessment of their son Arthur to determine whether Arthur might have a learning disability. The parents were concerned that weak academic progress and lack of behavior controls might be the result of frustration resulting from learning problems.

DEVELOPMENTAL HISTORY/FAMILY BACKGROUND

Arthur was delivered by cesarean section, 2 weeks post due date, weighing 8 pounds, 3 ounces. The pregnancy was reportedly normal with the exception of fluid retention, which was monitored over the course of five ultrasound assessments as well as pelvic X ray. Arthur was jaundiced at birth; however, this was treated and he was released from the hospital within the normal time frame.

Developmental motor milestones were delayed: sitting at 8-9 months; walking at 16 months. Language skills were also reported as delayed, and although he did say his first word at about one year, he reportedly did not speak much in his initial years. Descriptions of infant behaviors revealed that Arthur was not temperamental, nor was he overly active or colicky. Arthur experienced febrile convulsions, and he had a history of earaches, ear infections, and impacted ears due to wax build-up. There were difficulties with bed-wetting until Arthur was 11 years of age.

Family history reveals that Arthur is the oldest child in a family of three, having a younger sister (11 years) and brother (8 years). Arthur's siblings appear to be well adjusted both emotionally and academically. There is no known history of psychopathology in the families of either parent. Arthur's parents, Celia and Paul Watson, met at university and have been in a stable marital relationship for almost 20 years. Celia works as a counselor in a women's shelter, and Paul works as a financial consultant for the government.

Previous Assessment Results/School History

Arthur has had an extensive history of previous assessments, and his initial investigation was conducted by a developmental pediatrician when he was 3 years, 8 months of age. At that time, Arthur presented with articulation problems and developmental delays. An EEG was conducted and results were normal. The recommendation was for enrollment in a nursery school program, and Arthur began attending a Montessori program the next year. However, progress continued to be difficult and problems with aggression, overactivity, and following directions made the transition to kindergarten problematic. Arthur's behaviors continued to be problematic with a high level of overactivity, aggressive responding, and poor ability to follow directions. Arthur was reassessed by the developmental pediatrician at 5½ years of age. On this occasion Arthur presented with "silly" behaviors and appeared distractible and agitated, although he was able to score in the lower Average range on a picture vocabulary test. The recommendation was for a classroom with reduced pupil-teacher ratio and a trial of stimulant medication. However, the placement broke down and Arthur's parents were asked to remove Arthur from the kindergarten program midway through the academic year. Apparently, Arthur's behavior could not be maintained within the kindergarten program and administrative staff felt that Arthur required more supervision than could be provided in the regular program.

Mr. and Mrs. Watson were becoming increasingly frustrated with the public education system and took Arthur to a private psychologist for an assessment when he was 5 years, 9 months old. Results of the Weschler Preschool and Primary Intelligence Test (WPPSI-R) revealed Verbal functioning to be within the lower limits of the lower Average range, while Performance skills were within the Borderline range. Results from the picture vocabulary test were identical to those obtained 6 months earlier by the developmental pediatrician, indicating receptive vocabulary to be within the lower Average range. The recommendations were in support of a trial medication period, future assessment of central auditory processing, and the need for a structured behavioral management program. History repeated itself, however, and Arthur's continued behavioral outbursts resulted in his eventual removal from the regular class program in the public school. As a result, the school board recommendation was for future placement in a behavioral program. Parents appealed the decision, stating that Arthur had attention-deficit/hyperactivity disorder (ADHD) and that his needs would be better served in a program that addressed his learning needs. However, parents were unable to produce a clear diagnostic statement to confirm that Arthur had ADHD, and Arthur had not responded favorably to stimulant medication. Ultimately, the school board decision to place Arthur in a special program was upheld; however, the designation of exceptionality was changed from "Emotionally and Behaviorally Disordered (EBD)" to "Learning Disabled (LD)."

Over the course of the next 4 years, Arthur attended programs in several schools with limited success. At 7 years of age, he enrolled in a day treatment program affiliated with a local children's mental health center. While at the center, assessment of intellectual level was attempted; it was only partially completed, however, due to lack of compliance on Arthur's part. Although results of that intellectual assessment were inconclusive, it was reported that subtest scores ranged from average (general information, block design) to very delayed (oral math, visual sequencing). Arthur scored at the 8th percentile on a readministration of the picture vocabulary test, which was well below previous scores. It was suggested that Arthur's outbursts might be attempts to avoid academic difficulties and were likely developmental in nature. The following year, Arthur was discharged from day treatment and placed in a primary learning disability program in a community school. However, Arthur's transition to the program was not successful and parents ultimately removed Arthur from school; he was home-schooled the following year.

Parents enrolled Arthur in a local private school when he was 9 years of age; progress was minimal and the school was forced to shut down due to financial reasons. For the next 2 years, Arthur returned to the public school system and was placed in a Junior Special Learning Class. Despite continued problems with attention and concentration, Arthur demonstrated improved work habits, and aggressive acting out was replaced with a newly developed sense of humor. Arthur seemed to relate to his teacher in a very positive manner. However, the following year, when Arthur was moved to a Senior Special Learning Class, previous difficulties with aggression resurfaced and Arthur was removed once again and home-schooled. Parents hired a tutor to assist Arthur during this period and assessments conducted by the tutor revealed core academics to be at the first percentile (kindergarten/Grade 1 level). Reassessment on the picture vocabulary test revealed receptive language to be below the first percentile, and at 14 years of age, Arthur had a vocabulary that was approximately equivalent to a child half his age (7 years, 9 months).

Arthur was now becoming a teenager, and aggressive outbursts were becoming more threatening to his parents and younger siblings. Out of desperation, parents sent Arthur to a private boarding school in upstate New York. They were hopeful that the school would be able to provide the structure and behavior management that Arthur required and that he would return from the school with many positive changes. A review of reports suggests, however, that the facility was more of a prep school than geared to special needs and was highly inappropriate for Arthur. Parents have had little understanding of what transpired over the year, since Arthur has refused to share any information about his school experience with his parents. When Arthur returned home after one year in the program, he was more angry and resentful than ever. Behaviors continued to escalate, and Arthur was beginning to use threatening gestures toward his parents and physically and verbally abusive behaviors toward his siblings (kicking, swearing, hitting, pushing).

As a result of a recent violent outburst (Arthur chased his sister around the house with an electrical cord, saying he was going to get her), parents sought temporary placement for Arthur in a residential facility for youth with emotional and behavioral problems. At the time of the current interview, Arthur was being slowly integrated back into his home on weekends.

REASON FOR REFERRAL

Arthur's parents were desperate for any information that would help them with Arthur. They were requesting a formal assessment to clarify the nature of cognitive functioning, academic levels, and any other information that might assist in better understanding Arthur's social/emotional and behavioral difficulties. According to Mr. and Mrs. Watson, despite a number of previous attempts to assess Arthur's functioning, to their knowledge Arthur had not had a complete formal psychological assessment.

During the interview, Arthur appeared highly agitated. He shifted his position in the chair continuously, slouching down with his long legs dangling across the floor. At approximately 5 feet, 10 inches tall, Arthur towered over his parents when he stood up. Throughout the interview, Arthur would make grimacing faces, mimic his parents' comments, interrupt often, and correct his parents, especially his mother, in a loud and mocking voice. When asked about the private school he had returned from, Arthur said that he hated the school and he hated the kids at the school. In response to specific questions, Arthur was difficult to understand, partially due to poor articulation and sound substitutions ("s" for "t"), but mostly because he tended to be very tangential in his responses. Cluttered speech, a tendency to trail off at the ends of sentences, and a propensity to make "silly voices" also rendered communication difficult to understand.

When asked if he knew why he was at the clinic, Arthur said that he was "too violent" sometimes and added that lately he was "more bad than good." He did seem remorseful, however, and said that he wanted to be better. When asked if he might agree to take medication to help control his behavior and do better at school, Arthur responded that he was prepared to try, if it would work. He added that things were very difficult now, and he was getting into trouble a lot because of his temper. He said that he was also having trouble sleeping and falling asleep. In response to a question about what concerned him most, Arthur said that sometimes he did stuff that he wished he hadn't but then it was too late. He spontaneously added that he did not have any friends and that he hated his "zits" and wanted them to go away so he could get a girlfriend. He worried that he would not be able to get rich and find a wife when he got older.

Arthur was seen for three assessment sessions. Behavior varied across sessions with Arthur becoming more vocal and volunteering more personal information as time progressed. However, Arthur was quite agitated when he arrived for the third session, and muttered an obscenity as his father dropped him off at the office. When asked if he wanted to talk, he said that he just wanted to do his work with me for the day, but then spontaneously began to discuss what had occurred. Arthur was of the impression that he would not be able to go back to school because it cost too much money and that he would have to stay home and do jobs all day. When he was reassured that we were working together to find out which school he would be happiest at, he seemed to be very relieved and was eager to get back to the assessment. A fourth assessment session was scheduled; however, further assessment was pre-empted when Arthur's behavior again escalated at home, resulting in admission to the crisis unit at the regional children's hospital. On that occasion, Arthur had threatened harm to his parents, sister, and eventually himself and was admitted to the hospital for one month to allow for medication trials, observation, and behavioral stabilization.

While in the hospital, Arthur responded well to a combination of sertraline and thioridazine, his behavior stabilized, and he was discharged back to his home at the end of the month. A discharge planning meeting was held prior to Arthur's release from the hospital and parents again voiced their frustrations with the "system," complaining that they had been given very little direction regarding future placements for Arthur. Parents returned to the clinic to complete Arthur's assessment and for assistance regarding future planning.

ASSESSMENT RESULTS

The actual raw scores for Arthur's assessment are presented in Appendix A. The following is a summary of those findings. Information regarding specific assessment instruments can be found in Appendix C.

The Wechsler Intelligence Scale for Children (WISC-III) was administered over three sessions to allow for sufficient rapport building and to accommodate Arthur's tangential response style. Spontaneous digressions were frequent throughout the assessment session. Arthur's effort was considered optimum, and although anxiety and low frustration tolerance were evident, results were considered to be a valid index of functioning levels. Although Arthur's scores on the Performance Scale (IQ Range 63-79) were superior to his Verbal abilities (IQ Range 51-63), the discrepancy was not significant. Therefore, Arthur's Full Scale IQ (Range 53-64) is considered to be a good index of composite intellectual functioning. Academically, according to the Wide Range Achievement Test (WRAT-3), Arthur's academic performance was commensurate with his intellectual functioning, and Arthur scored consistently at the Grade One level across the core academic areas.

Parents completed the Adaptive Behavior Scale (ABS-S:2) and Vineland Adaptive Inventory. According to the ABS-S:2, Arthur was rated at age level in all areas of Personal and Personal-Social Responsibility. Similarly, parents also rated Trustworthiness and Social Engagement within the norm. Language Development, Hyperactive Behaviors, and Disturbing Interpersonal Behaviors were rated as minor problems. Ratings on the Vineland Interview were consistent with the ABS-S:2 and placed Daily Living Skills and Socialization within the Normal range for his age and Communication Skills at a low average level.

According to parent ratings on the Conners Scales (CPL) and Achenbach (CBCL), Arthur demonstrated significant problems in areas of Conduct (T = 96), Learning (T = 71), Impulsivity (T = 68), and Anxiety (T = 68).

Further Assessment: Psychiatric Consult

A psychiatric referral was initiated to assist in the monitoring of Arthur's medication following his release from the hospital. Resulting from the psychiatric consult, the possibility of Tourette's disorder was also raised due to some evidence of complex motor and vocal tics with associated mimicry. During his interview with the psychiatrist, Arthur admitted that although he sometimes would engage in swearing, facial grimaces, silly voices, and mimicry on his own accord, at other times, he had difficulty controlling these behaviors. Although recent evidence of depression with aggressive behavior patterns had responded to a combination of sertraline and thioridazine, the psychiatrist recommended that the family slowly wean Arthur off the thioridazine, which was causing excessive sedation. The psychiatrist indicated that future pharmacological treatment might include a combination of an SSRI (sertraline or Prozac) in combination with stimulant medication. Other areas to be addressed would include possible risperidone for the motor tic disorder and/or lithium to reduce aggressive behavior.

POST-CASE QUESTIONS

1. Would Arthur's profile warrant a diagnosis of mental retardation (MR)? Discuss this question from the perspective of each of the following classification systems: *DSM,* AAMR (American Association on Mental Retardation), and Educational System (see Appendix B).

2. Lalli, Kates, and Casey (1999) investigated the rates of problem behavior relative to academic demands in two boys with mild retardation. Results revealed that aggression was highest during spelling instruction, and that problem behavior was driven by negative reinforcement. Changes in instructional format produced a reduction in negative behaviors.

   a. Explain how these findings might be relevant to Arthur's case. How might a functional behavioral assessment of Arthur's behaviors have helped with programming?

      Based on information in the case presentation, develop a likely functional behavioral assessment for Arthur's disruptive classroom behaviors outlining: *possible behaviors* (suggest possible examples of disruptive behaviors); *precipitating conditions* (situations that trigger the behavior); *consequences of behavior* (situations/events that follow the behavior) and *functions of behavior* (underlying processes/motivations that sustain the behavior).

   b. Show how you would conduct a similar assessment to determine the extent to which behaviors were also occurring in other contexts: playground, after-school program, at home.

ISSUES IN TREATMENT

Behavioral Treatments

Treatments for children and adolescents with MR (mental retardation) often focus on two broad areas: (1) associated behavioral-emotional problems and (2) intellectual-adaptive deficits (Kronenberger & Meyer, 2001). Evidence-based treatment for associated behavioral difficulties is discussed first, followed by a discussion of the efficacy of educational treatments.

Behavior Management:
Behavioral and Emotional Problems

Treatment programs developed to assist with behavioral and emotional problems in MR populations have largely used methods of functional analysis based on applied behavior analysis (ABA). ABA has been defined as "the extension of experimental methods to applied settings" (Kazdin, 1994, p. 25). Behavior management programs can be simplistic (using praise to increase or ignoring to decrease behaviors) or very complex (contingency-based programs). Behavior management techniques are based on sound empirical support that have been documented in countless studies (for review see Lipsey & Wilson, 1993) and journals devoted specifically to behavioral research: *Behavior Modification, Journal of Applied Behavior Analysis, Behavior Therapy*, and others. However, successful behavior management programs require more than a knowledge of the mechanisms of behavioral change. They also require an understanding of how the child's different situational contexts contribute to the problem (Phares, Compas, & Howell, 1989).

Behavioral treatment programs can be developed to either increase deficit behaviors or decrease behavioral excess. Although it is always preferable to increase deficit behaviors, such as targeting increased compliance through the use of positive reinforcement or negative reinforcement, there are times when it is necessary to focus on reducing a behavioral excess (e.g., highly aggressive behavior) through the use of punishment or extinction. Behavioral principles of schedules of reinforcement, shaping behavior and behavior chaining, secondary rewards, and token economies have all been demonstrated as effective methods for managing behavioral change. Empirical studies have emphasized the need to assess baseline behavior rates and to monitor the effectiveness of programs (Jensen, 1988) and time-out techniques (Solnick, Rincover, & Peterson, 1977). Behavioral programs can benefit from the use of an empirical approach to select target behaviors (Weist, Ollendick, & Finney, 1991). For example, research has investigated how to create a reinforcer hierarchy (Christian, 1983); the selection of reinforcers for specific populations, such as adolescent populations (Reynolds, Salend, & Beahan, 1989, 1992); and techniques to promote generalization of outcomes across situations (Rutherford & Nelson, 1988; Stokes & Baer, 1977). The efficacy of using contingency management systems or token economies to improve behavior in children and adolescents has been demonstrated across many settings (Wielkiewicz, 1995). Children can be motivated to increase desirable behaviors by earning tokens or coupons to be traded in for concrete reinforcers. Contingency programs to increase deficit behaviors can be used in the regular classroom (Brantley & Webster, 1993), special classroom (Kratochwill, Elliott, & Rotto, 1990), and home (Clark, 1985). Contingency programs can also be developed to reduce excess behaviors. Programs that target reducing behaviors function on a response cost basis, where children lose tokens, coupons, and the like, when they demonstrate the undesirable behavior. Response cost programs can also be effectively introduced in the regular class (Rapport, Murphy, & Bailey, 1982), special class (Proctor & Morgan, 1991), and in the home (Little & Kelley, 1989). Other approaches to improving behavior in MR populations have included the use of relaxation training (Cautela & Groden, 1978; McPhail & Chamove, 1989), and functional equivalence training or teaching of replacement behaviors (Horner & Day, 1991), while behavior reduction can involve techniques such as performing restitution or undoing/overcorrection (Azrin & Besalel, 1980). Behavior programs for training in adaptive skills and social behaviors have also demonstrated successful positive change (Embregts, 2000).

Parent training programs have also been demonstrated to be an effective component for treatment of children with MR and other disabilities (Handen, 1998). It has been demonstrated that inclusion of parent treatment components in interventions can be superior to treatments conducted in clinics alone (Koegel, Schreibman, Britten, Burke, & O'Neill, 1982). Parent training programs have been proven effective whether administered in groups (Harris, 1983) or individually (Clark & Baker, 1983).

Parent training programs can also be helpful in increasing compliant behaviors in the home (Forehand & McMahon, 1981).

Educational Programs: Intellectual-Adaptive Deficits

Fundamental to the IDEA (Individuals with Disabilities Education Act) is the assurance that all children with disabilities in the United States receive a free and appropriate public education (FAPE) in the least restrictive environment (LRE). The IDEA also outlines procedures that should be followed by special education personnel, including obtaining informed written consent of the parents prior to assessment and the need to develop an individualized education program (IEP) for each disabled child. The IEP serves as the child's educational plan and outlines needs for meeting the child's educational goals through assessment, intervention, and monitoring of progress through annual reviews.

With regard to issues of placement, the IDEA focus on providing education for children with disabilities in the LRE resulted in a joint emphasis on providing services through special education programs as required to meet special needs, and *mainstreaming*, or the integration of disabled children into the regular class program, for as much time as possible. The underlying premise of this thrust was to provide normative models for exceptional children. Most recently, the Regular Education Initiative (REI) has taken the position that *full inclusion*, rather than mainstreaming, would be the best solution and that the needs of children with disabilities would be best served by full-time placement in the regular or general education program. Proponents of mainstreaming and inclusion frequently cite results from the Carlberg and Kavale (1980) meta-analysis comparing general with special education. Results of this analysis suggested that students with mild mental retardation (MMR) generally obtained better outcomes in regular programs. It has further been argued that placing students with MMR in contained special classrooms can actually place them at a disadvantage (Ysseldyke, Thurlow, Christenson, & Muyskens, 1991). Research concerning the effectiveness of special education relative to regular programming has come under more recent scrutiny. Hocutt (1996) reviewed more than 100 studies conducted over the last 25 years and suggests that claims of the efficacy of special education placement versus regular placement are difficult to substantiate. According to Hocutt, much of the research in the area is flawed methodologically, and/or outdated with respect to today's classification systems. On a more positive note, Hocutt (1996) suggests that it is the intervention program (intensive individualized instruction and monitoring of progress) rather than the placement that predicts success for students with MMR. The question remains, however, whether adequate monitoring and intervention are more likely to occur in a class with smaller enrollment. Mortweet (1997) studied the effect of classwide peer tutoring of EMR (educable mentally retarded) students within the regular program; results revealed positive gains academically and socially, although social interaction did not generalize to other settings outside the programmed instruction. However, Gottlieb, Alter, and Gotlieb (1991) found that mainstreaming did not have a positive impact on the academic achievement of EMR children, and Taylor (1986) cautions that mainstreaming EMR students without attention to direct training in areas such as social skills can have detrimental effects. A comparison of 34 mainstreamed EMR students with a sample of 34 nonretarded peers, matched for sex, race, and grade level (Grades 3 through 6) revealed that EMR children reported feeling more lonely and dissatisfied with their social relationships in school than their non-MR peers. Lack of social awareness and inappropriate social behaviors may result in students with disabilities not only having fewer friends, but being actively rejected by peers (Farmer & Rodkin, 1996: Nabasoku & Smith, 1993).

Although there has been attention paid to the possible positive and negative social implications of integration within the regular class program, there has been less attention paid to the longer-term and vocational implications of educational preparation for youth with MR. Polloway and his colleagues (Polloway, Patten, Smith, & Roderique, 1991) contend that the educational curriculum for the MR population should focus on community integration, starting as early as elementary school. The Hawaii Transition Project (Patton, Beirne-Smith, & Payne, 1990) provides an example of such a program geared to providing a bridge from school to community functioning.

REFERENCES

Azrin, N. H. & Besalel, V. A. (1980). *How to use overcorrection*. Lawrence, KS: H & H Enterprises.

Brantley, D. C., & Webster, R. E. (1993). Use of an independent group contingency management system in a regular classroom setting. *Psychology in the Schools, 30,* 60-66.

Carlberg, C., & Kavale, K. (1980). The efficacy of special versus regular class placement for exceptional children: A meta-analysis. *The Journal of Special Education, 14,* 295-308.

Cautela, J. R., & Groden, J. (1978). Relaxation: A comprehensive manual for adults, children, and children with special needs. Champaign, IL: Research Review.

Christian, B. (1983). A practical reinforcement hierarchy for classroom behavior modification. *Psychology in the Schools, 20,* 83-84.

Clark, D. B., & Baker, B. L. (1983). Predicting outcome in parent training. *Journal of Consulting and Clinical Psychology, 51,* 309-311.

Clark, L. (1985). *SOS! Help for parents*. Bowling Green, KY: Parents Press.

Embregts, P. J. C. (2000). Effectiveness of video feedback and self-management on inappropriate social behavior of youth with mild mental retardation. *Research in Developmental Disabilities, 21,* 409-423.

Farmer, T. W., & Rodkin, A. C. (1996). Antisocial and prosocial correlates of classroom social position: The social network centrality perspective. *Social Development, 5,* 174-178.

Forehand, R., & McMahon, R. (1981). Helping the noncompliant child: A clinician's guide to parent training. New York: Guilford.

Gottlieb, J., Alter, M., & Gottlieb, B. W. (1991). Mainstreaming mentally retarded children. In J. L. Matson & J. A. Mulick (Eds.), *Handbook of mental retardation* (pp. 63-73). New York: Pergamon.

Handen, B. L. (1998). Mental retardation. In E. J. Mash & L. G. Terdal (Eds.), *Treatment of childhood disorders*. New York: Guilford.

Harris, S. L. (1983). *Families of the developmentally disabled: A guide to behavioral intervention*. New York: Pergamon.

Hocutt, A. M. (1996). Effectiveness of special education: Is placement the critical factor? *The Future of Children, 6,* 77-102.

Horner, R. H., & Day, H. M. (1991). The effects of response efficiency on functionally equivalent competing behaviors. *Journal of Applied Behavior Analysis, 24,* 719-732.

Jensen, M. (1988). An unexpected effect: Restitution maintains object throwing. *Education and Treatment of Children, 2,* 252-256.

Kazdin, A. E. (1994). *Behavior modification in applied settings* (5th ed.). Pacific Grove, CA: Brooks/Cole.

Koegel, R. L., Schreibman, L., Britten, K., Burke, J., & O'Neill, R. (1982). A comparison of parent training to direct child treatment. In R. L. Koegel, A. Rincover, & A. L. Ege (Eds.), *Educating and understanding autistic children* (pp. 260-279). San Diego, CA: College-Hill Press.

Kratochwill, T. R., Elliott, S. N., & Rotto, P. C. (1990). Best practices in behavioral consultation. In A. Thomas & J. Grimes (Eds.), *Best practices in school psychology-II* (pp. 147-170). Silver Spring, MD: National Association of School Psychologists.

Kronenberger, W. G., & Meyer, R. G. (2001). *The child clinician's handbook* (2nd ed.). Boston: Allyn & Bacon.

Lalli, J. S., Kates, K., & Casey, S. D. (1999). Response covariation: The relationship between correct academic responding and problem behavior. *Behavior Modification, 23,* 339-357.

Lipsey, M. W., & Wilson, D. B. (1993). The efficacy of psychological, educational and behavioral treatment: Confirmation from meta-analysis. *American Psychologist, 48,* 1181-1209.

Little, L. M., & Kelley, M. L. (1989). The efficacy of response cost procedures for reducing children's noncompliance to parental instructions. *Behavior Therapy, 20,* 525-534.

McPhail, C. H., & Chamove, A S. (1989). Relaxation reduces disruption in mentally handicapped adults. *Journal of Mental Deficiency Research, 33,* 399-406.

Mortweet, S. (1997). The academic and social effects of a class-wide peer tutoring for students with educable mental retardation and their typical peers in an inclusive classroom (Doctoral dissertation, University of Kansas, 1997). *Dissertation Abstracts International: Section B: The Sciences & Engineering, 58,* 1515.

Nabasoku, D., & Smith, P. K. (1993). Sociometric status and social behavior of children with and without language difficulties. *Journal of Child Psychology and Psychiatry and Allied Disciplines, 34,* 1435-1448.

Patton, J. R., Beirne-Smith, M., & Payne, J. S. (1990). *Mental retardation*. New York: Macmillan.

Phares, V., Compas, B. E., & Howell, D. C. (1989). Perspectives on child behavior problems: Comparisons of children's self reports with parent and teacher reports. *Psychological Assessment, 1,* 68-71.

Polloway, E. A., Patten, J. R., Smith, J. D., & Roderique, T. W. (1991). Issues in program design for elementary students with mild retardation: Emphasis on curriculum development. *Education and Training in Mental Retardation, 26,* 144-150.

Proctor, M. A., & Morgan, D. (1991). Effectiveness of a response cost raffle procedure on the disruptive classroom behavior of adolescents with behavior problems. *School Psychology Review, 20,* 97-109.

Rapport, M.D., Murphy, H. A., & Bailey, J. S. (1982). Ritalin vs. response cost in the control of hyperactive children: A within-subject comparison. *Journal of Applied Behavior Analysis, 15,* 205-216.

Reynolds, C. J., Salend, S. J., & Beahan, C. L. (1989). Motivating secondary school students: Bringing in the reinforcements. *Academic Therapy, 25,* 81-90.

Reynolds, C. J., Salend, S. J., & Beahan, C. L. (1992). Reinforcer preferences of secondary school students with disabilities. *International Journal of Disability, Development and Education, 39,* 77-86.

Rutherford, R. B., Jr., & Nelson, C. M. (1988). Generalization of treatment effects. In J. C. Witt, S. N. Elliott, & F. M. Gresham (Eds.), *Handbook of behavior therapy in education*. New York: Plenum.

Solnick, J. V., Rincover, A., & Peterson, C. R. (1977). Some determinants of the reinforcing and punishing effects of timeout. *Journal of Applied Behavior Analysis, 10,* 415-424.

Stokes, T. F., & Baer, D. M. (1977). An implicit technology of generalization. *Journal of Applied Behavior Analysis, 10,* 349-368.

Taylor, A. (1986, April). *Loneliness, goal orientation and sociometric status: Mildly retarded children's adaptation to the mainstream classroom*. Paper presented at the annual meeting of the American Educational Research Association, San Francisco.

Weist, M. D., Ollendick, T. H., & Finney, J. W. (1991). Toward the empirical validation of treatment targets in children. *Clinical Psychology Review, 2,* 515-538.

Wielkiewicz, R. M. (1995). *Behavior management in the schools* (2nd ed.). Boston: Allyn & Bacon.

Ysseldyke, J. E., Thurlow, M. L., Christenson, S. L., & Muyskens, P. (1991). Classroom and home learning differences between students labeled as educable mentally retarded and their peers. *Education and Training in Mental Retardation, 26,* 3-17.

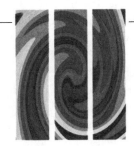

Case 4: Shirley Yong

Worried to Perfection

Shirley was referred to the clinic by her family physician, Dr. Long, to evaluate her emotional status. For the past 6 months Shirley has been suffering from alopecia (hair loss), which has resulted in a prominent bald spot on the side of her head. Shirley was wearing a hat when she came to the interview accompanied by her mother, Lilly. Shirley presented as a serious young girl who looked more mature than her age of 11 years. Shirley was currently attending Heartfield Middle School in the regular Grade 6 program. Shirley has one younger sibling, a brother, David, who is 4 years of age. Lilly Yong is a nurse and her husband, David, is a computer programmer. The Yongs came to the United States from China when David was offered a position as a senior computer programmer with an American-based firm. The move occurred approximately 4 years prior to Shirley's birth. Lilly began working soon after their arrival in the United States. With a background in nursing, Lilly was able to obtain a position very quickly, due to a nursing shortage.

DEVELOPMENTAL HISTORY/FAMILY BACKGROUND

Shirley weighed 7 pounds, 5.5 ounces at birth. Shirley's mother described the pregnancy as difficult and the labor as lengthy (12 hours). Although the delivery was normal, there were minor complications due to meconium aspiration, and Shirley stayed overnight in the pediatric critical care unit. Lilly said that to her knowledge, Shirley was relatively easy to manage as an infant, and for the most part slept well and had a good appetite. Mrs. Yong admitted, however, that Shirley's early years were spent primarily under the care of her mother, Shirley's grandmother.

Shortly after Shirley was born, Lilly's widowed mother came from China to live with the Yong family. This situation provided Lilly with a full-time care-giver for Shirley and, as a result, Lilly was able to return to work at the hospital almost immediately. The situation was also helpful for Lilly's mother, who was grieving the loss of her husband. When asked about other extended family, Lilly was not eager to discuss the extended family, saying that she had lost contact with most of her relatives. Lilly stated that to her knowledge there were no known mental or physical difficulties for any of the extended family members. With the exception of her mother, all other extended family continued to reside in China.

Although Lilly could not recall much information about Shirley's early development, she did believe that developmental milestones were generally achieved within the norm. There were some difficulties with speech, however, and Shirley did not say her first word until 18 months of age. Lilly remembered this vividly, since a colleague at work had an infant boy who was already saying words at 13 months, and Lilly felt that Shirley should have been talking by then as well. She had read that, generally, girls begin to speak earlier than boys and felt that the delay was unusual. The concern actually resulted in a fight between Lilly and her own mother, since Lilly began to blame her mother for Shirley's speech delay. Lilly was worried that Shirley's language delay may have resulted from the use of both Chinese and English in the home. Despite Lilly's protests, her mother continued to speak to Shirley exclusively in Chinese, while Lilly communicated with Shirley only in English.

Although Shirley was described as a relatively timid and passive toddler, Lilly admitted that there were times when Shirley could become quite irritable or fussy. On these occasions, Shirley would experience problems falling or staying asleep. Lilly recalled these incidents because they were very annoying and disruptive to her schedule. Being a nurse, Lilly needed her sleep to survive the lengthy shifts at the hospital. When Shirley had those fretful and irritable nights, it was impossible to get any sleep or to soothe Shirley.

Shirley remained very close to her grandmother, who was her primary care-giver, until the grandmother's death 7 years ago. Shirley's grandmother passed away in her sleep of natural causes when Shirley was 4 years of age. When asked how Shirley responded to her grandmother's death, Lilly said that the whole family was very distraught. Not only had they suffered a great personal loss, but now they had to face child care problems, as well. Shirley could not adjust to the new babysitters and would cry endlessly when her mother left for work, only to refuse being comforted upon her return. Fretfulness, eating difficulties, and sleeping problems were prominent during this period. After an endless parade of babysitters, Lilly eventually had to quit work and stay home to care for Shirley. Lilly readily admitted that this was not an easy time for both of them. Shirley's demands for consoling were exhausting and frustrating. Lilly enrolled Shirley in a half-day Montessori program, but Shirley would often say she felt sick and begged her mother to let her stay home. Lilly welcomed Shirley's sixth birthday, since this signaled mandatory schooling and some relief from parenting demands.

However, one year later, Lilly found out that she was pregnant again. David Jr. was born when Shirley was 7 years old. Shirley became very distressed that her brother David would now get to stay home with Lilly but she was forced to go to school. Mornings were often disruptive and chaotic. Shirley would compete with David's cries for food with her own complaints of stomachaches or headaches and asking to stay home from school. Shortly after the birth of David Jr., Lilly was diagnosed with postpartum depression. During this period of time, Lilly relied heavily on Shirley to help out with the baby and to assist with household chores. Often, Lilly would give in to Shirley's requests to stay home from school, especially when Lilly did not have the energy to engage in yet another battle. On these occasions, Shirley felt good about helping her mother and took her job of housecleaning very seriously.

Lilly says that all the cleaning Shirley did as a child may have backfired somewhat, because Shirley can now be "a real neat freak" to the extent that others find it annoying. Shirley will often become very upset at David Jr. for playing with toys in an area that she has cleaned. She is always at him to clean up and put his toys away before he has even had a chance to play with them. Shirley's own bedroom is arranged to perfection, with a place for everything and everything in its place. Shirley has asked for a lock for her door to make sure David Jr. does not go into her room or touch her things.

REASON FOR REFERRAL

Shirley was reticent throughout the initial part of the interview and did not volunteer any information spontaneously. Lilly said that she was concerned most recently because Shirley was demonstrating more tension and mood swings that she had seen before. The hair loss was particularly upsetting for both mother and daughter. She described her daughter as being more moody and short-tempered in the past few months. She also thought that her daughter was starting to be more secretive and not sharing information about what she was doing at school. Shirley would often come straight home after school and go right up to her room, where she locked the door. A call from Shirley's teacher last week revealed that Shirley was not handing in her assignments and that she was falling behind the class, especially in her journal writing.

When Lilly confronted Shirley about the missing assignments, Shirley stomped into her room and slammed the door. Lilly said that this was totally unacceptable behavior from her daughter. She also complained that Shirley was spending more and more time in her room and less time with the family. When asked what she was doing in her room, Shirley would say that she was working on her homework.

When asked about stress in her life, Shirley looked at her mother and then responded to the interviewer in a disgruntled manner. Attempts to engage Shirley in a conversation about her school life also met with minimal response. However, when asked how she was feeling, physically, Shirley said that she was not feeling very well and complained of headaches, stomachaches, and feeling very tired. Lilly interjected that Shirley was probably feeling tired because she wasn't sleeping much. Lilly added that she was not sleeping well herself; she had been awakened again last night by Shirley's making herself a snack at midnight. Lilly said that this seemed to be becoming a nightly ritual. (Although it was not addressed in the interview due to Shirley's guarded nature, Lilly had mentioned when making the appointment that Shirley was putting on much weight recently and had gained about 10 pounds in the past 2 months.) Shirley was obviously upset by her mother's comments and responded defensively, saying, "Well, I was hungry because I didn't like the tofu stuff you made for dinner. It was awful . . . like eating chalk." When asked if she could change one thing in her life, Shirley's eyes filled with tears and she said: "Everything."

With encouragement and patience, Shirley began to outline some of her worries about herself and her school situation. Shirley said that reading had become harder and harder because she couldn't concentrate. She would read a page and then not remember what she had read. She wanted to make her work very neat, and so she would print out all her assignments. Often she would work long hours making sure that the printing was perfect. Many times, she would have erased so many words that she would have to start all over again from the beginning on a fresh piece of paper. It took so long to print her work that she had problems finishing the assignments. Shirley said that she received only a "C" on the last assignment she handed in because it was incomplete. Shirley said she didn't tell her mother about the paper because she was embarrassed about her grade and felt guilty that her mother would be ashamed of her.

When asked about social life at school, Shirley admitted that she was miserable socially. Shirley said that she had no friends and the girls at school teased her. They were calling her names and laughing at her bald spot, saying that she was going to be a "bald old fat man." She had also found a note hidden in her desk from someone, with a drawing of a fat bald person with the label "Shirley" written across the top. One girl had started a rumor that Shirley was contagious and that if you touched her, your hair would fall out too. Now no one would even stand beside her in line. Shirley was so upset the other day that she just hid in the restroom during recess so she wouldn't have to go outside.

When asked if she was a worrier, Shirley looked concerned and said that she couldn't stop worrying and added: "I worry about doing poorly at school; I worry about being late for school; and I worry about making mistakes in my work. I worry so much that I keep waking up because I think I forgot to do something, or I am afraid I might sleep in and be late for school. I can't sleep so I straighten and clean my room or go to the kitchen and eat something. But then I can't remember if I have cleaned the kitchen, so I go back and check on it. Sometimes, I have to keep checking because I don't remember seeing it clean enough."

In response to Shirley's list of concerns, Lilly shook her head and said: "Kids today, what can you do about them." She then looked at Shirley and in an attempt to minimize her difficulties, stated that Shirley was exaggerating her problems. In China, she said, we did what we were told and worked hard at our schoolwork. That was our job. We didn't have time to complain about all these things. In our culture, we value emotional restraint, not self-indulgence.

ASSESSMENT RESULTS

The actual raw scores for Shirley's assessment are presented in Appendix A. The following is a summary of those findings. Information regarding specific assessment instruments can be found in Appendix C.

Shirley's responses to the WISC-III were notable. The examiner reported that Shirley lost bonus points due to slow task completion resulting from tendencies to waste time lining up edges to meet perfectly on the block designs or puzzle tasks. Multiple responses to verbal items were also observed, as if Shirley were unsure when to stop giving information. Requests for feedback were also frequent. Shirley's Full Scale IQ was in the Average range (84-92). Significant weaknesses in Freedom From Distractibility (working memory) and Processing Speed were evident. Shirley was academically at grade level in language arts, but she was approximately one year behind grade placement in math. Mother's response to CBCL noted significant elevations on all Internalizing scales: Withdrawn,

Anxious Depressed, Somatic, as well as Thought Problems (obsessions, repetition of acts) and Attention Problems (concentration). On the CPRS-R:L, Mrs. Yong also endorsed clinical levels for Inattention, Anxious-Shy, Perfectionism, Social Problems, and Psychosomatic concerns. Shirley's teacher responded to the TRF with clinical elevations on scales for Anxious-Depressed Mood and Thought Problems, and on the CTRS-R:L with significant concerns in areas of Inattention, Anxious-Shy, Perfectionism, and Social Problems. According to the YSR, Shirley self-reported significant concerns for all Internalizing scales: Withdrawn, Somatic, Anxious-Depressed, as well as Social Problems and Thought Problems. Shirley also endorsed significantly low levels of Self-Concept (4th percentile) and significantly high levels of anxiety (98th percentile) and Depression (95th percentile). Clinical levels of depression were also noted on the Child Depression Inventory (CDI; Kovacs, 1992) with significant concern in areas of Ineffectiveness, Anhedonia, and Negative Self Esteem. On the CDI, Shirley admitted that *she thinks about killing herself, but would not do it.* Shirley scored just below the threshold for high hopelessness on the Hopelessness Scale (Kazdin, Rodgers, & Colbus, 1986).

POST-CASE QUESTIONS

1. The co-occurrence of depression and anxiety in childhood is not unusual. In younger children, this co-occurrence is frequently associated with a Depressive-Anxious Syndrome (see CBCL: Achenbach). The features of this syndrome have also been referred to as *negative affectivity*. Research has demonstrated that while children in the sixth grade can demonstrate the separate syndromes for all three presentations of these disorders (anxiety, depression, and negative affectivity), children in the third grade are better represented by the combined syndrome of negative affectivity alone (Cole, Truglio, & Peeke, 1997). It has been suggested that developmentally, negative affectivity represents a less differentiated form of a syndrome primarily dominated by negative emotions. Developmentally, differentiation into anxious responses (physiological arousal) and depressed mood (deflated mood) would occur at a later date.

Given the above information, describe how Shirley's anxious and depressed symptoms can be conceptualized with respect to negative affectivity.

2. Gibbs and Huang (2001) outline three broad ways in which ethnicity can influence mental health in children and adolescents. First, ethnicity can shape beliefs about what constitutes mental illness at a general and specific

level. Next, cultures may also influence the manifestation of the symptoms (internalizing, through physical somatic symptoms, externalizing), as well as reactive patterns and defensive styles. Ultimately, ethnicity can also be highly influential in determining whether it is acceptable to seek assistance for mental health issues outside of the family, and who should be consulted for assistance (family elder, priest, minister, herbalist, etc.). Some high-risk factors related to cultural context include high risk for suicide in native populations and drop-out rates for ethnic minorities.

Huang and Ying (2001) discuss a number of potential stressors and conflicts that may face the bicultural child who is attempting to incorporate values from both the Chinese and the American cultures. While expression of feelings is often encouraged in Western cultures, the Chinese culture values emotional restraint, especially for negative emotions. The authors also suggest that although many children develop somatic complaints in response to stress, this particular form of symptom expression is often accompanied by sleep and appetite disturbances, followed by declines in academic performance in children of traditional Chinese American families. A major barrier to effective treatment for these children is that mental health service is highly underutilized by the Chinese American population. For those few families who seek treatment, drop out after the initial sessions is highly probable.

Discuss the potential impact of cultural contexts on Shirley's emotional status.

3. Children of depressed mothers are twice as likely to become depressed themselves (Peterson, Compas, Brooks-Gunn, Ey, & Grant, 1993). Possible suggestions for this linkage include lack of adequate models for emotion regulation; excessive use of controlling, irritable, and impatient parenting (Cicchetti & Toth, 1998); and lack of emotional availability (Malphurs et al., 1996). Girls seem to be at much higher levels of risk for transmission of depression than boys (Hops, 1992). Based on this information, discuss Shirley's depressive features relative to her mother's.

4. While boys are more likely to use bullying tactics, which rely on physical aggression, girls have been found to engage in forms of *relational aggression,* such as causing hurt to others through the propagation of rumors, ridicule, exclusion from a peer group, or withdrawal of friendship and support (Crick & Grotpeter, 1995). Research has demonstrated that girls are more relationally aggressive than males, and that relational aggression is associated with peer rejection and feelings of loneliness and isolation (Crick, Casas, & Mosher, 1997; Crick & Grotpeter, 1995).

Explain how relational aggression had an impact on Shirley's socialization. What could be done at a school level to counteract this behavior in peers?

ISSUES IN TREATMENT

Anxiety disorders represent one of the highest prevalence rates for disorders occurring in childhood and adolescence with a rate of up to 13% for one year prevalence (Costello et al., 1996). Although the *DSM-IV-TR* lists only two anxiety disorders, separation anxiety disorder and selective mutism, as "first diagnosed in infancy, childhood or adolescence," young children and adolescents can and do display many types of anxiety disorders. According to the *DSM*, when considering a diagnosis of general anxiety disorder (GAD) in children, "a thorough evaluation for the presence of other childhood anxiety disorders should be done to determine whether the worries may be better explained by . . . Separation Anxiety Disorder, Social Phobia and Obsessive Compulsive Disorder" (p. 474). There is also a likelihood that GAD symptoms of "restlessness" and "concentration problems" may be mistaken as symptoms of ADHD. In addition to the various forms of anxiety disorders, diagnosis in childhood is further complicated by some disorders appearing early and others manifesting at later developmental stages. One study reported an increase in prevalence rate for anxiety disorders from 7% at 11 years of age to almost 20% in early adulthood (Kovacs & Devlin, 1998). In addition, high rates of comorbidity are evident within the anxiety disorders, and studies report between 65% and 95% of the population demonstrating more than one anxiety or affective disorder (Last, Perrin, Jersen, & Kazdin, 1992). Many adults with anxiety and depressive disorders report that these problems had their onset in childhood, indicating that anxiety disorders can represent a stable construct across the lifespan (Ollendick & King, 1994). In their review of empirically supported treatments for children with phobic and anxiety disorders, Ollendick and King (1998) found several treatments to be effective in reducing fears and phobias. However, with respect to anxiety disorders, the authors found only one treatment method, cognitive-behavioral procedures, with or without family inclusion, that met criteria for the probably efficacious treatment category.

Despite the high rate of prevalence for anxiety disorders, until recently there have been relatively few studies regarding the treatment of childhood anxiety disorders. Cognitive-behavioral treatment (CBT) for childhood anxiety disorders has received increasing empirical support, with Ollendick and King (1998) citing several studies conducted by separate research teams in the United States and Australia. Kendall and colleagues (1992) have developed several treatment strategies, including a treatment manual called *Coping Cat* for children with generalized anxiety disorder, and the CBT treatment has been demonstrated effective in several studies. The CBT program focuses on four components: (a) training children to recognize feelings and physiological responses associated with anxiety; (b) awareness of self-defeating negative attributions/expectations; (c) reframing negative thoughts into positive constructive thoughts; and (d) evaluation of successful coping. Children are taught behavioral strategies over 16 sessions and increase their ability to manage anxious responses through the use of role play, modeling, in vivo exposure, and relaxation training (Kane & Kendall, 1989; Kendall et al., 1992; Kendall and Treadwell, 1996). In Australia, researchers investigated the combined effect of CBT for children and a family component (FAM). The FAM included a parallel 12-week program for parents to learn skills in areas such as supportive praise for courageous behavior and planned ignoring for excessive anxious responses. Results revealed that the Australian children treated with a 12-week CBT + FAM performed significantly better than children treated by CBT alone (Bartlett, Dadds, & Rapee, 1996).

The selective serotonin reuptake inhibitors (SSRIs) have been found to successfully alleviate symptoms of obsessive-compulsive disorder (OCD) in adolescents and children (Riddle, Subramaniam, & Walkup, 1998). Other treatments that are currently under increased investigation include: exposure with response prevention and cognitive behavioral therapy. Exposure procedures such as desensitization or flooding can bring the child into increased contact with the anxiety-provoking stimulus either in reality (in vivo) or through guided imagery or pictures. The child is taught a form of muscle relaxation that is incompatible with heightened anxiety in an attempt to link the object or situation that evokes anxiety with a lower level of arousal (relaxed state). Recently, Neziroglu, Yaryura-Tobias, Walz, and McKay (2000) found that combining an SSRI (fluvoxamine) with behavior therapy of exposure and response prevention was superior to medication alone and that children and adolescents in the study continued to show improvement 2 years later. March and Mulle (1998) have developed a cognitive-behavioral treatment manual for children and adolescents with OCD that provides a session-by-session guide for clinicians through the four stages of treatment: psychoeducational, cognitive training, mapping OCD, and graded exposure and response prevention. Initial studies of the effectiveness of the manualized program with adolescents are encouraging (Thieneman, Martin, Creggar, Thompson, & Dyer-Friedman, 2001).

REFERENCES

Bartlett, P. M., Dadds, M. R., & Rapee, R. M. (1996). Family treatment of childhood anxiety: A controlled trial. *Journal of Consulting and Clinical Psychology, 64,* 333-342.

Cicchetti, D., & Toth, S. L. (1998). The development of depression in children and adolescents. *American Psychologist, 53,* 221-241.

Cole, D. A., Truglio, R., & Peeke, L. (1997). Relation between symptoms of anxiety and depression in children: A multitrait-multimethod-multigroup assessment. *Journal of Consulting and Clinical Psychology, 65,* 110-119.

Costello, E. J., Angold, A. A., Burns, B. J., Stangl, D. K., Tweed, D. L., Erkanli, A., & Worthman, C. M. (1996). The Great Smoky Mountains study of youth. Goals, design, methods, and, the prevalence of *DSM-III-R* disorders. *Archives of General Psychiatry, 53,* 1129-1136.

Crick, N. R., Casas, J. F., & Mosher, M. (1997). Relational and overt aggression in preschool. *Developmental Psychology, 33,* 579-588.

Crick, N. R., & Grotpeter, J. K. (1995). Relational aggression, gender and social psychological adjustment. *Child Development, 66,* 710-722.

Gibbs, J. T., & Huang, L. N. (Eds.). (2001). *Children of color.* San Francisco: Jossey-Bass.

Hops, H. (1992). Parental depression and child behavior problems: Implications for behavioral family intervention. *Behavior Change, 9,* 126-138.

Huang, L. N., & Ying, Y. W. (2001). Chinese American children and adolescents. In J. T. Gibbs, N. L. Huang, et al. (Eds.), *Children of color.* San Francisco: Jossey-Bass.

Kane, M., & Kendall, P. C. (1989). Anxiety disorders in children: A multiple baseline evaluation of a cognitive-behavioral treatment. *Behavior Therapy, 20,* 499-508.

Kazdin, A. E., Rodgers, A., & Colbus, D. (1986). The Hopelessness Scale for Children: Psychometric characteristics and concurrent validity. *Journal of Consulting and Clinical Psychology, 54,* 241-245.

Kendall, P. C., Chansky, T. E., Kane, M. T., Kim, R. S., Kortlander, E., Ronan, K. R., Sessa, F. M., & Siqueland, L. (1992). *Anxiety disorders in youth: Cognitive-behavioral interventions.* Needham Heights, MA: Allyn & Bacon.

Kendall, P. C., & Treadwell, K. R. H. (1996). Cognitive behavioral treatment for childhood anxiety disorders. In E. D. Hibbs & P. S. Jensen (Eds.), *Psychosocial treatments for child and adolescent disorders: Empirically-based strategies for clinical practice.* Washington, DC: American Psychological Association.

Kovacs, M. (1992). *Children's Depression Inventory manual.* Toronto: Multi-Health Systems.

Kovacs, M., & Devlin, B. (1998). Internalizing disorders in childhood. *Journal of Child Psychology and Psychiatry and Allied Disciplines, 39,* 47-63.

Last, C. G., Perrin, S., Jersen, M., & Kazdin, A. E. (1992). *DSM III-R* anxiety disorders in children: Sociodemographic and clinical characteristics. *Journal of the American Academy of Child and Adolescent Psychiatry, 31,* 1070-1075.

Malphurs, J. E., Field, T. M., Larraine, C., Pickens, J., Lelaez-Nogueras, M., Yando, R., & Bendell, D. (1996). Altering withdrawn and intrusive interaction behaviors of depressed mothers. *Infant Mental Health Journal, 17,* 152-160.

March, J. S., & Mulle, K. (1998). *OCD in children and adolescents: A cognitive-behavioral treatment manual.* New York: Guilford.

Neziroglu, F., Yaryura-Tobias, J. A., Walz, J., & McKay, D. (2000). The effects of fluvoxamine and behavior therapy on children and adolescents with obsessive-compulsive disorder. *Journal of Child & Adolescent Psychopharmacology, 10,* 295-306.

Ollendick, T. H., & King, N. J. (1994). Diagnosis, assessment and treatment of internalizing problems in children: The role of longitudinal data. *Journal of Consulting and Clinical Psychology, 62,* 919-927.

Ollendick, T. H., & King, N. J. (1998). Empirically supported treatments for children with phobic and anxiety disorders: Current status. *Journal of Clinical Child Psychology, 27,* 156-167.

Peterson, A. C., Compas, B., Brooks-Gunn, J., Ey, S., & Grant, K. E. (1993). Depression in adolescence. *American Psychologist, 48*(2), 155-168.

Riddle, M. A., Subramaniam, G., & Walkup, J. T. (1998). Efficacy of psychiatric medications in children and adolescents: A review of controlled studies. *Psychiatric Clinics of North America: Annual of Drug Therapy, 5,* 269-285.

Thieneman, M., Martin, J., Creggar, B., Thompson, H., & Dyer-Friedman, J. (2001). Manual-driven group cognitive-behavioral therapy for adolescents with obsessive-compulsive disorder: A pilot study. *Journal of the American Academy of Child & Adolescent Psychiatry, 40,* 1254-1260.

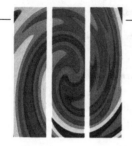

Case 5: Winnie Kent

Silence Is Not Golden

Winnie, a 5½-year-old girl, was referred for assessment by her pediatrician. Winnie was accompanied by her mother, Isabel. Despite being a seemingly normal and talkative youngster at home, Winnie had always been rather shy and reticent in larger group settings. Although her mother had anticipated some early reservations on Winnie's part regarding her initial school placement, Isabel was totally unequipped to deal with the current situation, which had developed over the past 6 months of enrollment in the kindergarten program.

DEVELOPMENTAL HISTORY/FAMILY BACKGROUND

Isabel Kent and her husband Frank were both in their early forties. They met and married while attending graduate school. Frank is an engineer, and Isabel is currently a "stay-at-home mom." Prior to Winnie's birth, Isabel was a research assistant for a pharmaceutical company. Isabel stated that there was no serious mental illness on either side of the family, although she described herself as "high-strung" and a bit of a loner. She felt that her husband was a workaholic, since he spent the majority of his time either working or thinking about working. She described their marriage "as successful as most enduring marriages."

Isabel stated that although Winnie is an only child, it was not by choice. The pregnancy was planned and it was decided that when the baby was born, Isabel would quit her job and devote her time to child rearing. Although the plan was to have two or three children, Isabel suffered a miscarriage when Winnie was about 14 months old, and then a second miscarriage about 5 months later.

Isabel described herself as depressed during this period with frequent bouts of crying and fatigue. Her physician suggested a trial of Prozac; however, Isabel developed headaches and nervousness/agitation as side effects. A trial of Paxil produced fewer side effects and eventually Isabel was coping much better. Because of the risk of complications in pregnancy, given Isabel's age, and fear of the depression returning if she had another miscarriage, the Kents decided to abandon any further attempts to conceive a child.

Winnie weighed 5 pounds, 6 ounces at birth, and although pregnancy and delivery were normal, complications developed later on. Immediately after the birth, an attempt to intubate a blocked nasal passage resulted in swelling. Winnie was fed intravenously and required an artificial airway until the swelling subsided and surgery could finally be performed to remove the membrane that was blocking the nasal passage. During this time, Winnie experienced what her mother described as "blue spells," a term she used to describe the color of Winnie's face and body resulting from lack of oxygen. Isabel said that this was a very emotionally draining time for her. Isabel was very fearful and anxious concerning Winnie's health, even though the medical staff assured her that Winnie would be fine. Winnie remained in the neonatal intensive care unit for 3 weeks before Isabel could take her home from the hospital.

As an infant, Winnie had bouts of being fretful and colicky, and she had some difficulties keeping her food down. Mrs. Kent recalled that at least twice a week, if not more, Winnie would lose almost half her intake in rather severe episodes of projectile vomiting. Mrs. Kent was concerned and asked the pediatrician about it, but his response was that it was likely due to a sensitive and immature digestive system. He suggested they change the baby formula; that helped somewhat, but the matter never really resolved itself until Winnie was totally on solid food. Mrs. Kent stated that even today, Winnie is a picky eater, and if she is upset, she tends to eat very little because her stomach is easily upset.

Motor milestones were slightly advanced developmentally, and Winnie was sitting independently at 4 months, standing at 7-8 months, and walking at 10 months of age. Language development lagged behind motor skills. Winnie did not say her first word until about 15 months, and simple sentences weren't produced until about 2½ years of age. Winnie had some articulation problems and substituted a few sounds, the most prominent of which were "w" for "r" (wabbit for rabbit) and "l" for "y" (lellow for yellow). The articulation errors stopped about a year ago. Currently, Isabel believes that Winnie's speech is normal for her age, based on conversations between Winnie and her best friend Kate's daughter, Molly, who is almost the same age as Winnie. At home, she described Winnie as very chatty and quite the conversationalist with speech far more adult-like than child-like.

Isabel described herself as somewhat aloof and not one to initiate a lot of social contact. She was fortunate that Kate lived across the street, since Winnie and Molly were about the same age and played very well together. Kate was more outgoing than Isabel and was often responsible for organizing activities for the foursome, such as outings to the park, or attending movies or concerts. Isabel and her husband Frank rarely went out in the evenings, due to Frank's long work hours, but when they did, Winnie would just go over and spend the night at Kate's house with Molly. Similarly, Molly would spend the night with them, whenever Kate and Brian went out for an evening. People often mistook Winnie and Molly for twins, since they were about the same age and looked somewhat alike. Unfortunately, about 9 months ago, Brian was suddenly transferred and the family moved out of state. Isabel said that until the separation, she never really realized how much time the four of them had spent together. Isabel said that she really misses Kate's company and she is sure that Winnie must really miss Molly, too, although she doesn't talk about Molly much. Isabel wondered if she were grieving in silence or just didn't feel as strongly as an adult might.

About 2 months after Kate and Molly left, Isabel decided to enroll in a Tuesday morning art class at the local gallery and enroll Winnie in a once-weekly preschool program for that morning. Isabel thought that this would be good for both herself and Winnie. However, when she tried to drop Winnie off at the preschool center, Winnie had a severe temper tantrum, attached herself to her mother's leg, and began sobbing uncontrollably. Isabel was in shock since she had never seen such behavior from Winnie before. Isabel stayed with Winnie for the next half hour hoping that Winnie would calm down. Eventually, sobs dissipated into heaving sighs and Isabel decided to make another attempt to leave. On cue, Winnie's sobs began again, this time even more violent with screaming and begging her mother not to go. The preschool staff encouraged Isabel not to give in to Winnie at this point, since it would only make matters worse. Isabel left, without looking back, afraid if she saw Winnie, she would not be able to carry on. When Isabel returned 3 hours later, Winnie looked like she was totally drained. She was engaged in subdued solitary play in the corner, rocking her doll. Her eyes were red and swollen from crying. The preschool staff said that she continued with her sobbing for quite some time after Isabel had left. That night, Winnie was like Velcro and refused to sleep alone. The whole ordeal was far more than Isabel had bargained for. The next night, had it not been for Frank's insistence that Winnie sleep in her own bed, the nightly ritual probably would have continued. As it was, Winnie started calling out at night, and often Isabel would have to go into Winnie's bedroom to comfort her. Isabel ended up sleeping in Winnie's room the next night because Winnie had a night-mare that her mom had gone away. Isabel started leaving the light on in Winnie's bedroom so she would not be afraid of the dark.

The following Tuesday, Winnie started crying when Isabel began to prepare to leave. Winnie started to complain that her stomach was hurting and held on tightly to her stomach saying: "It hurts, it hurts." Although Isabel could not be definite, she was pretty sure that Winnie was saying she was sick and wanted to stay home. Rather than give in, she picked Winnie up and carried her to the car, with Winnie sobbing and complaining about her aching stomach. The tears, the sobbing, the protests, and the aches and pains continued every Tuesday for the next 3 months. Eventually, Winnie would comply, but began to sit beside the preschool window waiting and watching for signs of her mother's return. When they were home, Winnie was constantly in need of reassurance that her mother was alright and that everything was OK.

Despite the difficulties, Isabel persisted in taking Winnie to preschool because kindergarten would be starting shortly, and Isabel knew Winnie had to become more prepared. Winnie was having considerable difficulty adjusting to preschool, which was only one day a week. How would she cope with kindergarten on a daily basis? She also needed more practice socially. She seemed so withdrawn at the preschool and didn't seem to interact with the other children. Her teachers said that she was very cooperative, but she didn't seem comfortable talking to anyone.

Isabel was thrilled when a new family moved in a few doors down because they had a daughter Winnie's age. Isabel really pushed herself to be more social and extended an invitation to the new mother and daughter to come over for afternoon tea. Winnie seemed to get along well with her new friend and soon they were playing together, much like she and Molly had. After a few months, Winnie was invited to a sleep over at Becky's. Although the girls had planned the event for some time, Winnie began to get anxious just before it was time to leave. She asked an endless series of questions about what her mother would be doing in her absence. Isabel continued to reassure her that she was just going to take a bath and watch television. Winnie immediately became concerned that her mother might slip in the bathtub and if nobody else was home, she could drown. Isabel continued to attempt to calm Winnie's fears. Finally, Becky and her mother came to pick Winnie up for the sleep over. Winnie's goodbye hug was more like a desperate attempt to carry her mother along with her. Two hours later, Winnie was standing at the door, sleeping bag in tow, complaining that she had to come home because she didn't feel well.

Kindergarten finally started and after much struggle and distress, Isabel finally got Winnie to walk to school with her friend Becky. Winnie would walk beside Becky with her head bent down, constantly looking sideways to see if her mother was still watching from the outside steps. The school was only a block away, and Winnie told herself that if she looked real hard, she could probably see her house between the trees. At school, Winnie just seemed to go through the motions until it was home time. On the playground, she was always peering through the fence, trying to see her house. Her teachers were very patient and encouraging, and Winnie was cooperative, but she would not participate verbally in any activities that were going on. For the first month, her teachers thought it was just a case of reluctance to talk in the new environment. After all, Winnie did appear to be very shy, and her mother had cautioned the kindergarten teachers that Winnie was slow to warm up. They anticipated that it might take a while for her to feel comfortable talking to the teachers and the other children. However, 4 months had gone by and Winnie had not said a word. When asked a question, Winnie would nod her head in the affirmative or shake her head to signal "no," but no words accompanied the gestures. Winnie would talk only to Becky at school, and then only in whispers, until they got far enough away from the schoolyard that no one could hear. Then she would talk to Becky as if they were at home.

REASON FOR REFERRAL

Isabel finally brought Winnie to the pediatrician for help, not understanding why her daughter was giving the school situation the silent treatment. The pediatrician suggested that Isabel take Winnie to see a child psychologist, who could evaluate the causes of Winnie's silent behaviors and suggest ways to best deal with this behavior in the school.

ASSESSMENT RESULTS

When Isabel contacted the psychologist at the clinic, prior to seeing Winnie in the clinic, the psychologist requested permission to observe Winnie in the classroom. Isabel was very much in agreement. After observing Winnie for a morning and interviewing her teachers, the psychologist sat beside Winnie and asked her to draw a picture for her. Winnie drew a picture of a little girl skipping. The psychologist found it interesting that the skipping rope surrounded the little girl's head, as if her head were in a space capsule. The drawing was sophisticated enough, however, to suggest that Winnie was likely, at least, of average intelligence. The psychologist contacted Isabel and suggested she bring Winnie to the clinic for additional assessment.

Isabel brought Winnie to the clinic the following week. Winnie would not go into the assessment room unless her mother came with her. Throughout the assessment, Winnie would not speak directly to the psychologist, or answer any questions verbally. On occasion, Winnie would bend over toward her mother and whisper something into her mother's ear. But even on these occasions, she would cup her hand around her mouth, blocking the psychologist from any entry into her verbal world.

Winnie's drawing of a person (Draw-A-Person) and Bender Visual Motor Gestalt designs were all within the Average range. Scores on the Peabody Picture Vocabulary Test (PPVT-III) also revealed an understanding of vocabulary that was above the expected level for her age (SS = 110). The psychologist asked Winnie's teacher and mother to complete the Behavioral Assessment System for Children (BASC) Preschool Scales. Based on Winnie's responses to the school setting, Mrs. Kent rated Winnie in the clinical range for Adaptability; however, all other ratings were within the norm. Winnie's teacher rated clinical elevations for: Anxiety, Atypicality, Adaptability, and Social Skills.

POST-CASE QUESTIONS

1. There are several models that can be advanced to explain the sequential development of internalizing disorders, such as anxiety disorders, and the factors that might be responsible for variable outcomes. From the perspective of the diathesis-stress model, an inherited genetic vulnerability to anxiety may remain dormant until environmental conditions are adverse (peer rejection; family conflict; parent psychopathology, e.g., depression), causing the disorder to become overt (Kazdin & Weisz, 1998). In addition, temperamental factors such as behavioral inhibition may also account for why one child may be more vulnerable to stressful or unfamiliar surroundings than another child (Kagan & Snidman, 1991). Discuss how Winnie's separation anxiety might be explained using the diathesis-stress model.

2. There are a number of possible theories that can be suggested to account for the etiology or development and onset of separation anxiety disorder (SAD). There is some support to suggest that children with SAD come from families that share a greater prevalence for anxiety and mood disorders (Black, 1995). Attachment theory might predict that an anxiously attached infant might be more prone to develop SAD than a securely attached or resistant infant. Discuss the onset and development of Winnie's separation anxiety disorder as a psychologist from each of the following perspectives: behavioral, cognitive, psychodynamic. Suggest possible treatment alternatives that might be developed for each of the above perspectives relative to probable cause.

3. Discuss how selective mutism might be influenced by the various contexts of development, using Bronfenbrenner's model: individual characteristics, immediate environment, social and economic factors, cultural factors.

4. Develop a case formulation for Winnie, based on factors considered in Table 1.3, from the perspectives of the family systems and attachment theories.

ISSUES IN TREATMENT

Treatments that have been successful for children's phobic disorders have also been successful for treating separation anxiety disorder (Werry & Wollersheim, 1991). In their extensive review of treatments for childhood phobic disorders, Ollendick and King (1998) found one well-established method (contingency management) and a number of probably efficacious treatments (systematic desensitization, modeling, cognitive behavioral). Contingency management relies on principles of operant conditioning and differs fundamentally from the other approaches discussed. Conceptually, while systematic desensitization, modeling, and cognitive-behavioral methods share a belief that reducing the fear is a necessary precursor to increasing the desired behaviors, contingency management focuses directly on increasing the desired behavior through rewarded practice. Using contingency management methodology, a child afraid of the dark would be rewarded for spending time in the dark, resulting in increased dark tolerance (Leitenberg & Callahan, 1973). Applying these methods to separation anxiety disorder (SAD), children would be rewarded for spending time away from their caregiver and for developing greater tolerance for separation. Using cognitive-behavioral methods to reduce fear of the dark might involve modeling and verbal rehearsal to assist children to generate positive self-statements. Graziano and Mooney (1980, 1982) combined parent reward for "brave statements" with "brave" self-statement training, relaxation training, and imagined positive scenes to successfully reduce fear of the dark in young children. Ollendick and King (1998) reviewed several modeling techniques and concluded that although modeling is generally successful, participant modeling (actual engagement with the feared object, in conjunction with observation of the model) is the superior method.

Systematic desensitization (Wolpe, 1958) was a procedure designed to incorporate two inherent assumptions: (a) fears are conditioned responses (learned behaviors) and can be de-conditioned (unlearned); (b) fear/anxiety and relaxation are two competing and incompatible responses. Although there are variations on the method, at its basis, systematic desensitization involves the following steps: (a) lessons in deep muscle relaxation; (b) creation of a fear hierarchy (least to most fearful); and (c) graduated pairings of the feared thought with deep muscle relaxation. Feared thoughts can involve actual behaviors ("in vivo") or "mental images."

An interesting variation that has been used successfully with children is emotive imagery (Cornwall, Spence, & Schotte, 1997; Lazarus & Abramowitz, 1962). In this variation, emphasis is placed on conquering the fear, rather than on pairing the feared responses with relaxation, and "child mastery" becomes the antidote to fear. Children participate in creating exciting stories, and as their heroes defeat the elements of the fear hierarchy, a new sense of control and mastery develops to replace the anxiety and fear.

Although initially thought to be a rare disorder, selective mutism may be more prevalent than previous estimates have suggested (e.g., fewer than 1% according to the *DSM-IV*). A recent study out of California found as many as 7 children in every 1,000 in kindergarten through second grade had the disorder (Bergman, Piacentini, & McCracken, 2002). Black and Uhde (1992) have suggested that since the onset of the disorder often coincides with initial school entrance for the majority of children, an underlying feature of the disorder may be school refusal. Issues regarding how the disorder should be conceptualized have impacted on research, diagnosis, assessment, and treatment.

Selective mutism was originally called elective mutism (*DSM-III*) because initially the disorder was thought to reflect an intentional refusal to speak outside of the family. However, current emphasis has focused on the situational aspect of the disorder. Refining the definition of the disorder from "elective" to "selective" has resulted in some theorists suggesting the need to retain the original and current conceptualizations in recognizing two different disorder types. It has been suggested that anxiety is the defining comorbid feature of the *anxious or compliant type* demonstrated in passive, shy, fearful, and insecure behaviors. This type of selective mutism can be contrasted to the willful, oppositional, manipulative, and aggressive behaviors evident in the *noncompliant or resistant type* (Lesser-Katz, 1988). Research suggests that the vast majority (90%) of children with selective mutism will conform to the anxious-compliant type. Of the anxiety disorders, social phobia is the most prevalent comorbid disorder and is evident in up to 90% of cases with selective mutism (Black & Uhde, 1995; Drummit et al., 1997). Oppositional defiant disorder and attention-deficit disorder have been linked as comorbid features with the less prominent, resistant form of selective mutism (Black & Uhde, 1995; Drummit et al., 1997). Finally, Beidel and colleagues (Beidel, Turner, & Morris, 1999) outline several areas of social anxiety in children that might be seen to overlap with selective mutism, such as fears of: reading aloud in class, joining in on conversations, speaking to adults, and starting conversations.

Currently, given the research findings, selective mutism is considered by most to be a form of anxiety disorder (Anstending, 1999). It is not surprising, then, that cognitive-behavioral therapies (CBT), which have been so successful in treating childhood anxiety disorders (Kendall, 1994), are under current investigation regarding their potential role in the treatment of selective mutism. Given the high rates of comorbidity with social phobia, behavior therapies often used in the treatment of phobias have also been adapted for use in treating selective mutism. A third avenue of treatment for the disorder is a pharmacological approach.

Various theories about selective mutism have been advanced, including psychodynamic (fixation at the anal stage), family systems (enmeshment and overprotection), behavioral (avoidance), and cognitive (maladaptive thinking). Success has been minimal for the psychodynamically oriented therapies, such as play therapy or family therapy (Dow, Sonies, Scheib, Moss, & Leonard, 1995). Behaviorally based treatments that combine multimodal techniques have been the most successful (Sluckin, Foreman, & Herbert, 1991). Kehle, Hintze, and DuPaul (1997) outline several behavioral interventions that have been successfully integrated into treatment programs, including: contingency management (rewarding speech and ignoring silence); shaping and fading (e.g., reward speech in school in the presence of mother; gradually remove mother's presence); escape and avoidance and self-modeling of videotaped presentations of desired behaviors (Kehle et al., 1997). Blum and colleagues (1998) investigated the potential use of audiotape recordings as a self-modeling technique. Results were very encouraging, suggesting that this easy-to-use and brief technique can provide a successful intervention approach for use in school settings. Fung (2002) recently adapted a CBT program for children (*Coping Bear Workbook;* Mendlowitz et al., 1999) into a Web-based Internet program for selective mutism and reports success in alleviating symptoms of selective mutism in a 7-year-old child. In cases where behavioral interventions are not successful, selective serotonin reuptake inhibitors (SSRIs) have met with success, especially if anxiety is a comorbid feature (Black & Uhde, 1994; Dow et al., 1995).

REFERENCES

Anstending, K. D. (1999). Is selective mutism an anxiety disorder? Rethinking *DSM-IV* classification. *Journal of Anxiety Disorders, 13,* 417-434.

Beidel, D. C., Turner, S. M., & Morris, T. L. (1999). Psychopathology of childhood social phobia. *Journal of the American Academy of Child and Adolescent Psychiatry, 38,* 643-650.

Bergman, R., L., Piacentini, J., & McCracken, J. T. (2002). Prevalence and description of selective mutism in a school-based population. *Journal of the American Academy of Child and Adolescent Psychiatry, 41,* 938-946.

Black, B., & Uhde, T. W. (1992). Treatment of elective mutism as a variant of school phobia. *Journal of the American Academy of Child and Adolescent Psychiatry, 31,* 1090-1094

Black, B., & Uhde, T. W. (1994). Treatment of elective mutism with fluoxetine: A double-blind, placebo-controlled study. *Journal of the American Academy of Child and Adolescent Psychiatry, 33,* 1000-1006.

Black, B., & Uhde, T. W. (1995). Psychiatric characteristics of children with selective mutism: A pilot study. *Journal of the American Academy of Child and Adolescent Psychiatry, 32,* 847-856.

Blum, N. J., Kell, R. S., Star, H. L., Lender, W. L., Bradley-Klug, K. L., Osborne, M., L., & Dowrick, P. W. (1998). Case study: Audio feedforward treatment of selective mutism. *Journal of the American Academy of Child and Adolescent Psychiatry, 37,* 40-43.

Cornwall, E., Spence, S. H., & Schotte, D. (1997). The effectiveness of emotive imagery in the treatment of darkness phobia in children. *Behavior Change, 13,* 223-229.

Dow, S. P, Sonies, B. C., Scheib, D., Moss, S. E., & Leonard, H. L. (1995). Practical guidelines for the assessment and treatment of selective mutism. *Journal of the American Academy of Child and Adolescent Psychiatry, 34,* 836-846.

Drummit, E. S., Klein, R. G., Tancer, N. K., Asche, B., Martin, J., & Fairbanks, J. A. (1997). Systematic assessment of 50 children with selective mutism. *Journal of the American Academy of Child and Adolescent Psychiatry, 36,* 653-660.

Fung, D. S. (2002, February). Web-based CBT for selective mutism [Letter to the editor]. *Journal of the American Academy of Child and Adolescent Psychiatry.*

Graziano, A. M., & Mooney, K. C. (1980). Family self-control instruction for children's nighttime fear reduction. *Journal of Consulting and Clinical Psychology, 48,* 206-213.

Graziano, A. M., & Mooney, K. C. (1982). Behavioral treatment of "Nightfears" in children: Maintenance of improvement at 2½ to 3 year follow-up. *Journal of Consulting and Clinical Psychology, 50,* 598-599.

Kagan, J., & Snidman, N. (1991). Temperamental factors in human development. *American Psychologist, 46,* 856-862

Kazdin, A. E., & Weisz, J. R. (1998). Identifying and developing empirically supported child and adolescent treatments. *Journal of Consulting Clinical Psychologist, 66,* 19-36.

Kehle, T., Hintze, J. M., & DuPaul, G. J. (1997). Selective mutism. In G. Bear, K. Minke, & A. Thomas (Eds.), *Children's needs II. Development, problems and alternatives* (pp. 329-386). Bethesda, MD: NASP.

Kendall, P. C. (1994). Treating anxiety disorders in children: Results of a randomized clinical trial. *Journal of Consulting and Clinical Psychology, 64,* 724-730.

Lazarus, A. A., & Abramowitz, A. (1962). The use of "emotive imagery" in the treatment of children's phobias. *Journal of Mental Science, 108,* 191-195.

Leitenberg, H., & Callahan, E. J. (1973). Reinforced practice and reduction of different kinds of fears in adults and children. *Behavior Research and Therapy, 11,* 19-30.

Lesser-Katz, M. (1988). The treatment of elective mutism as stranger reaction. *Psychotherapy, 25,* 305-313.

Mendlowitz, S., Manassis, K., Bradley, S., Scapiliato, D., Miezitis, S., & Shaw, B. F. (1999). Cognitive-behavioral group treatments in childhood anxiety disorders. *Journal of the American Academy of Child and Adolescent Psychiatry, 38,* 1223-1229.

Ollendick, T. H., & King, N. J. (1998). Empirically supported treatments for children with phobic and anxiety disorders: Current status. *Journal of Clinical Child Psychology, 27,* 156-167.

Sluckin, A., Foreman, N., & Herbert, M. (1991). Behavioral treatment programs and selectivity of speaking at follow-up in a sample of 25 selective mutes. *Psychologist, 26,* 132-137.

Werry, J. S., & Wollersheim, J. P. (1991). Behavior therapy with children and adolescents: A twenty year overview. In S. Chess & M. E. Hertzig (Eds.), *Annual progress in child psychiatry and child development, 1990* (pp. 413-447). New York: Brunner/Mazel.

Wolpe, J. (1958). *Psychotherapy by reciprocal inhibition.* Stanford, CA: Stanford University Press.

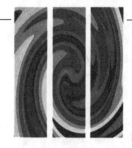

Case 6: Jordan Neeson

Let Me Count the Ways

Jordan appeared agitated and upset as he walked into the clinic, accompanied by his mother, Sally Neeson. The last thing Jordan wanted to do this morning was get dressed and go to a clinic. After all, he was on his summer vacation. Mrs. Neeson brought Jordan to the clinic because the school had recommended he be retained in the Grade 3 program due to academic difficulties and problems with attention and concentration. Work was rarely handed in or completed and Jordan was beginning to really hate school.

DEVELOPMENTAL HISTORY/FAMILY BACKGROUND

Sally Neeson completed the intake survey and was available for a telephone intake conversation prior to bringing Jordan in for his assessment session. In recalling Jordan's birth history, Sally stated that the pregnancy was very hard on her. She had considerable nausea in the first 3 months and was very fatigued throughout the majority of her pregnancy. The delivery was also difficult, and Jordan had a lowered Apgar score because of birth complications. During the delivery, there were knots in the umbilical cord that cut off or reduced the oxygen supply. It seemed to take forever, but he was finally breathing on his own. Jordan seemed to rebound, and Sally was able to bring Jordan home with her when she left the hospital. Sally reported that appetite and sleep habits were normal for the first year.

At one point in the rather lengthy telephone conversation, Sally seemed particularly agitated and wanted to know why the interviewer was asking her personal questions about her marriage and relatives. After all, she just wanted to have Jordan tested for school, there was absolutely nothing wrong with his behavior and he didn't have any "mental" problems. Sally described Jordan as a sensitive boy who was very aware of his academic difficulties. Sally was definitive in stating that Jordan did not have any behavior problems. Sally also was very sure that there was no mental illness in either her family or her husband's. However, Sally did recall an aunt, Bertha, who wouldn't leave her house. She remembered family members talking about Bertha at family functions, because she would never attend. They said she was afraid to go outside and that she even had to have groceries delivered to her door. Sally could not recall any more about Bertha, who died about 10 years ago. Sally described herself as a bit of a worrier and said that her husband, Ralph, was pretty easy going and just liked to watch sports on TV when he finished work at the office. Ralph sold insurance and Sally was a full-time homemaker. Jordan has an older sister, Susy, who is 2 years older than Jordan, but she is very mature for her age. Sally said that Susy is 11 years old, going on 20, while Jordan is 9 years old, going on 5.

Sally stated that Jordan's milestones were achieved on time and he walked at about 14 months and talked a bit later. Sally admitted that she was not a very good historian about dates and times. Jordan had some ear infections and had tubes inserted for drainage when he was about 3 years old. Sally described Jordan as a bit of a "mama's boy." She said that they were like "two peas in a pod," and when Jordan was a toddler, Sally took him everywhere with her. Jordan never went to preschool and Sally chose to home-school him rather than send him to kindergarten. Jordan was not eager to go to first grade. Most mornings, his sister Susy had to hold his hand all the way to school so that he would not try to run the other way. Jordan was finally starting to settle into Grade 1 by December, when the family had an opportunity to purchase a home in a better neighborhood across town. As a result, Jordan had to change schools in January. Jordan started to resist going to school all over again, and Susy was once again forced to drag him with her. One good thing about the relocation was that the house was within eyesight of the school. Jordan's mother told him that if he missed her, he could just look across the street and know that she was thinking about him. This seemed to comfort Jordan somewhat.

One day shortly after the move, Jordan's mother had an appendicitis attack and had to be rushed to the hospital. Unfortunately, shortly after the ambulance arrived, Jordan's class was let outside for recess. Jordan was terrified when he saw the ambulance in his driveway, and he ran across the street just as the ambulance pulled away. Jordan ran down the street, yelling and crying, until he was retrieved by the school principal. For the next 5 months, Jordan was very fearful of leaving the house. He was afraid that something might happen to his mother if he left. Often he would ask to stay home, saying that he wasn't feeling very well. Sally said that she felt to blame because she had scared him with her appendicitis attack. Often she felt sorry for him, and would let him stay home.

By the end of first grade, Jordan's teachers were becoming concerned. He had missed quite a bit of school (21 days) and did not have a firm grasp of the fundamentals. His handwriting was very poor and most of his letters and numbers were reversed or upside down.

The following year, Sally tried to keep Jordan's absences in check by making promises that they would do things together after class. Jordan went to school, but his midyear report was very poor. Jordan was falling farther and farther behind. Sally tried reading with him at home, but Jordan seemed to have a very poor memory for the words, and each day it was like he had not seen the word before. Recently, the school recommended that Jordan repeat Grade 3. Sally finally decided to have him assessed.

Sally noted that Jordan's health has been good except for frequent complaints of headaches and stomachaches. Vision and hearing had been recently tested and were within the Normal range. Jordan's mother had not sent her responses to the BASC and Conners to the clinic ahead of time, so it was not possible to score these instruments until after Jordan's first assessment session. In hindsight, having this information beforehand would have provided significant insight into Jordan's emotional profile. On a positive note, Sally was able to locate Jordan's Grade 3 teacher, who volunteered to complete the teacher forms during her summer break.

REASON FOR REFERRAL

Sally brought Jordan to the clinic because she wanted to know why he was having academic problems, and if Jordan had this "attention deficit" problem that his teacher had mentioned. It was important to Mrs. Neeson that Jordan have an assessment completed before the new school year, because she was very concerned about his success in the Grade 4 program, and Jordan's growing reluctance to attend school.

ASSESSMENT RESULTS

Information regarding specific assessment instruments used in this assessment can be found in Appendix C.

The examiner found Jordan to be a very cautious participant in the assessment process. Jordan took a long time to respond to open-ended questions, and it was often difficult to determine whether he was formulating a response to a question, not comprehending the question, or lost in his own thoughts. During the first assessment session, Jordan participated in a semistructured clinical interview, and completed the WISC-III and Bender Gestalt.

Jordan obtained a Full Scale IQ within the Average range (86-97) with a minimal 2-point discrepancy between his Verbal and Performance IQ. There were a number of relative weaknesses: Arithmetic (SS 6), Comprehension (SS 7), Digit Span (SS 6), and Coding (SS 6). Freedom from Distractibility was at the 7th percentile. Jordan seemed to be very anxious when the stopwatch was introduced and became visibly upset, saying that he would not be able to do his work on time. Jordan was hesitant and tentatively approached each task in an approach-retreat style. Requests for question repetition were frequent, and Jordan also evidenced word-finding problems throughout. On the mental arithmetic task, Jordan was observed tapping on his leg with his index finger, three times, before he would verbalize a response. When he saw that I had noticed this, he pulled himself farther under the desk to conceal his legs from view. Other mannerisms were noted, such as touching his shoe before lifting his pencil and touching his ear before writing. However, Jordan was very subtle and secretive in performing these touching and counting compulsions. Likely, these rituals had escaped detection in most situations. Jordan also demonstrated perfectionistic tendencies when performing the block design and object assembly tests. He failed to earn any bonus points, wasting much time fitting the parts together so that the edges were perfectly aligned.

Jordan took 25 minutes to complete the Bender Gestalt test. Although the resulting reproductions were very poor, due to his weak visual motor integration skills, the majority of time was spent checking and re-checking the number of dots on the cards, rather than actually executing the designs. Jordan would count the dots and start to draw, then recount to make sure that he had remembered the number correctly. On one design, Jordan re-counted the dots 15 times before he completed the drawing. In addition, execution time was further delayed by a ritualistic tendency to punctuate each drawing by the touching and tapping compulsions noted previously.

Jordan's response to the Woodcock Johnson-III Test of Achievement was also enlightening. It took an entire assessment session (almost 2 hours) to complete this instrument, which usually takes about 40 minutes. Prior to starting tasks, Jordan had a series of questions he asked to make sure that he understood what was required. As far as spelling dictation was concerned, dictated words did not look correctly spelled until they were written, erased, and rewritten a number of times. Each mathematical calculation had a pizza drawn beside it (he called them "pizza faces"), with pepperoni slices indicating the number. For example, in order to perform the calculation 5 + 6, Jordan drew two pizzas: one with five slices of pepperoni and one with six slices of pepperoni. He then added up the pepperoni slices to obtain the final answer. Reading was also performed very hesitantly, with much doubting as to the correct pronunciation. Jordan continually requested feedback about his performance. On tasks that were not timed, Jordan demonstrated functioning about 2 years behind his grade level in all areas. Timed tasks resulted in even more pronounced academic lags, with very poor scores for academic fluency across all areas. Jordan continued to demonstrate the touching and tapping rituals noted during his previous assessment session.

After Jordan's first assessment session, it became evident from clinical observations that Jordan was experiencing many symptoms of obsessive-compulsive disorder and that these ritualistic compulsions were likely causing significant problems at school and at home. Subsequent assessment sessions and behavioral reports would confirm the extent to which Jordan's secret world would be revealed.

Mrs. Neeson completed three behavioral rating scales: the Achenbach CBCL, BASC, and Conners Scales. Clinical elevations were noted on the Thought Problems and Anxious Depressed scales of the Child Behavior Checklist (CBCL); the Atypicality Scale (BASC), and the Perfectionistic Scale (Conners). Teacher reports noted elevations on the Attention and Thought Problems Scales (Achenbach TRF); Atypicality, Adaptability, Learning Problems, Social Problems, and Attention Problems (BASC), and Attention (Conners Scale).

■ Further clinical interviews with Mrs. Neeson confirmed several other OCD behaviors and possible family history for the disorder. Mrs. Neeson said that Jordan could be superstitious, much like her mother who seemed to have a superstitious saying for everything. Her mother was also what she called a "clean freak" and "checking perfectionist." Often they would make several attempts to get out of the driveway because her mother would constantly get out of the car and return to the house to make sure that the stove and coffee maker were turned off, or the door was locked securely. Although Sally did not consider these behaviors to be mental health problems, she did say it was very annoying to try to do anything with her mother. During the course of the conversation, Sally began to discover several likenesses between Jordan and his grandmother.

■ Sally was aware that Jordan did have some superstitions like counting or touching rituals; however, she did not know the extent to which Jordan engaged in these behaviors. Sally became aware of these rituals when she caught him on occasion and questioned his repetitive behaviors. Jordan explained that it was about "threes." Apparently, he had some system worked out that if he repeated an action three times or tapped three times, then it would prevent something from happening. Sometimes, he had to do more than one count of "threes," for example, count to 3 two or three times in a row, before he was satisfied. Further conversation revealed that Jordan also hoarded useless items under his bed and had other peculiar habits involving arranging and placement of certain items in very specific places. At the dinner table, the family had just accepted the fact that Jordan's fork and knife had to be perfectly aligned on the stripe of the place mat before he would begin eating. They were also accustomed to his odd mannerism of eating his food starting at the outside of the plate and working toward the center. Sally had just accepted these behaviors as "Jordanisms" and reasoned to herself that he would eventually outgrow the habits, or they would later develop into other orderly and beneficial ways of organizing his world.

Jordan completed the BASC but had considerable difficulty with the yes/no response format. He had trouble making up his mind and was very uncomfortable not being able to use "sort of" as a response. On the Personality Inventory for Youth (PIY), the Feelings of Alienation scale was somewhat elevated due to Jordan's endorsement of items referring to repetitive and distressing thoughts and behaviors. Jordan did not endorse significant symptoms on the Child Depression Inventory (CDI), which was in the normal range for his age. Jordan did, however, admit to having a significant number of symptoms that were indicative of Worry/Attentional Concerns and Physiological Indicators on the Revised Child Manifest Anxiety Scale (RCMAS).

Based on clinical interviews, observations, and assessment results, increasing confirmation and support were obtained to suggest that Jordan suffered from an obsessive-compulsive disorder. Jordan evidenced a number of compulsions: repeating, checking, touching, counting, arranging, and hoarding. Obsessive thoughts that seemed to drive these compulsions included concerns regarding: doubts, disorder, and danger. Upon completion of the Children's Yale Brown Obsessive-Compulsive Scale (CY-BOCS), the examiner felt that Jordan's compulsions were time-consuming (likely involving more than 1 hour a day) and were interfering significantly with his school work and social relationships. Furthermore, Jordan seemed to have very little control over his compulsions, nor was he able to resist the acts.

POST-CASE QUESTIONS

1. It is possible to explain obsessive-compulsive disorder (OCD) from a number of theoretical positions. Develop a case formulation to explain the development of obsessions and compulsions based on the following theoretical perspectives, in light of Jordan's history: biomedical, behavioral, psychodynamic, cognitive, and family systems. Provide the specific treatment implications for Jordan's OCD based on each of the case formulations derived.

2. Behavioral Interventions for OCD often include exposure techniques designed to elicit the anxiety (either gradually or completely) by either direct exposure (in vivo) or in an imagined state. Graduated levels of anxiety can be predetermined by the construction of an anxiety hierarchy (from least to most stressful situation). Anxiety can be reduced by pairing increasing levels of anxiety-provoking situations with a relaxation response (muscle relaxation exercises). Another intervention for OCD involves exposure followed by response prevention. In this technique, the child would be limited in performing the compulsion (e.g., checking, counting), when he or she has an obsessive thought. The child would agree to limit the response and would be rewarded for following through.

Design a behavioral intervention plan for Jordan's use in the classroom, using exposure and response prevention.

3. Discuss the relationship between separation anxiety and obsessive-compulsive disorder in Jordan's developmental history.

ISSUES IN TREATMENT

Despite prevalence rates of about 1% (Valleni-Basile et al., 1994), obsessive-compulsive disorder (OCD) in young children and adolescents is often undiagnosed. Because the disorder involves distressing and often unpleasant thoughts (obsessions) that drive unwanted acts or behaviors (compulsions) that can often appear embarrassing to children, OCD may be hidden by young children and adolescents, who suffer in silence. According to Leonard, Swedo, and Rappaport (1991), some indicators that OCD behaviors may be occurring in children and adolescence include: hoarding of useless objects, repeated touching of objects, taking an inordinate amount of time to complete tasks, and constant erasures or reworking of homework assignments. The long-term consequences of OCD have long been established, and the disorder is also often associated with other comorbid disorders (Bolton, Luckie, & Steinberg, 1995). Research evidence supports the importance of early intervention in childhood and adolescence in reducing the long-term severity of OCD (Leonard et al., 1993).

Some of the most frequently occurring compulsions in child and adolescent populations include: hand-washing, checking, counting, touching, rearranging, and hoarding. The following obsessions have also been identified as occurring most frequently in child and adolescent populations: doubts, danger, contamination, aggression, and sexual impulses (King, Leonard, & March, 1998; Leonard et al., 1991).

OCD is classified as an anxiety disorder by the *DSM-IV*. Though OCD was once thought to have a primarily psychological basis, many who suffer from it show evidence of a biological basis for the disorder. Two areas of research have investigated biological explanations for the disorder: one explanation involves relating OCD behaviors to low levels of the neurotransmitter serotonin; the other explanation looks to malfunctioning in a key area of the brain. Support for the serotonin theory has come from clinical trials that have established SSRIs such as fluoxetine (which serve to increase serotonin levels) as a successful treatment approach for OCD in adults and children/adolescents (Riddle et al., 1992). Other biological theorists suggest that regions of the brain that convert sensory information into thoughts and actions (orbital region of the frontal cortex and caudate nuclei) may be overactive in people with OCD. Because the system malfunctions, impulses that should be filtered pass on to the thalamus and the person becomes driven to perform the acts (Peterson et al., 1998).

Implications of the basal ganglia in OCD have also been suggested due to the high rates of comorbidity between OCD and Tourette's syndrome (King et al., 1998). Recently, research has amassed increasing support for some children who develop acute OCD symptoms resulting after a strep infection. These children, who demonstrate OCD symptoms from an autoimmune response to streptococcal infection (PANDAS), may require a very different method of treatment. Murphy and Pichichero (2002) monitored 12 cases of OCD with new-onset PANDAS and found that antibiotic treatment was effective in alleviating symptoms of OCD in all the children on first trial, and re-administration successfully resulted in symptom remission for the 7 children who suffered a future relapse. The PANDAS-related OCD symptoms included hand-washing behaviors and preoccupation with germs, and are thought to result from an inflammation of specific regions of the brain.

The two treatments of choice for adult populations with OCD, medical management and behavioral therapy, have also demonstrated success with children and adolescents. Medical treatment with SSRIs such as fluoxetine (Geller et al., 2001; Riddle et al., 1992) have assisted some children in reducing OCD symptoms, and behavioral therapy, using techniques of exposure and response prevention (ERP) have also demonstrated success (March, Mulle, & Herbel, 1994). Recently, Thieneman, Martin, Cregger, Thompson, and Dyer-Friedman (2001) reported significant reduction of OCD symptoms measured by the Children's Yale-Brown Obsessive Compulsive Scale for adolescents involved in a group Cognitive Behavioral Therapy (CBT) Program. March and Mulle (1998) have recently published a manual for the treatment of OCD in children and adolescents based on their empirical research. The manual provides a guide to assessment and treatment planning around four stages of treatment: education/awareness, cognitive training, mapping OCD, and graded exposure and response prevention (13-20 structured sessions).

In another recent research program designed to compare the effects of combined treatments, Neziroglu, Yaryra-Tobias, Walz, and McKay (2000) found that children who received a combination of fluvoxamine and exposure and response prevention demonstrated more immediate improvement and continued improvement 2 years later, than either condition in isolation. However, Sabine (2001) argues that CBT may be at least as effective and a less stressful alternative than ERP for children and adolescents with OCD. Techniques commonly used in CBT programs include: cognitive restructuring, psychoeducation (to dispel irrational fears of contamination, etc.), distraction, and relaxation. The importance of family involvement in the treatment program has also been investigated recently. Waters, Barrett, and March (2001) found that including the family in cognitive-behavioral treatment can also be an effective treatment component for children with OCD; they recommend further research to compare treatment with and without family involvement.

REFERENCES

Bolton, D., Luckie, M., & Steinberg, D. (1995). Long-term course of obsessive-compulsive disorder treated in adolescence. *Journal of the American Academy of Child and Adolescent Psychiatry, 34,* 1441-1450.

Geller, D. A., Hogg, S., Heiligenstein, J., Ricardi, R., Tamura, R., Kluszynski, S., & Jacobson, J. G. (2001). Fluoxetine treatment of obsessive-compulsive disorder in children and adolescents: A placebo-controlled clinical trial. *Journal of the American Academy of Child and Adolescent Psychiatry, 40,* 773-779.

King, R. A., Leonard, H., & March, J. (1998). Practice parameters for the assessment and treatment of children and adolescents with obsessive-compulsive disorder. *Journal of the American Academy of Child and Adolescent Psychiatry, 37,* 27-45.

Leonard, H. L., Swedo, S. E., & Rappaport, J. L. (1991). Diagnosis and treatment of obsessive compulsive disorder in children and adolescents. In M. T. Pato & J. Zohar

(Eds.), *Current treatments of obsessive compulsive disorder* (pp. 87-102). Washington, DC: APA Press.

Leonard, H. L., Swedo, S. E., Lenane, M. C., Rettew, D. C., Hamburger, S. D., & Bartko, J. J. (1993). A 2- to 7-year follow-up study of 54 obsessive-compulsive children and adolescents. *Archives of General Psychiatry, 50,* 429-439.

March, J. S., & Mulle, K. (1998). *OCD in children and adolescents: A cognitive behavioral treatment manual.* New York: Guilford.

March, J. S., Mulle, K., & Herbel, B. (1994). Behavioral psychotherapy for children and adolescents with obsessive-compulsive disorder: An open trial of a new protocol-driven treatment package. *Journal of the American Academy of Child and Adolescent Psychiatry, 33,* 333-341.

Murphy, M. L, & Pichichero, M.E. (2002). Prospective identification and treatment of children with pediatric autoimmune neuropsychiatric disorder associated with Group A streptococcal infection (PANDAS). *Archives of Pediatric and Adolescent Medicine, 156,* 356-361.

Neziroglu, F., Yaryra-Tobias, J., Walz, J., & McKay, D. (2000). The effect of fluvoxamine and behavior therapy on children and adolescents with obsessive-compulsive disorder. *Journal of the American Academy of Child and Adolescent Psychiatry, 10,* 295-306.

Peterson, B. S., Leckman, J. F., Arnsten, A., Anderson, G. M., Staib, L. H., Gore, J. C., Bronen, R. A., Malison, R., Scahill, L., & Cohen, D. J., (1998). Neuroanatomical circuitry. In J. F. Leckman, D. J. Cohen, et al. (Eds.), *Tourette's syndrome—Tics, obsessions, compulsions: Developmental psychopathology and clinical care.* New York: John Wiley.

Riddle, M. A., Scahill, L., King, R. A., Hardin, M. T., Anderson, G. M., & Ort, S. I. (1992). Double-blind, crossover trial of fluoxetine and placebo in children and adolescents with obsessive-compulsive disorder. *Journal of the American Academy of Child and Adolescent Psychiatry, 31,* 1062-1069.

Sabine, W. (2001). Obsessive compulsive disorder. In W. Lyddon & J. V. Jones, Jr. (Eds.), *Empirically supported cognitive therapies: Current and future applications* (pp. 118-133). New York: Springer.

Thieneman, M., Martin, J., Cregger, B., Thompson, H., & Dyer-Friedman, J. (2001). Manual-driven group cognitive-behavioral therapy for adolescents with obsessive-compulsive disorder: A pilot study. *Journal of the American Academy of Child and Adolescent Psychiatry, 11,* 1254-1260.

Valleni-Basile, L. A., Garrison, C. Z., Jackson, K. L., Waller, J. L., McKeown, R. E., & Addy, C. L. (1994). Frequency of obsessive-compulsive disorder in a community sample of young adolescents. *Journal of the American Academy of Child and Adolescent Psychiatry, 33,* 782-791.

Waters, T., Barrett, P. M., & March, J. S. (2001). Cognitive-behavioral family treatment of childhood obsessive-compulsive disorder: Preliminary findings. *American Journal of Psychotherapy, 55,* 372-387.

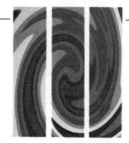

Case 7: Sandy Smith

Marching to the Tune of a Different Drummer

When Eileen opened the clinic door, it was as if she were facing her worst fears head on.

Sandy's pleas and verbal exchanges could be heard by the office staff all the way from the elevator at the other end of the building. Although Sandy was physically small for her 8 years, her stiff posture almost anchored her mother's arm to the ground. Eileen was embarrassed by Sandy's behavior, but Sandy's reaction only served to confirm her resolve to finally seek professional help. As Eileen approached the receptionist's desk, Sandy bumped into the desk and slid onto the couch awkwardly beside her mother, with her legs entwined around each other like a pretzel. In the waiting room, Eileen tried to collect her thoughts about her daughter's development in anticipation of the many interview questions that might be asked.

DEVELOPMENTAL HISTORY/FAMILY BACKGROUND

Eileen had hoped for a daughter her entire pregnancy, even though Tom's family lineage had produced predominantly males. Against the odds, Eileen's hopes were answered and miraculously Sandy was born 8 years ago. The pregnancy and delivery were uneventful. Sandy was a beautiful baby, and Tom was proud to be the father of a baby girl. Sandy was also adored by her two older brothers, Jason, 6 years, and Sean, 4 years of age. Everything seemed to be going well. There were some minor stresses initially when Eileen had to give up attempts to nurse Sandy. Eileen had no problem nursing her other two infants, but due to Sandy's erratic sleep habits and irritability, her doctor recommended switching to the bottle. This switch proved difficult; Sandy's poor coordination meant that propping the bottle wouldn't work, since she often lost the bottle if her mother was not holding it. Sandy was a very active baby and she seemed to require little sleep. Eileen reasoned that perhaps the fact that the baby needed less sleep was a sign of curiosity and intelligence. Eileen placed a brightly colored mobile over the bed and added the crib activity center that her infant sons had enjoyed so much. However, Sandy had no interest in the mobile or in exploring the activity center. Sandy actually became very agitated with the crib additions, and Eileen responded by removing everything from the crib, which seemed to calm Sandy down. Through trial and error, Eileen eventually found that the sound of a wind-up merry-go-round on the dresser could be helpful in soothing Sandy. To this day, Sandy listens to music to help calm her down when she is anxious.

Despite her difficulties adjusting to any changes in her environment or schedule, Sandy did demonstrate one extremely advanced area of development. She was a very early talker and had amassed an amazing vocabulary by the time she was 2. At 2½ years of age, Sandy was sounding more like a miniature adult than a child and would repeat her grandmother's phrases "verbatim." Sandy would surprise on-lookers in the grocery store with her pseudo-adult comments on the quality of the fruits and vegetables. By 3 years of age, Sandy could repeat stories from taped texts, verbatim, and Sandy often recited these stories riding in the car, during dinner, or when playing by herself.

Sandy's strong verbal skills were in sharp contrast to her slower developing motor skills. Sandy was a highly verbal but very awkward toddler. Initially, Eileen worried about her muscle coordination, since Sandy was slow to sit and would fall over if not securely propped with a pillow. When Sandy began to walk, she looked like she was drunk, swaying to the left and with an off-balance gait. Sandy's legs were black and blue from falling down and bumping into things. At first, Eileen thought that Sandy was so preoccupied with talking that she wasn't looking where she was going. She eventually had Sandy's vision checked, but results came back negative. Sandy's poor coordination also seemed to influence her choices of play activities. Unlike the boys, Sandy had little interest in Lego, blocks, or puzzles. Sandy was definitely much more interested in chatting than doing. Eileen tried to enroll Sandy in a preschool gymnastics program to improve her coordination. But this backfired, since Sandy was unable to reproduce many of the tumbling movements, couldn't touch her toes to her head, and repeatedly fell off the balance beam. The other children were soon making fun of Sandy, imitating her awkward movements, and

Eileen removed her from the program. Eileen was becoming concerned about Sandy's fears of going anywhere new and her increasingly clingy behavior. Sandy was soon going to be kindergarten age, and Eileen worried about the transition. She enrolled Sandy in a morning preschool program 2 days a week. Each day was torture, getting Sandy into the car and over to the day-care center. Sandy did not want to go and would scream, hide, and run away (often running into something) in a frenzied panic. Eileen was determined to persist, however, knowing that it would only be worse to give in.

Sandy's preschool experience was not very successful. As long as she could sit and read by herself or play on the flannel form board, spelling words with preformed letters, Sandy was quite content. However, other children did not seem to want to play with Sandy and during free playtime, Sandy was often left alone. On the few times that she did try to enter a group activity, her awkward sense of timing and poor social skills usually resulted in a negative experience, and Sandy would withdraw once again. She did not seem to profit from experiences, either. The following day, Sandy would approach the same child in the same way, setting herself up for another rejection and subsequent retreat. In kindergarten, Sandy continued to struggle socially.

Social skills were very immature and Sandy did not seem to take nonverbal communication (facial expressions, conversational tone) into consideration at any time. Her sense of social-personal space was also poor, and Sandy would often stand too close and encroach on other children's sense of comfort. Eventually, Sandy preferred to shadow the teacher instead of interacting with the other children. She gained her rewards when she could read aloud to the class and write words on the board in big letters. However, a lot of kindergarten activities were very difficult for Sandy: cutting and pasting, tracing, drawing, painting, and the big shoe with the lace to be tied and untied. Sandy often cried at home, asking if she could stay home from school.

Sandy continued to experience problems with coordination. At 8 years of age, Sandy had yet to learn how to ride a two-wheeler. She never made the transition from training wheels and even with the training wheels on, Sandy continued to lose her balance and fall over. Had it not been for the bicycle helmet, Eileen was sure that Sandy might have also had a head injury to deal with. Luckily, to Eileen's knowledge, Sandy never bumped her head in the falls, although she did sustain many bruises on her arms and legs. Recently, Sandy's teacher had complained that Sandy was trying to get out of gym classes by making excuses. Sandy had begged her mother to write a note to the teacher to get her out of gym class, but Eileen refused. Sandy's lack of coordination and clumsiness also seemed to permeate her total appearance. Despite her mother's extensive efforts at home to coordinate and organize Sandy's outfits for the next day, Sandy always looked somewhat disheveled and thrown together: buttons would not match the right button holes; shoe laces were dangling from her feet. Eileen eventually refurbished Sandy's wardrobe, removing button-up shirts and replacing lace-up shoes with Velcro-strap shoes. Sandy's lack of organization and messiness was pervasive. If Sandy wanted to remove an object from her dresser drawer, half the drawer often spilled over onto the floor. It was the same with her desk at school, which was jammed with papers crumpled and rolled into little balls.

Although Sandy's messiness and disorganization were annoying, they were not the reasons that brought Eileen to the clinic. Eileen was frustrated and confused. Sandy was a real puzzle and Eileen was now very motivated to find out what could possibly explain how her daughter's abilities could be so extreme: seemingly so very bright in some areas, yet totally lost in others. Sandy had an excellent vocabulary and wonderful memory for words. As a result, she could read beautifully and spell most words she had seen, without error. However, despite Sandy's excellent vocabulary, spelling and reading skills, she was having increasing problems with reading comprehension. Sandy could recall a passage verbatim, but she seemed to have real problems answering any questions that required an inference going beyond information presented in the passage. Eileen recalled last night's homework assignment involving a reading passage that described a family eating breakfast together. Sandy had to answer a number of comprehension questions about the story. Sandy had no idea how to answer one question, which asked: "What time of day is it?" Even with Eileen's help and questions directed at passage clues, Sandy was unable to answer the question, saying: "I read it over and over. It doesn't tell you the time of day!" Eileen wondered if Sally's problems telling time could somehow be related to her difficulties with comprehension. Sandy was still unable to tell time on an analogue clock. Even if she could tell you the time on a digital clock, she seemed oblivious to how time related to activities. Eileen recalled an incident where Sandy wanted to have some ice cream for breakfast. When Eileen told Sandy, "You don't have ice cream for breakfast," Sandy's response was: "Fine. Then I'll have dinner, now!" Initially, she thought Sandy was joking, but she was completely serious. There were other situations as well, where Sandy's odd thinking caught Eileen completely off guard. Sandy seemed to take things very literally, all the time. Sandy could be very gullible, and Eileen had to monitor her brothers carefully so they would stop playing tricks on Sandy. Eileen remembered one time that Sean told Sandy if she ate her ice cream cone from the bottom of the cone, she would get more ice cream. Eileen came in to find Sandy trying to eat the ice cream cone upside down with it melting all over the place. Eileen recalled another incident when they were watching a TV movie about an odd character and Tom mentioned that, "He certainly marches to the tune of a different drummer." Sandy looked up and said: "Where's the parade?" Tom tried to explain the expression, but Sandy just didn't get it and continued to ask about the drummer in the parade. She was very upset that she missed the parade. She eventually went to bed that evening, upset, talking about the parade and how drummers march. At school, Sandy's literal interpretations often were not appreciated by her teacher, who thought that Sandy was just being smart.

Mathematics was another area of real difficulty for Sandy. It was as if mathematics involved a foreign language. Homework was an endless struggle involving hours and hours of explanations and discussions. Sandy didn't seem to be able to perform the same task twice in a row without having it all explained over and over again. The next day, it was as if she had never heard the explanation. Academic problems were compounded by Sandy's poor handwriting. Numbers as well as letters were often scrawled across the page without attention to writing between the lines, spacing, or direction. Often, her writing was impossible to decipher. As a result of her problems with math, comprehension, and writing, Sandy was falling farther and farther behind. At a recent school conference, Eileen was informed that the school was recommending that Sandy repeat the third grade.

Socially, Sandy seemed to have few friends at school. At the parent-teacher conference, Eileen asked Sandy's teacher what was keeping Sandy from forming more friendships with the other children. According to Sandy's teacher, it was Sandy's poor sense of timing that often turned the other kids off. Sandy often made comments at inappropriate times or out of context, and the other girls seemed to respond by ignoring and excluding her. Sandy also talked nonstop and didn't give the other girls a chance to get a word in. Eileen was very disappointed last week by the poor showing of classmates at Sandy's birthday party. After Sandy struggled for hours making invitations to her birthday party (cutting, coloring, and pasting were never Sandy's strengths), only one child showed up. Ann, a 5-year-old who lives next door, was the only one who attended the party. Although initially upset, Sandy soon became absorbed in playing a new audiotape she received as a gift and totally ignored Ann for the rest of the party. When Ann finally left, Sandy seemed to have no idea as to where she went or why she might have left.

REASON FOR REFERRAL

Eileen had talked to Sandy's pediatrician, hoping to gain insight into Sandy's "odd" ways of thinking and marginal school progress. Eileen had always thought that Sandy would outgrow her awkward ways, but she was now beginning to fear that her daughter's difficulties were more permanent. Her concerns were also escalating because of the lack of social contacts in her daughter's life and how this might impact negatively on her social development later on. Finally, Eileen decided that "knowing" was better than "not knowing," and she brought Sandy to the clinic in the hopes that she could find some answers to her questions.

ASSESSMENT RESULTS

Information regarding specific assessment instruments can be found in Appendix C.

The psychologist administered the Weschler Intelligence Scale for Children (WISC-III) and noted the following test behaviors. Sandy was very verbal throughout the assessment and comments often resulted in digressions away from the target task. Sandy often had to be redirected to the task at hand. When verbal responses were required, such as on the Vocabulary and the Comprehension tests, Sandy tended to overelaborate, giving verbose responses far in excess of what was required. When nonverbal tasks were presented, Sandy used self-talk to work her way through the task. Sandy frequently requested feedback regarding her performance and seemed to become somewhat agitated when informed by the examiner that he was unable to tell her how she was doing. Sandy seemed to be somewhat comforted, however, when the examiner expressed comments of encouragement and praised her effort in general. Visual tasks were very difficult for Sandy. She was able to reproduce the initial block designs by placing the blocks on top of the designs in the model booklet. However, as the designs increased in complexity and external cues were reduced, Sandy became visibly upset. She wanted to know where the lines went in the sixth design: "There are supposed to be lines to tell you where the blocks go!" Similarly, Sandy also encountered significant problems with the Object Assembly subtest and became very frustrated with the more difficult puzzles, spending considerable time trying randomly to locate matching lines.

Responses to the WISC-III revealed a significant, 26-point split between Verbal IQ 117 (Range 110-122) and Performance IQ 91 (Range 84-100). Less than 1% of the population would have had a discrepancy of this extent between these two components. The Full Scale IQ was not calculated, since it would be rendered meaningless due to the extreme discrepancy noted between the Verbal and Performance Scales. The discrepancy between the Verbal Comprehension Index (Index = 122) and Perceptual Organization Index (Index = 91) was even more pronounced. The Verbal IQ, which was at the 87th percentile, revealed a significant strength in Vocabulary (SS = 16) with a relatively strong score in Information (SS = 14). A relative weakness was noted in Arithmetic (SS = 9). Performance IQ was at the 27th percentile and noted very weak performance on Block Design (SS = 7) and Object Assembly (SS = 7).

Academically, Sandy's scores on the Wide Range Achievement Test (WRAT-3) revealed Reading and Spelling to be above grade level (Standard Scores of 115 and 110), but Arithmetic was at only a Grade 2 level (Standard Score 74). Since Sandy's mother mentioned problems with comprehension, additional academic assessment was conducted and the Woodcock Johnson III Test of Achievement was administered. On this test, although Sandy's Reading Fluency (Grade 4.2) and Letter-Word Identification (Grade 4.5) were above her current Grade 3 placement, Passage Comprehension was at an early Grade 2 level. Broad Math was at a 2.1 level with difficulties noted in computation, word problems, and math reasoning. Sandy demonstrated some letter and number reversals, especially on the fluency tests, which were timed tests. Handwriting was very poor.

Sandy's response to the Bender Gestalt test revealed a visual motor perception score to be equivalent to a child of 5 years, 5 months, two standard deviations below her expected age level. Sandy's drawings were extremely immature, despite taking excessive time to complete the task (in excess of 15 minutes). Although Sandy counted and recounted dots, and often traced designs with her finger before execution, the resulting reproductions were poor due to problems with rotations, design integration, substitution of circles for dots, and tendencies to run designs into each other. When asked to "draw a person," Sandy seemed to take forever to produce the finished product, and after many erasures, the resulting image was very immature. Somewhat embarrassed by the lack of results, and partially as an evasive tactic, Sandy eventually produced a stick figure. She compensated for her poor motor skills, however, by creating an elaborate story about what the stick figure was doing and how he came from the "land of stick people."

Parent responses to the Achenbach, Child Behavior Checklist (CBCL) revealed significant elevations on Withdrawn, Social Problems, Thought Problems, and Attention Problems, while Conners Scale responses (CPRS-R:L) noted elevations for Cognitive Problems/Inattention, Anxious/Shy and *DSM-IV* Inattentive. Teacher responses to the Achenbach, Teacher Report Form (TRF) revealed significant concerns in Social Problems, Thought Problems, and Attention, while responses to the Conners Scale (CTRS-R:L) revealed significant elevations on scales measuring Opposition, Cognitive Problems/Inattention, and Social Problems.

Sandy's responses to the Revised Child Manifest Anxiety Scales (RCMAS) revealed significant elevations in areas of Worry/Oversensitivity, and Attention/Social Concerns. There were no significant elevations on the Child Depression Index (CDI).

POST-CASE QUESTIONS

1. Children who demonstrate a nonverbal learning disability (NLD) may pose a particular problem for diagnosis and intervention since their symptoms do not conform to the traditional concept of a language-based learning disability. Discuss some of the difficulties of diagnosis of NLD with respect to how learning disabilities are defined by (a) the *DSM,* (b) Education, and (c) National Joint Committee on Learning Disabilities (NJCLD) (see Appendix B).

2. Discuss how a nonverbal learning disability might be differentiated from Asperger's syndrome or Asperger's disorder.

3. Discuss case formulations from the following theoretical frameworks: biomedical, psychodynamic, behavioral, cognitive, family systems, and attachment/parenting style.

4. Social skills are often an area of weakness for children with NLD. Using a social information processing model, develop a case formulation for Sandy's social skills deficits and explain how you would target specific areas for treatment.

ISSUES IN TREATMENT

Descriptions of the syndrome called nonverbal learning disability (NLD), nonverbal learning disorder, or developmental right-hemisphere syndrome (DRHS) can be found in Harnadek and Rourke (1994), Rourke (1989), Strang and Casey (1994), and Gross-Tsur, Shalev, Manor, and Amir (1995). The core symptom presentation includes: social problems due to interpersonal skill deficits, motor slowness, weak visual-perceptual organization, difficulties with nonverbal problem solving, and especially weak arithmetic ability. Soft neurological signs can also be evident on the left side of the body (Gross-Tsur et al., 1995). Often symptoms of ADHD are comorbid with the disorder. Results of a recent investigation by Garcia-Sanchez, Estevez-Gonzalez, Suarez-Romero, and Junque, (1997) suggest that visuo-spatial deficits associated with right-hemisphere dysfunction are more pronounced in those youth who had attention-deficit disorder without hyperactivity, compared to youth with ADHD hyperactive-impulsive type.

In a recent investigation of the clinical characteristics associated with NLD or DRHS, Gross-Tsur et al. (1995) found the following characteristics that were shared by children in their sample: 65% demonstrated left-sided soft-neurological signs; the mean Verbal IQ was approximately 20 scale score points higher than the mean Performance IQ of 85; the lowest Verbal scale score was Arithmetic, followed by Comprehension; the lowest Performance Scale Score was for Coding; 94% had at least one specific learning disability, and 67% had discalcula. In this particular sample, 90% demonstrated graphomotor impairment evidenced by weak performance on Coding and the Bender Visual Motor Gestalt Test, and 80% were referred for slow cognitive and motor performance. Descriptions of slow cognitive and motor output were noted in an inability to complete schoolwork, sluggish response to activity, and slow to initiate and complete routine tasks. All children demonstrated poor social skills, often evident in inadequate or inappropriate facial expression, eye contact, weak pragmatic language, and poor comprehension of social rules. Children with NLD display considerable difficulties in nonverbal problem solving. According to Harnadek and Rourke (1994), deficits in concept formation and hypothesis testing result in poor ability to profit from environmental reinforcers that normally shape our behavior. These children do not readily establish a cause-and-effect relationship, which brings structure and contextual meaning to our experiences. These children fare poorly in complex or novel situations and can appear scripted and inappropriate in their responses.

A recent literature review revealed that all of the 26 studies reported in the past 12 years concerning nonverbal learning disabilities were concerned with issues of identification of nonverbal learning disability or differential diagnosis relative to other disorders (e.g., semantic pragmatic disorder, Asperger's disorder, etc.). Therefore, empirically supported interventions for NLD continue to remain a high-need area for research. Despite the lack of empirically supported programs for NLD, a number of recommendations have been suggested as clinically effective in remediating neuropsychological deficits (visual-perceptual organization; psychomotor and concept-formation skills) responsible for problems in areas of: social skills, mathematical abilities, and responses to novel problem-solving situations (Rourke, 1993). Treatment suggestions involve direct instruction and guided practice. The following list summarizes some of the suggested directions for treatment (Rourke, 1995):

- teach the child, in a predictable, step-by-step, rote manner
- encourage the application of problem-solving strategies and their transfer to new situations

- teach a problem-solving format, or template, that the child can use to structure the situation (e.g., STOP: Stop and see what is happening; Think about what I am going to do now; Observe how others are responding to me; Practice and improve).
- use direct instruction to teach appropriate verbal social responses and how to read verbal cues
- provide many opportunities for practicing these new skills and applying them to new situations until the responses become more fluid and automatic
- teach the child to link visual information (facial expression, body posture) with auditory information—not only what is said, but how (tone, inflection) it is said
- teach visual-organizational skills
- teach comprehension directly

Despite increasing awareness of NLD, Thompson (1997) suggests that many school districts have not recognized NLD because the syndrome does not conform to the more traditional concept of a language-based learning disability. In these cases, students may not receive appropriate CAMS (compensations, accommodations, modifications, and strategies). The dangers and risks of not detecting or providing early intervention can be found in retrospective studies of adults with NLD. These retrospective studies (Rourke, Young, & Leenaars, 1989; Rourke, Young, Strang, & Russell, 1986) suggest that undetected children with NLD demonstrate a greater degree of developing internalizing disorders, such as depression; are at greater risk for suicidal behaviors; and report a greater incidence of loneliness and social isolation as adults.

REFERENCES

Garcia-Sanchez, C., Estevez-Gonzalez, A., Suarez-Romero, E., & Junque, C. (1997). Right hemisphere dysfunction in subjects with attention-deficit disorder with and without hyperactivity. *Journal of Child Neurology, 12,* 107-115.

Gross-Tsur, V., Shalev, R. S., Manor, O., & Amir, N. (1995). Developmental right hemisphere syndrome: Clinical spectrum of the nonverbal learning disability. *Journal of Learning Disabilities, 28,* 80-86.

Harnadek, M. C. S., & Rourke, B. P. (1994). Principal identifying features of the syndrome of nonverbal learning disabilities in children. *Journal of Learning Disabilities, 27,* 144-153.

Rourke, B. P. (1989). *Nonverbal learning disabilities: The syndrome and the model.* New York: Guilford.

Rourke, B. P. (1993). Arithmetic disabilities, specified and otherwise: A neuropychological perspective. *Journal of Learning Disabilities, 26,* 214-226.

Rourke, B. P. (1995). Treatment program for the child with NLD. In B. P. Rourke (Ed.), *Syndrome of nonverbal learning disabilities: Neurodevelopmental manifestations.* New York: Guilford.

Rourke, B. P., Young, G. C., & Leenaars, A. A. (1989). A childhood learning disability that predisposes those afflicted to adolescent and adult depression and suicide risk. *Journal of Learning Disabilities, 22,* 169-175.

Rourke, B. P., Young, G. P., Strang, J. D., & Russell, D. L. (1986). Adult outcomes of childhood central processing deficiencies. In I. Grant & K. M. Adams (Eds.), *Neuropsychological assessment of neuropsychiatric disorders* (pp. 244-267). New York: Oxford University Press.

Strang, J. D., & Casey, J. E. (1994). The psychological impact of learning disabilities: A developmental neurological perspective. In L. F. Koziol & E. E. Scott (Eds.), *The neuropsychology of mental disorders: A practical guide* (pp 171-186). Springfield, IL: Charles C Thomas.

Thompson, S. (1997). Nonverbal learning disorders revisited in 1997. Retrieved September 17, 2002, from http://www.nldline.com/nld.htm

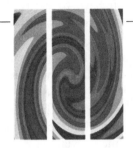

Case 8: Dylan Bach

The World According to Dylan

Dylan's behavior was discussed at a school intervention meeting shortly after Dylan enrolled in the kindergarten program at Cyprus Springs Elementary School. His teacher was concerned because Dylan displayed very "odd" behaviors and despite being very verbal seemed to be in "his own world." Dylan's speech was indistinct, and although he seemed to chatter a lot, it was very difficult to comprehend what he was saying. Often he would talk to himself, in a singsong refrain, reciting entire monologues. Dylan was a spontaneous reader, and he would take great pleasure in reading everything from book titles to footnotes. He could also spell his name. However, Dylan preferred solitary activities and it was very difficult to engage Dylan in the normal classroom routines and group activities. Dylan could be very resistant. Not only did the teacher have problems engaging Dylan in regular classroom activities, it was equally as difficult trying to disengage Dylan from an activity that he was involved in. When asked to participate in activities not to his liking, Dylan had thrown a number of temper tantrums. On these occasions, he would scream a very loud and persistent "No!!!!"

Dylan was awkward, poorly coordinated, and often seemed to walk into things. Dylan seemed to be in constant motion and was very fidgety. During quiet times, like story or circle time, Dylan's constant motion (rocking, squirming, fidgeting) was often disturbing to the other children. This, coupled with Dylan's poor coordination, would often result in his falling into other children or tripping over things in the classroom.

DEVELOPMENTAL HISTORY/FAMILY BACKGROUND

The school social worker met with Dylan's mother, Celeste Bach, to discuss the school's concerns and to obtain a social history. Celeste and her husband Arnold were both 23 years of age when Dylan was born. They had been married for 2 years. The Bachs owned an art studio and made their living through the sale of their own creative art pieces. Celeste was an oil painter and Arnold was a sculptor. They supplemented their income from the sale of their artwork by giving art lessons and selling art supplies. Celeste described a difficult and unpleasant pregnancy. She was nauseated through most of the pregnancy and also developed toxemia midway through the pregnancy. Dylan was born 2 weeks ahead of schedule after a very long labor (40 hours) and weighed almost 9 pounds (8 lbs., 10 oz.). The delivery was uneventful.

Celeste described Dylan as cheerful, affectionate and sociable during his first year. He had a good appetite but was difficult to put on a schedule. He experienced many colicky bouts, and sleep was often disrupted. When he woke, it was difficult to get him back to sleep. Milestones were achieved within the norm, and Dylan was walking and saying his first words by one year of age. Mrs. Bach admitted to difficulties with toilet training, and at almost 5 years of age, Dylan continued to exhibit occasional bed-wetting incidents. Accidental soiling stopped about a year ago. Health was described as good, with the exception of vulnerability to ear infections and food allergies (dairy products). Dylan is rarely ill; however, when he gets sick he tends to develop a fever and requires monitoring.

Family history notes a paternal uncle with cerebral palsy and mental retardation. There is a history of bipolar disorder with obsessive-compulsive disorder in the family (maternal grandmother), as well as anxiety (paternal aunt). Celeste stated that Dylan's pediatrician felt that Dylan might be autistic, however, no further assessment was conducted. She added that Dylan can be stubborn at home, but that he will comply when necessary. Dylan gets along well with their adult neighbors, who have all been very impressed with Dylan's reading and writing abilities. Celeste added that they currently live in an area that has no children Dylan's age and that he has had very little practice socializing with peers.

Toward the end of the kindergarten program (Dylan was 5 years, 6 months of age) a brief assessment was conducted by the school psychologist to obtain information regarding Dylan's cognitive functioning. The Differential Ability Scales (DAS) were administered and revealed a Verbal Cluster Standard Score of 56, and a Nonverbal Cluster Score of 86. The psychologist noted that rapport was very difficult to establish and cautioned interpretation of the assessment results due to Dylan's immaturity, lack of compliance, low frustration tolerance, and insistence on doing things his own way.

The school convened a staffing meeting to determine eligibility for special education programming and decided upon the following course of action. Due to difficulties with standard assessment, at this time Dylan was given a temporary designation as Developmentally Delayed. The temporary designation would not lapse until Dylan's 6th birthday, allowing an additional 6 months to conduct a more valid and in-depth evaluation of his ability levels. Dylan would be provided with interim services from Occupational Therapy, Speech and Language, and the Special Programs teacher while awaiting his reevaluation.

Dylan's parents moved over the summer holidays, and Dylan began attending Lawton Elementary School for the next academic year. In order to accommodate Dylan's special needs, a decision was made to have Dylan attend the kindergarten program for a half day and receive specialized services in a class for children with varying exceptionalities (VE Program) for the remainder of the day. Speech was provided on a daily basis by the school speech pathologist, and occupational therapy was received once weekly. The move to a new school was difficult for Dylan and initially he did not want to get on the bus. However, his resistance mellowed and after about 3 weeks Dylan began to settle into his new routines. Recently, he has been experiencing difficulties, and resistance to riding on the school bus has resurfaced. Just prior to his formal reassessment, Dylan was observed throwing himself to the ground and refusing to get on the school bus. Investigation is under way to determine the nature of Dylan's refusals.

REASON FOR REFERRAL

A referral for re-evaluation was initiated by Dylan's school to remove his temporary placement designation, as developmentally delayed. A full assessment was requested to update intellectual estimates of Dylan's abilities and to determine how to best meet Dylan's academic, social, and emotional needs within the school system.

ASSESSMENT

Dylan's assessment was conducted on several levels, including obtaining several observations of Dylan within the different classroom environments and attempts to engage Dylan in more formal psychometric tasks.

Classroom Observations

The school psychologist began a series of observations of Dylan in the two classroom settings. Observation of Dylan in kindergarten revealed a number of interesting behaviors. On one occasion, Dylan was observed while his teacher read a story to the class. The children were sitting on the floor, gathered around the teacher's chair. Although Dylan seemed attentive initially, he soon began a series of excessive movements (fidgeting, rocking, sprawling on the floor, hanging upside down) that were distracting to the other children. He spontaneously got up and walked to the back of the classroom in search of paper and crayons. For the next 15 minutes, the teacher would redirect Dylan back to the circle and Dylan would comply momentarily, then get up and return to the back of the classroom. At one point he was very insistent on leaving the circle saying: "I want to do my work!" The teacher responded by saying: "You *will* sit and listen to the story!" Dylan's responded by saying: "I *won't* sit and listen to the story!" At this point, the teacher reminded him of good and bad choices and the consequence of losing a star for bad choices. If he did not do as he was told, he would lose a "star." (The star chart was a classroom behavior merit program. Children earned stars for good behavior and lost stars for poor behavior. Stars could be traded in for activities and small prizes at the end of the day.) Dylan immediately complied and remained on the floor. However, his constant motion eventually resulted in his kicking another child (by accident), resulting in the child breaking into tears. Dylan seemed oblivious to his role in the event and clearly did not understand the teacher's request to apologize to the other child for the infraction. Within the kindergarten program, the teacher's goals and expectations for Dylan were the same as for all children in her classroom. Dylan struggled with the lack of flexibility and did not understand the need to be involved in activities that held little interest for him.

For Dylan, the Varying Exceptionalities (VE) Program had several advantages: fewer children, older children (7-9 years of age), and a teacher trained in special education. In this environment, Dylan seemed to enjoy the freedom of being allowed to work on a task at his own pace. Dylan worked very quickly and seemed to thoroughly enjoy coloring in pictures, drawing animated cartoons, and writing captions beside the drawings. He was highly productive and was not distracted by the grouped activities that were going on around him. Since the children were of varying levels of ability (slow learners, learning disabled), they were often grouped for instructional purposes. Due to Dylan's uniqueness, his instruction was most often in a 1:1 with the teacher, or involved independent learning (computer access) or individual seatwork. While he worked, Dylan often sang to himself what seemed to be lyrics from various audio computer programs: for example, "Rock and Roll, ABC's." He would repeat refrains over and over in a singsong fashion while he worked.

Although reluctant to disengage from a task when requested to do so, he did comply and brought his work to the teacher for her remarks. He followed routines relatively well and enjoyed his times when called on to read to the teacher, which he did flawlessly. He was rewarded for following routines and for completed work with individual computer time. Dylan very quickly became totally absorbed in the computer programs during his free time, repeating the monologue as if he were narrating the program himself.

Comments on Classroom Observations

The psychologist noted that many behaviors demonstrated by Dylan fit descriptions in the literature on Asperger's disorder: idiosyncratic areas of interest, odd and peculiar behaviors, intense interest in specific areas, poor coordination, and lack of social reciprocity. Watching his behavior in the two classroom settings was also very revealing. While Dylan constantly desired to return to solitude and independent work in the kindergarten class, he was forced to comply with group-oriented activities. In his specialized program, he was allowed to work within the confines of his own little world, without attempts to draw him into any group activities.

ASSESSMENT RESULTS

Dylan was seen for three assessment sessions. The psychologist decided to conduct Dylan's assessment in a small resource room off the VE classroom. Dylan was familiar with the room because he received his language and occupational therapy in the same room; also, he could readily see his teacher through the glass windows. By this time Dylan was also familiar with the psychologist and willingly accompanied her into the room. Since Dylan seemed to enjoy artwork, as an introductory task Dylan was asked to draw a person. Dylan responded by saying that he would draw a pig. Which he did. The pig had a big sign on its neck: "Babe." Apparently, Dylan has been watching the movie over and over and is very interested in pigs at this time. He did comply with a request to copy Bender Designs and completed the drawings in a short period of time. Dylan used a whole-hand pencil grip for all drawing and printing.

Throughout the assessment sessions Dylan's enthusiasm waxed and waned, as did his interest in compliance. Dylan was very excited about doing the Picture Completion subtest of the WISC-III, and repeated the phrase "What is missing!" over and over again. He wanted to draw in the missing parts in the Picture Completion booklet and the examiner had to confiscate writing materials to ensure this did not happen. Dylan's enthusiasm for visual materials far outweighed his interest in responding to verbal questions, and assessment results reflect this disparity. Despite a predominance of fidgety and tense behaviors, Dylan became very focused, deliberate, and methodical working with block designs. He carefully moved each block with precision, checking and rechecking with the stimulus card to ensure accuracy. Dylan also made humorous comments, and when the 11th block design was revealed, he said: "Scary!" and laughed. Then he added, "You will have to help me on this one." Throughout the assessment, when one subtest was completed, Dylan repeatedly asked if he could play "What is Missing!" again. Eventually, the examiner had to remove the stimulus book from the room, since Dylan kept trying to find it.

In her article on Asperger's syndrome (AS), Williams (1995) talks about the impact of sensory overload on children with AS. She states that these children can be overwhelmed by very little change and that sensory overload can throw these children off balance. During the course of this first session, Dylan fell off his chair three times. A combination of poor coordination and becoming overstimulated served to throw him off balance, literally and figuratively.

When the examiner arrived in the classroom for the second session, Dylan jumped up from his seat (almost falling into the desk) and greeted her with an enthusiastic and loud announcement: "You're back! You're back!" He spontaneously took her hand and led her to the assessment room. The Woodcock Johnson Test of Achievement (WJ-III) was introduced and Dylan completed the Letter Word Identification Subtest with ease. The Passage Comprehension subtest was next, and it was anticipated that this would be another area of high interest for Dylan. However, what transpired was not expected. The Passage Comprehension subtest requires that the student orally fill in the blank to complete the sentence exposed in the stimulus book. When this task was introduced, Dylan was insistent on filling in the blanks by writing the answer in the stimulus book. Although the psychologist made several attempts to explain why Dylan could not write in the book, it was not possible to console him. He became visibly upset and started to shake, was on the verge of tears, and repeatedly stated: "You must fill in the blank with the missing word! . . . You must fill in the blank with the missing word!" Dylan was extremely distraught. At this point, the examiner removed the book from the room and brought in sheets of paper and crayons, allowing Dylan to draw and color his favorite cartoons. Drawing seemed to be an activity that served to sooth Dylan in times of stress; this discovery could play an important role in the development of a treatment plan.

After Dylan calmed down, the examiner accompanied Dylan to kindergarten, where he was supposed to go after lunch. However, when they arrived, the other students had already left for PE and the examiner began to walk Dylan over to the playground to join his class. Given Dylan's poor coordination and reluctance to engage in group activities, it is not surprising that PE is his least favorite subject. He became very upset about going to PE and began clinging to the examiner's arm, refusing to let go. The examiner talked to him about all the good choices he had made that day and added that he might earn a star for joining his class, because this was a very good choice indeed. Reluctantly, he separated and joined his class in session. The examiner talked to his teacher to ensure that he did receive a star for compliance.

In order to complete the academic assessment the following day, the examiner photocopied the Passage Comprehension and Applied Problems Subtests of the WJ-III. The plan was to provide Dylan with worksheets that would allow him to fill in the blanks, on the actual pages, rather than respond orally. Although this technique was not part of the standardized procedure, the psychologist wanted to avoid unduly upsetting Dylan, who was "locked into" a "filling in the blanks" mode of operation. The psychologist considered the deviation in protocol a minimal concession, and it avoided the risk of another emotional upset for Dylan. In addition, the task actually became more difficult, since Dylan now had to spell the words to complete the sentences, rather than just provide the answers orally. When presented with the sheets, Dylan proceeded to fill in a large number of blanks correctly, and also spelled the words appropriately. He was rewarded by being allowed to color in the pictures and then draw another series of cartoon animals. As he was drawing, Dylan recited, verbatim, an entire dialogue from a computer program that he had previously heard:

> "This CD program is a Random House Production. As a special bonus feature, be sure to try our newsletter and programs for kids. . . . Each issue is packed with behind-the-scenes action and fun-filled games for kids. Your first issue is free. . . . To obtain your free issue send the enclosed postcard to Random House Productions, P.O. Box 1478, Chicago, Illinois, Postal Code 68374. So don't miss an issue. Send your postcard in today!"

Dylan's drawings were quite remarkable and very well done. He titled his drawing of animated characters as the "Wakabe Rabbit Collection." Dylan also drew another picture, this time of the Windows 2000 logo, complete with copyright. Ultimately, Dylan completed the academic assessment, although it required considerable redirection to task. Dylan fell out of his chair again during this assessment session.

Dylan was able to engage with the examiner socially, albeit within a restricted range. Although eye contact was established, at times he would actually open his eyes wide with a penetrating stare, but at other times visual distance and lack of eye contact was far more comforting. Dylan displayed a sense of humor and could be very engaging; however, laughter would often escalate quickly out of control. Dylan preferred to engage the examiner on his own terms, and could become totally absorbed in paper-and-pencil tasks or verbal monologues that effectively excluded social contact. Dylan was able to request help when needed for a cognitive problem-solving task (puzzles, blocks); however, he experienced difficulty eliciting assistance when emotionally upset, due to a very high level of anxiety and distress. On these occasions, Dylan seemed to respond either by clinging or by attempting to escape (tantrums).

ASSESSMENT RESULTS

Information regarding specific assessment instruments can be found in the Appendix.

Dylan's responses to the Weschler Intelligence Scale for Children—Third Edition (WISC-III) revealed a Verbal Score of 92 (Range 86-99) and a Performance Score of 115 (Range 106-122). Both scores were considered to be an underestimate of global cognitive reasoning, yet likely an adequate picture of day-to-day functioning. Verbal tasks were responded to poorly, and despite an excellent base vocabulary, Dylan's responses to verbal tasks were lower than anticipated, but in the predicted direction for Asperger's disorder. A relative strength was noted in Vocabulary (12), while weaknesses were noted in Comprehension (4) and Arithmetic (5). Performance noted significant strengths on Block Design (16) and Object Assembly (14) with a weakness noted in Picture Completion (8). Dylan's WISC-III profile of superior Visual to Verbal ability was not in the predicted direction (Klin et al., 2001), however, Dylan was also more compliant on visual tasks, which may have altered overall scores. Despite this fact, subtest scatter actually did conform to suggested patterns in the literature on Asperger's disorder: Vocabulary and Information much higher than Comprehension and Arithmetic scores; Picture Arrangement one of the lower Performance scores (Klin et al., 2001).

Although Dylan's error score of 9 for reproductions of Bender Designs was within age expectations, his substitution of lines for dots in designs 2, 3 and 5 is highly associated with brain dysfunction.

Standard scores for academic performance on the Woodcock Johnson Achievement Test (WJIII) revealed Broad Reading to have a Standard Score of

133. Broad Reading is comprised of Letter Word Identification (SS = 135), Reading Fluency (SS = 119) and Passage Comprehension (SS = 128). Spelling (SS = 148) and Writing Samples (SS = 140) were noted strengths. Calculation (SS = 94) and Applied Problems (SS = 84) were Dylan's weakest areas of performance. Academic consistency was noted in Dylan's performance on the Wide Range Achievement Test (WRAT3) for Reading (SS = 133), and Math Calculations (SS = 131), although the Spelling (SS = 131) score was lower on this particular instrument.

Dylan's mother completed the Vineland Adaptive Behavior Scale, the Gilliam Autism Rating Scale (GARS), and the Asperger Syndrome Diagnostic Scale (ASDS). Mrs. Bach's ratings placed Dylan within the normal range of behaviors on the GARS, (SS = 87) which would suggest Below Average indicators for autism. Ratings on the ASDS indicated an overall Asperger's Syndrome Quotient of 105, suggesting a likely diagnosis of Asperger's disorder. A significant elevation was noted for the Social Behavior scale on the ASDS. According to Dylan's mother, overall adaptive behavior on the Vineland was within the expected range for his age level.

Dylan's teachers also completed the GARS and the ASDS. Since Dylan was observed to behave very differently in the two classroom environments, it was not surprising that the kindergarten teacher and the Special Programs teacher rated Dylan differently. On the GARS, the kindergarten teacher rated Dylan as having an Average probability of autism (SS = 91), with only Communication slightly elevated. The special programs teacher rated Dylan much higher on the Autism Scale (SS = 126), suggesting a "high" probability of autism with elevations on the Communication Scale (Scale Score = 14) and Social Interaction Scale (SS = 19). Teachers reported better agreement on the ASDS, suggesting a Likely (SS = 97) and Very Likely (SS = 111) probability of Asperger's syndrome. According to the ASDS, the kindergarten teacher noted significant escalation on the Cognitive Scale (SS = 13), while the Special Program teacher noted significant elevations on the Social (SS = 13) and Sensorimotor Scales (SS = 13).

POST-CASE QUESTIONS

1. Discuss how some of Dylan's symptoms conform to a diagnosis of Asperger's disorder and how some symptoms and behaviors are not in the predicted direction.

2. In terms of differential diagnosis, how do Dylan's behaviors fit with an Asperger profile relative to that of high functioning autism or nonverbal learning

disability? Use illustrations from Sandy's case profile (Case 7) and Dylan's case presentation to compare and contrast the most salient features.

3. Provide some possible explanations for the wide discrepancies in ratings between the three raters (two teachers and parent). Discuss these potential differences relative to various levels of influence, or developmental contexts, suggested by Bronfenbrenner's model. Design an intervention program drawing on the strengths of both classroom programs.

ISSUES IN TREATMENT

Prior to the fourth edition of the *DSM*, published in 1994, Asperger's disorder was not a recognized Axis I disorder. Currently, Asperger's disorder is listed under pervasive developmental disorders (PDDs), which are characterized by severe and lifelong impairments in a number of areas. The term *autistic spectrum disorders* has been used to refer to disorders that have autistic-like features. There is much confusion in the area because many disorders have overlapping features, and given the relative newness of Asperger's disorder as an official category, considerable research on treatment planning is needed.

Asperger's disorder involves a severe impairment in the area of reciprocal social interaction skills, and two broad criteria are required for diagnosis, namely: severe, sustained impairment in social interaction; and the demonstration of restricted and repetitive, stereotypical behavior pattern. Two additional criteria are listed for differential diagnosis relative to autism: Asperger's disorder is ruled out if there is indication of a significant language delay or significant cognitive or adaptive delays (other than social). The severe social impairment noted in Asperger's disorder is described similarly for autism, but is often manifested in a different manner. With Asperger's disorder, lack of reciprocity often takes the form of a self-sustained monologue in an area of self-interest and preoccupation, regardless of the interest or positive response from others. Often there is an intense preoccupation with specific areas of interest. Unlike autism, Asperger's disorder is often accompanied by a well-developed vocabulary basis with the deficit in communication evident at the level of social-pragmatic speech. Associated features can include relative strengths in verbal areas and weaknesses in visual-motor or visual-spatial skills. Motor clumsiness may also be evident. Often the disorder may not be fully recognized until the child is enrolled in a peer group setting, such as preschool or kindergarten (*DSM-IV*).

Prior to the inclusion of Asperger's disorder in the *DSM*, there was considerable controversy regarding differential diagnoses among disorders and syndromes that shared common features, such as autism, Asperger's syndrome, and semantic pragmatic disorder (Bishop, 1989). More recently, diagnostic difficulties continue within the spectrum of pervasive developmental disorders regarding children who do not fit neatly into more "classic" examples of the disorder. Schreier (2001) notes two areas in which diagnostic confusions are particularly pronounced. Difficulties exist in distinguishing Asperger's disorder from "high-functioning autism" (HFA), an informal subcategory of autism for children who score above the mentally retarded range (approximately 25%). The distinction between Asperger's children and children with a nonverbal learning disability (NLD: See Case Study 7, Sandy, for a comparison) is also difficult because both share similar features of a social disability due to poor understanding of the pragmatics of social communication, inability to read social cues, and poor understanding of nonverbal social indicators. Klin and colleagues (1995) suggest that it is most likely that these disorders represent different perspectives on a heterogeneous set of disorders that share some overlapping features. They emphasize the need for future research to employ more rigorous definitions and criteria to better understand the nature of Asperger's disorder, and the similarities and differences between these seemingly related conditions. Although they note that little research has been published regarding interventions for Asperger's, Klin and colleagues suggest that interventions developed to address nonverbal learning disabilities might also be helpful for this population. The Asperger Syndrome Diagnostic Scale (Smith Myles, Jones, Bock, & Simpson, 2001) is a recent advancement toward providing a more reliable method of assessing the degree to which observed behaviors match criteria for Asperger's disorder as defined in the *DSM-IV* and *International Classification of Diseases and Related Health Problems—Tenth Edition* (ICD-10: World Health Organization, 1992). The scale provides an Asperger Syndrome Quotient derived from observer ratings for 50 behaviors distributed over four behavioral indexes: Language, Social, Maladaptive, Cognitive, and Sensorimotor behaviors. The potential value of this scale in providing direction for future research and outcomes for treatment planning is yet to be determined.

Currently, no definitive cause has been isolated; however, researchers continue to examine the possibilities of genetic links. According to Szatmari, (1991), Asperger's disorder has a developmental-neurological etiology, like other PDDs, although the precise nature of the relationship is not clear. Studies suggest a higher proportion of males with Asperger's and less evidence of organic impairment compared to other PDDs (Volkmar, Cohen, & Hoshino, 1988). Complications during pregnancy have also been reported more frequently in the literature on autism (Gillberg, 1989). Because some studies have found Asperger's and autism co-existing in the same families, there are questions about possible common genetic pathways (Gillberg, 1989). There is some support for close family members sharing milder forms of some of the personality traits noted in the child with Asperger's (Klin et al., 1995). Results from neurological research have revealed that when children with autism and Asperger's are presented with tasks that involve decoding facial expressions and vocal tone, their brains are activated in areas used to identify objects in normal populations (Schultz et al., 2000). Future studies will continue to investigate the role of genetics, neurological factors, and pregnancy/birth complications that may explain genetic vulnerabilities in some children.

In her review of empirically supported comprehensive treatments for young children with autism, Rogers (1998) did not find a program that met the stringent requirements of the APA Task Force on evidence-based treatments. Rogers did note, however, that positive outcomes were published for eight comprehensive treatments programs. Programs that were intensive (ranging from 15 to 40 hours per week), targeted children under 5 years of age, and used treatment methods based on behavioral, center-based programs [or a developmental behavioral curriculum indicated positive outcomes]. However, wide variations were noted in whether IQ ranges were reported or how rigidly autistic criteria were adhered to (e.g., diagnostic vs. "autistic-like" subjects). Given the wide variations in intellectual functioning between severe autistic and Asperger's populations, severity of problems exhibited, and the range of areas targeted for improvement, it becomes difficult to generalize results from these studies readily to an Asperger's population.

The importance of treating social skills deficits in Asperger's disorder is self-evident. Therefore, programs that have been successful in the remediation of social skill deficits (Forman, 1993; LeCroy, 1994) may be particularly relevant sources for remediation with this special population. Marriage, Gordon, and Brand (1995) developed a social skills intervention program for Asperger's children, targeting skill deficiencies peculiar to the Asperger's population. The program of eight weekly 2-hour sessions was followed by six weekly 1-hour reinforcement sessions. Multimodal techniques (role play, video taping, games, show and tell) were practiced during the sessions and homework was assigned to provide carry-over into the home. To assist skill-generalization, sessions were varied across a number of different settings within the clinic. Parents met for an informal discussion group while the children attended the sessions. Although results did not reveal significant positive outcomes, the authors suggest that lack of positive outcomes may have been an artifact of the measurement process, since anecdotal comments and observation pointed to overall social gains. The authors recommended future studies include increased generalization of the program within an actual school setting.

On a more practical note, Williams (1995) suggests several guidelines for teachers of students with Asperger's disorder. A number of school-based programming suggestions are provided that target seven defining characteristics of Asperger's disorder: insistence on sameness, impairment in social interaction, restricted range of interests, poor concentration, poor motor coordination, academic difficulties, and emotional vulnerability. Describing children with Asperger's as "easily stressed, and emotionally vulnerable" (p. 9), Williams states that although there are no precise recipes for success due to the diverse nature of the disorder, broad strategies can be adapted to meet the needs of the individual child. Williams suggests that Insistence on Sameness can be counteracted by: giving the student sufficient warning or pretraining regarding pending changes; incorporating consistent routines; minimizing transitions and providing a safe and predictable environment. Impairment in Social Interaction can be assisted through: direct modeling and practice of appropriate social interactions, encouragement to participate in social activities, and limitation of time spent in solitary activity. To increase Range of Interests, gradually introduce other topics of interest, while at the same time reducing time spent on areas of intense interest (relegate to specific time of day, etc.). Suggestions to Increase Concentration include: preferential seating, shortened assignments, and use of a buddy system. Issues of Emotional Vulnerability can be addressed by skill-building exercises to reduce stressful responding. The introduction of step-by-step problem-solving exercises can be very helpful in providing a structured plan to adopt in times of stress: Many Asperger's children will readily commit a ritualized list or scripted response set to memory. Ultimately, Williams (1995) cautions about the onset of depression in older youth and adolescents with Asperger's, since these children often want to establish social relationships and may have very few resources at their disposal, especially those who have not had the benefit of applied social interventions.

REFERENCES

Bishop, D. V. M. (1989). Autism, Asperger's syndrome and semantic-pragmatic disorder: Where are the boundaries? *British Journal of Disorders of Communication, 24,* 107-121.

Forman, S. G. (1993). *Coping skills interventions for children and adolescents.* San Francisco: Jossey-Bass.

Gillberg, C. (1989). Asperger's syndrome in 23 Swedish children. *Developmental Medicine and Child Neurology, 81,* 520-531.

Klin, A., Sparrow, S. S., Marans, W. D., et al. (2001). Assessment issues in children and adolescents with Asperger syndrome. In A. Klin, F. R. Volkman, & S. S. Sparrow (Eds.), *Asperger syndrome.* New York: Guilford.

Klin, A., Sparrow, S. S., Volkmar, F. R., Cicchetti, D. V., & Rourke, B. P. (1995). Asperger syndrome. In B. P. Rourke (Ed.), *Syndrome of nonverbal learning disabilities: Neurodevelopmental manifestations.* New York: Guilford.

LeCroy, C. W. (1994). Social skills training. In C. W. LeCroy (Ed.), *Handbook of child and adolescent treatment manuals.* New York: Lexington Books.

Marriage, K. J., Gordon, V., & Brand, L. (1995). A social skills group for boys with Asperger's syndrome. *Australian and New Zealand Journal of Psychiatry, 29,* 58-62.

Rogers, S. J. (1998). Empirically supported comprehensive treatments for young children with autism. *Journal of Clinical Child Psychology, 27,* 168-179.

Schreier, H. (2001). Socially awkward children: Neurocognitive contributions. *Psychiatric Times, 17*(9). Retrieved March 30, 2003, from http://www.mhsource.com/pt/srchild.html

Smith Myles, B., Jones Bock, S., & Simpson, R. L. *Asperger Syndrome Diagnostic Scale (ASDS): Examiner's manual.* Austin, TX: Pro-ed.

Szatmari, P. (1991). Asperger's syndrome: Diagnosis, treatment and outcome. *Journal of the Psychiatric Clinics of North America, 14,* 81-93.

Volkmar, F. R., Cohen, D. J., & Hoshino, Y. (1988). Phenomenology and classification of the childhood psychoses. *Psychological Medicine, 18,* 191-201.

Williams, K. (1995). Understanding the student with Asperger syndrome: Guidelines for teachers. *Focus on Autistic Behavior, 10,* 9-16.

World Health Organization. (1992). *International classification of diseases and related health problems* (10th ed.). Geneva, Switzerland: Author.

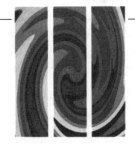

Case 9: Matthew Morgan

Out of Control and In Control

Since Matthew's mother left, when he was only one year old, Tom has struggled continually to meet his son's escalating needs. Being a single father was a very difficult task, especially with all of Matthew's problems. In fact, Tom couldn't believe that Matthew would be celebrating his ninth birthday soon. For Tom, Matthew's childhood was just a blur, like watching a roller coaster speed down the track at 100 miles an hour. The highs and the lows were beginning to run into each other more and more. There were days when Matthew seemed to be able to handle things, and then he would just fall apart, crying and saying he hated himself.

DEVELOPMENTAL HISTORY/FAMILY BACKGROUND

Matthew had always been difficult, even as a baby. As an infant, he seemed to spit up more food than went down and then he would wake up crying in the middle of the night because he was hungry. Then he would overeat and cry again, his little stomach distended with gas. Matthew's mother would have had problems handling the best of babies. With Matthew, she didn't have a chance. Tom worked nights and would often arrive early in the morning after the night shift to hear Matthew screaming in the crib and his wife sleeping through it on the couch.

Eventually, she left, saying that she just wasn't cut out for motherhood. In the first 3 years, Tom struggled with Matthew's mother coming and going out of his life. Matthew would wait patiently for her visits, and then she would either not show up or come in one of her moods. Her erratic behavior was what caused the marriage break-up in the first place. Ultimately, she stopped coming for visits altogether and it had now been 4 years since Matthew had seen his mother. In the beginning, Matthew talked about his mother incessantly, asking why she would not see him. Often he would cry himself to sleep at night. Although Matthew finally seemed to accept the fact that his mother would not return, Tom felt that he never really understood why.

Matthew did not get along with his stepsister, Emily. Emily was 14 years old and Tom's daughter from his first marriage. Matthew and Emily were like night and day. While Matthew was extremely temperamental and hard to get along with, Emily was sweet, soft-spoken, and eager to please. Emily did well in school and had many friends. Often Matthew would deliberately set out to annoy Emily, as if he were angry that she seemed so happy. When Tom started dating again, Matthew went ballistic. One night when Emily was baby-sitting, Matthew went totally out of control. He started smashing things in Tom's room. Emily called her father on his cell phone and he came home immediately, but not before Matthew had made a complete mess of his room. Drawers were dumped on the floor and the lamp was smashed against the wall. Tom tried to restrain Matthew, who was flailing his arms and behaving like a human tornado. After this frenzied burst of activity, Matthew collapsed on the floor and began sobbing. He told his father he was sorry and felt very badly about the damage he had done. The pattern repeated itself again and again. Angry outbursts would be followed by remorse and guilt. Matthew seemed to have little control over his emotions in either direction. On days when he was having a good time, his exuberance would also spiral out of control. Tom remembered the day that Matthew got his new bike. He went right out into the traffic and was almost hit by a truck. Matthew also had few friends because he always seemed to overreact and either get in fights with other kids or blame them if things were not going well. His behavior was often unpredictable and bossy. Often he would come home from the playground in tears.

Although Matthew's behaviors made it difficult for Tom to have a social life, Tom eventually met Eileen and despite Matthew's efforts to come between them, Eileen moved in.

The next 2 years were horrible for everyone in the house. Matthew was very easily upset and seemed to have a continual chip on his shoulder. Eileen initially thought that Matthew would warm up to her in time; however, anytime she attempted to get close to him, Matthew would do something to draw the line. Matthew's irritable disposition also made it difficult for anyone to get close to him. Discipline was very difficult, because Matthew had problems handling criticism at any level. Anytime Eileen would reprimand Matthew, he would break into tears, saying that she was not his mother and had no business acting like it. In time, Matthew's behavior became the focal point for arguments between Tom and Eileen. Matthew was also spending an inordinate amount of time in the garage working on his go-cart. On several nights in succession, Eileen found Matthew in the garage painting and putting decals on the cart well after bedtime. He was getting up at all hours of the night, seemingly obsessed with these late-night activities. Eileen and Tom argued about how to curtail these activities, with the result that nothing was done. Homework assignments were not handed in and homework became another battleground for Matthew and Eileen. Finally, Eileen refused to get involved with Matthew's schoolwork and the job fell to Tom, who was often very tired after working a long day at the trucking firm. Matthew began to complain of headaches and stomachaches and wanted to stay home from school. While doing his homework, Matthew would make self-deprecating comments, calling himself stupid and a dummy. He complained frequently of feeling ill, and he was not eating or sleeping very well.

Eileen eventually left, saying that she could no longer tolerate the family situation. She said that Matthew was spoiled and that Tom did nothing to control his behavior. Their constant fights about Matthew had finally taken their toll. Matthew said that he was happy the "witch" was gone. Tom wondered, however, if Matthew felt that he had just lost another mother, or worse yet, that he had caused another mother to leave.

Matthew was also beginning to get into more trouble at school. His teacher had called Tom twice in the past week, and Tom attended a parent conference. At the school's suggestion, Tom agreed to have the school psychologist observe Matthew in class and to conduct a full assessment to determine if Matthew might also be having learning problems that were adding to his difficulties. When the school psychologist observed Matthew in the classroom, it was readily apparent which child she was there to observe. Matthew was sitting at his desk, slouched down with his arms folded around himself in one enormous pout. Apparently, his teacher had reprimanded Matthew on the way back from lunch because he was running in the hall. Matthew continued to glare at the teacher with his eyes bearing down on her and his lips pursed tightly. The teacher asked the class to break into small groups of six for the next activity, which was a math game. Matthew quickly got out of the chair and gleefully joined his group, hopping and bouncing up and down.

In the groups, children rotated the leadership role by selecting the next child to take the math lead. For a brief time, Matthew seemed to be doing well and getting along with the others in his group, until it was his time to pick another child to be the group leader. Instead of picking another child, Matthew began teasing the others in the group, pretending to pick someone, and then changing his mind, pointing at them with his chalk and then retracting it. Finally, Matthew's group began to ignore him and selected another leader. At this point, Matthew threw the chalk on the floor, sulked, stomped his feet, and returned to his chair and resumed his position of master pouter. Matthew's teacher intervened, once again, and directed Matthew back to his group. At this point, Matthew returned to the group, but laid down on the floor in the middle of the group that was ignoring him. He managed to get the chalk away from the leader and would not give it back. At this point, the group was becoming very upset with Matthew and asked the teacher to intervene. This time the teacher walked Matthew back to his seat, and Matthew sat quietly while the other children returned to their seats as well. When the teacher asked for volunteers to write their group's response on the board, Matthew's hand shot up and he started saying "Me . . . me!!" When he was not picked, Matthew threw his book on the floor and resumed the pout position.

Prior to the outburst that landed Matthew in the alternate school placement, Matthew started repeatedly asking if he could see his mother again. He was very disturbed that no one seemed to know where she was. Matthew was obsessed with finding her and would spend long hours, at night, searching for her on the Internet. At school, Matthew was getting into trouble on a regular basis. He was not sleeping well, and was now irritable most of the time. He was having problems concentrating on schoolwork, and he seemed unable to cope with other children or school demands. Matthew would frequently burst into tears and had to be removed from the classroom on several occasions. Socially, other children would either tease him or ignore him. Matthew's responses were very unpredictable: volatile and aggressive at one moment; at another time, crying and saying that he wished he were dead. Tom attended another school conference, and the school psychologist shared concerns regarding her observations of Matthew in class and around the school on her regular visits. It was the psychologist's belief that Matthew might have bipolar disorder. A psychiatric appointment was scheduled, but it would take 2 months for Matthew to be seen. In the interim, Tom agreed to take Matthew to his family physician for his medical opinion.

REASON FOR REFERRAL

Tom took Matthew to his family physician and the physician prescribed imipramine, hoping that is would reduce Matthew's anxiety. The physician said that he also felt that Matthew had attention-deficit/hyperactivity disorder, which might explain why he tended to be so impulsive and demonstrate such poor behavioral controls. Four days later, in response to teasing from peers, Matthew ran out in front of the school and impulsively ran into the traffic. When the teachers retrieved him and tried to get him back into the classroom, he began kicking and screaming. Matthew grabbed a chair and threw it at one of the teachers. Matthew was removed from the school and placed in an alternative placement for the next 45 days. While in the alternative setting, the imipramine was discontinued since there were concerns that the medication might have escalated the behaviors. The consulting psychiatrist diagnosed Matthew with child onset bipolar disorder, and over the next several months tried various medications to stabilize Matthew's behavior. Eventually, a trial of lithium proved relatively successful in reducing the depressive episodes and emotional volatility. Matthew was referred for assessment to determine intellectual potential, academic progress and emotional status.

ASSESSMENT RESULTS

While in the alternate school placement, Matthew was assessed by the psychologist, who found that Matthew's intelligence was in the High Average range overall, with very little discrepancy between his Verbal and Performance Scores. Academically, Reading and Math were at grade level, although Written Expression was about a year behind and in need of remediation. During his clinical interview, Matthew talked at length about his real mother and said that he was having problems because she left. He said that he was sure he would be better if she would return.

POST-CASE QUESTIONS

1. Using the framework for a Functional Behavioral Assessment (Table 1.2), develop a case formulation outlining the precipitating and maintaining variables regarding Matthew's behavior. Working from this assessment information, develop a behavioral intervention plan for use in Matthew's school to assist in monitoring his behaviors.

2. Develop a case formulation from the perspective of an attachment theorist. What treatment plan would best accommodate Matthew's needs using this approach?

3. Develop a case formulation from the perspective of a family systems therapist. How would you attempt to restore the balance of power in this family?

4. Develop a case formulation for Matthew, relating his behaviors to developmental theory and contexts (Bronfenbrenner's model), using the framework of risks and protective factors.

5. The IDEA definition of emotional disturbance is highly controversial (see Appendix B: Special Topics in Classification). Based on the IDEA, would Matthew qualify for an exceptional designation as an emotionally disturbed or seriously emotionally disturbed child? If not, why not?

ISSUES IN TREATMENT AND REFERENCES

Note: Issues in Treatment and References for child onset bipolar disorder are included in Case Study 10: Jenny: The All-American Girl, on adolescent onset bipolar disorder.

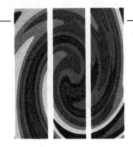

Case 10: Jenny Sloan

The All-American Girl

Jenny, a strikingly attractive 16-year-old, arrived at the clinic with her mother, Stella. Jenny was recently released from the hospital after an unsuccessful suicide attempt. Jenny's mother had found her on the bathroom floor, unconscious, amid empty bottles of nonprescription drugs: Advil, Tylenol, Sudafed. Fortunately, the ambulance arrived in time. What scared Stella the most was that there were no warning signs of depression and suicide. Or were there?

DEVELOPMENTAL HISTORY/FAMILY BACKGROUND

Jenny was a beautiful baby—bright, alert, and very easy to manage. Stella and Carl, both in their mid-thirties, were very proud of their baby girl and were especially thankful that they were able to conceive a child after so many years of trying. Although Carl was a successful banker, he kept his priorities in check and was often more interested in family life than corporate life. Stella did a lot of volunteer work in the community and the local school. They had a strong marriage and were well suited to each other. It seemed that parenthood was all that was missing. Stella, who was an avid reader, had purchased several books on child rearing and charted Jenny's milestones diligently in her daughter's journal. Jenny developed perfectly in tune with what the books would say. She began walking on her first birthday and actually was saying words before she was walking.

As a preschooler, Jenny was very social and loved attending school and playing with the other children. It seemed that the other children were drawn to Jenny by her infectious laughter, something that would continue throughout her school years. Jenny was very well coordinated, and Stella enrolled her in kinder-gym, dance, and swimming. Jenny embraced each new activity with vigor and enthusiasm and was an excellent gymnast, dancer, and swimmer.

In elementary school, Jenny won awards for track and field and was voted most popular girl in her class in Grade 5. She continued dance lessons and gymnastics and competed in several regional meets with relative success. Jenny seemed to be a born leader, and her popularity with the other children was readily apparent. It seemed like there was no stopping her.

When Stella thought back, there may have been early warning signs that all was not well. Middle school seemed to launch Jenny into early adolescence, and her responses to change or adjustments in her life started to trigger more intense and extreme reactions. Stella recalled when Jenny's class schedule was changed by the guidance counselor, Jenny came home extremely irritated and agitated, complaining that the counselor had no right to do this to her. She demanded that her parents go to the school and have the schedule changed. Stella and Carl tried to reason with Jenny after they talked to the guidance counselor on the telephone. However, Jenny said they were all in on the conspiracy against her. She was up most of the night on the telephone to classmates, trying to organize a protest. The next day she was very agitated and angry at her friends for not supporting her in the protest. Were it not for the fact that Jenny was so popular, Stella was sure that these behaviors would have cut off all her social contacts. However, Jenny continued to be very popular with her peers. She was a formidable leader, who was beautiful, full of life, and assertive. Many of her classmates may have cowered in her wake, but they secretly desired to be just like her.

Stella and Carl were concerned about Jenny's escalating behaviors; however, Stella had read several books on adolescence and convinced Carl that Jenny was probably just being a difficult adolescent. When it came to parent-teacher conferences, some of Jenny's teachers were not pleased with her confrontational nature, but others seemed to admire her perseverance. Jenny's grades were good, and she excelled in extracurricular activities. She was beautiful, bright, and motivated. These were qualities to be admired. She was the "all-American girl." These comments left Stella and Carl uncertain about how to deal with Jenny's behaviors, and they wondered if they were overreacting or maybe doing something wrong at home. They discussed whether they should take Jenny to a child psychiatrist or psychologist, but other parents convinced them that Jenny was just being a teenager, and that they would readily change places with them. How great it must be to have a teenager as motivated as Jenny.

In her final year at middle school, Jenny had just turned 14 and tried out for the cheerleading squad. When she was selected, she was elated about making the team. However, halfway through the school year, Jenny decided that the cheerleading uniforms needed to be revamped: the skirts were too long and the design on the front of the sweater was outdated. For the next month, Jenny was relentless. She became obsessed with getting the uniforms changed. She spoke on the phone most of the night. Jenny's mother picked up the extension by mistake one time, and couldn't believe Jenny's rambling on about buying material and sewing patterns, pantsuits, designs, and European fashion trends and megaphones. Much of what Jenny was rambling on about seemed to make no sense. Of course, when her mother questioned her about the conversation, Jenny was furious at her mother for picking up the extension and eavesdropping on her. Eventually, Jenny's friends stopped calling. Jenny was now spending more and more time on the Internet at night when she was supposed to be doing her homework. She told her parents that she was doing "research"; what she didn't reveal was that her research was focused on trying to locate a uniform designer that the school could hire to redesign the uniforms. Ultimately, she began drawing her own designs and spending countless hours at night cutting out patterns and trying new designs. She was convinced that she had the talent to become a world-famous uniform designer and ran up expensive phone bills trying to contact clothing manufacturers across the United States who might support her line of uniforms: Jeunesse by Jenny. She got the name from the French word for "youth."

When the telephone bills arrived at the end of the month, Jenny had amassed hundreds of dollars in international phone calls. Her parents were furious and Jenny was upset, saying that they didn't support her. Maybe they would believe her when she became famous.

No one seemed to understand how intense Jenny could be. Her parents were the only windows on her all night vigils, extensive phone bills, and constant diatribes at home. Yet her parents somehow felt powerless to intervene because they were constantly being reminded by parents of other teenagers that Jenny was "the all-American girl" and that they were fortunate to have such a talented and motivated daughter.

Jenny had now graduated and was in high school. Her mother thought that, in hindsight, it was amazing how Jenny was able to contain her more bizarre outbreaks to the home front and appear relatively normal at middle school. Once Jenny was in high school, however, things began to go noticeably out of control. Socially, Jenny began pushing the limits with her parents and dressing very provocatively despite their protests. Jenny's behavior became more erratic. Highs were followed by lows. Jenny loved the highs. They were addictive. The highs were great. Jenny thrived on the highs. When she was on a high, it was as if she were wearing magical senses: Colors were more intense; sounds were more reverberating; and touch was more penetrating. But then the crash . . . the awful crash. The mood swings were swift and devastating.

In the hospital, Jenny admitted to her parents that she was beginning to feel out of control about a week before the suicide attempt. Jenny had been on the phone for hours frenetically attempting to organize a party that would be the biggest and best party ever, but by the time the party began, her mood had spiraled into a deep depression. It was as if someone had pulled the floor out from under her. Jenny felt riveted to the bed, immobile, as if her feet were stuck in buckets of poured concrete. The horrible pain of the black hole. It was as if someone had vacuumed out her very soul. The emptiness and the pain were unbearable. On that night, the pain hurt so much, she woke up in a panic, ran to the bathroom, and devoured bottles of painkillers, anything she could find to end the pain once and for all.

A review of the intake information showed a history of bipolar disorder in Jenny's paternal grandmother, and alcohol abuse in the maternal grandfather. There were also several cousins with a history of depression and suicidal behavior.

REASON FOR REFERRAL

When Jenny was in the hospital, a comprehensive clinical assessment was conducted to determine her functioning on several levels including intellectual, academic and social/emotional status.

ASSESSMENT RESULTS

Information regarding specific assessment instruments can be found in Appendix C.

When Jenny arrived at the clinic, she brought with her the results of the assessment conducted in the hospital. Results of the WISC-III revealed average intellectual ability, although scores may have been somewhat depressed, given her mood state at the time. Low scores were noted on the Freedom from Distractibility Index. Academically, Jenny scored at grade level, with the exception of arithmetic, which was approximately 2 years below grade level. Her mother's responses to the CBCL revealed clinical elevations for Attention, Anxious-Depressed, and Thought Problems. Scores for Delinquent Behaviors and Aggression were elevated but not significant. Jenny completed the Revised

Child Manifest Anxiety Scale (RCMAS) and the Youth Self Report (YSR). Jenny's responses indicated extreme elevations on the Physiological Indicators Scale on the RCMAS, and clinical elevations on the Anxiety-Depression and Thought Disorder Scales of the YSR. The semi-structured diagnostic interview (K-SADS) revealed positive endorsement of manic and depressive symptoms.

POST-CASE QUESTIONS

1. Matthew and Jenny provide examples of how bipolar disorder may appear different from two developmental perspectives. Explain the differences in presenting symptoms. Discuss how developmental context might influence not only the symptom presentation, but the treatment goals, as well.

2. How would theorists from each of the following schools develop a case formulation to describe bipolar disorder: psychodynamic, biophysiological, behavioral, cognitive, attachment/parenting, family systems?

3. Design a treatment program for Jenny to ensure that she is compliant with her medical regime.

4. In addition to medication, what other treatments might you recommend for Jenny, and why? What other comorbid disorders would you be concerned about Jenny demonstrating?

ISSUES IN TREATMENT

Until recently, bipolar disorder in children and adolescents has received little attention (Rapoport & Ismond, 1996). However, between 20% and 40% of adults with the disorder (Joyce, 1983; Lish, Dime-Meenan, Whybrow, Price, & Hirschfeld, 1994) reported onset in childhood and adolescence. Therefore, it is possible that bipolar disorder in childhood was largely underdiagnosed in the past. However, increased interest in the area has also led to the fear that the pendulum has swung in the opposite direction, resulting in current tendencies to overdiagnose bipolar disorder when children and youth may more appropriately be diagnosed with attention-deficit/hyperactivity disorder (ADHD) with comorbid substance abuse or conduct disorder (Weller, 2000).

There has been an increasing need to address developmental issues in the assessment, diagnosis, and treatment of bipolar disorder (Geller & Luby, 1997). Egeland (2000) compared features from social histories of 58 patients diagnosed with bipolar disorder with a "contrast group" of siblings and peers from the same Amish community. Egeland found evidence of prodromal features in 22% of the sample by 6 years of age, and more than half (59%) had evidence of the symptoms between 7 and 10 years of age. Prodromal symptoms were identified as episodes of depressed mood (53%), increased energy (47%), and decreased energy (38%). Other features included anger dyscontrol/quick temper and argumentativeness (38%), and irritable mood (33%). In reviewing cases of bipolar disorder across development, Carlson (1983) found that young bipolar children (under the age of 9) tended to have chronic rather than acute episodes; irritability, crying, and motor agitation compared to older bipolar youth. However, older youth tended to manifest more classic bipolar symptoms of "mania," such as euphoria or grandiosity, and "depression." Other early identifiers may come from neurobiological data, which suggest that manic individuals may also have right-hemisphere impairments (Sackeim & Decina, 1983), lower Performance IQs than Verbal IQs (Decina, Kestenbaum, & Farber, 1983), and decrease in math performance in pre-bipolar adolescence (Kutcher, 1993). Young children at risk for developing bipolar illness demonstrate moods of intense emotional responses, both positive and negative, and behaviors that are under-controlled and disinhibited (Akiskal, 1995). Predictors of bipolar disorder in adolescents with depression include: family history of bipolar disorder, psychomotor retardation, hypersomnia, sudden onset of symptoms, and delusions (Akiskal, Walker, & Puzantian, 1983; Strober, 1992).

The diagnosis of bipolar disorder in childhood and adolescence is problematic for several reasons, including: the diversity of how the disorder presents within and across episodes (Cogan, 1996); symptoms of mania overlapping with other disorders of childhood; and the diversity of symptom presentation due to developmental stage (Bowring & Kovacs, 1992).

Presentation of bipolar symptoms in childhood may differ from the sudden onset of bipolar disorder in adult or older adolescent populations. In childhood and early adolescence, bipolar disorder may involve a more insidious pattern of brief rapid cycling and involve multiple brief episodes (Kutcher, 1993). In addition to the subtle waxing and waning of episodes, childhood onset bipolar disorder may also include disruptive behavior, moodiness, irritability, impulsivity, difficulty sleeping, and hyperactivity. In addition to short attention span and low frustration tolerance, some young children may also demonstrate episodes of explosive anger followed by guilt, remorse, depression, and subsequent decline in academic performance (Weller, Weller, & Fristad, 1995). This almost continuous cycling pattern challenges differential diagnoses between bipolar disorder and ADHD. Diagnostic uncertainty between these two disorders is often due to overlapping symptoms of: inattention, impulsivity, distractibility, and hyperactivity. Furthermore, children may simultaneously demonstrate bipolar disorder and ADHD, in which case more intense and severe symptom presentation would be expected.

In younger children, although symptom presentation may not be as severe as in adolescent populations, the ongoing and possibly daily interference in functioning and anger outbursts would certainly influence mastery of normal developmental tasks such as regulating behavioral self-control and interfere with the establishment and maintenance of social relationships (Cogan, 1996). In children and adolescents, displays of aggression have also been noted as a common feature of bipolar disorder. Steiner (2001) reports displays of affective, reactive, and defensive aggression in children and adolescents with bipolar disorder. He further subdivides aggressive types into escalating types and intermittent types, with adolescents tending to demonstrate more of the escalating type of aggression.

In older children, differential diagnosis between bipolar and conduct disorder may be difficult in the case of a youth who impulsively shoplifts, is sexually promiscuous, and engages in risky behavior. However, differential diagnosis would recognize that in the bipolar adolescent, these behaviors represent high-risk and stimulation-seeking behaviors devoid of the vindictive and antisocial elements noted in conduct disorder (Bowring & Kovacs, 1992). Similarly, delusions of grandeur, paranoia, irritability, and flight of ideas might be difficult to distinguish from schizophrenia. Geller and colleagues (1995) studied 26 children (13 were aged between 7 and 13 years; 13 were adolescents) with bipolar disorder. Results revealed that 80% of the sample had rapid cycling patterns (100% of the younger group and 70% of the adolescent group). The authors also found a prevalence of hallucinations in the older group (hearing voices), delusions (grandeur, persecutory, somatic), and ideas of reference that may lead to misdiagnosis of this group as schizophrenic. Whether these patterns that resemble bipolar disorder II are an age-specific and developmental antecedent to bipolar disorder I in adulthood, remains to be seen (Geller, Fox, & Clark, 1994).

Lithium has been the main pharmacological treatment for bipolar disorder in adults. Geller and Luby (1997) caution, however, that it may be unreasonable to expect that treatments for adults will work for children. The authors draw on the lack of success of tricyclic antidepressants for child and adolescent populations (Geller, 1996). Recently, Tueth, Murphy, and Evans (1998) reviewed research concerning lithium treatment for children and adolescents and concluded that results have been promising. Geller and colleagues (1998) have also reported success using lithium with bipolar adolescents. However, lithium does not appear to be as effective for children as for adult populations, and there is wide variation on the success rate, which is reported to be between 33% and 74% (Weller et al., 1995). Furthermore, the use of lithium in child and adolescent populations has not been without problems. Frequent monitoring of blood levels is essential, and relapse rate is high when medication is discontinued (Strober, Lampert, & Burrough, 1990). Geller and Luby (1997) also warn of the dangers of prescribing lithium for children of chaotic families or where there is a bipolar parent, due to the need for consistent monitoring of lithium levels to avoid toxicity. The association of pediatric bipolarity with greater familial loading, early aggressive hyperactivity, and greater resistance to lithium has also been noted by Strober and his colleagues. Side effects of lithium (gastrointestinal upset, nausea, weight gain, tremor, and acne) may also be particularly upsetting to adolescents and interfere with treatment compliance. Valproate (Depakote) and carbamazepine (Tegretol) have also met with successful trials; however, variations in effectiveness have also been reported (Bezchlibnyk-Butler & Jeffries, 1997; Weller et al., 1995). Frazier, Meyer, and Biederman (1999) noted risperidone (Risperdal) to be effective in 82% of the 28 adolescent cases surveyed in a retrospective chart review. The use of methylphenidate (stimulant medication) has been known to worsen symptoms of bipolar disorder in some children (Koehler-Troy, Strober, & Malenbaum, 1986), and more research is required given the similarity between manic symptoms and symptoms of ADHD.

As an adjunct to medication, there are several other treatment goals that need to be incorporated in intervention programs for children and adolescents with bipolar disorder. Psychotherapy needs to address strategies for improving interpersonal relationships, stress management, as well as management of medication regimes. Cogan (1996) emphasizes the need to monitor and reduce potentially stress-inducing events, as well as normalization of sleep habits. Cogan suggests that sleep deprivation may actually trigger a manic episode in adolescents. Collaboration with school personnel is also an essential component of the treatment process (Cogan, 1996; Kronenberger & Meyer, 2001). In *The Bipolar Child,* Papolos and Papolos (2000) present a mock-up IEP (Individual Education Plan) for a hypothetical bipolar student, Elan. The plan is an practical example of how interventions can address children's needs across developmental contexts, such as the school environment. Elan's IEP is developed to incorporate six goals in his school programming aimed at learning and applying strategies to: divert inappropriate thoughts, reduce anxiety, increase on-task behaviors, increase communication skills, increase academic competence, and reduce explosive outbursts. The plan is written in behavioral terms that allow Elan to earn points for meeting goals on a daily basis.

Kronenberger and Meyer (2001) suggest a five-step intervention plan for children and adolescents with bipolar disorder, including: psychoeducation, rules for medication compliance, depression treatments (such as cognitive behavioral methods: see Case Study 11, David), family therapy, and collaboration with the school regarding behavioral plans and educational interventions.

REFERENCES

Akiskal, H. S. (1995). Developmental pathways to bipolarity: Are juvenile-onset depressions pre-bipolar? *Journal of the American Academy of Child and Adolescent Psychiatry, 34,* 754-763.

Akiskal, H. S., Walker, P., & Puzantian, V. R. (1983). Bipolar outcomes in the course of depressive illness. *Journal of Affective Disorders, 5,* 115-128.

Bezchlibnyk-Butler, K. Z., & Jeffries, J. J. (1997). *Clinical handbook of psychotropic drugs.* Toronto: Hogrefe & Huber.

Bowring, M. A., & Kovacs, M. (1992). Difficulties in diagnosing manic disorders among children and adolescents. *Journal of the American Academy of Child and Adolescent Psychiatry, 31,* 611-614.

Carlson, G. A. (1983). Bipolar affective disorders in childhood and adolescence. In D. P. Cantwell & G. A. Carlson (Eds.), *Affective disorders in childhood and adolescence* (pp. 61-84). New York: S. P. Medial Science Books.

Cogan, M. B. (1996). Diagnosis and treatment of bipolar disorder in children and adolescents. *Psychiatric Times, 13*(5). Retrieved September 28, 2002, from http://www.mhsource.com/pt/p960531.html

Decina, P. Kestenbaum, C. J., & Farber, S. (1983). Clinical and psychological assessment of children of bipolar probands. *American Journal of Psychiatry, 140,* 548-553.

Egeland, J. (2000). Prodromal symptoms present a decade before diagnosis of bipolar disorder. *Journal of the American Academy of Child and Adolescent Psychiatry, 39,* 1245-1252.

Frazier, J. A., Meyer, M. C., & Biederman, J. (1999). Risperidone treatment for juvenile bipolar disorder: A retrospective chart review. *Journal of the American Academy of Child and Adolescent Psychiatry, 38,* 960-965.

Geller, B. (1996). The high prevalence of bipolar parents among prepubertal mood-disordered children necessitates appropriate questions to establish bipolarity. *Current Opinions in Psychiatry, 9,* 239-240.

Geller, B., Cooper, T. B., Sun, K., Zimerman, B., Frazier, J., Williams, M., & Heath, J. (1998). Double-blind and placebo-controlled study of lithium for adolescent bipolar disorder with secondary substance dependency. *Journal of the American Academy of Child and Adolescent Psychiatry, 37,* 171-178.

Geller, B., Fox, L. W., & Clark, K. A. (1994). Rate and predictors of prepubertal bipolarity during follow-up of 6- to 12-year-old depressed children. *Journal of the American Academy of Child and Adolescent Psychiatry, 33,* 461-468.

Geller, B., & Luby, J. (1997). Child and adolescent bipolar disorder: A review of the past 10 years. *Journal of the American Academy of Child and Adolescent Psychiatry, 36,* 1168-1176.

Geller, B., Sun, K., Zimerman, B., Luby, J., Frazier, J., & Williams, M. (1995). Complex and rapid-cycling in bipolar children and adolescents: A preliminary study. *Journal of Affective Disorders, 34,* 259-268.

Joyce, R. R. (1983). Age of onset in bipolar affective disorder and misdiagnosis as schizophrenia. *Psychology of Medicine, 14,* 145-149.

Koehler-Troy, C., Strober, M., & Malenbaum, R. (1986). Methylphenidate-induced mania in a prepubertal child. *Journal of Clinical Psychiatry, 47,* 278-279.

Kronenberger, W. G., & Meyer, R. G. (2001). *The child clinician's handbook* (2nd ed.). Needham Heights, MA: Allyn & Bacon.

Kutcher, S. (1993). Bipolar disorder in an adolescent cohort. *Paper presented at the Annual Meeting of the American Academy of Child and Adolescent Psychiatry,* San Antonio.

Lish, J. D., Dime-Meenan, S., Whybrow, P., Price, R., & Hirschfeld, R. M. (1994). The National Depressive and Manic-Depressive Association (DMDA) survey of bipolar members. *Journal of Affective Disorders, 31,* 281-294.

Papolos, D., & Papolos, J. (2000). School: A child's world beyond home: Hypothetical baseline information and draft IEP for a bipolar student. In D. Papolos & J. Papolos, *The bipolar child* (pp. 280-284). New York: Broadway Books.

Rapoport, J. L., & Ismond, D. R. (1996). *DSM-IV training guide for diagnosis of childhood disorders.* New York: Brunner/Mazel.

Sackeim, H. A., & Decina, P. (1983). Lateralized neuropsychological abnormalities in children of bipolar probands. In P. Flor-Henry & J. Gruzelier (Eds.), *Laterality and psychopathology.* New York: Elsevier Science.

Strober, M. (1992). Bipolar disorders: Natural history, genetic studies and follow-up. In M. Shafii & S. L. Shafii (Eds.), *Clinical guide to depression in children and adolescents* (pp. 251-268). Washington, DC: American Psychiatric Press.

Strober, M., Lampert, C., & Burrough, J. (1990). Relapse following discontinuation of lithium maintenance therapy in adolescents with bipolar I illness: A naturalistic study. *American Journal of Psychiatry, 147,* 457-461.

Tueth, M. J., Murphy, T. K., & Evans, D. L. (1998). Special considerations: Use of lithium in children, adolescents and elderly populations. *Journal of Clinical Psychiatry, 59,* 66-73.

Weller, E. (2000, May). *Bipolar children and adolescents: Controversies in diagnosis and treatment.* Paper presented to the American Psychiatric Association 153rd Annual Meeting, Chicago.

Weller, E. B., Weller, R. A., & Fristad, M. A. (1995). Bipolar diagnosis in children: Misdiagnosis, underdiagnosis and future directions. *Journal of the American Academy of Child and Adolescent Psychiatry, 34,* 709-714.

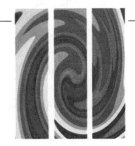

Case 11: David Steele

Hopelessness and Despair

David sat at his desk staring off into space. When he glanced back down at the paper in front of him, he realized that he had been drawing boxes for the last half hour. Each box connected to the next. Just like his life. There was no way out and there was no way in. He was boxed into a corner. There was no escape.

David hated school and he hated the kids. They were all a bunch of phonies. No one understood anything that mattered. He could hear them at their lockers, talking and laughing. They were all so ridiculous, so shallow. They were all full of themselves. They didn't see life like he did. They never would. He was sick and tired of the whole damn thing. He had done his thing. He had tried it their way. But they always wanted something from him. There was always a catch. Either they needed to borrow money, or they needed a ride somewhere. They always wanted something. He was sick of being used. He hated them anyway. Better this way.

His mother's voice talked at him from the other side of the closed door. She said something about going out for the evening, something about making sure his homework was done, and then he heard the front door close behind her. Good, she was gone. He didn't need her interruptions, either. She was always going out somewhere. No wonder his father left. She was never home. Life was just one big party. She was as shallow as the rest of them. She didn't understand him, either. She said he was just a moody teenager. Laughed at him. Called him "James Dean, tortured teen." The funny thing was, that didn't even upset him anymore. He was beyond upset. Upset needed feelings. He felt nothing.

He looked back down at the drawings of the boxes; they were all empty too. Just sides. Nothing inside. Empty boxes.

It was very quiet now. Just four walls with emptiness inside. Dead air. Death. He thought about death a lot. They put dead people in boxes. Was he dead already? There was no noise. There was no feeling. Ah . . . the betrayal. Thoughts. Dead people don't think. Dead people don't have to listen to the same damned thoughts echoing in their heads over and over and over. What was the noise in his head? Was that a voice talking to him from the grave? A dead person calling to claim him? Or was it just the sound of his own voice, caught in his head and bouncing back and forth in the emptiness. . . . Dead people are better off. If he were dead, would anyone care? Would anyone notice that he wasn't in class? He thought about the philosophical argument about the tree falling in the forest. How did it go? If a tree falls in the forest and no one is there to hear it . . . did it make a noise? If he killed himself, and no one cared . . . did he even exist?

David started to write a suicide note but gave up because he couldn't think of anyone who would be interested in his thoughts. He berated himself, because he couldn't even make his mind up about this. He was pathetic. He would wait for another day. He didn't even have the energy to figure out how to do it. Maybe just walk into the traffic. But then, what if you screw up with that, too, and only get run over and lose a leg or something. That would be worse. He walked into the living room and poured himself another shot of rye. At least he knew one thing, the rye would stop the thinking soon, and he would pass out. Passing out worked. You stopped thinking, at least for a while . . .

David's case is typical of many adolescents who live in a private world of despair. The majority never end up in a psychologist's office or a clinic. Some suffer in silence. Others end their suffering.

ISSUES IN TREATMENT

The *DSM-IV* categorizes adult depression in terms of severity and duration. Major depressive disorder (MDD) is a pervasive feeling of depressed mood or loss of pleasure for at least 2 weeks and is accompanied by at least five of nine other symptom from the following areas: emotional (sadness, guilt, emptiness); motivational (loss of interest); behavioral (insomnia or hypersomnia); cognitive (recurrent thoughts of suicide, death, diminished concentration), and physical (psychomotor retardation/agitation, fatigue, loss of appetite/increase appetite, loss of energy). Minor depression, or dysthymia, is a low-grade depression involving fewer symptoms (2 instead of 5) over a longer duration of time (2 years for adults; 1 year for children). Children and adolescents may have symptoms similar to adults', however, depressed mood can often appear as "irritable mood," and symptom presentations will vary given different developmental levels.

In their investigation of empirically supported treatments for children and adolescents with symptoms of depression, Kaslow and Thompson (1998) found that although a number of group interventions, mostly using cognitive-behavioral therapy (CBT), demonstrated success in alleviating depressive symptoms in children and adolescents, none of the studies met with the stringent criteria for well-established treatments. Furthermore, the authors noted that most of the interventions had been adapted from adult treatments and neglected to include any reference to the child's or adolescent's developmental stage. Reviews of the studies with children revealed that only two child studies and two adolescent studies met criteria for probably efficacious interventions set forth by the APA Task force (APA Task Force on Psychological Intervention Guidelines, 1995). The child studies that met the standard were two studies conducted by Stark and colleagues (Stark, Reynolds, & Kaslow, 1987; Stark, Rouse, & Livingston, 1991) demonstrating the benefits of CBT self-control therapy. Adolescent studies meeting the standard included studies by Lewinsohn and colleagues (Lewinsohn, Clarke, Hops, & Andrews, 1990; Lewinsohn, Clarke, Rhode, Hops, & Seeley, 1996). In the first study (Lewinsohn et al., 1990), both adolescents who received a 14-week CBT program and adolescents whose parents conjointly received a 7-week CBT program reduced more symptoms of depression than the wait-list control group. Replication of the study (Lewinsohn et al., 1996) with some modifications revealed similar results with maintenance of reduced depressive symptoms on 2-year follow-up. Kaslow and Thompson (1998) concluded their review by emphasizing the need to recognize developmental differences in the study of treatment outcomes and greater sensitivity to incorporating cultural perspectives.

It is estimated that 20% of all adolescents will experience at least one episode of depression by age 18, and 65% will report less severe, transient symptoms (Lewinsohn, Hops, & Roberts, 1993). Prevalence rates vary according to type of depression (major depression vs. dysthymia) and whether the population sampled is normative or clinical. According to Kovacs and colleagues (Kovacs, Devlin, Pollock, Richards, & Mukerji, 1997), major depression in children and adolescents usually lasts from 7 to 9 months, while the average duration for dysthymia is 4 years. Although children and youth may experience many of the same symptoms as adults (loss of interest, apathy, sadness, self-doubt, feelings of worthlessness, guilt, and despair), young children may also experience feelings of separation anxiety and a wide variety of physical complaints (Mitchell, McCauley, & Burke, 1988; Ryan, Puig-Antich, & Ambrosini, 1987). In adolescent populations, depression may appear as irritability mixed with features of anxiety or anger (Compass, Connor, & Hinden, 1998). Depression in children and adolescents may go undiagnosed due to a failure to recognize irritability, anxiety, and physical complaints (headaches, body pains, and stomachaches) as signs of depression. In addition, adolescent "mood swings" may be considered as normal teenage angst by some parents. Auditory hallucinations may also accompany an episode of severe depression in children and adolescents (Birmaher, Ryan, Williamson, Brent, & Kaufman, 1966). Comorbidity is also a common feature of child and adolescent depression. Between 40% and 60% (Angold & Costello, 1993; Rohde, Lewinsohn, & Seeley, 1994) of depressed children and youth have at least one other comorbid disorder, the most common of which are: anxiety, substance abuse, and disruptive behavior disorders. The risks for developing bipolar disorder are high (20%).

Depression in children and adolescents has been linked to multiple causes, including: family history (Kovacs, Obrosky, Gastonis, & Richards, 1997); biological factors (low levels of serotonin, high levels of cortisol); and cognitive factors (negative and maladaptive thought processes). Studies have also isolated situational/environmental factors that can be linked to depressive episodes in children and adolescents, such as: stress (Lewinsohn, Rogdem, & Seeley, 1998); loss of a parent or loved one (Wells, Deykin, & Kierman, 1985); romantic break- up (Monroe, Rohde, & Seeley, 1999); and school problems (Gould et al., 1996).

Suicide is the third leading cause of death among 10- to 19-year-olds (Borowsky, Ireland, & Resnick, 2001). Twice as many females attempt suicide, but males are four times more likely to succeed. Although risk factors are similar for both genders, the emphasis placed on each of the factors differs by gender. Although major depression seems to be the most prominent risk factor for suicide in girls (Shaffer et al., 1996), somatic symptoms, peer suicide attempt, and illicit drug use were all found to increase the risk of suicide in white, Hispanic, and black females (Borowsky et al., 2001). Previous suicide attempt is the most lethal risk factor for males (Shaffer et al., 1996), along with weapon carrying at school and same-sex romantic attraction (Borowsky et al., 2001). Other risk factors that cut across gender and ethnicity include: violence victimization, violence perpetration, alcohol use, marijuana use, and school problems. In their examination of adolescent profiles for more than 13,000 students (Grades 7-12) between 1995 and 1997, Borowsky and colleagues (2001) found that having three protective factors reduced suicide attempts by between 70% and 85%. Protective factors were identified as: parent and family connectiveness, emotional well-being (girls), and high grade point average (boys). Although acting on suicidal impulse has been linked to serotonin malfunction in adults, this association has not been confirmed in children and adolescents. Children and adolescents who contemplate suicide feel intense emotional distress and choose death as a means of ending severe psychological pain. Based on historical data from 50 adolescents who had attempted suicide, Jacobs (1971) suggests a 5-step model of the hypothetical factors leading to progressive suicide ideation: (1) History of family and school problems; (2) intensification of problems in adolescence (increased family and academic problems); (3) increased withdrawal, and isolation from social contacts and family members; (4) severing of social ties; and (5) justification of suicide as the conclusion.

Unfortunately, mass approaches to suicide prevention, such as suicide hot lines (Shaffer, Garland, & Bacon, 1989), and in-school awareness programs (Shaffer et al., 1991), have not been demonstrated to be successful in preventing suicide and run the risk of increasing suicide ideation in some youth. At a global level, however, it is possible that routine screens can serve to identify at-risk students for more intensive services (Shaffer & Craft, 1999). Borowsky et al. (2001) suggest that targeting protective factors in intervention programs is an important key to developing successful suicide prevention programs. Targeting risk factors such as substance abuse, stress, and lack of social support, and protective factors such as family cohesiveness, academic success, and emotional well-being may well be important ingredients in future prevention programs for these children of despair.

Psychotherapy, especially cognitive behavioral approaches (CBT) and pharmacotherapy, have been shown to be effective treatments for depression in children and adolescents. Although initial studies concerning medical treatments for adolescent depression revealed contradictory results, these studies involved trials of tricyclic antidepressants. Recently, trials of SSRIs point to more persuasive evidence for the benefits of fluoxetine (Prozac) and paroxetine (Paxil). In two separate controlled studies, fluoxetine has proven effective for children and adolescents (Emslie, Rush, & Weinberg, 1997), while paroxetine has proven successful with adolescents (Keller, Ryan, & Strober, 2001).

REFERENCES

APA Task Force on Psychological Intervention Guidelines. (1995). *Template for developing guidelines: Interventions for mental disorders and psychosocial aspects of physical disorders.* Washington, DC: American Psychological Association.

Angold, A., & Costello, E. J. (1993). Depressive comorbidity in children and adolescents: Empirical, theoretical, and methodological issues. *Journal of the American Academy of Child and Adolescent Psychiatry, 150,* 1779-1791.

Birmaher, B., Ryan, N. D., Williamson, D. E., Brent, D. A., & Kaufman, J. (1996). Childhood and adolescent depression: A review of the past 10 years. Part II. *Journal of the American Academy of Child and Adolescent Psychiatry, 35,* 1575-1583.

Borowsky, I. W., Ireland, M., & Resnick, M. D. (2001). Adolescent suicide attempts: Risks and protectors. *Pediatrics, 107,* 485-502.

Compass, B. E., Connor, J. K., & Hinden, B. R. (1998). New perspectives on depression during adolescence. In R. Jessor (Ed.), *New perspectives on adolescent risk behavior.* Cambridge, UK: Cambridge University Press.

Emslie, G. J., Rush, A. J., & Weinberg, W. A. (1997). A double-blind, randomized, placebo-controlled trial of fluoxetine in children and adolescents with depression. *Archives of General Psychiatry, 54,* 1031-1037.

Gould, M. S., Fisher, P., Parides, M., Flory, M., & Shaffer, D. (1996). Psychosocial risk factors of child and adolescent completed suicide. *Archives of General Psychiatry, 53,* 1155-1162.

Jacobs, J. (1971). *Adolescent suicide.* New York: John Wiley.

Kaslow, N. J., & Thompson, M. P. (1998). Applying the criteria for empirically supported treatments to studies of psychosocial interventions for child and adolescent depression. *Journal of Clinical Child Psychology, 27,* 146-155.

Keller, M. B., Ryan, N. D., & Strober, M. (2001). Efficacy of paroxetine in the treatment of adolescent major depression: A randomized, controlled trial. *Journal of the American Academy of Child and Adolescent Psychiatry, 40,* 762-772.

Kovaks, M., Devlin, B., Pollock, M., Richards, C., & Mukerji, P. (1997). A controlled family history study of childhood-onset depressive disorder. *Archives of General Psychiatry, 54,* 613-632.

Kovacs, M., Obrosky, D. S., Gastonis, C., & Richards, C. (1997). First-episode major depressive and dysthymic disorder in childhood: Clinical and sociodemographic factors in recovery. *Journal of the American Academy of Child and Adolescent Psychiatry, 36,* 777-784.

Lewinsohn, P. M., Clarke, G. N., Hops, H., & Andrews, J. (1990). Cognitive-behavioral treatment for depressed adolescents. *Behavior Therapy, 21,* 385-401.

Lewinsohn, P. M., Clarke, G. N., Rhode, P., Hops, H., & Seeley, J. (1996). A course in coping: A cognitive-behavioral approach to the treatment of adolescent depression. In D. Hibbs & P. S. Jensen (Eds.), *Psychosocial treatments for child and adolescent disorders: Empirically based strategies for clinical practice* (pp. 1109-135). Washington, DC: American Psychiatric Association.

Lewinsohn, P. M., Hops, H., & Roberts, R. E. (1993). Adolescent psychopathology: Prevalence and incidence of depression and other *DSM III-R* disorders in high school students. *Journal of Abnormal Psychology, 102,* 133-144.

Lewinsohn, P. M., Rogdem, P., & Seeley, J. R. (1998). Major depressive disorder in older adolescents. Prevalence, risk factors, and clinical implications. *Clinical Psychology Review, 18,* 765-794.

Mitchell, J., McCauley, E., & Burke, P. M. (1988). Phenomenology of depression in children and adolescents. *Journal of the American Academy of Child and Adolescent Psychiatry, 27,* 12-20.

Monroe, S. M., Rohde, P., & Seeley, J. R. (1999). Life events and depression in adolescence: Relationship loss as a prospective risk factor for first onset of major depressive disorder. *Journal of Abnormal Psychology, 108,* 606-614.

Rohde, P., Lewinsohn, P. M., & Seeley, J. R. (1991). Comorbidity of unipolar depression: II. Comorbidity with other mental disorders in adolescents and adults. *Journal of Abnormal Psychology, 100,* 214-222.

Rohde, P., Lewinsohn, P. M., & Seeley, J. R. (1994). Are adolescents changed by an episode of major depression? *Journal of the American Academy of Child and Adolescent Psychiatry, 33,* 1289-1298.

Ryan, N. D., Puig-Antich, J., & Ambrosini, P. (1987). The clinical picture of major depression in children and adolescents. *Archives of General Psychiatry, 44,* 854-861.

Shaffer, D., & Craft, L. (1999). Methods of adolescent suicide prevention. *Journal of Clinical Psychiatry, 60,* 70-74.

Shaffer, D., Garland, A., & Bacon, K. (1989). Prevention issues in youth suicide. In D. Shaffer, I. Philips, & N. Enzer (Eds.), Prevention of mental disorders, alcohol and drug abuse in children and adolescents (*OSAP Prevention Monograph, 2,* pp. 373-412). Rockville, MD: Alcohol, Drug Abuse and Mental Health Administration.

Shaffer, D., Garland, A., Vieland, V., Underwood, M., & Busner, C. (1991). The impact of curriculum-based suicide prevention programs for teenagers. *Journal of the American Academy of Child and Adolescent Psychiatry, 30,* 588-596.

Shaffer, D., Gould, M. S., Fisher, P., Trautment, P., Moreau, D., Kleinman, M., & Flory, M. (1996). Psychiatric diagnosis in child and adolescent suicide. *Archives of General Psychiatry, 53,* 339-348.

Stark, K. D., Reynolds, W. M., & Kaslow, N. J. (1987). A comparison of the relative efficacy of self-control therapy and a behavioral problem-solving therapy for depression in children. *Journal of Abnormal Child Psychology, 15,* 91-113.

Stark, K. D., Rouse, L., & Livingston, R. (1991). Treatment of depression during childhood and adolescence: Cognitive-behavioral procedures for the individual and family. In P. Kendall (Ed.), *Child and adolescent therapy* (pp. 165-206). New York: Guilford.

Wells, V. E., Deykin, E. Y., & Kierman, G. L. (1985). Risk factors for depression in adolescence. *Psychiatric Development, 3,* 83-108.

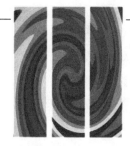

Case 12: Sarah Burke

Food for Thought

Sarah, a 16-year-old teenager, came to the clinic accompanied by her mother, Ann. Sarah presented as a typical teenager of average height and weight. There was a tension between mother and daughter that was readily recognizable to the clinic staff from the outset. Shouting had accompanied the car ride all the way to the clinic and both looked like they had been through an emotional war. Ann was biting her lip as they walked through the door, while Sarah gave a sideways glance that could have knocked her mother over. Sarah's behavior was escalating out of control.

DEVELOPMENTAL HISTORY/FAMILY BACKGROUND

During the telephone intake interview, Ann reported the following background information. Sarah's birth was natural and unremarkable. Developmental milestones were all within the normal range with the exception of speech/language acquisition. Sarah was a quiet baby with a good appetite, and she had no serious health problems. There was a history of tonsillitis and severe throat infections about twice a year, but surgery has never been done to correct this due to Sarah's reluctance to have the procedure. There is no history of mental illness in the family, although Sarah's father did abuse alcohol and drugs, which Ann believes contributed to his eventual heart disease and untimely death when Sarah was 12 years of age.

Sarah was relatively easy to manage as a toddler and she has always been soothed by music. Ann added that as late as 3 years of age, Sarah's speech was largely still unintelligible due to articulation difficulties. As a result, Sarah tended to be very unwilling to speak, especially if strangers were within hearing range. Ann wondered if some of Sarah's speech delay might have been attributed to the fact that Sarah's father was a boisterous, loud, and verbally abusive man. The marriage was rocky for some time, and when Sarah was 4 years of age, the marriage finally crumbled. The tension in the home was horrible, because they all had to continue living under the same roof until her father found other accommodations. During this time, Ann tried to avoid any interaction with Sarah's father, since every incident turned into another eruption. Ann feels that Sarah might have been fearful and reticent to speak around her father and this made her nervous about speaking, period. Ann still feels that Sarah continues to have very conflicted feelings about her dad. Arguments in the household were common, and the children seemed to shrink from their father at times. Sarah's older sister, Cindy, coped by literally living at a neighbor's house with her friend, Tammy. Eventually, Sarah's dad moved out.

Once her dad left, it seemed that Sarah's behavior took a turn for the worse. After that time, Sarah began to have temper tantrums when she did not get her own way. She would scream so loud that Ann was sure the neighbors thought she was killing her. These incidents were often precipitated by Ann's denying something Sarah wanted, but sometimes there seemed to be no apparent reason for the outburst. During these times, Ann would plead, make deals, cajole, or threaten punishment if Sarah would not desist. These methods usually failed, and she would eventually give in to Sarah's demands. Sometimes, Sarah would stop on her own, without any intervention. Given Sarah's difficult behaviors, delayed speech, and late birthday, Ann was very tempted to delay Grade 1 school entrance for a year to allow Sarah more time to mature. Since Ann is a teacher, she even thought about home schooling, but decided against it. Ann wonders if she did the right thing, since Sarah has always lagged somewhat behind her peers academically and socially.

Sarah and her older sister, Cindy, who is 18 years of age, have never really gotten along. Cindy has always been a very good student and one who has not had to apply herself too arduously in order to make good grades. Ann feels that Sarah resents her sister for this, and Sarah feels that her older sister sometimes makes fun of her and her struggles with academics. The parent adds that Sarah and her older sister, a senior in high school, argue very frequently, and their arguments sometimes become physical. During one episode, Sarah slammed a door on her sister's hand, causing her sister considerable pain.

Although Sarah is a cheerleader and drill team member at school and appears to be popular enough to be voted into these activities, Ann feels that she can be very domineering with her friends. Ann has heard Sarah engage in very intense disagreements with friends on the phone. She has overheard Sarah cursing and shouting at people on the phone, and Sarah sometimes speaks of "fronting" someone; meaning that she confronts them angrily or in a hostile way. Ann also stated that she believes Sarah sometimes feigns illness, giving some vague physical complaint, either in order to get sympathy or to stay home from school.

Sarah is currently enrolled in the 11th grade at Truman High School. Her grades are passing, but presently she has particular problems with math and chemistry. Sarah has always struggled in math and Ann is concerned that this will negatively affect Sarah's college prospects. Sarah has also verbalized some insecurity about her academic abilities and she worries about her future in college. However, when Ann tries to help Sarah with her homework, Sarah reacts very belligerently, resulting in arguments and accusations about Ann interfering in her life. On the one hand, Sarah wants her mother out of her life. On the other hand, Sarah can be a very demanding child whose needs have to be met, immediately. On these occasions, Sarah expects her mother to "be on call" when Sarah needs something. The parent states that she is constantly "running here and there" on errands for Sarah, and she wishes that Sarah could take more responsibility for herself.

Ann also revealed several factors that have caused her to be increasingly concerned about Sarah's welfare and motivated her to make contact with the clinic. Recently, many fights between Sarah and her mother have centered on Sarah's boyfriend. When Ann tries to broach the subject of the boyfriend, Sarah can become very defensive and verbally aggressive. She has thrown things and cursed her mother. Sarah accuses her mother of meddling in her affairs and of being unfair and domineering. Ann states that she has legitimate concerns because she knows some of the boyfriend's history, which includes involvement with drugs and of possibly having fathered an illegitimate child. The boyfriend can also be quite thoughtless and mean. He has made comments on more than one occasion about Sarah putting on weight, which has reduced Sarah to tears. As a result, Sarah will go off food for days, until she is literally starving, and then break down and clean out the fridge. Ann has begun to worry about Sarah's eating habits, since she found a bottle of diet pills hidden in Sarah's room. Ann has not confronted Sarah about this, since Sarah would certainly "throw a fit" about her mother sneaking into her room and invading her privacy. Ann is also concerned that Sarah is having sexual relations with the boyfriend, given his past history.

Sarah's father died of complications due to heart disease when Sarah was 12 years old. Upon the death of her father, Sarah was inconsolable for a time and seemed to withdraw into herself. She was often irritable and moody during this time and had difficulty sleeping. Her weight fluctuated from weight loss to weight gain. Due to the history of divorce and the subsequent death of the father, Ann believes she may have overindulged Sarah's behaviors and minimized some difficulties in order to avoid confrontation with her. Ann wonders why Sarah is not more like her sister; she feels frustrated and unappreciated when Sarah accuses her of meddling.

Ann summed up the telephone interview outlining her present concerns by saying that she wished Sarah could behave more tactfully with friends in resolving problems and she wished that Sarah could understand that what seems like meddling is genuine motherly concern. Ann added that Sarah's academic difficulties worry her as well as Sarah and this seems to add to the tension between them. While she does not approve of Sarah's present boyfriend, she does not forbid Sarah's seeing him. On the other hand, the mother does not hide her disdain for him, either. She can see the negative influence the boy has on Sarah and how he impacts negatively on her self-image and confidence. In her final comments, Ann added that she is tired of everyone having to "tiptoe around Sarah" in order to avoid a confrontation with her. Ann added, "I would like to go through just one normal week with Sarah."

Sarah was well dressed for the interview and immediately stated that she was pleased that her mother had to wait outside and wasn't going to be part of the interview. Sarah's speech still reflects some slight articulation difficulties, but her speech is intelligible. Sarah tends to speak rather rapidly, and the examiner had to ask her to repeat herself on occasion. Sarah seemed at ease during the interview and was forthcoming with information. She was somewhat animated but generally appropriate. Sarah admitted to having difficulties with peer relations and said when she gets into fights, she confronts people, and then writes them off: "I just pretend they don't exist!" Sarah was very vocal about her resentment regarding her mother's involvement in her personal matters. Sarah also seemed to be sensitive about her academic abilities, said that she never did well in math and said that she "hated it." When describing her social contacts, Sarah said that she most admired Ashley because she was smart, pretty, tanned, and thin. She also wished she could live in her house because her parents were rich and they had a pool. She spoke at length about her boyfriend, saying that her mother doesn't understand him at all. She added that she thinks her mother is jealous because her mother doesn't have a boyfriend and she does. Sarah admits to being sad sometimes, and she wishes her dad were still alive. She wishes her mom would just "chill" and stay out of her business. When asked about the one thing she would change about herself, Sarah said her appearance. She said she wished she were taller and thinner, like Ashley. She admitted to going on diets to lose weight, and said that she has tried just about every diet in the teen magazines and some of her mother's diets as well. She described her mother as "anorexic" and obsessed with weight, saying she eats a piece of cheese for lunch. Sarah was asked how she felt after she ate a big meal. She said, "I feel disgusting, like a blimp. I get really mad at myself for being so grotesque." She said she makes a bargain with herself that if she doesn't eat any more that week, she will be able to binge again the next weekend. When asked if she ever took pills or vomited to get rid of the food, Sarah flatly denied doing either, then retracted, saying she had tried vomiting once, but didn't like it. The examiner was not convinced that Sarah was being completely honest, especially since her mother had discovered the diet pills.

REASON FOR REFERRAL

Ann had finally acted on her instincts to get help for Sarah, since Sarah was becoming very verbally abusive to her mother, somewhat reminiscent of the abuse Ann had sustained from her husband in the failed marriage. Were it not for the abusive situation, Ann might have missed the other cues that suggested that Sarah was having many more difficulties than were apparent on the surface. However, it was Ann's feelings of helplessness and fears of confronting Sarah that finally resulted in the referral to the clinic.

ASSESSMENT RESULTS

Information regarding specific instruments can be found in the Appendix.

The examiner noted that Sarah's test behaviors revealed a tendency toward impulsive responding and poor check-back skills (misreading math calculation signs). Frustration tolerance was also low, and Sarah tended to give up easily. These behaviors, however, were considered to be consistent with Sarah's everyday approach to challenging tasks and results were considered to be a valid index of her current functioning levels.

Sarah's overall score on the Weschler Intelligence Scale for Children (WISC-III) revealed a Verbal IQ of 89 (Range 83-96) and a Performance IQ of 83 (Range 76-93). Verbal weaknesses were noted in mental arithmetic (S = 6) and general information (S = 7). On the Performance scale, Sarah had significant problems sequencing visual pictures to tell a story (S = 4) and reproducing block designs (S = 5). Given this profile, it would be anticipated that Sarah would encounter academic difficulties, especially in math. Academically, according to the Woodcock Johnson III Achievement Test (WJIII), Sarah was approximately 1 year behind her present grade placement in Broad Reading and Broad Written Expression, but almost 3 years behind across all math areas (calculation, fluency, and reasoning).

Sarah completed the Eating Disorder Inventory-2 (EDI-2) and demonstrated significant elevations on the Desire for Thinness and the Body Dissatisfaction Scales. An elevated Bulimia Scale also supported suspicions regarding Binge Eating/Purging Behaviors, and scores for Impulse Regulation were also of concern. In response to interview questions and in her responses to the Child Depression Inventory (CDI), Sarah did not endorse symptoms of depression to any significant degree; however, scores for Ineffectiveness and Interpersonal Problems were in the At-Risk level. On the Revised Child Manifest Anxiety Scale (RCMAS), scores for Worry/Oversensitivity and Social Concerns were also within the At-Risk range. Responses to the Beck Youth Scales noted concerns in areas of elevated Anger Expression score and lowered scores for Self-Esteem.

Sarah's mother completed the Conners Parent Rating Scale (CPRS:L), which yielded several subscales elevated to the Clinically Significant level: Oppositional Behavior (T = 74); Anxious-Shy (T = 78), Perfectionism (T = 72), Social Problems (T = 99), Psychosomatic (T = 99), and Emotional Lability (T = 77). Sarah's mother's responses suggest that difficulties are evident in having few friends, feelings of being socially detached, and lacking in self-confidence. In view of suspected bulimic activity, there is a cautionary note regarding the significant number of physical complaints endorsed. Overall, the parent's rating of Sarah represents an elevated general profile that might represent global problematic behavior or comorbid functioning.

POST-CASE QUESTIONS

1. Within family systems theories, four characteristics have been observed in "anorexic families": enmeshment, overprotectiveness, rigidity, and denial of family conflict (Minuchin, Rosman, & Baker, 1978). "Bulimic families," on the other hand, tend to have greater tendencies toward predisorder conflict with parents; greater incidence of family pathology, especially substance abuse or depression; and more perceived intense family conflict (Neuman & Halvorson, 1983).

Discuss how Sarah's family characteristics support or contrast with this theory.

2. Discuss some reasons why Sarah's sister Cindy did not develop an eating disorder, while Sarah did. Support your discussion from the viewpoint of a theorist from each of the following models: biomedical, psychodynamic, behavioral, cognitive, family systems, and attachment/parenting style. How might developmental contexts interact to create greater risk or protective factors for the two sisters?

3. Bruch (1991) has developed a theory linking parenting style to eating disorders that combines facets of psychodynamic and cognitive theories. Bruch argues that severe and frequent mother-daughter conflicts result in lack of adequate ego development in the child (poor sense of independence and control) and cognitive distortion regarding eating habits. Developing this line of thought, Bruch suggests that effective parents correctly identify their child's internal state and match comfort needs with appropriate responses. If a child is hungry, food is provided; if a child is emotionally upset, emotional comfort is provided; and if a child is cold, the parent provides a warm blanket or clothing. However, ineffective parents do not attend appropriately to the child's internal cues and provide inappropriate responses, such as trying to comfort an anxious child with food. Children who grow up in these environments do not learn to recognize their own internal signals and confuse feelings of anxiety, anger, or distress with feelings of hunger. Feeling helpless and out of control, adolescent girls may respond by taking excessive measures to assert their control over their own bodies. Research has provided some support for Bruch's theory. Studies have shown that bulimics often equate anxiety with hunger (Rebert, Stanton, & Schwarz, 1991). In addition, bulimics' desire to please often results in their reliance on others' opinions and views, consequently feeling less sense of control in their lives (Walters & Kendler, 1995). Describe how Bruch's theory might be used to explain Sarah's eating disorder.

ISSUES IN TREATMENT

Contemporary preoccupation with thinness has been referred to as "the new age of eating disorders" (Rodin, Striegel-Moore, & Silberstein, 1990). As a result, there is growing concern about the development of eating disorders in adolescent female populations. The *DSM* outlines three main categories of eating disorders: anorexia nervosa, bulimia nervosa, and binge eating disorder. The onset for anorexia can be earlier (range 14-19 years) than onset for bulimia (range 15-21 years). There are several differences between these two disorders, such as the dynamics inherent in personality and family systems and the fact that anorexics maintain a body weight less than 85% of the normative weight, while bulimics are more likely to be of average weight or slightly overweight. There are two types of anorexics: restrictors, who reduce their total food intake, and the binge-purge type. Bulimics can also be divided into two groups based on the type of compensatory behavior exhibited: purge type and non-purge type. Purging activities can involve induced vomiting, laxatives, or diuretics; examples of non-purge behaviors include fasting and excessive exercise. Anorexics and bulimics are both subject to faulty cognitions; however, the bulimic's thought processes serve to perpetuate a self-destructive cycle of anger and guilt. Pre-binge thought patterns of anger, guilt, and loss of control are followed by binge eating. Binge eating serves to increase the sense of anger, guilt, and loss of control. Post-binge feelings of depression, disgust, and self-depreciation follow, which can be alleviated only by getting rid of the excess food. Once compensatory measures are taken and the food is expelled, the bulimic once again feels a sense of calm and self-control. The cycle perpetuates behaviors that are inherently self-rewarding and compulsive. Tendencies for bulimics to also exhibit comorbid disorders of depression and anxiety are well documented (Herzog, Keller, Sacks, Yeh, & Lavori, 1992); however, Geist, Davis, and Heinman (1998) also found high comorbidity rates (15%) for oppositional defiant disorder (ODD) in adolescent girls with binge-purge features in their eating disorder population.

Studies of the etiology of eating disorders have suggested strong family connections, both genetically and from a psychosocial perspective. Research concerning familial linkages to eating disorders has revealed that relatives of anorexics and bulimics had a 7 to 12 times greater risk of having an eating disorder than nonrelatives. In addition, this population also had greater prevalence of other comorbid disorders, such as major depression, obsessive-compulsive disorder, and anxiety disorders (Lilenfeld, Kay, & Greenco, 1998).

In seeking treatments for bulimia, investigation of potential biological factors has led researchers to suggest a link between eating disorders and low levels of serotonin (Carrasco, Diaz-Marsa, Hollander, Cesar, & Saiz-Ruiz, 2000) or chemicals such as GLP-1 that serve as a natural appetite suppressant (Turton et al., 1996). In support of genetic and biological theories, studies of monozygotic twins with eating disorders have revealed concordance rates as high as 23% compared with only 9% for fraternal twins (Walters & Kendler, 1995). One treatment for bulimia has focused on the use of antidepressants like SSRIs, which have had some measure of success (Jimerson, Herzog, & Brotman, 1993).

The role of family dynamics in eating disorders has also been investigated in research. In analyzing the responses of mother-father-daughter triads in response to the Structural Analysis of Social Behavior, Humphrey (1989) found that parents communicated very different messages to anorexics and bulimics. Families of anorexics tended to be controlling and allowed little room for their daughter's self-expression. They communicated a mixed message of nurturance but no tolerance for expression of feelings. Families of bulimics, on the other hand, demonstrated more overt signs of emotional conflict and often blamed and berated their daughters.

As would be anticipated given the bulimic cycle of self-defeating thought patterns, cognitive therapy as been one of the more successful avenues for treating adolescent bulimics (Lewandowski, Gebing, Anthony, & O'Brien, 1997). Cognitive behavioral interventions with family support would involve development of a treatment plan that included built-in monitoring and reinforcements. Strategies would include introduction of relaxation techniques and coping strategies (e.g., response prevention, cognitive restructuring, etc.) to manage maladaptive thought processes and curb impulsive responding. Including a relapse prevention component is also important due to the high rate of relapse, which may be as high as 33% within the first 2 years (Olmstead, Kaplan, & Rockert, 1994).

REFERENCES

Bruch, H. (1991). The sleeping beauty: Escape from change. In S. I. Greenspan & G. H. Pollock (Eds.), *The course of life: Vol. 4. Adolescence*. Madison, CT: International Universities Press.

Carrasco, J. L., Diaz-Marsa, M., Hollander, E., Cesar, J., & Saiz-Ruiz, J. (2000). Decreased platelet monamine oxidase activity in female bulimia nervosa. *European Journal of Neuropsychopharmacology, 10,* 113-117.

Geist, R., Davis, R., & Heinman, M. (1998). Binge/purge symptoms and comorbidity in adolescents with eating disorders. *Canadian Journal of Psychiatry, 43,* 507-512.

Herzog, D. B., Keller, M. B., Sacks, N. R., Yeh, C. J., & Lavori, P. W. (1992). Psychiatric comorbidity in treatment-seeking anorexics and bulimics. *Journal of the American Academy of Child and Adolescent Psychiatry, 31,* 810-818.

Humphrey, L. L. (1989). Observed family interactions among subtypes of eating disorders using structural analysis of social behavior. *Journal of Consulting and Clinical Psychology, 57,* 206-214.

Jimerson, D. C., Herzog, D. B., & Brotman, A. W. (1993). Pharmacologic approaches in the treatment of eating disorders. *Harvard Review of Psychiatry, 1,* 82-93.

Lewandowski, L. M., Gebing, T. A., Anthony, J. L., & O'Brien, W. H. (1997). Meta-analysis of cognitive behavioral treatment studies for bulimia. *Clinical Psychology Review, 17,* 703-718.

Lilenfeld, L. R., Kay, W. H., & Greenco, C. G. (1998). A controlled family study of anorexia nervosa and bulimia nervosa: Psychiatric disorders in first-degree relatives and effects of proband comorbidity. *Archives of General Psychiatry, 32,* 1031-1038.

Minuchin, S., Rosman, B. L., & Baker, L. (1978). *Psychosomatic families: Anorexia nervosa in context.* Cambridge, MA: Harvard University Press.

Neuman, P. A., & Halvorson, P. A. (1983). *Anorexia nervosa and bulimia: A handbook for counselors and therapists.* New York: Van Nostrand-Reinhold.

Olmstead, M. P., Kaplan, A. S., & Rockert, W. (1994). Rate and prediction of relapse in bulimia nervosa. *American Journal of Psychiatry, 151,* 738-743.

Rebert, W. M., Stanton, A. L., & Schwarz, R. M. (1991). Influence of personality attributes and daily moods on bulimic eating patterns. *Addictive Behaviors, 16,* 497-505.

Rodin, J., Striegel-Moore, R. H., & Silberstein, L. R. (1990). Vulnerability and resilience in the age of eating disorders. Risk and protective factors for bulimia nervosa. In J. Rolf, A. S. Masten, D. Cicchetti, K. H. Nuechterlein, & S. Weintraub (Eds.), *Risk and protective factors in the development of psychopathology* (pp. 361-383). Cambridge, MA: Cambridge University Press.

Turton, M. D., O'Shea, D., Gunn, I., Beak, S. A., et al. (1996, January 4). A role for glucagon-like peptide-1 in the central regulation of feeding. *Nature, 379,* 69-72.

Walters, E., E., & Kendler, K. S. (1995). Anorexia nervosa and anorexia-like syndromes in a population based female twin sample. *American Journal of Psychiatry, 152,* 64-71.

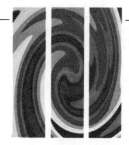

Case 13: Jason Coleman

Disconnected Connections

Jason was almost 16 years of age when he was brought to the clinic by his social worker, accompanied by his foster mother, Mrs. Belcour.

DEVELOPMENTAL HISTORY/FAMILY BACKGROUND

Little is known of Jason's early history, but according to reports, Jason's parents died when he was 4½ years of age. There were reported stories of a murder-suicide as both parents were found in a submerged car that had crashed through a bridge. As had happened on other occasions, Jason was not in the car, since he had been left with an aunt while his parents frequented the local bar. Jason's mother was barely a teenager when he was born and had a troubled history of substance abuse and running away from an abusive home situation. Jason's father was also a runaway who had his own history of substance abuse and reckless behavior. Although they never married, they lived together and fought often. There were concerns that Jason's father was abusive physically when he was drinking, which was often, and after his death, it was learned that he was also a registered sex offender.

After his parents' tragic death, Jason was initially cared for by a maternal aunt; apparently the aunt was also physically abusive, and Jason moved in with his maternal grandparents 2 years later. At 6½ years of age, Jason's behavior was becoming more and more difficult to control. Despite his impulsive behaviors, which were often reckless and dangerous, Jason also demonstrated intense fears, such as a fear of the dark and fear of water. He would scream hysterically if the grandparents turned the lights out in his room or even tried to pull his shirt over his face to get dressed or undressed. Often he would awake in the middle of the night, screaming in terror. Because of his fears of water, he was afraid to go in the bathtub and cleanliness became an ongoing issue. At school, children would call him names and Jason would retaliate by hitting, punching, and kicking. Temper tantrums were frequent at home, and intense. Jason would often throw himself on the floor, arching his back, kicking, and screaming. He would also bang his head on the floor or walls or anything he could find. His grandparents were increasingly concerned about safety issues. When upset, Jason could not be comforted or consoled. Mood shifts were frequent, and at times Jason seemed to be out of reach and "in a world of his own." On these occasions, he would "zone out" and seem to lose contact with everyone around him. The grandparents eventually went to child protection services to seek help in managing Jason's behavior and in obtaining weekend relief. Ultimately, they gave him up altogether when he set a fire in their bedroom.

Jason went through a series of foster placements like a revolving door, breaking down each placement in succession. It was as if he would destroy the placement before the placement could reject him. His life became a self-fulfilling prophecy. During this time, Jason was seen for psychotherapy at a regional treatment center. His behavior was described as "chronically hostile," and play sessions were directed toward assisting Jason to understand his behavior and to relate more positively to those around him. Jason's themes in play therapy were full of violence and destruction. He would smash cars together, bury toy dolls in the sand, and put ropes around the stuffed animals and dangle them from clothes hooks. While Jason was receiving treatment, his social worker continued to search for a stable therapeutic foster placement and eventually found such a placement in a city 90 miles away. In order to assist with his transition, Jason was assessed at the center. Intellectual assessment revealed that despite average intelligence, Jason did evidence significant difficulties with short-term memory, attention, concentration, and visual motor functioning. Academically, Jason was below the expected level in the core academic areas. The psychologist who did the assessment also noted that Jason was emotionally distraught, depressed, and fearful about his move so far away. Ritalin was prescribed to assist Jason with attention and concentration in his new school placement.

Jason joined the Belcour family just prior to his 10th birthday. He would be the only child in the home, since the Belcours agreed not to take in any additional foster children at that time. Throughout his history with the Belcour family, behavioral difficulties would be evident whenever Jason felt threatened or insecure. During the initial stages of his placement, the foster parents were trained to recognize that Jason would test his new placement in ways that would test the limits of their patience and endurance. Jason had developed a highly predictable pattern of self-defeating behaviors that were designed to break down the foster placement. However, these behaviors were motivated by his highly anxious fears of abandonment and constant need for reassurance. Eventually, the behaviors lessened and Jason looked as if he was beginning to settle into the family. Although Jason's behaviors continued to challenge the Belcours, these behaviors began to escalate about 18 months ago. Jason began staying out late, and had been truant from school. When confined to his bedroom, Jason sneaked out the bedroom window and was found wandering the streets with a friend. Despite coming home smelling of cigarettes, Jason denied that he was smoking. Mrs. Belcour sought the assistance of the social worker, and Jason began to take part in weekly counseling sessions in an attempt to get his behavior in check. Ritalin dosage was also increased at that time.

Recently Jason's behaviors were escalating out of control. He managed to obtain Mrs. Belcour's pin number (looking over her shoulder while she withdrew money from her account), removed her ATM card from her purse and withdrew $500 from her bank account. Jason also manipulated the new foster child, who was of limited intellectual capacity, to assist him in breaking into the house across the street, saying that the boy who lived there had stolen his CD collection. Eventually, it was also learned that alcohol was missing from the Belcours' liquor cabinet, although the bottles were cleverly filled with soda pop to avoid immediate detection. Jason had also recently earned a 3-day suspension from school for being rude to one of his teachers.

Jason, a tall and lean adolescent, 15 years, 6 months of age, presented well and was cooperative and congenial throughout the assessment. He offered to carry the testing materials from the car and assisted the psychologist in clearing excess paper from her desk to get ready for the assessment. He was not overly spontaneous in response to open-ended conversation; he responded better to direct questions and then proceeded to elaborate and embellish his responses. In response to questions directed toward areas of interest in school, Jason cited welding, auto work, and woodworking. When asked what he would like to do when he finished school, Jason stated that he would like to become a "pyrotechnician." Jason then asked if the psychologist if she knew what a "pyrotechnician" was. The psychologist asked Jason what type of schooling would be required for such a position. Jason stated that this was a job that required a 4-year university degree and that it involved staging "blow-ups" for television and the movies. If this was not a possible career, he said, his next choices were to be a trucker or a racecar driver. At this point in the interview, Jason began asking the psychologist about becoming a "shrink" and wondered how long it takes to get such a degree. He said that he figured that this was a profession that probably made lots of money. Conversation then was directed to where a psychologist might live in the city. When this was not responded to directly, Jason said that he lived in a section of town where people lived who had less money than psychologists.

Throughout the assessment, Jason attempted to become more familiar with the examiner and often asked questions that pushed the boundaries of the relationship, but never quite went beyond the bounds of decorum. When asked about his recent episode of being caught for a "break and enter," Jason denied any direct involvement and stated that he was only waiting outside for his friend. He was upset that the police would not believe him.

REASON FOR REFERRAL

Given Jason's escalating behaviors, there were concerns that Jason might act out to the extent that he would have to leave the Belcour home and be placed with juvenile justice. A comprehensive assessment was requested to determine what was causing Jason's recent behaviors and how best to intervene on his behalf.

ASSESSMENT RESULTS

Although Jason's responses to the WISC-III revealed an overall level of intellectual functioning within the "Average range" (Full Scale IQ Range 99-107), this global picture did little to represent the wide range of scatter on his profile. There was a 16-point discrepancy between his Verbal IQ (95) and his Performance IQ (111), and the gap was even wider when the Verbal Comprehension Index (SS = 100) was compared to the Perceptual Organization Index (SS = 119). Freedom from Distractibility (SS = 75) was a significant area of weakness, and Processing Speed (SS = 86) also surfaced as an area of weakness. Jason demonstrates some surprising strengths, given several years of interrupted schooling and lack of consistent exposure to formal education. Scores in areas of general knowledge, abstract reasoning, vocabulary development, and practical reasoning were all within the average range for his age.

Jason's High Average to Superior ability in areas of Perceptual Organization (IQ Range 114-125) suggests skills well above the expected level for his age in areas of: attention to visual detail (perceptive/observation skills), understanding the nuances of social interaction, and solving visual puzzles (all above the

90th percentile). A significant weakness was noted in his ability to copy symbols within a given time frame, a task that was only at the 9th percentile.

Further assessment with the Wide Range Assessment of Memory and Learning (WRAML) revealed that despite excellent visual problem-solving skills, Jason had a very weak memory for visual sequence (1st percentile), which often is associated with poor spelling. Considering the memory weakness in conjunction with poor copying speed, it was not surprising that Jason would be highly frustrated and resistant to producing written work. Academically, although Jason was currently enrolled in Grade 10, he was functioning at the following levels according to the WRAT-3: Decoding, Grade 8; Spelling, Grade 4; and Math calculations at a Grade 6 level. Reading comprehension and speed of reading were at a mid Grade 6 range.

Jason and his foster mother completed the Jesness Inventory and the Jesness Behavior Checklist. Although Jason presented as a candid and cooperative respondent, there were wide and significant discrepancies between his self-rating scales and ratings completed by his foster mother. The profiles presented a mirror image: According to Jason, all behaviors were within the Average to High Average Positive range; according to his foster mother, the majority of behaviors were well below average, in the very negative range. Mrs. Belcour endorsed the following behaviors below the second percentile: ability to take responsibility for his actions; ability to avoid engaging others in negative inter-actions; lack of depression/withdrawal; lack of stealing; lack of adherence to rules; weak frustration tolerance/resistance to teasing, and more. According to Mrs. Belcour, only two areas of behavior were within the normative range: independence and sociability.

In addition to weak agreement between ratings on the Jesness scales, ratings on the Depression and Anxiety Scales for Youth (DAYS) revealed self-ratings for depression (16th percentile) and anxiety (50th percentile) to be within normative expectations, compared to his foster mother's clinically significant ratings for Depression (98th percentile) and Anxiety (91st percentile).

POST-CASE QUESTIONS

1. Jason's intellectual profile presents several possible implications regarding his overall approach to problem solving that may be highly relevant to his interaction with others. As a youth who is highly observant (Picture Completion S = 15), Jason's hyper-vigilance may cause him to select the best features of others, or may result in tendencies to be overly critical of perceived flaws or weaknesses in others. Jason is also very aware of the subtle nuances

in social relations (Picture Arrangement S = 15), and at its best, this skill could result in Jason being able to lead others in a positive direction. In the worst scenario, these skills could provide a strong base to influence others in a more negative direction, through "conning" or manipulation of others.

Discuss the above suggestions and any other features of Jason's cognitive style that might impact on his social relationships.

2. The following is an excerpt from the psychologist's written report concerning Jason:

> Jason's responses to the Jesness Inventory suggest that he may utilize his strong visual perceptive skills in ways which may be highly effective in a manipulative and controlling manner. Jason's profile suggests a tendency to perceive the world in terms of power and control, both in very subtle ways and in ways which may be more directive in their controlling influence. At the extreme, the use of manipulation may be used to satisfy his own needs and in this manner, become satisfying in and of itself. To this end, misbehavior may be evident in "conning," or deception which is often a means of self gratification in its ability to "outsmart" others. Unfortunately, given Jason's intellectual capacity, his strong skills may be misdirected towards influencing others who may not be his intellectual equal. Jason's Jesness Profile also suggests strong tendencies towards denial of responsibility for actions/consequences of his behaviors.

Discuss the above with reference to how the following models would interpret Jason's underlying processes: biomedical, psychodynamic, family systems, cognitive, behavioral, and theories of attachment and parenting. Include references to how these processes would interact with various developmental contexts: individual, family and school, social and economic, and cultural.

3. The psychologist felt that history would predict that in times of perceived change or uncertainty, Jason would act out in a misdemeanor roughly equivalent in intensity to the amount of anxiety he was feeling. Furthermore, since thefts involved large amounts of money taken from the foster household, it was important to look at what changes or perceived changes were happening in that environment: the introduction of a new foster child; a pending move farther out into the country; impact of turning 16 as a potential threat to loss of his foster placement. Discuss how these factors might be explained in driving Jason's self-defeating behaviors.

4. Develop case formulations for Jason from three different perspectives. How might you integrate community resources in your treatment planning for Jason?

ISSUES IN TREATMENT

One issue in determining appropriate treatment for a conduct disordered (CD) youth involves how to conceptualize CD relative to oppositional defiant disorder (ODD). Should these behaviors be conceptualized along a continuum of disruptive behavior disorders, or be considered as two separate disorders? In support of a continuum theory, it can be argued that ODD occurs earlier (usually in preschool) and is a milder form of CD, which occurs later (middle childhood or adolescent onset). However, two bodies of research evidence support retaining two separate identities for these disorders. Although 90% of youth with CD also had ODD, only 25% of all children with ODD go on to develop CD (Rey, 1993). Furthermore, a meta factor analytic study by Frick and his colleagues (1993) revealed behavior clusters that would be more supportive of the two-disorder distinction with ODD type behaviors of aggression and opposition representing more overt and nondestructive forms of behavior, versus property and status violations or covert and destructive behaviors more typical of CD behaviors. With respect to the case study, Jason's conduct in the past 6 months had involved aggression (fighting at school), theft, breaking into someone's house, conning others, lying to avoid punishment, and staying out all night. These behaviors are of sufficient magnitude to warrant a diagnosis of conduct disorder according to the *DSM* criteria.

The previous discussion of empirically supported treatments for behaviorally disordered children (see Case Study 2: Scott) revealed that parent training programs can be an effective way of treating children with ODD. What about youth with more serious forms of CD? Few treatments have demonstrated effectiveness with this difficult-to-serve population, and furthermore, some treatments involving peer aggregation have been found to have iatrogenic effects. Frick (2001) suggests that based on our current understanding of the complexity of CD, in order for treatment to be effective it must attempt to address the vast range of factors within the child (genetic and environmental history) and within the child's developmental contexts (family, school, societal and economic, cultural) that serve to precipitate and maintain the symptoms. In addition, Frick emphasizes the need to individualize the treatment, taking into account the developmental pathway involved. Frick cites the FAST Track Program (McMahon & Slough, 1996) and MST (Borduin, Mann, Cone, & Henggeler, 1995; Henggeler, Schoenwald, Borduin, Rowland, & Cunningham, 1998) as having considerable promise to deliver this type of intervention. Increasing emphasis on community-based interventions has generated recent research initiatives comparing community-based treatment alternatives. Further support for the importance of including community-based resources in this difficult-to-serve population can be found in studies by Chamberlain and Reid (1991, 1998) and Wilmshurst (2002). Chamberlain and Reid (1991, 1998) found that juveniles assigned to specialized foster care programs (SFC) were more successful than peers assigned to residential treatment centers or family/relatives homes; Wilmshurst (2002) found significantly better outcomes for youth with severe emotional and behavioral problems when the youth received interventions provided by family preservation workers in the home, compared to youth who were removed to a 5-day residential program for treatment. Furthermore, the Wilmshurst study found that while children and youth in the community-based program demonstrated significant improvement in all areas one year post treatment, youth who had attended the residential program revealed poorer outcomes and significant increases in internalizing symptoms (e.g., depression).

Recently, several theorists have turned to attachment theory to assist in understanding the disturbed interpersonal relations of youth with CD. There is an emerging body of literature addressing the relationship of attachment theory to traumatic experiences (see Cassidy & Mohr, 2001, for review). According to Bowlby's (1988) adaptation theory, human infants are pre-wired to form early attachments to maintain proximity with their caregivers to ensure their survival and protection in times of fear. In a secure relationship, the infant uses the caregiver as a point of social referencing: a secure base from which to explore. However, the security of these early attachments can vary widely. Based on early experiences, defining relationships as either responsive and secure or as nonresponsive and insecure, the infant develops an *internal working model* or template of expectations for future relationships.

Through the use of the "strange situation," Ainsworth, Blehar, Waters, and Wall (1978) were able to measure the quality of infant-mother attachments by observing babies' responses to a stranger in their mothers' absence and subsequent behaviors when reunited with their mothers. Initially, Ainsworth's research suggested three possible attachment styles: secure, insecure-avoidant, and insecure-ambivalent. Matching these infant responses to maternal behaviors, Main (1990) suggests that infants adapt their behaviors to maximize the opportunity to maintain proximity to their caregiver. Therefore, avoidant babies have learned that avoidant behaviors will maintain proximity to caregivers who are uncomfortable with closeness, while ambivalent babies have learned that excess distress is needed in order to maximize the caregiver's response.

In their work with traumatized infants, Main and Solomon (1986) discovered a set of behaviors that did not fit any of Ainsworth's categories. Unlike normal infants who seek security and proximity to the caregiver in times of stress, traumatized infants were demonstrating distress or fright in the caregiver's presence. They identified these random disoriented behaviors as "disorganized behavior," including such behaviors as: contradictory behaviors, odd movements, freezing, fear responses, and/or incomplete movements. Furthermore, Main and Hesse (1990) have suggested that disorganized behaviors can later manifest in relationships as controlling behaviors based on hostile and punitive control or on oversolicitous control. The need for attachment is highly activated during times of stress when the normal infant seeks solace through proximity to the caregiver. For the disorganized infant, however, fear sets up an approach-avoidance conflict, where infants simultaneously seek to attach and to flee the caregiver. Situations that have been linked to the development of disorganized attachment behaviors include those in which the parent is viewed as frightening, as in child abuse (Lyons-Ruth & Jacobvitz, 1999) or as frightened, as in cases of unresolved loss or trauma (Main & Hesse, 1990). Another possible pathway to disorganized behavior may involve infant temperament and arousal level (see Spangler & Grossmann, 1999, for a review). Research from a biomedical perspective has suggested that children with disorganized attachment patterns demonstrate a greater rise and maintenance of elevated cortisol levels when placed in the strange-situation test environment. With the advent of position emission tomography (PET) and magnetic resonance imaging (MRI), investigators began to link attachment theory to neurological development. Studies by Chiron, Jambaque, and Nabbout (1997) suggest that the right brain is dominant at a time (first 3 years of life) when attachment formation is a predominant developmental task. To support the connection between caregiver and brain response, studies have demonstrated that EEGs of infants whose mothers are depressed mirror their mother's right frontal asymmetries (Field, Fox, Pickens, & Nawrocki, 1995). Clearly, further research is indicated in this area.

Based upon work with children in the foster care system, Steinhauer (1998) suggests that precursors of neglect, abuse, and/or multiple moves, and/or caregivers set the stage for a reactive attachment disorder resulting in attachment resistant children. These children will develop pseudo-relationships with others that on the surface appear engaging, but in actuality are highly manipulative and self-serving, lacking the warmth and empathy necessary to sustain any true bonding. When adults attempt to encourage closeness, these children will become anxious and attempt to erect barriers through withdrawal or will invite punishment and subsequent rejection. The attachment resistant youth may develop intimacy avoidant behaviors that impact on another person and ultimately sabotage any possibilities for mutual reciprocity. Examples of attachment-disordered behaviors of CD children include behaviors that involve contact without allowing reciprocity: manipulation, promiscuity, instigating conflict, and theft. Steinhauer (1996) argues for consideration of attachment disorder as an Axis 2 diagnosis. According to Steinhauer, it is imperative that treatment for conduct disordered youth recognize the underlying dynamics of disturbed attachment responsible for creating a self-defeating working model focused on: self-concept as worthless/unacceptable; perception of others as unavailable/abusive; and an inability to self-soothe or turn to others for comfort. Although there is minimal empirical support regarding interventions for youth with CD that is based on attachment theory, a program developed by Holland, Moretti, Verlaan, and Peterson (1993) has produced some encouraging results.

REFERENCES

Ainsworth, M. D., Blehar, M., Waters, E., & Wall, S. (1978). *Patterns of attachment.* Hillsdale, NJ: Lawrence Erlbaum.

Borduin, C. M., Mann, B. J., Cone, L. T., & Henggeler, S. W. (1995). *Family therapy and beyond: A multisystemic approach to treating the behavior problems of children and adolescents.* Pacific Grove, CA: Brooks/Cole.

Bowlby, J. (1988). *A secure base.* New York: Basic Books.

Cassidy, J., & Mohr, J. J. (2001). Unresolved fear, trauma and psychopathology: Theory, research and clinical considerations related to disorganized attachment across the life span. *Clinical Psychology Science Practice, 8,* 275-298.

Chamberlain, P., & Reid, J. (1991). Using a specialized foster care community treatment model for children and adolescents leaving the state mental hospital. *Journal of Community Psychology, 19,* 266-276.

Chamberlain, P., & Reid, J. (1998). Comparison of two community alternatives to incarceration for chronic juvenile offenders. *Journal of Consulting and Clinical Psychology, 66,* 624-633.

Chiron, C., Jambaque, I., & Nabbout, R. (1997). The right brain hemisphere is dominant in human infants. *Brain, 120,* 1057-1065.

Field, T., Fox, N., Pickens, J., & Nawrocki, T. (1995). Relative right frontal EEG activation in 3- to 6-month-old infants of depressed mothers. *Developmental Psychology, 31,* 358-363.

Frick, P. J. (2001). Effective interventions for children and adolescents with conduct disorder. *Canadian Journal of Psychiatry, 46,* 597-608.

Frick, P. J., Lahey, B. B., Loeber, R., Tannenbaum, L., Van Horn, Y., Christ, M. A., Hart, E. L., & Hanson, K. (1993). Oppositional defiant disorder and conduct disorder: A meta-analytic review of factor analyses and cross-validation in a clinic sample. *Clinical Psychology Review, 13,* 319-340.

Henggeler, S. W., Schoenwald, S. K., Borduin, C. M., Rowland, M. D., & Cunningham, R. B. (1998). *Multisystemic treatment of antisocial behavior in children and adolescents.* New York: Guilford.

Holland, R., Moretti, M. M., Verlaan, V., & Peterson, S. (1993). Attachment and conduct disorder: The response program. *Canadian Journal of Psychiatry, 38,* 420-431.

Lyons-Ruth, K., & Jacobvitz, D. (1999). Attachment disorganization: Unresolved loss, relational violence and lapses in behavioral and attentional strategies. In J. Cassidy & P. R. Shaver (Eds.), *Handbook of attachment: Theory, research, and clinical applications* (pp. 520-554). New York: Guilford.

Main, M. (1990). Cross-cultural studies of attachment organization: Recent studies, changing methodologies, and the concept of conditional strategies. *Human Development, 33,* 48-61.

Main, M., & Hesse, E. (1990). Parents' unresolved traumatic experiences are related to infant disorganized attachment status: Is frightened and/or frightening parental behavior the linking mechanism? In M. T. Greensberg, D. Cicchetti, & E. M. Cummings (Eds.), *Attachment in the preschool years: Theory, research, and intervention* (pp. 161-182). Chicago: University of Chicago Press.

Main, M., & Solomon, J. (1986). Discovery of an insecure-disorganized/disoriented attachment pattern: Procedures, findings and implications for the classification of behavior. In T. B. Brazelton & M. Yogman (Eds.), *Affective development in infancy* (pp. 95-124). Norwood, NJ: Ablex.

McMahon, R. J., & Slough, N. M. (1996). Family-based intervention in the FAST Track Program. In R. deV. Peters & R. J. McMahon (Ed.), *Preventing childhood disorders, substance abuse, and delinquency.* Thousand Oaks, CA: Sage.

Rey, J. M. (1993). Oppositional defiant disorder. *American Journal of Psychiatry, 150,* 1769-1777.

Spangler, G., & Grossmann, K. (1999). Individual and physiological correlates of attachment disorganization in infancy. In J. Solomon & C. George (Eds.), *Attachment disorganization* (pp. 95-126). New York: Guilford.

Steinhauer, P. D. (1996). The diagnosis, prevention and management of attachment disorders in children. *P.R.I.S.M.E., 6,* 604-617. (Original in French)

Steinhauer, P. D. (1998). *Separation and attachment—Treatment issues.* Paper presented to The Children's Aid Society of the County of Perth, Stratford, Ontario.

Wilmshurst, L. (2002). Treatment programs for youth with emotional and behavioral disorders: An outcome study of two alternate approaches. *Mental Health Services Research, 4*(2), 85-96.

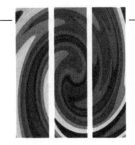

Case 14: Neesha Williams

Phoenix Rising: A Story of Resilience

Neesha Williams, a 10-year-old African American girl, was referred for assessment to the school psychologist as a result of a child study team meeting held at the school in May 2001. Presenting problems included poor school progress and escalating behavioral concerns. It was the school's impression that Neesha might qualify for special education assistance as a child with an emotional disorder. Currently, Neesha has an older brother attending another school in a special program for emotionally disturbed children.

DEVELOPMENTAL HISTORY/FAMILY BACKGROUND

The school social worker completed Neesha's initial work-up just prior to the end of the academic term; intake information is summarized as follows. Neesha lives with her 13-year-old brother, Steven, and her mother in a two-bedroom apartment. The social worker described the apartment as tiny but very well kept. Neesha has her own bedroom, and Steven sleeps on the couch, which folds out into a bed. The social worker noted that it was difficult to book an appointment with Mrs. Williams, who was reportedly working two jobs: cleaning offices and working as a hair stylist. Mrs. Williams graduated from hairstylist classes last year. Although her career as a hairstylist has a lot of potential, she is only beginning to develop a clientele. She also works part-time cleaning offices when her sister is unable to work. Despite the lack of financial resources, the children were clean, well dressed, and did not miss any meals. The children were on the free lunch program at the school. According to Mrs. Williams, Neesha's early history was unremarkable and motor and language milestones developed on schedule.

An immediate concern of the social worker's centered around who cared for the children when their mother, Tanya, had to work evenings cleaning offices. Tanya stated that it was not a problem for her because she would either send the children to her sister's apartment a few blocks away, or have a cousin who lived in the building check in on the kids. Also, Steven was 13 so he was capable of watching his sister.

Neesha's mother described Neesha as an easy baby and said that she never really had any problems with her. She added that it was Steven who was giving her all the problems, not Neesha. Neesha's father, Tyrone, left the family about 3 years ago, when Neesha was in Grade 1. At that time, they had to move because Tanya could no longer afford to live in the apartment they had. Neesha was very upset with the marriage breakdown and misses her father very much. Tyrone has since moved in with his girlfriend and they now have a one-year-old baby. Neesha has visited with her dad and his new family on a few occasions, but is very disappointed that the visits are neither consistent nor more frequent. According to Tanya, Neesha often talks about wanting to see her father and continues to set herself up for disappointment.

Tanya described the previous 2 years as very difficult for her and the kids. As Tanya spoke, the social worker noted on the file that the mother's affect was very flat. She also seemed preoccupied with her financial situation and said, at times, she just wasn't sure she would make the rent. They have struggled to survive financially, and Tanya often gets depressed and either goes to bed early or cries herself to sleep. On these occasions, Neesha is very quiet and tries to comfort her mother. Tanya said that when she woke up the other morning, Neesha had placed a handmade card on her pillow. The card was decorated with hearts and bows and huge letters: "I love you, Mom. Neesha." Tanya said she didn't understand why Neesha was doing so poorly in school, because she seemed to love to "play school" on the weekends and in the evening. When asked about Neesha's behavior problems, Tanya said she is not a behavior problem at home. Her brother is the problem; Neesha is more like a little adult. She described Neesha as a sweet and loving child who always tries to please.

The social worker expressed her concern to Tanya about her own symptoms of depression and fatigue, and wondered if Tanya might see her physician for a referral to talk to a counselor. The social worker stated that she was concerned because Tanya seemed overwhelmed by all the financial stresses the family faced that seemed to be taking their toll on her, emotionally. However, Tanya was quick to say that she had a very supportive family and that her two sisters were always there for her to talk to when she needed it. She also said that her church was a continued source of comfort and support for herself and the children. In addition to information obtained from the clinical interview, the social worker also had Tanya complete the Behavioral Assessment System for Children (BASC).

In August, at the beginning of the new term, the school psychologist completed a review of Neesha's cumulative school record and obtained teacher BASC ratings from her previous years' teachers, which were on file in the guidance office. Neesha's school record contained the following additional information. Neesha began her formal schooling at Franklin Elementary School but transferred schools midway through the Grade 1 program. She completed Grade 1 and Grade 2 at Vista Springs Elementary. She has been attending Heartfield Elementary since her enrollment in the Grade 3 Program. Neesha is currently repeating the fourth grade. Neesha's records reveal that her Grade 3 teacher was concerned because Neesha was repeatedly falling asleep in class. As a result, Neesha's mother apparently took Neesha to a physician; however, no medical reason was evident to explain her fatigue. Last year, Neesha was absent 15 days. On the days she attended school, Neesha was late more than one third of the time (51 days). Classroom observations conducted at that time revealed Neesha to be off-task for the majority of time, and work was not completed or handed in. On one independent classroom observation, Neesha completed only 4 out of 25 items assigned for seatwork in a 25-minute span. Neesha's lack of attention to task could also result in class-disturbing behaviors such as humming, playing with articles on her desk, and socializing. Interventions included sending a daily agenda regarding Neesha's behavior for home signature, providing extra time for task completion, and seating proximity to the teacher's desk. Ultimately, the decision was made to have Neesha repeat the Grade 4 program, since she had not completed any assigned tasks during her Grade 3 year.

The school psychologist saw Neesha for an initial assessment session. Neesha was very well groomed, with matching accessories and her hair stylishly braided in a way that must have taken hours to complete. When asked about her hair, Neesha was very proud to say that her mother had done it for her, and that her mother was a very good hairdresser. Neesha was very polite and cooperative. Neesha's responses and demeanor suggested a precocious maturity for her 10 years. The psychologist felt that Neesha tried her best on all tasks presented, but questioned the validity of overall Intellectual scores.

REASON FOR REFERRAL

The school was requesting assessment due to Neesha's escalating academic and behavioral problems. There were concerns that Neesha might warrant placement in a program for children with emotional problems.

ASSESSMENT RESULTS

Information concerning specific assessment instruments can be found in Appendix C.

Responses to the Wechsler Intelligence Scale for Children-III revealed Neesha's overall Intellectual Score of 92, which was within the Average range (IQ Range 87–98). However, there were several indicators to suggest that this score was likely an underestimate of her "true potential." Neesha's mature conversational tone, insight, and academic levels obtained on standardized testing suggested intellectual functioning more appropriately suited to the upper Average to High Average range.

Based on her overall obtained score, Neesha performed in the Average range of ability at the 30th percentile when compared with children her age. A 5-point difference between the Verbal (IQ = 90) and Performance (IQ = 95) sections was not significant. Based on this score, she would be expected to be performing approximately at grade level. An analysis of the individual pattern of test results indicated that Neesha had relative strengths in the areas of Freedom from Distractibility, which involves the manipulation of mental information and short-term working memory and processing speed, measuring speed, and accuracy of completing written tasks. An analysis of the individual pattern of subtest scores indicated that Neesha had relative strengths in the sequencing of visual-social information and in mental arithmetic. Weaknesses were noted in vocabulary development, social judgment, and part-to-whole visual organization (puzzle completion).

Academically, according to the Woodcock Johnson III Test of Achievement, Neesha's current functioning levels were far in excess of her current grade placement and also exceeded predicted levels according to the WISC-III (which was considered as an underestimate of her intellectual potential). Overall, Neesha was performing at a Grade 7.2 level in Broad Reading (Age Score of 12.7); 5.8 level in Broad Math (Age Score 11.4); and Grade 7.9 in Broad Written Expression (Age Score 13.2). Overall, Neesha was achieving in the High Average range when scores were compared with those of other children her age, who would be enrolled in a regular Grade 5 Program. When compared with other children enrolled in a Regular Grade 4 Program (which Neesha was currently repeating), her scores represented functioning in the Superior range.

Neesha was cooperative during the clinical interview, and provided thoughtful and conscientious responses to the interviewer's questions. When asked what types of things or situations made her feel happy, sad, angry, or frightened, Neesha provided the following information. Neesha stated that "compliments, surprises, and visits with her Dad" were all things that could make her "happy." She said she felt "sad" when kids threaten her or people say bad things about her or her family. She also stated that she gets very sad when her mother cries, because she doesn't know how to make it better. Neesha looked sad as she spoke about her mother, and her voice trailed off as she swallowed hard. Neesha admitted to feeling angry and upset when her older brother (13 years of age) hits her, and she is "frightened" when she visits her aunt's neighborhood, because the kids are loud and scary. In response to what worries her presently, Neesha said that she is worried that she won't be able to advance to the fifth grade this year. She said that she asked her mother to talk to the principal because she is working very hard and wants to go to Grade 5.

When asked why she was falling asleep in class, Neesha said that in the past she had lots of problems falling asleep, but added that was 2 years ago and things were different then. She said that at that time she would come home from school very tired and fall asleep after dinner. Then she would wake up at night and not be able to go to sleep again. She said that she has stopped taking naps in the afternoon and now she doesn't wake up at night anymore. Neesha volunteered that she also worried a lot about things and that sometimes when she worries she has a hard time falling asleep. Not so much now, but it was bad then because she missed her dad and wanted him to come home. She said that last year she got in trouble for being late so many times, but it was hard to wake up. Neesha said that she was tired and had trouble getting herself ready for school. Her mom was sleeping late because she was working more nights cleaning the offices. Neesha said it was a very hard year. She was tired and cranky and just couldn't seem to concentrate on her work. She said she would read a page and then not remember what she read. Neesha said that she got so far behind that she just gave up. When I asked what made the difference this year. Neesha said, for one, she now has an alarm clock. She sets the clock and lets her mom sleep in. The school bus picks the kids up on the corner, so she just goes and waits with the other kids who live in the apartment building.

When asked about schoolwork, Neesha stated that she was very proud of her reading ability and said that she is now concentrating on finishing her work and that keeps her going.

Neesha completed several self-report inventories. Overall response to the Revised Children's Manifest Anxiety Scale (RCMAS) revealed total anxiety to be within normal limits. However, there was a significant elevation on the Physiological Indicator Scale, and Neesha endorsed several items indicating a generalized heightened state of arousal often associated with stressful conditions, such as: trouble getting her breath, feeling sick to her stomach, and hands feeling sweaty. She also admitted to worrying a lot of the time, and having problems falling asleep. An elevated validity scale (the Lie Scale on the RCMAS) was suggestive of Neesha's tendency to try to project a good image. Neesha's responses to the Children's Depression Inventory (CDI) revealed overall depression level to be within the norm when compared to girls of a similar age. However, the elevation on the Negative Mood Scale was significant, indicating problems with sleeping, fatigue, and worry about aches and pains. Neesha also completed the Personality Inventory for Youth (PIY), a 270-item questionnaire that assesses emotional and behavioral adjustment and family characteristics and interactions, as well as school adjustment. The instrument also includes validity scales that identify a respondent's level of consistency and/or defensiveness. Neesha's scores on the validity scales suggest that her profile was an honest attempt to reflect her current emotional and behavioral concerns. Scores indicated normal concerns typical of girls her age in most areas. However, consistent with the RCMAS, Neesha endorsed a significant number of items indicating Somatic Concern (T = 73). Scores in this range suggest a large and varied number of somatic symptoms and health concerns such as: fatigue, headache, stomachache, back pain, dizzy spells, trouble breathing, and the like. Results of this kind are often seen in children who worry about and are preoccupied with illness and may become emotionally upset when they are sick. Often these symptoms represent the physical aspects of anxiety and tension. Neesha's particular pattern of endorsement suggests that symptoms are likely connected to feelings of psychological distress within the home.

Projective assessment was also conducted. The characters in Neesha's stories, developed in responses to the Robert's Apperception Test, revealed difficulties in the following areas: conflicts with siblings, fear of being punished for doing something wrong, fear of being ill, and concerns regarding school performance. Family matters included a mother having a new baby and a young girl being a bridesmaid for her parents' wedding. Neesha's drawings for the House-Tree-Person indicated a positive openness to communication and were generally free of suggested pathology.

Two of Neesha's teachers from last year, her current teacher, and her mother completed the Behavioral Assessment System for Children (BASC). It should be noted that although the BASC suggests that rating be conducted by individuals who have known the child for at least 6 months, the desire to have a current behavioral rating for comparison violated this suggestion since her current teacher has known Neesha only since the beginning of August (less than 2 months). Therefore, results should be interpreted with caution. The BASC is a comprehensive measurement of common behavioral and emotional problems in children. Ratings of children are interpreted to indicate behavioral concerns that are normal, at risk, or clinical. Behaviors falling within the At-Risk range represent an emerging problem area that needs attention but does not warrant a formal diagnosis, while behaviors within the Clinical range are problem that warrant attention and intervention. It should be noted that these ratings are based on the observations and interpretations of the informant. It is not unusual for children to behave differently in various situations. Therefore, inconsistencies between informants are not unusual. According to Neesha's teachers last year, there was agreement in several areas on the BASC ratings. The two teachers rated her behaviors as Clinically Significant in the following areas: Aggression (physical and verbal), Conduct Problems (rule breaking behaviors), and overall Externalizing Problems. They also agreed that the following behaviors were At Risk: Attention Problems, Leadership, Social Skills, and Study Skills. At-Risk or Clinically Significant elevations were also noted for: Composite Adaptive Skills (Adaptability, Social Skills, Leadership, Study Skills). Neesha's current teacher and Neesha's mother have indicated all behaviors currently to be within the Normal range.

In the final assessment session, Neesha appeared very positive about her school successes this year and said that she was working very hard to go to the next grade level. When asked if she would like to meet with the school psychologist once in a while, just to talk about her worries, Neesha said that she would like that very much. As she left the office, she turned and thanked the psychologist for working with her, and added, "You know, sometimes, it's hard being a kid."

When Neesha's mother came to talk to the school psychologist about the test results, the psychologist mirrored the social worker's earlier concerns about mother being depressed and preoccupied. Affect was very flat despite the excellent news she was receiving regarding her daughter's academic skills and behavioral turnaround. Her mother reported that what Neesha had accomplished, she had done on her own. She stated that Neesha had received no help from her. Mother appeared preoccupied with the interview making her late for work and asked if she could please leave quickly.

POST SCRIPT

Three weeks later, at 10:00 am, the school principal received a call from Neesha's mother, who asked that her daughter not be sent home from school because she was going to kill herself. As she spoke on the telephone, she explained that she was holding a loaded gun to her head and that she had to do it, because she was not going to make this month's rent. She could not take it any longer, but she did not want Neesha to come home and find her dead. While the guidance counselor continued to keep mother talking, the school contacted the police, who apprehended mom while was talking on her cell phone from her car in the driveway of the apartment building. The loaded gun was on her lap. Mother was Baker Acted (taken into custody due to fears regarding danger to self) and taken to the local psychiatric facility. Currently, mother is on medication for depression.

POST-CASE QUESTIONS

1. In discussing the plight of resilient children, Luthar (1993) contrasts earlier concepts of the invulnerable child with present concepts of the resilient child. Luthar observed that children who survived difficult circumstances without developing maladaptive outcomes often presented with more subtle internalizing problems. In Luthar's study, 85% of the resilient children had clinically significant symptoms of anxiety and depression. Similarly, longitudinal data from studies by Werner and Smith (1992), also noted that resilient children in adulthood were plagued with somatic complaints (headaches, backaches) and feelings of dissatisfaction.

Discuss Neesha's current clinical profile in light of the information provided by these studies on resilience.

2. In a study of developmental response patterns to maternal depression, Solantaus-Simula (2002) found four response patterns: active empathy, emotional overinvolvement, indifference, and avoidance. Of the four types, children in the emotional overinvolvement and avoidance groups demonstrated the most internalizing and externalizing symptoms, independent of mother's level of depression. Furthermore, children in the active empathy group fared best. They did not feel guilty about their parent's depression and were able to discriminate their experiences from those of the depressed parent, supporting Beardslee's theory (1989) of the protective function of self-understanding. The most

common response to maternal depression in the active group was to make some effort to cheer up the parent.

Discuss these findings in relation to Neesha's case.

3. The way in which a child responds to distress can be strongly influenced by the cultural context in which the circumstance is embedded.

Discuss this comment with respect to Neesha's case.

ISSUES IN TREATMENT

Considering Neesha's case within the framework of developmental contexts and environmental influences, there are several risk factors that are impacting on her development that are not within Neesha's immediate control, including poverty and her mother's mental illness.

Several researchers have focused on the role of protective factors in buffering some children living in high-risk environments. Emphasis has shifted from focusing on risks to determining environmental resources and adaptive strengths in children who do not show early signs of deviance (Richters & Weintraub, 1990). Rutter (1987) noted several years ago that instead of searching for broadly defined protective factors, emphasis needed to be placed on better understanding "why and how some individuals manage to maintain high self-esteem and self-efficacy in spite of facing the same adversities that lead other people to give up and lose hope" (p. 317). Further, Rutter (1990) suggests that we go beyond listing risk factors to looking at the underlying processes or mechanisms that are instrumental in producing the buffering effect. Rutter defines these processes as: reduction of risk impact, reduction of negative chain reactions, factors that promote self-esteem and opening of opportunities. The role of timing (life events) in changing the trajectory away from vulnerability is also discussed.

Durlak (1998) reviewed 1,200 outcome studies concerning prevention programs for children and identified several common risk and protective factors across eight major outcome areas: behavior problems, school failure, poor physical health, physical injury, pregnancy, drug use, and AIDS. Analysis of risk and protective factors linked each factor with the appropriate developmental context, including: individual, immediate (family, school, peers), and community. Durlak found multiple factors playing a protective role for more than one outcome. For example, attending a "high quality school" protected against behavior problems, school failure, early pregnancy, drug use, and AIDS, and having "positive peer models" also protected across the same five areas. Having a good parent-child relationship and good personal and social skills protected across all eight major outcomes. High risk factors included: living in an impoverished neighborhood, low family SES, parental psychopathology, marital discord, and punitive parenting. Stress was considered to be a risk factor that crossed all levels of development, while social support was a protective factor that crossed all developmental levels.

When discussing risk and protective factors, the risks of being in an ethnic minority have rarely been addressed. Gibbs and Huang (2001) emphasize that when ethnic identity is combined with membership in a minority race, children are faced with a dual challenge. The authors also note that ethnic minority status has often been associated with restricted range of opportunities, and children growing up in minority families may be exposed to circumstances and experiences very different from the majority of the community. In addition, there is often an interaction among factors of ethnicity, race, and social class (SES), with upper status comprised of white, Anglo-Saxon, middle-class families, and lower status associated with nonwhite, ethnic minority, and lower-class families (Hacker, 1992). According to the 1994 census, approximately 43% of African American youth under 18 years of age live below the poverty line (U.S. Bureau of the Census, 1996). Within this context, the role of the family has assumed a position of strength and resilience. One central value that is cultivated by African American families is the importance of being "independent" and the value of independence. In this manner, the family unit is sustained by members who are self-reliant. Other strong family values often include: obedience, respect for elders, and emphasis on obtaining a good education. However, culture clash may be evident in the way in which family members or children whose sense of time is fluid and event oriented interact with largely white establishments where time is determined by the clock, calendar, or school agenda (Lynch & Hanson, 1998).

The importance of considering cultural context in determining child abuse and neglect is an area that has had little research emphasis. Aptekar and Stocklin (1997) discuss the need to recognize ethnocentric perspectives in defining abuse and neglect. According to the authors, the way in which a child responds to trauma can be strongly influenced by the cultural context in which the circumstance is embedded. Children can respond to difficult circumstances by developing extreme forms of psychopathology or improved mental health. Children who grow up in less-than-ideal conditions may accept these conditions as part of the "normalcy" of their life and learn to cope with what they have. Others may develop a sense of positive self-esteem and independence that may serve to buffer them from more negative outcomes (Cicchetti & Rogosch, 1997).

REFERENCES

Aptekar, L., & Stocklin, D. (1997) Children in particularly difficult circumstances. In J. Berry, P. Dasen, & T. S. Saraswathi (Eds.), *Handbook of cross-cultural psychology: Vol. 2. Basic processes and human development* (2nd ed., pp. 377-412). Needham Heights, MA: Allyn & Bacon.

Beardslee, W. R. (1989). The role of self-understanding in resilient individuals: The development of a perspective. *American Journal of Orthopsychiatry, 59,* 266-278.

Cicchetti, D., & Rogosch, F. A. (1997). The role of self-organization in the promotion of resilience in maltreated children. *Development and Psychopathology, 9,* 797-815.

Durlak, J. A. (1998). Common risk and protective factors in successful prevention programs. *American Journal of Orthopsychiatry, 68,* 512-520.

Gibbs, J. T., & Huang, L. N. (2001). Framework for the psychological assessment and treatment of minority youth. In J. T. Gibbs & L. N. Huang (Eds.), *Children of color* (pp. 112-142). San Francisco: Jossey-Bass.

Hacker, A. (1992). *Two nations: Black & white, separate, hostile, unequal.* New York: Scribner.

Luthar, S. S. (1993). Annotation: Methodological and conceptual issues in research on childhood resilience. *Journal of Child Psychology and Psychiatry, 34,* 441-453.

Lynch, E. W., & Hanson, M. J. (1998). *Developing cross-cultural competence* (2nd ed.). Baltimore, MD: Brooks.

Richters, K., & Weintraub, S. (1990). Beyond diathesis: Toward an understanding of high-risk environments. In J. Rolf, A. Masten, D. Cicchetti, K. Nuechterlein, & S. Weintraub (Eds.), *Risk and protective factors in the development of psychopathology* (pp. 67-96). New York: Cambridge University Press.

Rutter, M. (1987). Psychosocial resilience and protective mechanisms. *American Journal of Orthopsychiatry, 57,* 316-330.

Rutter, M. (1990). Psychosocial resilience and protective mechanisms. In J. Rolf, A. Masten, D. Cicchetti, K. Nuechterlein, & S. Weintraub (Eds.), *Risk and protective factors in the development of psychopathology* (pp. 181-214). New York: Cambridge University Press.

Solantaus-Simula, T. (2002). Children's responses to low parental mood: Balancing between active empathy, overinvolvement, indifference, and avoidance. *Journal of American Academy of Child and Adolescent Psychiatry, 41,* 278-286.

U.S. Bureau of the Census. (1996). *Statistical abstract of the United States, 1996* (116th ed.). Washington, DC: U.S. Department of Commerce.

Werner, E. E., & Smith, R. S. (1992). *Overcoming the odds: High risk children from birth to adulthood.* Ithaca, NY: Cornell University Press.

Appendix A

Supplemental Case Information

Colby: Results from Psychological Testing

Results of the multimodal assessment battery are presented below in the form of standard scores, T scores, and/or percentiles. Interns will be expected to evaluate, interpret, and integrate findings to formulate a more refined diagnostic impression. Anecdotal comments from the clinic psychologist (e.g., comments on test behaviors, etc.) are presented in parenthesis whenever these comments might aid in interpretation of the findings. In addition, a list of endorsed items is provided for any scales (checklists & rating scales) elevated to clinical levels to facilitate interpretation of behavioral patterns within and across sources of information.

Results are presented in their entirety rather than in summarized form to provide the intern with maximum opportunity to develop independent skills in the analysis and synthesis of information from multiple sources.

General Cognitive (WISC-III) and Academic (WRAT-3)

Wechsler Intelligence Scale for Children—Third Edition (WISC-III)

Verbal Scale	SS	Performance Scale	SS		IQ/Index	%tile
Information	18	Picture Completion	18	Verbal IQ	150	99
Similarities	19	Coding	10	Performance IQ	141	99
Arithmetic	17	Picture Arrangement	17	Full Scale IQ	150	99
Vocabulary	19	Block Design	19	Verbal Comprehension	150	99
Comprehension	19	Object Assembly	17	Perceptual Organization	147	99
(Digit Span)	(14)	(Symbol Search)	(11)	Freedom from Distractibility	129	97
		(Mazes not given)		Processing Speed	104	61

Administrator Comments: Excellent speed and dexterity on puzzles & block design, intuitive holistic learner. Excellent effort, good sense of humor. Very articulate. Frustration evident on lower scored tasks.

Wide Range Achievement Test (WRAT-3)

Subject	Standard Score	%tile	Grade Level
Reading (Decoding)	134	99	Post High School
Spelling	131	98	Post High School
Arithmetic	122	93	High School

Administrator Comments: Fluent decoder, handwriting very difficult to read, awkward pencil grip. Arithmetic questions required extra paper to compute; used unusual strategies but got the correct answers.

Check Lists and Rating Scales

Checklists: Child Behavior Checklist (CBCL)/Teacher Report Form (TRF) and Youth Self-Report

Note: Bold-faced numbers indicate scales in the significant range. Individual items endorsed by the respondent are listed for each of the significant scales.

	CBCL (T Score)	TRF (T Score)	YSR (T Score)
Syndromes			
I Withdrawn	65	62	64
II Somatic	**72**	59	**72**

Tired, Aches, Headaches, Eye, Skin, Stomach (CBCL)   *Dizzy, Tired, Aches, Headaches, Nausea, Eye, Skin, Stomach* (YSR)

	CBCL	TRF	YSR
III Anxious/Depressed	**70**	62	63

Need to be perfect, Fearful, Others out to get him, Worthless, Self-conscious, Worries

	CBCL	TRF	YSR
IV Social Problems	50	54	50
V Thought Problems	**67**	58	61

Mind wanders off, Repeats things, Stares

	CBCL	TRF	YSR
VI Attention Problems	**70**	63	59

Problems with concentration, Restless, Confused, Day-dreams, Impulsive, Poor school work, Blank stares

	CBCL	TRF	YSR
VII Delinquent Behavior	50	53	50
VIII Aggressive Behavior	**65**	62	61
Total Internalizing	73	63	68
Total Externalizing	60	60	56
Total Problems	61	63	63

Other Problems:
Accident prone, Sleeps less, Stores stuff, Trouble sleeping

(Continued)

(Continued)

Competence Scales	CBCL	TRF	YSR
	Activities T = 48	Adaptive T = 39	Activities T = 55
	Social T = 55		Social T = 54
	School T = 39		

Anecdotal Comments–Teacher: Additional effort is needed, achievement below ability, weak study skills, inconsistent effort, assignments not completed, frequent lates. Good natured, well liked.

Conners Rating Scales

	Parent (CPRS-R:L) (T Score)	Teacher (CTRS-R:L) (T Score)	Youth (CASS:L) (T Score)
Oppositional	58	57	NA*
Cognitive Problems/ Inattention	62	72	60

Avoids/reluctant to engage in tasks of sustained mental effort, Fails to finish what he starts, Lacks interest in schoolwork

Hyperactivity	54	57	52
Anxious/Shy	44	67	NA
Perfectionism	48	46	NA
Social Problems	45	48	NA
Psychosomatic	72	NA	NA

Stomachaches; Aches & pains; Aches before school; Frequent complaints

Conners ADHD Index	57	68	63
Conners Global Index: Restless/Impulsive	65	64	NA
Conners Global Index Emotional Lability	67	79	NA

Temper; Easily frustrated; Quick mood swings

Conners Global Index Total	67	68	NA
DSM-IV: Inattentive	60	70	72

Note: Teacher & Youth agreed for same six items

*Careless errors, misses details-----------> **
Avoids sustained mental effort---------->
Difficulty organizing---------------------->
Loses necessary items-------------------->
Poor follow-through---------------------->
Easily distracted-------------------------->

(Continued)

Continued	Parent (CPRS-R:L) (T Score)	Teacher (CTRS-R:L) (T Score)	*Note: Youth also endorsed Forgetful* Youth (CASS:L) (T Score)
DSM-IV: **Hy/Impulsive**	54	59	47
DSM-IV: Total	58	67	61
Family Problems	NA	NA	52
Emotional Problems	NA	NA	58
Conduct Problems	NA	NA	50
Anger Control Problems	NA	NA	61

NOTE: *NA (not applicable); items do not appear on this scale

Beck Youth Inventories of Emotional and Social Impairment

Self-Concept Inventory for Youth   T = 44   25 %tile

> *Items endorsed for Negative Self-Concept*
> **(Ratings for 0: Never or 1: Sometimes)**
> *Feel strong; Like myself; Do things well;*
> *Happy to be me; Proud of self; Good*
> *at remembering*

Depression Inventory for Youth   T = 63   93 %tile

> **(Ratings for 2 = Often, or 3 = Always)**
> *Think life is bad; Trouble sleeping (3); Feel sorry*
> *for myself; Feel like crying; Feel sad*

Anxiety Inventory for Youth   T = 67   95 %tile

> **(Ratings for 2 = Often, or 3 = Always)**
> *Worry about school; Get nervous; Worry I will get bad grades (3);*
> *Worry about the future (3); Worry others will get mad; Worry I*
> *might lose control (3); I worry always (3); Problems Sleeping (3);*
> *My heart pounds (3); Fear I might get sick (3)*

Anger Inventory for Youth   T = 50   62 %tile

Disruptive Behavior Inventory for Youth   T = 44   31 %tile

Colby: Case Formulation and Discussion

Assessment Report for Colby Tyler

Reason for Referral. Colby was referred for assessment due to presenting complaints of "poor school outcomes" and "temper outbursts."

Assessment Instruments

Weschler Intelligence Scale for Children (WISC-III)

Wide Range Achievement Test (WRAT-3)

Child Behavior Checklist (CBCL)

Teacher Report Form (TRF)

Youth Self-Report (YSR)

Conners Parent Rating Scale (CPRS-R:L)

Conners Teacher Rating Scale (CTRS-R:L)

Conners-Wells Self-Report Scale (CAAS:L)

Beck Youth Inventories

Clinical Interviews

Background Information. Colby was a full-term baby who weighed 6 lb. 2 oz. Labor was lengthy (12 hours) and forceps were used for delivery. Mother stated that she was under much stress during pregnancy due to marital conflict, and admitted to smoking as well as having an occasional drink.

Colby was difficult to manage as an infant due to eating problems (often hungry, sensitive stomach, vomiting) and sleeping problems (difficulties falling asleep and staying asleep). However, he was a good natured and inquisitive toddler. Developmental milestones were within the norm, with the exception that Colby spontaneously began to read words at 2 years of age, a skill that continued to develop and progress at a rapid rate. Colby's health has been good, with the exception of a severe outbreak of hives at 5 years of age shortly after he entered kindergarten. The cause remained undiagnosed and there has not been a recurrence. Hearing and vision have been assessed and results indicate that hearing is normal. Colby wears glasses for distance vision. There is a family history of mood disorders, anxiety disorders (maternal grandmother), family violence, and aggressive impulses, likely related to alcohol abuse (maternal grandfather).

Colby's parents have recently separated (6 months ago), however, marital conflict has been ongoing throughout the 15-year marriage. There was a previous brief separation 7 years ago. Colby and his sister Susy (7 years of age) are living with their mother and visit their father every Wednesday and every second weekend. Colby gets along well with his mother, but the relationship with his father is often strained and conflicted. Colby has stated that his father is often critical of what he does and will often make sarcastic remarks about him in front of his friends. Colby feels that he cannot please his father. Colby often appears very agitated on Wednesday evenings and after returning from weekend visits with his father. Colby's young sister, Susy, is also having transition problems.

Colby gained entrance to the gifted program in the fourth grade as a result of a districtwide screening program. Colby scored in the very superior range (Full Scale IQ 151) on the intellectual assessment conducted at that time. The gifted program was offered for students from Grades 4-8 one day a week at a regional school that served the needs of gifted students from all district schools. Colby was very successful in the program, which offered extensive computer access and various activities emphasizing higher order functioning (e.g., mindbender logic games). However, school reports concerning regular school programming were very disappointing, noting problems in areas of inconsistent effort, incomplete assignments, late for class, not bringing required materials to class, and poor work habits. Colby's most recent report card for his first high school term was extremely disappointing with one A, four C's, and one D (Chemistry). Colby has also been late many times for classes, since he is having difficulty getting up in the mornings due to staying up very late in the evenings.

Present Assessment Results and Interpretation

Colby was seen for two assessment sessions. Rapport was readily established and effort was good throughout. Therefore, results are considered to be a valid estimate of current functioning levels. Test behavior was notable in the following ways. Colby was able to complete puzzles and block designs very quickly with an intuitive holistic learning style. Some frustration was noted on paper-and-pencil tasks, and on these exercises Colby was much slower to respond and used an awkward pencil grasp. Colby seemed to fatigue when required to complete a series of three rating scales. Colby stopped halfway through the exercise to start a spontaneous conversation, unrelated to the forms he was completing. Colby was also easily distracted by extraneous noises in the room, which was relatively quiet by normal standards. When he would return his attention to the questionnaires, he had some difficulty with re-orienting to task and finding his place in the booklet.

Colby scored in the Superior range on the WISC-III (Full Scale IQ range 142-154) at the 99th percentile relative to similar aged peers. Although Verbal IQ (range 141-154) was better than Performance IQ (range 129-145), the difference was not significant. Colby's score on the Coding subtest was significantly lower than the mean of all other subtests. A difference of this magnitude would only be seen in less than 5% of the population. Colby's score on the Freedom from Distractibility Index (range 116-134) was significantly lower than Colby's score on the Verbal Comprehension Index (range 141-154), while his score for Processing Speed (range 94-113) was significantly lower than all other indices. The Freedom from Distractibility Index, which is comprised of the Arithmetic and Digit Span subtests, can provide a measure of working memory involving processes of attention, concentration, sequential processing, and short-term memory. The Processing Speed Index includes a symbol search task, which taps mental speed and a coding task, which taps psychomotor speed and is considered to measure visual-motor coordination, visual memory, and planning ability.

Academically, according to the WRAT-3, Colby's reading (decoding) and spelling skills were commensurate with his intellectual ability and indicated functioning at or above the 98th percentile. Colby scored at the 93rd percentile for arithmetic computation, which is slightly below the expected level. Colby used unusual strategies to assist in recalling multiplication tables (e.g., for 7×8, Colby added eight 7s together to get 56), however, he was able to obtain correct answers using these methods. Colby was a fluent decoder and was able to successfully read all words presented. Colby used an awkward pencil grasp for paper-and-pencil tasks and handwriting was difficult to decipher due to poor number and letter formations. Although there was no formal test of written expression, Colby was asked to write a short story about any topic of his choice. Colby experienced much difficulty getting started and after a few false starts (writing and erasing sentences) Colby began a story about "The first man on the moon." However, he abandoned this effort after about 10 minutes and changed the topic to "My Perfect Vacation." His final product was a brief, but well-written, account of a fantasy vacation to Mars.

Information concerning behavioral and emotional functioning was obtained from clinical interviews and from responses to Rating Scales and Checklists completed by Colby (YSR, CAAS, Beck Inventories), his mother (CBCL, CPRS), and homeroom teacher (TRF, CTRS).

Colby's mother rated Total Internalizing (CBCL) within the clinically significant range (T = 73), while Colby's self-rating (YSR) placed Total Internalizing within the borderline clinical range (T = 68). Colby (T = 72) and his mother (T = 72) both endorsed significant levels of Somatic Complaints, while Colby's mother also noted clinically significant levels for Anxious/Depressed (T = 70) behaviors (Feeling worthless, Self-Conscious, Fearful, Worried), and Attention Problems (T = 70) noted in problems with concentration, restlessness, day-dreaming, poor school progress, and weak impulse control. Although Colby's teacher did not indicate any syndromes to be within the clinical or borderline clinical ranges, further analysis revealed that Inattention on the Attention Problems Subscale was at the 95th percentile, indicating problems with concentration, failure to finish tasks, day-dreaming, lack of motivation, underachievement, and poor school work. Anecdotal comments from the teacher revealed that Colby was late for classes 18 times in the first term and that effort was very inconsistent. Although his teacher also noted overall Adaptive Functioning was within the borderline clinical range (T = 39), this was mainly due to low scores for effort and performance. Ratings also noted strengths in areas of behavior (TRF), social competence (CBCL, YSR), and participation in nonacademic activities (sports, hobbies, part-time job).

Parent responses to the Conners Rating Scale (CPRS) revealed significant elevation on the Psychosomatic Subscale (T = 72) noting problems with stomachaches, aches and pains, and frequent before-school complaints. Therefore, parent responses were consistent in endorsing somatic or psychosomatic complaints across both the CBCL and the CPRS. Colby's mother also noted significant problems in emotional responsiveness on the Emotional Lability subscale (T = 67) evident in temper outbursts and abrupt mood changes. In addition, parent responses to the Conners Global Index Total (T = 67) endorsed the following behaviors occurring much of the time: excitable and impulsive, failure to finish tasks, inattentive, easily distracted, temper outbursts, fidgeting, easily frustrated, and abrupt mood swings.

Teacher ratings on the Conners scales (CTRS) noted significant elevations for Cognitive Problems/Inattention (T = 72) noted in behaviors of: avoidance/reluctance to engage in tasks requiring sustained mental effort, failure to finish tasks, and lacks interest in schoolwork. Teacher ratings for the *DSM-IV* Inattentive Scale (T = 70) were also indicative of significant problems: careless errors/misses details, avoids sustained mental effort, difficulty organizing information, loses necessary items, poor follow through, and ease of distractibility. Emotional Lability (quick temper, ease of frustration, quick mood swings) was also noted to be within the clinically significant range (T = 79) by Colby's teacher. Colby also rated himself as having significant problems on the

DSM-IV Inattentive Scale (T = 72) of the CASS and endorsed "forgetful in daily activities" in addition to all items that his teacher had indicated for the same scale.

Colby's responses to the Beck Youth Inventories revealed that Anxiety (T = 67) and Depression (T = 63) were moderately elevated, while Self-Concept (T = 44) was lower than average, at the 25th percentile. Colby admitted to having many worries about school, getting bad grades, and his future. He also endorsed fears of becoming ill and admitted to having fears about losing control. Trouble falling asleep and staying asleep were also noted as problematic, often resulting in being late for school in the mornings. Although there were no indications of suicide ideation, the Child Depression Inventory (CDI) was also administered to obtain additional information concerning possible depressive features. Colby's overall level of Depression on the CDI (T = 47) was within normal limits with no significant findings for any of the subscales. The most elevated scale on the CDI was predictably on the Ineffectiveness Scale (T = 59), although this was not out of the normal range.

Summary and Diagnostic Impressions

Colby is a 14-year-old teenager who was referred for assessment by his mother due to concerns regarding poor school outcomes and temper outbursts. Colby is currently enrolled in the Grade 9 program and reports received at the end of his first term suggest that he is underachieving significantly based on his intellectual functioning, which is within the Very Superior range. In the past 6 months, in addition to a transition to high school from elementary school, Colby has also had to deal with the recent split-up of his parents. These stressors have likely caused preexisting problems to escalate, evident in increased levels of anxiety, depression, and emotional reactivity (frustration, temper tantrums).

Although it is possible that Colby's current reactions might be interpreted as an adjustment reaction to current life stressors (transition to high school; parents' separation), given the current assessment findings, family history, and chronic nature of Colby's academic difficulties, a diagnosis of attention-deficit disorder—predominantly inattentive type—is suggested. According to *DSM-IV* criteria, Colby presents with at least six of the behaviors required to warrant such a diagnosis, noted in behaviors of inattention, distractibility, problems with completing assignments, poor organizational skills, avoidance of activities requiring sustained mental effort, and forgetful in daily activities. These behaviors have appeared at home and at school and have been evident since Colby enrolled in formal education. Lack of diagnosis to date, however, can likely be attributed to Colby's extremely high level of intelligence, which has allowed him to cope in the earlier grades and served to mask the severity of his problem. However, with increased emphasis on written and independent work, Colby's inability to engage in planned, meaningful, and goal-directed behavior, and his reluctance to sustain effort in tasks that are long, arduous, and often group oriented, has resulted in increasingly poor school performance.

Given the disparity between Colby's intellectual ability and his poor performance, and in view of continued family conflict, it is not surprising that Colby would also present with symptoms of anxiety, depression and lowered self-concept. Assessment results also reveal that Colby has a high level of emotional reactivity to stressors that is primarily internalized and likely to find expression in somatic complaints (sleep problems, digestive complaints, headaches). However, when frustration tolerance is especially low, Colby may also be prone to externalize feelings of frustration in outbursts of anger. When Colby expresses his feelings in an angry outburst, however, venting of feelings is often only temporary and often results in negative feelings of loss of control and erosion of his self-concept.

Based on the above diagnostic impressions, the following recommendations are suggested:

The importance of considering stimulant medication to assist with enhancing school performance was thoroughly discussed with Colby and his mother.

It is essential that Colby's father also attend a session to receive feedback concerning this assessment to ensure understanding of Colby's difficulties.

Colby should receive supportive psychotherapy to provide an outside venue to express his feelings regarding his ADHD and family problems and to receive relaxation training to assist in reducing anxiety levels and difficulties falling asleep.

Engage the family as a whole (father, mother, and son) or as two dyads (father-son; mother-son) in a training program to develop problem-solving skills to address key areas of conflict, such as responsibilities, boundaries (rights), and curfews. A program similar to that developed by Robin and Foster (Robin, 1990) is suggested to develop consistent problem-solving approaches that will focus on using behavioral techniques to reduce the potential for engaging in emotionally reactive patterns.

Results of the assessment should also be discussed with school officials to provide greater understanding of how the school might address Colby's needs for support in several areas. Organizational aids (day timer; school mentor) should be provided to help Colby remain on task and to provide guidelines for breaking tasks down into smaller segments to assist with sustaining goal-directed behavior, and to assist Colby in monitoring his performance. Greater use of home and school communication would also be helpful. Colby would also benefit from being given additional time to complete tests, due to slow writing and processing skills.

Remediation in handwriting skills and/or keyboarding skills would assist in improved speed of written expression. If obtaining one is possible, the use of a laptop would likely greatly enhance performance. Provide extra time during test-taking activities.

Case Discussion and Differential Diagnosis

Evidence in support of a diagnosis of ADHD, primarily inattentive type:

Colby demonstrated at least six of the required diagnostic criteria of the *DSM-IV* for *attention deficit disorder—predominantly inattentive type*, evident since at least 7 years of age and across at least two settings (home, school): *difficulty sustaining attention, fails to finish, difficulty organizing tasks, avoids tasks with sustained mental attention, loses necessary items, easily distracted,* and *often forgetful.*

Associated features often linked with ADHD were also noted: low frustration tolerance, temper outbursts, mood lability, poor self-esteem, and dysphoria.

Negative parent-child interactions (especially father) were also evident. *Academic deficits and school problems* often associated with ADHD-Inattentive were also noted in the presenting problems (American Psychiatric Association, 2000, pp. 87-88).

Other behavioral risks linked to ADHD:

a. *sleep difficulties* such as falling asleep, frequent waking, tiredness due to sleep-wake schedule (Barkley, 1991)

b. *Increased rates of academic failure and depression reported at adolescence* due to demands for greater independent work in the light of ADHD; failure to compete assignments based on poor organization skills and work habits (Cantwell, 1996).

Cognitive associations linked to ADHD:
Colby's scores on the WISC-III were extremely high overall (Very Superior range); however, his *weakest scores were on the Coding and Symbol Search*

subtests, which comprise the *Processing Speed (PS)* factor, which was significantly lower than all other Indices. The next lowest subtest was the *Digit Span,* with *Freedom From Distractibility (FD)* factor significantly lower than Verbal Comprehension Index.

Freedom From Distractibility (FD). There is much conflicting evidence as to whether the FD factor can successfully discriminate between children with ADHD and other populations (LD, normal). While there is consensus that the FD factor should not be used as an exclusive marker for ADHD (Kaufman, 1994; Kaufman & Lichtenberger, 2000), Schwean and Saklofske (1998) found that the FD factor was the lowest index score for children with ADHD across three separate studies (Anastopoulos, Spisto, & Maher, 1994; Prifitera & Dersh, 1993; Schwean, Saklofske, Yackulic, & Quinn, 1993).

Processing Speed (PS). In their three-study comparison, Schwean and Saklofske (1998) also noted that the PS factor was within two points of the FD factor and the next lowest index score for children with ADHD.

Subtest Scores. Schwean and Saklofske (1998) also report that among individual subtests, two of the studies (Prifitera & Dersh , 1993; Schwean et al., 1993) reported *Coding* to be the lowest score, whereas *Digit Span* was recorded lowest in the third study (Anastopoulos et al., 1994). However, since gifted children also tend to score lowest on the PS factor (Wechsler, 1991), interpretation of this result to support ADHD is not as clear in Colby's case.

Risks: Prenatal Influences/Birth History

Difficult delivery by forceps

Early eating and sleeping difficulties

Differential Diagnoses:

Rationale in ruling out other comorbid or competing diagnoses

ADHD-Combined Type. ADHD combined type was ruled out, since Colby did not present with sufficient symptoms (6) of impulsivity and hyperactivity.

ADHD + Depressive Disorder (Major Depressive Disorder; Dysthymia, or Bipolar Disorder). Since depressed patients also note diminished concentration and sleep difficulties, and bipolar patients can elicit irritability, poor impulse control, physical hyperactivity, distractibility, and excessive talking when in a manic state, there is a need to rule out the possibility of comorbid mood disorders. Mood disorders and ADHD co-occur in approximately 20% to 30% of the population. Since ADHD without hyperactivity is associated with higher levels of internalizing symptoms, including depression (Schmidt, Stark, Carlson, & Anthony, 1998), investigating the possibility of a mood disorder is essential in the current evaluation. In this case, *major depressive disorder, dysthymia,* and *bipolar disorder* were ruled out because symptoms of sleep problems, concentration problems, and low self-esteem were better accounted for by associated features of ADHD and related to lack of academic progress or positive feedback regarding academics. Test results support this assumption.

ADHD-Anxiety Disorder. ADHD and anxiety have been found to overlap or co-occur in 25% to 40% of the population. Anxiety is thought to positively moderate for more impulsive behaviors through mechanisms of behavioral inhibition (Wenar & Kerig, 2000). Anxiety in childhood can take the form of *separation anxiety (SAD), phobias, panic attacks, obsessive-compulsive disorder (OCD), general anxiety disorder (GAD), acute stress disorder,* or *post traumatic stress disorder (PTSD).* In this case, although Colby did not present with symptoms of any of the anxiety disorders, he shared many of the symptoms suggestive of *GAD* (restless, fatigued, irritable, difficulty concentrating, sleep disturbance). However, GAD was ruled out because the focus of the anxiety was confined to performance anxiety associated with ADHD.

Given Colby's tendencies to internalize, however, there is a possibility that Colby might develop more pronounced symptoms of anxiety and/or depression or a *somatoform* disorder in the future, if the ADHD cannot be managed more successfully.

ADHD-LD. Although Colby presented with significant underachievement relative to his intellectual potential, and handwriting was immature, a specific *learning disorder (LD)* such as *disorder of written expression* was ruled out since Colby's difficulties with written expression were primarily due to problems with organizing information due to ADHD.

Developmental Coordination Disorder. Although handwriting was poor, due to poor pencil grip, Colby was well coordinated in all other activities, was good in sports, and achieved developmental milestones within the norm.

REFERENCES

American Psychiatric Association. (2000). *Diagnostic and statistical manual of mental disorders* (4th ed., TR). Washington, DC: Author.

Anastopoulos, A., D., Spisto, M. A., & Maher, M. C. (1994). The WISC-III freedom from distractibility factor: Its utility in identifying children with attention deficit hyperactivity disorder. *Psychological Assessment, 6,* 368-371.

Barkley, R. A. (1991). The ecological validity of laboratory and analogue assessment methods of ADHD symptoms. *Journal of Abnormal Child Psychology, 19,* 149-178.

Cantwell, D. P. (1996). Attention deficit disorder: A review of the past 10 years. *Journal of the American Academy of Child and Adolescent Psychiatry, 35,* 978-987.

Kaufman, A. S. (1994). *Intelligent testing with the WISC-III.* New York: John Wiley.

Kaufman, A. S., & Lichtenberger, E. O. (2000). *Essentials of WISC-III and WPPSI-R assessment.* New York: John Wiley.

Prifitera, A., & Dersh, J. (1993). Base rates of WISC-III diagnostic subtest patterns among normal, learning-disabled and ADHD samples. *Journal of Psychoeducational Assessment,* 43-55.

Robin, A. R. (1990). Training families with ADHD adolescents. In R. A. Barkley (Ed.), *Attention-deficit hyperactivity disorder: A handbook for diagnosis and treatment* (pp. 462-497). New York: Guilford.

Schmidt, K. L., Stark, K. D., Carlson, C. D., & Anthony, B. J. (1998). Cognitive factors differentiating attention deficit-hyperactivity disorder with and without a comorbid mood disorder. *Journal of Consulting and Clinical Psychology, 66,* 673-679.

Schwean, V. L., & Saklofske, D. H. (1998). WISC-III assessment of children with attention deficit hyperactivity disorder. In A. Prifitera & D. Saklofske (Eds.), *WISC-III: Clinical use and interpretation* (pp. 91-118). San Diego, CA: Academic Press.

Schwean, V. L., Saklofske, D. H., Yackulic, R. A., & Quinn, D. (1993). WISC-III performance of ADHD children. *Journal of Psychoeducational Assessment,* 56-70.

Wechsler, D. (1991). *Wechsler Intelligence Scale for Children* (3rd ed.). San Antonio, TX: Psychological Corporation.

Wenar, C., & Kerig, P. (2000). *Developmental psychopathology: From infancy through adolescence* (4th ed.). New York: McGraw-Hill.

CASE OF SCOTT

Scott: Results from Psychological Testing General Cognitive (WISC-111) and Academic (WRAT-3)

Wechsler Intelligence Scale for Children-Third Edition (WISC-III)

Verbal Scale	SS	Performance Scale	SS		IQ/Index	%tile
Information	6	Picture Completion	10	Verbal IQ	84	14
Similarities	8	Coding	7	Performance IQ	93	32
Arithmetic	8	Picture Arrangement	8	Full Scale IQ	87	19
Vocabulary	6	Block Design	9	Verbal	83	13
		Comprehension				
Comprehension	5	Object Assembly	6	Perceptual Organization	94	34
(Digit Span)	(7)	(Symbol Search)	(10)	Freedom from Distractibility	90	25
		(Mazes not given)		Processing Speed	96	39

Administrator Comments: Requested many repetitions for arithmetic questions. When he repeated questions out loud, mixed up information (e.g., 4 boys had 2 candies = 2 boys had 4 candies). Word-finding problems evident on Picture Completion. Vocabulary very limited. As comprehension questions got longer, he got more confused and required much prompting to expand verbal responses. Often off-target or peripheral in responses. Responded to "lost" as if responding to "found" in comprehension question and exchanged meanings for interrogatives (e.g., responded to a what question with a when response). Slow to complete visual tasks (e.g., earned very few bonus points for time)

Wide Range Achievement Test (WRAT-3)

Subject	Standard Score	%tile	Grade Level
Reading (Decoding)	95	37	3
Spelling	87	19	2
Arithmetic	103	58	4

Ekwall Reading Inventory (Comprehension)

Instructional Level: Grade 3

Administrator Comments: Visual whole word speller; poor phonetic speller and sound substitutions (correct = qurecht; circle = curcal). Reading comprehension, poor recall for factual information and sequential information (altered meaning of story).

Check Lists and Rating Scales

Child Behavior Checklist (CBCL)/Teacher Report Form (TRF) & Youth Self Report

Note: Boldfaced numbers indicate scales in the significant range. Individual items endorsed by the respondent are listed for each of the significant scales.

	CBCL (T Score)	TRF (T Score)
Syndromes		
I Withdrawn	67 *Borderline*	64
	Won't talk, Secretive, Shy, Sulks, Prefers to be alone	
II Somatic	56	57
III Anxious/Depressed	65	61
IV Social Problems	65	69 *Borderline*
		Acts young, Lonely, Not get along, Worthless, Not liked, Prefers younger
V Thought Problems	65	58
VI Attention Problems	70	69 *Borderline*
	Acts young, Concentration, Confused, Day-dreams, Impulsive, Poor school work	*Acts young, Hums, Fails to finish, Concentration problems, Fidgets, Day-dreams, Problems with directions, Impulsive, Nervous, Problems learning, Not motivated, Poor school work, Messy, Inattentive, Underachieves*
VII Delinquent Behavior	65	56
VIII Aggressive Behavior	73	63
	Argues, Brags, Mean, Demands attention, Destroys own, Disobeys at home & school, Jealous, Fights, Attacks, Screams, Shows off, Stubborn, Mood changes, Temper, Loud play	
Total Internalizing	68 *Clinical*	62 *Borderline Clinical*
Total Externalizing	71 *Clinical*	62 *Borderline Clinical*
Total Problems	70 *Clinical*	67 *Clinical*

Teacher Attention Problems Subscale:	Raw Score	Percentile
Inattention	19	95 %ile
Hyperactive-Impulsive	19	95 %ile

Anecdotal Comments–Teacher: Starting to get more argumentative. Can be bossy at times. Academics starting to slide. Good sense of humor (can be sarcastic). Good when he is doing what he wants to do. Can be stubborn and immature.

Conners Rating Scales

Items listed for Scales: T = 66-70   Moderately Atypical (Indicates significant problem)

T = 70+   Markedly Atypical (Indicates significant problem)

Items listed are rated as occurring Very Often (3) or Often (2)

	Parent (CPRS-R:L) (T Score)	Teacher (CTRS-R:L) (T Score)
Oppositional	71	65
Argues, Loses temper, Irritable, Defies, Touchy/annoyed, Blames others, Annoys others		
Cognitive Problems/ Inattention	60	70
		Forgets what he has already learned, Careless mistakes, Avoids tasks of sustained effort, Doesn't listen, Problems with organization, Loses things, Poor follow through
Hyperactivity	66	62
Problems with quiet play, Restless		
Anxious/Shy	50	60
Perfectionism	52	49
Social Problems	53	64
Psychosomatic	42	NA
Conners ADHD Index	60	58
Conners Global Index: Restless/Impulsive	54	57
Conners Global Index Emotional Lability	72	54
Cries often & easily, Rapid mood shift		

(Continued)

(Continued)

	Parent (CPRS-R:L) (T Score)	Teacher (CTRS-R:L) (T Score)
Conners Global Index Total	62	57
DSM-IV: Inattentive	59	65
DSM-IV: Hy/Impulsive	**68**	**66**
	Fidgets, Squirms, Problems with quiet play, Problems remaining seated	*On the go; Leaves seat; Problems waiting turn; Fidgets, Interrupts*
DSM-IV: Total	64	64

Note: *NA (not applicable) items do not appear on this scale

Beck Youth Inventories of Emotional and Social Impairment

	T Score	Percentile
Self-Concept Inventory for Youth	T = 57	75 %tile

Items endorsed for Negative Self-Concept
(Ratings for 3: Always)
*Feel strong, Like myself, Just as good as
others, Normal, Good person, Do things well,
Good at things, A nice person, Tell the truth,
Proud of self; Like my body, Happy to be me.*

Depression Inventory for Youth	T = 39	11 %tile

(Ratings for 2: Often, or 3: Always)
*Feel like bad things happen to me, I want
to be alone.*

Anxiety Inventory for Youth	T = 40	15 %tile

(Ratings for 2: Often, or 3: Always)
*My dreams scare me. I'm afraid I might get hurt.
Afraid something bad might happen to me.*

Anger Inventory for Youth	T = 86	>99 %tile

(Ratings for 2: Often, or 3: Always)
*People try to cheat me. I feel like screaming. People
are unfair. Try to hurt me. Life is unfair. Bully me.
People . . . make me mad, bother me, try to control
me, put me down, are against me. I get angry.
When I get mad, I stay mad & have trouble getting
over it.*

Disruptive Behavior Inventory for Youth	T = 68	>94 %tile

(Ratings for 2: Often, or 3: Always)
*Others get me into trouble. I fight with others.
I like getting people mad. I hate listening to
others. I argue with adults. I like it when others
are scared of me. I like to trick people. I break
things when angry. I swear at adults.*

CASE OF ARTHUR

Results from Psychological Testing

Results of the multimodal assessment battery are presented below in the form of standard scores, T scores, and/or percentiles. Interns will be expected to evaluate, interpret, and integrate findings to formulate a more refined diagnostic impression. Anecdotal comments from the clinic psychologist (e.g., comments on test behaviors, etc.) are presented in parentheses whenever these comments might aid in interpretation of the findings. In addition, a list of endorsed items is provided for any scales (checklists & rating scales) elevated to clinical levels to facilitate interpretation of behavioral patterns within and across sources of information.

Results are presented in their entirety rather than in summarized form to provide the intern with maximum opportunity to develop independent skills in the analysis and synthesis of information from multiple sources.

General Cognitive (WISC-III) and Academic (WRAT-3)

Wechsler Intelligence Scale for Children-Third Edition (WISC-III)

Verbal Scale	SS	Performance Scale	SS		IQ/Index	%tile
Information	4	Picture Completion	6	Verbal IQ	55	0.1%
Similarities	1	Coding	2	Performance IQ	68	2%
Arithmetic	1	Picture Arrangement	4	Full Scale IQ	57	0.2%
Vocabulary	1	Block Design	4	Verbal Comprehension	59	0.3%
Comprehension	3	Object Assembly	7	Perceptual Organization	73	4%
(Digit Span) Distractibility	1	(Symbol Search)	NA	Freedom	50	>.1%
		(Mazes not given)		Processing Speed	(Not given)	

Administrator Comments: Left-handed. Arithmetic questions asked for numerous repetitions; used fingers for counting. Slow to process instructions and lengthy questions (comprehension). Picture Arrangement and Block

Design, thought he was doing very well. All-or-nothing approach. Said he did lots of puzzles at home. Word-finding difficulties (Picture Completion), pointed rather than providing label.

Wide Range Achievement Test (WRAT-3)

Subject	Standard Score	%tile	Grade Level
Reading (Decoding)	52		1.5
Spelling	57		1.5
Arithmetic	Below 45		1.2

Administrator Comments: Very frustrated. Said he forgot because it was summer. Upset with arithmetic test, said it wasn't fair because he didn't take it yet. Printing very large and immature.

Child Behavior Checklist (CBCL)/Teacher Report Form (TRF) & Youth Self Report

Note: Boldfaced numbers indicate scales in the significant range. Individual items endorsed by the respondent are listed for each of the significant scales.

	CBCL (T Score)
Syndromes	
I Withdrawn	65
II Somatic	67
Complains of headaches, Tired, Aches	
III Anxious/Depressed	69
Lonely, Feels others are out to get him, Worthless, Nervous, Sad, Worries	
IV Social Problems	70
Acts young, Not get along, Not liked, Clumsy	
V Thought Problems	65
VI Attention Problems	85
VII Delinquent Behavior	55
VIII Aggressive Behavior	75
Demanding attention, Attacking others, Temper outbursts, Teasing, Threatening, Argues, Jealous, Mood changes, Loud	
Total Internalizing	71 Clinical
Total Externalizing	68 Clinical
Total Problems	72 Clinical
Other Problems: *Speech Problems, Sleep Problems, Bites nails*	
Competence Scales: CBCL: T = 16 Clinical	

Anecdotal Comments: Teacher form not available since Arthur is not currently attending school. Youth report not done due to comprehension/attention problems.

Vineland Adaptive Behavior Scales

	Raw Score	Standard Score	Age Equivalent
Receptive	26		
Expressive	61		
Written	38		
Communication Domain	**125**	83	12'6
Personal	77		
Domestic	36		
Community	48		
Daily Living Skills	**161**	99	15'3
Interpersonal Skills	46		
Play & Leisure	38		
Coping Skills	33		
Socialization Domain	**117**	96	14'9

AAMR Adaptive Behavior Scale-School: ABS-S:2

Part 1: Domain Scores	Raw Score	Standard	Percentile	Age Score
Independent Functioning	116	17	99	16+
Physical Development	24	10	50	16+
Economic Activity	21	11	63	16+
Language Development	37	7	16	8'6
Numbers & Time	14	11	63	16+
Prevocation/Vocational	10	10	50	16+
Self-direction	20	20	37	16+
Responsibility	9	11	63	16+
Socialization	24	9	37	16+

Part 2: Domain Scores (higher standard scores indicate higher adjustment)

Part 2: Domain Scores	Raw Score	Standard	Percentile
Social Behavior	25	9	37
Conformity	4	10	50
Trustworthiness	0	14	91
Stereotyped & Hyperactive	3	8	25
Self-Abusive Behavior	0	63	11
Social Engagement	1	10	50
Disturbing Interpersonal Behavior	10	7	16

CASE OF SHIRLEY

Results from Psychological Testing

Results of the multimodal assessment battery are presented below in the form of standard scores, T scores, and/or percentiles. Interns will be expected to evaluate, interpret, and integrate findings to formulate a more refined diagnostic impression. Anecdotal comments from the clinic psychologist (e.g., comments on test behaviors, etc.) are presented in parenthesis, whenever these comments might aid in interpretation of the findings. In addition, to facilitate interpretation of behavioral patterns within and across sources of information, a list of endorsed items is provided for any scales (checklists & rating scales) elevated to clinical levels.

Results are presented in their entirety rather than in summarized form to provide the intern with maximum opportunity to develop independent skills in the analysis and synthesis of information from multiple sources. General Cognitive (WISC-III) and Academic (WRAT-3)

Wechsler Intelligence Scale for Children-Third Edition (WISC-III)

Verbal Scale	SS	Performance Scale	SS		IQ/Index	%tile
Information	10	Picture Completion	11	Verbal IQ	97	42
Similarities	9	Coding	7	Performance IQ	89	23
Arithmetic	8	Picture Arrangement	8	Full Scale IQ	92	30
Vocabulary	11	Block Design	7	Verbal Comprehension	99	47
Comprehension	9	Object Assembly	8	Perceptual Organization	91	27
(Digit Span)	7	(Symbol Search)	7	Freedom from Distractibility	84	14
		(Mazes not given)		Processing Speed	86	18

Administrator Comments: Methodical approach to Block Design, Picture Arrangement, and Object Assembly. Slow to complete visual motor tasks. Wasted time lining up edges to meet perfectly. Multiple responses to verbal items, as if unsure of when to stop descriptions. Frequent requests for feedback. Changed answers repeatedly on Arithmetic Test.

Wide Range Achievement Test (WRAT-3)

Subject	Standard Score	%tile	Grade Level
Reading (Decoding)	92	30	Grade 5
Spelling	106	66	Grade 6
Arithmetic	90	25	Grade 4

Administrator Comments: Word decoding was not fluid. Often stopped to check for feedback. Read very slowly. Arithmetic questions noted several erasures and changed answers. Used stick counters in margins to check on accuracy of multiplication tables. Used her fingers to check addition. Did not attempt many items. Spelling also took time due to perfectionistic tendencies, toward "perfect" printing. Did not use cursive writing. Said printing was neater.

Checklists and Rating Scales

Child Behavior Checklist (CBCL)/Teacher Report Form (TRF) & Youth Self Report (YSR)

Note: Boldfaced numbers indicate scales in the significant range. Individual items endorsed by the respondent are listed for each of the significant scales.

	CBCL (T Score)	TRF (T Score)	YSR (T Score)
Syndromes			
I Withdrawn	**68**	66	**69**
	Secretive, Underactive		*Secretive, Shy, Underactive, Withdrawn*
II Somatic	**74**	66	**69**
	Tired, Aches, Nausea		*Tired, Aches, Headaches, Stomach Problems*
III Anxious/Depressed	**73**	**72**	**72**
	Fearful, Self Conscious	*Fear of mistakes, Conforming*	*Cries, Feels guilty, Self-conscious*

NOTE: All three raters endorsed the following items: Perfectionistic, Nervous, Worries on the Anxiety Depressed Scale

IV Social Problems	57F	63	**70**
			Not get along, Teased, Not liked, Withdrawn
V Thought Problems	**73**	**70**	**70**
	Obsessions, Repeats acts,	*Obsessions, Repeats acts,*	*Obsessions, Repeats acts, Collects stuff, Strange behavior*

(Continued)

(Continued)

	CBCL (T Score)	TRF (T Score)	YSR (T Score)
VI Attention Problems	70	60	67
	Concentration, Confused, Nervous		*Concentration, Confused, Day-dreams, Nervous, Poor school work*
VII Delinquent Behavior	50	50	50
VIII Aggressive Behavior	50	50	50
Total Internalizing	75 Clinical	72 Clinical	77 Clinical
Total Externalizing	44	42	27
Total Problems	58	58	52
Other Problems:	*Fears, Nail biting, Nightmares, Sleeps less*		*Fears, Fears school, Get hurt a lot, Bite nails, Nightmares, Eat too much, Overweight, Sleep less, Sleep problems (wakes up)*

Anecdotal Comments: None

Conners Rating Scales

Endorsed Items (for "Often" & "Very Often") are listed for scales in the Moderately Atypical (T = 66-70) and the Markedly Atypical (T = 70+) Ranges

	Parent (CPRS-R:L) (T Score)	Teacher (CTRS-R:L) (T Score)
Oppositional	62	46
Cognitive Problems/ Inattention	70	69

Difficulty with homework, Sustained mental effort, Fails to complete work, Trouble concentrating, Needs supervision, Fails to finish	*Forgets what learned, Fails to finish, Not reading as expected, Poor in arithmetic*

Hyperactivity	44	46
Anxious/Shy	85	78

Timid, Afraid of people, Afraid of new situations, Lots of fears, Shy withdrawn, Clings to adults	*Feelings easily hurt, Timid, Easily frightened, Sensitive to criticism, Shy withdrawn*

Perfectionism	88	85

Everything must be just so, Keeps checking and re-checking, Fusses about cleanliness, Must be done same way, Has rituals, Sets high goals for self, Upset if things are re-arranged	*Perfectionist, Everything must be just so, Keeps checking & re-checking, Over-focused on details, Likes neat & clean, Things done same way every time*

Social Problems	84	90

Loses friends quickly, Doesn't know how to make friends, Feels inferior to others	*Unaccepted by group, Last to be picked, No friends, Doesn't know how to make friends, Poor social skills*

	Parent (CPRS-R:L) (T Score)	Teacher (CTRS-R:L) (T Score)
Psychosomatic	90	NA
Stomachaches, Aches & pains, Aches before school, Headaches, Complaints without cause, Tired/fatigued		
Conners ADHD Index	67	62
Problems with sustained mental effort, Concentration problems, Fails to finish, Inattentive		
Conners Global Index Restless/Impulsive	62	46
Conners Global Index Emotional Lability	60	58
Conners Global Index Total	62	
DSM-IV: **Inattentive**	62	66
DSM-IV: **Hy/Impulsive**	43	45
DSM-IV: **Total**	54	58

NOTE: *NA (not applicable) items do not appear on this scale

Beck Youth Inventories of Emotional and Social Impairment

	(T Score)	*Percentile*
Self-Concept Inventory for Youth	28	<4.5% population

Items endorsed for Negative Self-Concept
(Ratings for 0: Never)
*Just as good as other kids, Good
at jokes, People think I am good
at things, Like my body.*

Anxiety Inventory for Youth	79	98.5%

(Ratings for 2: Often, or 3: Always)
*Worry might be hurt at home, Scary dreams,
Worry at school, Think of scary things, Worry
about being teased, Afraid of making mistakes,
Get nervous, Afraid of being hurt, Worry about
grades, Worry about future, Worry people might
get mad at me, I worry, Problems sleeping, Heart
pounds, Afraid bad things will happen to me, Afraid
might get sick.*

Depression Inventory for Youth	70	95 %tile

(Ratings for 2: Often, or 3: Always)
*Trouble sleeping, Feel no one loves me, Stomach
hurts, Feel bad things will happen, Feel stupid,
Do things badly, Feel bad about what I do, Feel
like crying, Feel sad.*

Anger Inventory for Youth	57	82 %tile

(Ratings for 2: Often)
*Think people are unfair, Think others try to hurt me,
Life is unfair, People bully me, People try to put me
down*

Disruptive Behavior Inventory for Youth	47	47 %tile
(No ratings 2 or higher)		

Additional Assessment Instruments: Child Self Ratings	*Standard Scores*
Child Depression Inventory (CDI) Kovacs, 1992	
Total CDI Score	74
Negative Mood	64
Interpersonal Problems	67

> *Not like being with people many times,*
> *Get into fights many times.*

Ineffectiveness   70

> *Do many things wrong, Push myself to do*
> *schoolwork, Schoolwork not as good as before,*
> *Can never be as good as other kids.*

Anhedonia   69

> *Fun in some things, Trouble sleeping every night,*
> *Tired all the time, Many days not feel like eating,*
> *Worry about aches & pains, Feel alone many times,*
> *Fun at school only once in awhile, Do not have any*
> *friends.*

Negative Self Esteem   73

> *Not sure if things will work out for me,*
> *Do not like myself, Think about killing myself, but*
> *would not do it, Look ugly, Not sure if anybody*
> *loves me.*

Hopelessness Scale: Kazdin, 1983

Endorsed

Want to grow up because . . . things will get better (F); Can imagine my life 10 years from now (F); I will get more good things in life than most other kids (F); Things just don't work out the way I want them to (T); Tomorrow seems unclear and confusing to me (T);

Score = 5   Just below threshold for High Hopelessness (5)

Appendix B

Case Formulation and Classification

Given the complexity of issues involved in child and adolescent psychopathology, it is not surprising that clinicians may reveal wide variations in how they conceptualize maladjustment in childhood. The case of Jeremy provided a living example of the myriad explanations that could be presented for Jeremy's noncompliant behavior, based on the assumptions inherent in different theoretical perspectives. This disparity is evident in how terms are defined, how processes are conceptualized, and the relative weight certain factors are assigned in the overall design.

Although most clinicians would agree that a major goal of child assessment is to determine where the child's presenting behavior fits within the realm of adaptive and maladaptive behaviors, there are several issues regarding how to categorize or classify the behavior within the broad scheme of other mental disorders or maladaptive behaviors.

There are at least three major clinical approaches to organizing and classifying information concerning child and adolescent disorders or problem behaviors: categorical classification (*DSM*); empirical or dimensional classification (e.g., behavioral rating scales: ASEBA: Achenbach & Rescorla, 2001; BASC: Reynolds & Kamphus, 1992), and comparing behaviors to normative expectations or developmental psychopathology. It is assumed that information regarding these classification systems will be well documented in any number of other clinically relevant courses, and it is not the intention of this text to provide additional coverage in these areas.

However, a major intent of the text is to provide the student with information that will assist in understanding the complexity of the child's environment and to assist in the application of that understanding to contextually relevant materials. To this end, presentation of information on Educational Classification is considered to be highly relevant to practice in the real world and an area that is likely to have minimal coverage in other clinical courses. Questions at the end of each case study will reinforce the presentation by addressing some of the variations between the clinical and educational systems of classification regarding the classification of four primary disorders: mental retardation, learning disabilities, serious emotional disturbance, and attention-deficit/hyperactivity disorder.

A CLINICIAN'S GUIDE TO EDUCATIONAL CLASSIFICATION

Historical Background and Theoretical Information

Education and the Law

Given the nature and impact of the child's environment on issues of assessment and treatment, the importance of having a working knowledge of legislation impacting on the rights of the disabled child within the educational system cannot be understated. Three laws are of particular importance in this regard: The Americans with Disabilities Act of 1990 (ADA); Section 504 of the Rehabilitation Act of 1973; and Individuals with Disabilities Education Act (IDEA), amended in 1997. From a perspective of governance, the U.S. Department of Education (DOE) is responsible for overseeing public school compliance with laws pertaining to issues of civil liberties (ADA, Section 504) and educational rights (IDEA).

ADA and Section 504

Very briefly, the ADA and Section 504 are civil rights laws that prohibit discrimination against individuals with disabilities. The ADA prohibits discrimination on the basis of disability in employment, public services, and accommodation. Under the ADA, reasonable accommodations are required for individuals with disabilities to enable them to perform essential job functions. Some examples of reasonable accommodations include: removing transportation barriers, redesigning equipment, assigning aides, and providing communication in various formats. ADA also covers accommodations to students who may be involved in community job placements. Under Section 504, individuals with disabilities who are employed in the public and private sector, and school-aged children enrolled in public and private schools, have a right to an "appropriate and free" education equivalent to that of a child without disabilities. These educational accommodations may be in the regular or special education setting, and disabled students who do not qualify for services under IDEA may receive similar services under Section 504. Safeguards for parents and guardians under Section 504 include prerequisite permission for assessments and informed notice of any significant placement changes. The local education agencies (LEA) are required to provide due process hearings if parents disagree with the identification, evaluation, or placement decisions (see Henderson, 2001, for an overview of ADA and Section 504).

Critique

Both civil rights laws provide vague descriptions of who may qualify as disabled. Under each law, any individual with a disability who (a) has a physical or mental impairment that substantially limits one or more life activities, or (b) has a record of such impairment, or (c) is regarded as having such an impairment, qualifies. The federal government does not provide direct funding to implement either of the civil rights laws. There are limited tax credits available to remove architectural barriers, and federal agencies provide grants to public and private institutions supporting training and technical assistance. Section 504 is also the fiscal responsibility of the State. Funds from IDEA may not be used to service children who are eligible solely under Section 504.

IDEA

The Individuals with Disabilities Education Act (IDEA) of 1990 was a revision of what was first enacted in 1975 as PL 94-142 (The Education for All Handicapped Children Act). In May 1997, the U.S. House of Representatives and the U.S. Senate passed legislation reauthorizing and amending IDEA. The final regulations were published in the *Federal Register* in March 1999. The IDEA is an education act that provides federal funding assistance to state and local education agencies to guarantee that special education services (individualized educational programs, IEP) and related services (e.g., speech and language pathology, physical and occupational therapy) are available for children (3 to 21 years of age) who are deemed disabled. Under IDEA, there are 13 possible categories of eligibility for disabilities: autism; deaf-blindness; deafness; emotional disturbance; hearing impairment; mental retardation; multiple disabilities; orthopedic impairment; other health impairment; specific learning disability; speech or language impairment; traumatic brain injury; and visual impairment, including blindness. Under the 1990 revision of PL 42-142, children (3 to 9 years of age) who experience developmental delays may also be eligible for additional services. Infants and toddlers (birth through 2 years of age) were also added as part of the Early Intervention Initiative and may also qualify for funding and an Individualized Family Service Plan. IDEA safeguards the rights of parents and children through several procedures: parental involvement that includes consent to evaluation and placement, and due process hearings. Two changes of note in the most recent revision include (a) the addition of attention deficit disorder (ADD) and attention deficit hyperactivity disorder (ADHD) to the list of conditions eligible under Other Health Impairments; and the change in designation from seriously emotionally disturbed to emotionally disturbed. Both of these revisions are discussed in the section on special topics in classification.

Critique

There have been several criticisms regarding IDEA that have been directed toward (a) problems of definition or classification of disabilities and (b) issues of inconsistencies in interpretation or compliance with federal guidelines at the state and local levels. Three of the 13 categories of disabilities eligible for funding under IDEA have been especially problematic and have generated significant research and controversy: mental retardation (educable mentally retarded [EMR] or mild mental retardation [MMR]), learning disabilities, and emotional and behavioral disturbance/serious emotional disturbance (SED/EBD). MacMillan and Reschly (1998) have referred to these three categories as the "judgmental categories" because classification reliability for these three categorical groups is considerably less than that for the more biologically based and well-defined disabilities (e.g., disabilities of physical or sensory impairment). Issues in the classification/identification of attention-deficit/hyperactivity disorder (ADHD) are addressed.

Applications, Limitations, and Special Topics in Classification

Mental Retardation

With the development of intelligence tests in the early 1900s, increasing emphasis was placed on using IQ scores as the single defining feature of mental retardation (MR). By the mid-1900s this practice was receiving increasing criticism for two important reasons: (a) concentration on IQ scores placed minimal emphasis on the role of social adaptation in defining MR populations, and (b) the growing belief that IQ scores were biased with respect to psychosocial and cultural influences. Proponents of including social adaptive factors in the definition of MR cited cases of the "6-hour retardates" who might encounter significant cognitive problems during their 6-hour school day, but whose social adaptive skills allowed them to function successfully outside the school system. In 1959, the American Association on Mental Retardation (AAMR) officially stated that determination of mental retardation should include consideration of deficits in adaptive behavior as well as subnormal intellectual functioning. Despite AAMR's attempts to lobby in favor of de-emphasizing IQ scores as the sole determinants of MR, the practice continued for several years.

During the 1960s and 1970s, disproportionate numbers of minority students in special education programs increased concerns regarding the efficacy of IQ tests for minority populations, resulting in several lawsuits during this period. One such class action suit, *Larry P. v. Riles,* resulted in significant restrictions on the use of intellectual assessments for placing African American children in special education programs in California. In 1975, the passing of PL 94-142 (The Education for All Handicapped Children Act) provided the necessary support for the rights of the disabled and reaffirmed the need to incorporate both adaptive and intellectual features in the definition of mental retardation.

Today there are still concerns regarding the identification of disproportionate numbers of ethnic minorities who are placed in special education. Using data from 4,902 school districts sampled in the 1992 School Civil Right Compliance Report survey, Oswald, Coutinho, Best, and Nguyen (2001) found that African American students were nearly 2½ times as likely to be identified as MMR and about 1½ times as likely to be identified as seriously emotionally disturbed (SED) compared to their non-African American peers. The study also revealed that poverty had a significant relation to this skewed representation; however, the direction of effects differed by condition for African American children. While African American children living in poverty were more likely to be identified as MMR, African American children in more affluent areas were more likely to be identified as SED.

Currently there are three systems of classification regarding mental retardation (MR): *DSM-IV,* AAMR, and Education.

DSM-IV. There are three criteria necessary for a diagnosis of mental retardation according to the *DSM-IV:* significantly subaverage intellectual functioning (below an IQ of approximately 70, approximately two standard deviations below the mean), concurrent deficits or limitations in adaptive functioning in at least two areas, and onset before the age of 18 years. The *DSM* further codes the degree of retardation according to level of intellectual functioning: mild (IQ 50-55 to 70), moderate (IQ level 35-40 to 50-55), severe (IQ level 20-25 to 35-40), and profound (IQ below 20-25). Approximately 85% of all MR falls within the mild range. Lack of adaptive skills must be demonstrated in 2 areas from a list of 11 possible sources: communication, self-care, home living, social skills, community youth resources, self-direction, functional academic skills, work, leisure, health, and safety.

AAMR. The classification system of the AAMR includes the same three criteria as the *DSM* with respect to IQ cutoff, adaptive functioning, and age of onset. However, the two systems differ in subsequent specifications. While the *DSM* codes MR relative to degrees of severity, the most recent classification of the AAMR (1992) profiles types of MR based on the degree of support services required: intermittent, limited, extensive, or pervasive.

Furthermore, while the *DSM* suggests that it is possible to diagnose MR in individuals whose IQ is between 71 and 75 (measurement error of ±5 points) if they have sufficient adaptive behavior deficits, the AAMR is lobbying to raise the IQ cutoff from 70 to 75.

Education. Although the educational system also recognizes the need to include social and adaptive features of MR, most state education codes allocate funds for special education to children with disabilities, such as MR and learning disabled (LD), based on IQ score cutoffs to determine eligibility for services. Initially, children who had an IQ between 55 and 80 were classified as educable mentally retarded (EMR), sometimes also referred to as educable mentally handicapped (EMH), while children who had an IQ between 25 and 55 were considered trainable mentally retarded (TMR), or trainable mentally handicapped (TMH). Currently, there is variation across states with most states accepting an IQ cut off between 70 and 75 to designate MR, although some states, like Iowa, have retained higher cutoff levels (IQ 85; MacMillan & Forness, 1998). Within education, there has been continued controversy regarding how students are to be identified as MR and how these students are best serviced, once identified.

Investigation of classification procedures or how students are identified has revealed both inconsistencies in the application of classification procedures and concerns regarding the impact of minority status and poverty levels on the decision-making process. Regarding classification, MacMillan and Forness (1998) found that of the 150 students (Grades 2, 3, and 4) referred to the student study teams (SST) from five school districts in California, only 6 of the 43 children who scored below 75 on the WISC-III (and met diagnostic criteria for MR) were classified/identified as MMR, while 19 were classified as LD; despite the fact that the mean academic levels were approximately 2½ standard deviations (SDs) below the mean. The authors suggest that comorbid externalizing problems in the 6 children identified as MR likely influenced placement decisions. Using this same subject sample of 150 students, MacMillan, Gresham, and Bocian (1998) also investigated outcomes for Borderline students (IQ 71-85) and found that almost half (48%) of children referred to the SST were within the Borderline range, and of this number, 27, or 41%, were ultimately categorized as LD. Of the 19 students who were within an acceptable limit for MR designation (71-75), only 1 was identified as MR. Results from these and other studies have led MacMillan and colleagues to question the direction of special education, which has become increasingly insistent on assigning children to specific categories to meet compliance issues. IDEA requires that student eligibility for special education be linked to only one disability category. As a consequence, children are assigned to only one category of disability, despite the fact that high rates of comorbidity exist between categories. Problems are most pronounced in what MacMillan and Reschly (1998) have called the "judgmental categories"—mild mental retardation (MMR), learning disabilities (LD), and emotionally and behaviorally disordered (EBD).

Learning Disabilities

The definition of learning disabilities (LD), also referred to as specific learning disabilities (SLD), has remained a highly controversial area of debate. Currently there are several conflicting sources available for purposes of classification:

DSM: Learning Disorders and Communication Disorders. The *DSM* considers learning disorders (formerly called academic skills disorders) in three primary areas: reading disorder, mathematics disorder, and disorders of written expression. A fourth category, learning disorder NOS (not otherwise specified) might be diagnosed when significant impairment is evident but criteria are not met for the individual disorders. A learning disorder is diagnosed when measures of achievement (standardized assessments) are substantially below (discrepancy of more than two standard deviations between achievement and IQ) what is expected based on age, schooling, and level of intelligence. However, the discrepancy criteria are somewhat flexible (between 1 and 2 SDs) if other factors (cognitive, comorbid mental disorder, ethnic or cultural background) might compromise IQ scores. In keeping with other diagnostic features of the *DSM*, level of impairment is a key determining factor in defining learning disorders, and the impairment must significantly interfere with academic achievement or with functions of daily living. The definition is also exclusionary in that if sensory deficits are present, they must be ruled out as the primary cause of the learning difficulties. According to the *DSM*, it is expected that 5% of children in the public school system might be identified as having a learning disorder. Although disorders of reading and mathematics are somewhat self-explanatory, it is important to note that disorders of spelling or of handwriting alone are excluded from a diagnosis of disorders of written expression. The key defining feature between learning disorders (LD) and mental retardation is that for most MR cases achievement is commensurate with IQ, while LD cases are defined by the discrepancy criterion. If significant discrepancy exists between IQ and achievement, then a dual diagnosis of MR and LD is possible.

The *DSM* also defines communication disorders, which consist of disorders of expressive language, mixed expressive-receptive disorder, phonological disorder (developmental articulation disorder), and stuttering.

Education: Specific Learning Disabilities (SLD). The federal definition of a learning disability appears in the Individuals with Disabilities Education Act (IDEA, 1999), which was published in the Federal Register, March 12, 1999:

(i) General

A disorder in one or more of the basic psychological processes involved in understanding or in using language, spoken or written, in which the disorder may manifest itself in an imperfect ability to listen, think, speak, read, write, spell, or to do mathematical calculations.

(ii) Disorders Included/Not Included

The definition subsumes terms such as "perceptual handicap, brain injury, minimal brain dysfunction, dyslexia and developmental aphasia," while ruling out learning problems primarily due to problems of "vision, hearing, or motor handicaps, mental retardation, emotional disturbance, environmental, cultural or economic disadvantage." (p. 12422)

The guidelines suggest that a child may be determined as having a specific learning disability if, (a) the child does not achieve commensurate with his or her ability levels in the areas listed above and (b) there is a severe discrepancy between achievement and IQ, and (c) the severe discrepancy is not primarily a result of sensory, motor, mental retardation, emotional disturbance, or other environmental or economic factors.

National Joint Committee on Learning Disabilities (NJCLD). The NJCLD defines *learning disabilities* as a general term referring to a heterogeneous groups of disorders manifested by significant difficulties in the acquisition and use of listening, speaking, reading, writing, reasoning, or mathematical abilities. These disorders are intrinsic to the individual, presumed to be due to central nervous dysfunction, and may occur across the life span. Problems in self-regulatory behaviors, social perception, and social interaction may co-occur, but themselves do not constitute a learning disability. Although learning disabilities may occur with other handicapping conditions (e.g., sensory deficits, emotional disturbance, mental retardation, or cultural differences), they are not the result of those conditions or influences (NJCLD, 1988).

Learning Disabilities Generically and Specifically Defined. Byron Rourke has conducted numerous studies concerning subtypes of LD based on discrepancy response patterns evident on the Wechsler Intelligence Scale for Children (WISC-III). As a result of his work, Rourke suggests a generic definition of LD is most appropriate. Although this "generic" definition supports the NJCLD definition in general, a major point of difference is evident in Rourke's view that "the term LD is also appropriately applied to instances where persons exhibit significant difficulties in mastering social and other adaptive skills and abilities" (Rourke, 1989, p. 215). Furthermore, according to Rourke, it is possible that emotional disturbances and other adaptive deficiencies may arise from the same patterns of central processing assets and deficits that generate the manifestations of academic and social LD.

Issues in the Definition and Classification of Children and Adolescents With Learning Disabilities

Definitions of learning disabilities have been criticized on several fronts. The *DSM* definition has been faulted for being too narrow and considering only disorders of reading, mathematics, and written expression (excluding spelling) as true academic disorders. The definition has also been criticized theoretically in defining LD by exclusion (ruling out other disorders), thereby implying that coexisting disorders cannot occur. The NJCLD definition improves upon the *DSM* by ruling-in the possibility of co-occurring disorders and by introducing the heterogeneity of learning disorders; however, it fails to provide any operable guidelines for how to measure "significant difficulties in the acquisition" of academic skills. Although Rourke's generic definition also remains vague with respect to measurement of "significant difficulties in mastery" of academic skills, his definition improves upon other definitions in the recognition of the existence of LD in areas of social and adaptive functioning. The federal definition (IDEA) has also been criticized for usage of vague terms such as *basic psychological process* and lack of guidance regarding measurement of the "manifestation of an imperfect ability." In addition, definition by exclusion also implies that disorders cannot coexist with LD. The *DSM's* is the only definition that provides an objective measurement to define a significant discrepancy between IQ and achievement, and suggests a 2 *SD* rule be applied as a general guideline, although this criterion can be reduced to between 1 and 2 *SD*s if other factors compromise IQ level. However, as will be discussed shortly, there are several differences of opinion regarding the use and measurement of a discrepancy-based model.

Considering the differences evident in the four definitions presented, it is not difficult to understand why the concept of learning disabilities has met with such controversy. According to Kavale, Forness, and MacMillan (1998), the major problem in obtaining an agreed-upon definition of LD stems from the fact that the "concept" of LD has been severed from its biophysical roots. It is the authors' contention that the nature of LD has been reduced from a central nervous system (CNS) impairment to a categorical construct that has become equated in the schools with a generalized failure to perform academically. Inherent in this problem of definition and vague terminology, the LD category has become the catchall category that presently holds approximately 52% of all children with disabilities. The authors note that since 1976-1977, the LD population has increased 198%.

Although problems of definition have been cited as the likely culprit for substantial increases in identified LD, concerns have also been noted, even when prescribed procedures are clearly defined. MacMillan and Forness (1998) reviewed identification decisions for 113 students referred to the school support team (SST). Using an assessment battery, the research team tested, then matched, eligible candidates according to two clearly defined state-mandated criteria for LD: (a) aptitude-achievement discrepancy of 22 points and (b) exclusion of MR students. Results revealed that the SST identified 61, or 54%, of the population as LD. When matched to the state criteria, however, only one third met the full criteria for LD (assessment matched state guidelines). The authors conclude that there is often a lack of compliance between procedures at the state and local levels, and results supported the notion that many students are misidentified as LD.

Discrepancy Model

Inherent in the majority of definitions of LD is the notion of a significant discrepancy between intellectual functioning and academic performance.

However, there is much less agreement on what constitutes a "significant" discrepancy (Shaw, Cullen, McGuire, & Brinckerhoff, 1995).

Some clinicians define the discrepancy between achievement and age expectations by comparing current grade level to current functioning level. A 2-year rule has been used in several instances; for example, a child in Grade 4 is functioning at least 2 years behind his or her current grade placement. However, using a fixed criterion may penalize students in the early grades while being too lenient for students in the later grades. Sattler (2002) states that some definitions attempt to address this issue by using a gradient of discrepancy based on grade level: 1 year for Grades 1 and 2; 1.5 years for Grades 3 and 4; 2 years for Grades 5 through 8; and 3 years for secondary school performance levels. However, Sattler cautions against comparing achievement grade scores with actual grade scores since the practice is not sound statistically and is likely to lead to invalid conclusions.

Another method of defining discrepancy is to compare standard scores obtained on IQ tests with standard scores available from achievement tests. A common criterion applied to this method is to use discrepancies between 15 and 22 points (1.5 to 2 SDs) as significant. However, this method has also been criticized at the upper and lower levels. Comparisons at the upper levels may note a significant discrepancy, yet it is arguable whether this discrepancy would define a disability (e.g., IQ 145; Achievement 125). At lower IQ levels, students who tend to score lower on IQ tests (low SES) may not reveal significant discrepancy in the other direction (e.g., IQ 85; Achievement 75). Furthermore, according to Sattler (2002), processing difficulties that impact on achievement (e.g., vocabulary, comprehension, factual information) may also serve to reduce scores for intellectual functioning that requires the same processing abilities. Another difficulty arises when a significant discrepancy exists between IQ components, for example, Verbal IQ (IQ = 85) and Performance IQ (IQ = 115). Under these conditions, the Full Scale IQ is rendered meaningless, since it represents only a numeric average of discrepant scores (Kaufman & Lichtenberger, 2000). Some clinicians would select the higher of the two IQs (in this case, Performance IQ), arguing that this score is the most representative of the child's true ability; others might select the Verbal IQ, stating Verbal IQ correlates better with academic performance. Research has demonstrated that decisions regarding which scales to use (Full Scale, Verbal, Performance) can be instrumental in determining eligibility (MacMillan et al., 1998).

Despite these limitations and other statistical problems inherent in making comparisons between different test instruments (Sattler, 2002), Sattler's conclusion is in agreement with that suggested by Kavale et al. (1998), which supports the need to retain a discrepancy model as a necessary ingredient in determining eligibility for LD. However, more research is needed to determine how best to employ this model (Sattler, 2002).

There is an alternate school of thought, however, that runs contrary to this opinion. In his presentation to the National Association of School Psychologist Convention in March 2002, Assistant Secretary Robert Pasternack, Office of Special Education and Rehabilitation Services of the U.S. Department of Education, presented his "Distinguished Lecture" on the *Demise of IQ Testing for Children with Learning Disabilities.* Drawing on findings from recent meta analyses, Pasternack put forth the position that the IQ-Achievement Discrepancy is not a valid method for identifying individuals with LD. According to Pasternack, research has failed to support the hypothesis that IQ-discrepant and IQ-consistent populations differ with respect to either characteristics, prognosis, or response to intervention.

Emotional Disturbance

A complete description of the definitions for IDEA, CMHS, and SSA can be found in the module titled *Students With Emotional Disturbance,* produced by the Center for Effective Collaboration and Practice (CECP; 2000). CECP is one of several research centers funded by the Office for Special Education Programs (OSEP). The OSEP is responsible for monitoring compliance by the state to ensure that federal funds will not be withheld.

Educational: IDEA. Although the IDEA provides guidelines and definitions for categories of disabilities, there continues to be wide variation at the state level concerning how categories are defined. In addition, many of the disabilities that fall under IDEA are defined in educational terms, which can be at odds with more clinical definitions of childhood disorders: One such area is the category of emotional disturbance (previously called seriously emotionally disturbed). Within IDEA, emotional disturbance is defined as a long-lasting condition causing significant educational impairment manifested in the following characteristics:

1. learning difficulties not explained by intellectual, sensory, or health factors

2. difficulties maintaining satisfactory interpersonal relationships with peers and teachers

3. inappropriate behaviors or feelings in response to normal circumstances

4. pervasive mood of unhappiness or depression

5. tendencies to develop physical symptoms in response to personal problems or problems at school

Although the category of emotional disturbance includes schizophrenia, children who are socially maladjusted are excluded from this category, unless it can be determined that they have an emotional disturbance.

Center for Mental Health Services (CMHS). The CMHS is a federal agency that provides mental health services for children under 18 years of age. According to CMHS, service is provided to children and youth who present with a diagnosable mental, behavioral, or emotional disorder meeting criteria set out in the *DSM-IV.* The disorder must also meet criteria of duration and functional impairment as defined in the DSM.

Social Security Administration (SSA). The federal guidelines of the SSA define a mental condition as one that can be medically proven and that results in marked and severe functional limitations of substantial duration.

DSM. Given descriptions in the IDEA, it is possible that children who qualify under the category of emotional disturbance may be found in the *DSM* disorders represented by: mood disorders, anxiety disorders, somatic disorders, and schizophrenia.

Council for Exceptional Children. The Council for Exceptional Children has lobbied for a new and improved definition that changes the label to emotional or behavioral disorder (EBD) and defines the disorder as a condition in which behavioral or emotional response is so different from the generally accepted, age-appropriate, ethnic or cultural norms as to adversely affect self-care, social relationships, personal adjustments, academic progress, classroom behavior, or work adjustment. Despite strong support, the definition has not been incorporated into the latest revisions of IDEA.

National Mental Health and Special Education Coalition. The coalition has also actively lobbied for changes in the federal definition of emotional disturbance. The National Association of School Psychologists has adopted and endorsed the definition put forth by this group (Dwyer & Stanhope, 1997). This definition adopts the label of emotional or behavioral disorder (EBD) for responses that are so different from expectations (age, cultural, ethic norms) that they adversely compromise educational performance. The responses are demonstrated in more than one setting (at least one of which is school related) and are unresponsive to direct intervention in a general educational setting. EBD can coexist with other disabilities. The category may include: schizophrenia, affective disorders, anxiety disorders, or other sustained disturbances of conduct or adjustment.

Issues in the Definition and Classification of Children and Adolescents With Emotional Disturbance

The IDEA definition of emotional disturbance is highly controversial and is problematic for several reasons:

First, although the category of emotional disturbance would apply to children who had evidence of internalizing disorders, such as anxiety, depression, or withdrawal, the definition is problematic because the category excludes those children who exhibit socially maladaptive behaviors such as aggressive behaviors that are antisocial and violate the rights of others (e.g., conduct disorder).

Therefore, despite the fact that children with conduct disorder represent one of the largest diagnostic groups, this definition has led some states to exclude children with conduct disorder from identification within this category, while others have not (Gonzalez, 1991). Wide variations in rates of reporting children within this category (Connecticut reported 2.06% with SED in 1996, and Arkansas reported 0.09%) suggest different qualification criteria as well as the severity of children included (MacMillan, 1998).

Next, terms used to define duration (long period of time) and intensity (marked degree) are not operationally defined and provide no guidelines for measurement.

Third, in addition, although states must designate criteria that do not conflict with the federal guidelines of IDEA, there is wide interpretive leeway in how emotional disturbance is defined by various states (McInerney, Kane, & Pelavin, 1992). In addition, some states have adopted labels other than emotional disturbance for this category, and labels of behavior disordered (BD) or emotionally and behaviorally disordered (EBD) have been frequently substituted.

Fourth, studies have demonstrated that children with labels of serious emotional disturbance (SED) are not a homogenous population (Rosenblatt et al., 1998; Walrath et al., 1998), and investigators have questioned the usefulness of labels such as SED and EBD with respect to defining treatments (Kershaw & Sonuga-Barke, 1998). One study by Duncan, Forness, and Harsough (1995) suggests that the LD label may be the preferred starting point for intervention and often the first label of choice regardless of the nature of the problem. In their investigation, they found that the majority of children labeled as SED were initially classified as LD, until the requirement for more intensive service resulted in reclassification.

Attention-Deficit/Hyperactivity Disorder

Educational Definition of ADHD. The most recent revision of IDEA has added "attention deficit disorder" and "attention deficit hyperactivity disorder (ADHD)" to the list of disabilities. Prior to this change in regulations, ADHD children were able to receive special education assistance under Section 504 of the Rehabilitation Act of 1973, a broader piece of anti-discrimination legislation. Children with ADHD can now be deemed disabled under the category of Other Health Impairments, which are defined as "having limited strength, vitality or alertness, including a heightened alertness to environment stimuli, that results in limited alertness with respect to the educational environment" (IDEA, 1999). Other disabilities in the same category include acute health problems such as asthma, diabetes, epilepsy, a heart condition, hemophilia, lead poisoning, leukemia, and rheumatic fever. A diagnosis of ADHD alone does not guarantee services under IDEA. The ADHD must adversely affect education to warrant special education.

Issues in the Definition and Classification of Children and Adolescents With ADHD. Children with ADHD often have comorbid features of emotional or behavioral disturbance and learning disabilities. Children with ADHD may also qualify under other IDEA categories, such as LD or ED. At early developmental levels, ADHD features may overlap and share symptom features of developmental delay, a noncategorical option of IDEA available for children 3 to 9 years of age. Problems exist concerning how to assess children with ADHD, and high rates of overlap in symptoms between ADHD and other disorders/conditions (anxiety, abuse, post traumatic stress disorder, etc.).

REFERENCES

Achenbach, T. M., & Rescorla, L. A. (2001). *Manual for the ASEBA School-Age Forms & Profiles.* Burlington, VT: ASEBA.

American Association on Mental Retardation. (1992). *Mental retardation: Definition, classification, and systems of support* (9th ed.). Washington, DC: Author.

Center for Effective Collaboration and Practice. (2000). *Students with emotional disturbance.* Retrieved March 24, 2002, from http://cecp.air.org/resources/20th/eligchar.htm

Duncan, B. B., Forness, S. R., & Harsough, C. (1995). Students identified as seriously emotionally disturbed in day treatment: Cognitive, psychiatric and special education characteristics. *Behavioral Disorders, 20,* 238-252.

Dwyer, K. P., & Stanhope, V. (1997). IDEA "97": Synopsis and recommendations. *NASP Communique, 16*(1) [Handout supplement]. Washington, DC: National Association of School Psychologists.

Gonzalez, P. (1991). *A comparison of state policy of the federal definition and a proposed definition of "serious emotional disturbance."* Washington, DC: National Association of State Directors of Special Education.

Henderson, K. (2001, March). *An overview of ADA, IDEA and Section 504: Update 2001*. The Eric Clearinghouse on Disabilities and Gifted Education. Retrieved March 21, 2002, from http://www.ldonline.org/ld_indepth/legal_legislative/update_504_2001.html

IDEA practices. (1999). Retrieved March 20, 2002, from www.ideapractices.org

Kaufman, A. S., & Lichtenberger, E. O. (2000). *Essentials of WISC-III and WPPSI-R assessment*. New York: John Wiley.

Kavale, K., Forness, S., & MacMillan, D. L. (1998). The politics of learning disabilities: A rejoinder. *Learning Disability Quarterly, 21,* 306-317.

Kershaw, P., & Sonuga-Barke, E. (1998). Emotional and behavioral difficulties: Is this a useful category? The implications of clustering and comorbidity, the relevance of a taxonomic approach. *Educational and Child Psychology, 15,* 45-55.

MacMillan, D. L., & Forness, S. R. (1998). The role of IQ in special education placement decisions: Primary and determinative or peripheral and inconsequential. *Remedial and Special Education 19,* 239-253.

MacMillan, D. L., Gresham, F. M., & Bocian, K. M. (1998). Current plight of borderline students: Where do they belong? *Education and Training in Mental Retardation and Developmental Disabilities, 33,* 83-95.

MacMillan, D. L., & Reschly, D. J. (1998). Over-representation of minority students: The case for greater specificity or reconsideration of the variables examined. *Journal of Special Education, 19,* 239-253.

MacMillan, R. C. (1998). A longitudinal study of the cost effectiveness of educating students with emotional or behavioral disorders in a public school setting. *Behavioral Disorders, 25,* 65-75.

McInerney, M., Kane, M., & Pelavin, S. (1992). *Services to children with serious emotional disturbance*. Washington, DC: Pelavin Associates.

National Joint Committee on Learning Disabilities. (1987). Learning disabilities: Issues on definition. *Journal of Learning Disabilities, 20,* 107-108.

Oswald, D. P., Coutinho, M. J., Best, A. M., & Nguyen, N. (2001). The impact of socio-demographic characteristics on the identification rates of minority students as mentally retarded. *Mental Retardation, 39,* 351-367.

Pasternack, R. H. (2002, March). *The demise of IQ testing for children with learning disabilities*. Distinguished Lecture presented to National Association of School Psychologists annual convention, Chicago. Retrieved March 24, 2002, from Louisiana State University Health Sciences Center Web site: http://www.hdc.lsuhsc.edu

Reynolds, C. R., & Kamphaus, R. W. (1992). *BASC: Behavior Assessment System for Children manual*. Circle Pines, MN: American Guidance Service.

Rosenblatt, J. A., & Furlong, M. J. (1998). Outcomes in a system of care for youth with emotional and behavioral disorders: An examination of differential change across clinical profile. *Journal of Child and Family Studies, 7,* 1217-1232.

Rourke, B. P. (1989). *Nonverbal learning disabilities: The syndrome and the model*. New York: Guilford.

Sattler, J. (2002). *Assessment of children: Behavioral and clinical applications* (4th ed.). San Diego, CA: Jerome M. Sattler.

Shaw, S. F., Cullen, J. P., McGuire, J. M., & Brinckerhoff, L. C. (1995). Operationalizing a definition of learning disabilities. *Journal of Learning Disabilities, 26,* 586-597.

Walrath, C., Nickerson, K., Crowel, R., & Leaf, P. (1998). Serving children with serious emotional disturbance in a system of care. Do mental health and non–mental health agency referrals look the same? *Journal of Emotional and Behavioral Disorders, 6,* 205-213.

Appendix C

List of Assessment Instruments and Resources

Achenbach, T. M. (1991). *Manual for the Child Behavior Checklist 4-8 and the 1991 profile*. Burlington: University of Vermont, Department of Psychiatry.

Comment: Parent, Teacher and Youth Self Report (11 years +) measuring behaviors on eight syndrome scales.

Achenbach, T. M., & Rescorla, L. A. (2001). *Manual for the ASEBA School-Age Forms & Profiles*. Burlington, VT: ASEBA.

Comment: Revised and re-normed Parent, Teacher and Youth Self Report (11 years +) measuring behaviors on eight syndrome scales with *DSM* scale scoring.

Barkley, R. A. (1997). *Defiant children: A clinician's manual for assessment and parent training* (2nd ed.). New York: Guilford.

Barkley, R. A. (1987). *Defiant children: Parent-teacher assignments*. New York: Guilford.

Comment: Contains many excellent resources and handouts for parents, as well as scales and parent & teacher questionnaires.

Beck, A., & Beck, J. (2001). *The Beck Youth Inventories*. San Antonio, TX: Psychological Corporation.

Comment: Five brief (20-question) self-report scales measuring Self-Concept, Depression, Anxiety, Anger, and Disruptive Behavior, in children and youth, from 7 years of age.

Conners, C. K., (1998). *Conners Rating Scales-Revised technical manual.* North Tonawanda, NY: Multi-Health Systems.

Comment: Contains long, and short versions of Parent and Teacher Rating forms for Attentional and Behavioral Problems. Manual also provides information about the Conners-Wells Self Report Scale for Adolescents (C. K. Conners & K. Wells, 1997).

Dunn, L. M., & Dunn, L. M. (1997). *Peabody Picture Vocabulary Test— third edition.* Circle Pines, MN: American Guidance Service.

Elliott, C. D. (1990). *Differential Ability Scales.* San Antonio, TX: Psychological Corporation.

Gardner, D. M. (1991). *The Eating Disorder Inventory-2.* Odessa, FL: Psychological Assessment Resources.

Comment: A 91-item self-report scale measuring traits associated with eating disorders; yields 8 scales, such as Body Dissatisfaction, Drive for Thinness, and Perfectionism.

Gilliam, J. E. (1995). *Gilliam Autism Rating Scale: GARS.* Austin, TX: Pro-Ed.

Comment: Autism Quotient derived from ratings on four scales: Stereotyped Behaviors, Communication, Social Interaction, & Developmental.

Goodman, W., Rasmussen, S., & Price, L. (1988). *The Children's Yale Brown Obsessive Compulsive Scale (CY-BOCS).* New Haven, CT: Connecticut Mental Health Center, Clinical Neuroscience Research Unit.

Jesness, C. F. (1988). *JBC: Jesness Behavior Checklist.* North Tonawanda, NY: Multi-Health Systems.

Comment: A multiple rating scale for youth (13 to 20 years) at risk for antisocial behavior. Self Report and Observer Rating Scale measures behavior across 14 scales including: Social Control, Anger Control, and Conformity.

Jesness, C. F. (1996). *Jesness Inventory.* North Tonawanda, NY: Multi-Health Systems.

Comment: Self-report scale for youth ages 8 and older measuring Conduct Problems and Anti-Social Behaviors, yielding 10 trait scores, and indices of asocial tendencies and nine personality subscales: Social Maladjustment, Value Orientation, Immaturity, and Manifest Aggression.

Kazdin, A. E., Rodgers, A., & Colbus, D. (1986). The Hopelessness Scale for Children: Psychometric characteristics and concurrent validity. *Journal of Consulting and Clinical Psychology, 54,* 241-245.

Comment: A 17-item true-false questionnaire measuring hopelessness based on future expectations. Research supports hopelessness as a correlate of depression and suicide.

Kovacs, M. (1992). *Child Depression Inventory*. North Tonawanda, NY: Multi-Health Systems.

Comment: Self-report measure for children and youth 7 to 17 years of age. In addition to Total Depression Score, rates depressive symptoms in five areas: Negative Mood, Interpersonal Problems, Ineffectiveness, Anhedonia, and Negative Self-Esteem.

Lachar, D., & Gruber, C. P. (1995). *Personality Inventory for Youth (PIY) manual*. Los Angeles: Western Psychological Services.

Comment: Objective, multidimensional, self-report measure for children and youth 9 to 18 years of age. Assesses emotional and behavioral adjustment, family and school impressions, and academic adjustment. Includes validity and consistency scales.

Lambert, N., Nihira, K., & Leland, H. (1993) *ABS-S:2: The Adaptive Behavior Scale–School* (2nd ed.). Austin, TX: Pro-Ed.

Comment: Rating scale to assess adaptive functioning and maladaptive behaviors in children and youth.

Myles, B. S., Bock, S. J. & Simpson, R. L. (2001). *ASDS: Asperger Syndrome Diagnostic Scale examiner's manual*. Austin, TX: Pro-Ed.

Comment: Asperger's Quotient derived from ratings on five scales: Language, Social, Maladaptive, Cognitive, and Sensorimotor.

Newcomer, P. L., et al. (1994). *DAYS: Depression and Anxiety in Youth Scale*. Austin, TX: Pro-Ed.

Comment: Parent, Teacher, and Child Self-Report Scale with 22 items (true/false format) suitable for children and youth 6 to 19 years old.

Reich, W., Welner, Z., Herjanic, B., & MHS Staff. (1997). *Diagnostic Interview for Children and Adolescents computer program (DICA-IV)*. North Tonawanda, NY: Multi-Health System.

Reynolds, C. R., & Kamphaus, R. W. (1992). *BASC: Behavior Assessment System for Children manual*. Circle Pines, MN: American Guidance Service.

Comment: Multiple informant (parent, teacher, child) rating scales for adaptive and maladaptive behaviors, from 4 years to adolescence. Includes validity indexes to screen for excessive positive or negative response profiles.

Reynolds, C. R., & Richmond, B. O. (1994). *Revised Child Manifest Anxiety Scale*. Los Angeles: Western Psychological Services.

Sattler, J. M. (2001). *Assessment of Children: Cognitive Applications* (4th ed.). La Mesa, CA: Jerome M. Sattler.

Sattler, J. M. (2002). *Assessment of Children: Behavioral and Clinical Applications* (4th ed.). La Mesa, CA: Jerome M. Sattler.

Sparrow, S. S., Balla, D. A., & Cicchetti, D. V. (1984). *Vineland Adaptive Behavior Scales*. Circle Pines, MN: American Guidance Service.

Wechsler, D. (1991). *Manual for the Wechsler Intelligence Scale for Children–Third Edition*. San Antonio, TX: Psychological Corporation.

Wilkinson, G. S. (1993). *WRAT3: The Wide Range Achievement Test administration manual*. Wilmington, DE: Wide Range.

Woodcock, R. W., McGrew, K. S., & Mather, N. (2001). *Woodcock-Johnson III, Tests of Achievement*. New York: Riverside.

References

Achenbach, T. M., & Rescorla, L. A. (2001). *Manual for the ASEBA School-Age Forms & Profiles*. Burlington, VT: ASEBA.

Ainsworth, M. D., Blehar, M., Waters, E., & Wall, S. (1978). *Patterns of attachment*. Hillsdale, NJ: Lawrence Erlbaum.

Akiskal, H. S. (1995). Developmental pathways to bipolarity: Are juvenile-onset depressions pre-bipolar? *Journal of the American Academy of Child and Adolescent Psychiatry, 34,* 754-763.

Akiskal, H. S., Walker, P., & Puzantian, V. R. (1983). Bipolar outcomes in the course of depressive illness. *Journal of Affective Disorders, 5,* 115-128.

Alexander, J. F., & Parsons, B. V. (1973). Short-term behavioral intervention with delinquent families: Impact on family process and recidivism. *Journal of Abnormal Psychology, 81,* 219-225.

American Association on Mental Retardation. (1992). *Mental retardation: Definition, classification, and systems of support* (9th ed.). Washington, DC: Author.

Angold, A., & Costello, E. J. (1993). Depressive comorbidity in children and adolescents: Empirical, theoretical, and methodological issues. *Journal of the American Academy of Child and Adolescent Psychiatry, 150,* 1779-1791.

Anstending, K. D. (1999). Is selective mutism an anxiety disorder? Rethinking *DSM-IV* classification. *Journal of Anxiety Disorders, 13,* 417-434.

APA Task Force on Psychological Intervention Guidelines. (1995). Template for developing guidelines: Interventions for mental disorders and psychosocial aspects of physical disorders. Washington, DC: American Psychological Association.

Aptekar, L., & Stocklin, D. (1997) Children in particularly difficult circumstances. In J. Berry, P. Dasen, & T. S. Saraswathi (Eds.), *Handbook of cross-cultural psychology: Vol. 2. Basic processes and human development* (2nd ed., pp. 377-412). Needham Heights, MA: Allyn & Bacon.

Azrin, N. H. & Besalel, V. A. (1980). *How to use overcorrection*. Lawrence, KS: H & H Enterprises.

Barkley, R. A. (1997a). Attention deficit hyperactivity disorder. In E. J. Mash & L. G. Terdal (Eds.), *Assessment of childhood disorders* (pp. 71-129). New York: Guilford.

Barkley, R. A. (1997b). Behavior inhibition, sustained attention and executive function. *Psychological Bulletin, 121*, 65-94.

Barkley, R. A. (1998). *Attention deficit hyperactivity disorder: A handbook for diagnosis and treatment* (2nd ed.). New York: Guilford.

Bartlett, P. M., Dadds, M. R., & Rapee, R. M. (1996). Family treatment of childhood anxiety: A controlled trial. *Journal of Consulting and Clinical Psychology, 64*, 333-342.

Beardslee, W. R. (1989). The role of self-understanding in resilient individuals: The development of a perspective. *American Journal of Orthopsychiatry, 59*, 266-278.

Beidel, D. C., Turner, S. M., & Morris, T. L. (1999). Psychopathology of childhood social phobia. *Journal of the American Academy of Child and Adolescent Psychiatry, 38*, 643-650.

Bergman, R., L., Piacentini, J., & McCracken, J. T. (2002). Prevalence and description of selective mutism in a school-based population. *Journal of the American Academy of Child and Adolescent Psychiatry, 41*, 938-946.

Bernal, M. E., Klinnert, M. D., & Schultz, L. A. (1980). Outcome evaluation of behavioral parent training and client-centered parent counseling for children with conduct problems. *Journal of Applied Behavior Analysis, 13*, 677-691.

Bezchlibnyk-Butler, K. Z., & Jeffries, J. J. (1997). *Clinical handbook of psychotropic drugs*. Toronto: Hogrefe & Huber.

Billings, A. G., & Moos, R. H. (1983). Comparison of children of depressed and nondepressed parents: A social-environmental perspective. *Journal of Abnormal Child Psychology, 11*, 463-486.

Birmaher, B., Ryan, N. D., Williamson, D. E., Brent, D. A., & Kaufman, J. (1996). Childhood and adolescent depression: A review of the past 10 years. Part II. *Journal of the American Academy of Child and Adolescent Psychiatry, 35*, 1575-1583.

Bishop, D. V. M. (1989). Autism, Asperger's syndrome and semantic-pragmatic disorder: Where are the boundaries? *British Journal of Disorders of Communication, 24*, 107-121.

Black, B., & Uhde, T. W. (1992). Treatment of elective mutism as a variant of school phobia. *Journal of the American Academy of Child and Adolescent Psychiatry, 31*, 1090-1094.

Black, B., & Uhde, T. W. (1994). Treatment of elective mutism with fluoxetine: A double-blind, placebo-controlled study. *Journal of the American Academy of Child and Adolescent Psychiatry, 33*, 1000-1006.

Black, B., & Uhde, T. W. (1995). Psychiatric characteristics of children with selective mutism: A pilot study. *Journal of the American Academy of Child and Adolescent Psychiatry, 32*, 847-856.

Blum, N. J., Kell, R. S., Star, H. L., Lender, W. L., Bradley-Klug, K. L., Osborne, M. L., & Dowrick, P. W. (1998). Case study: Audio feedforward treatment of selective mutism. *Journal of the American Academy of Child and Adolescent Psychiatry, 37*, 40-43.

Bolton, D., Luckie, M., & Steinberg, D. (1995). Long-term course of obsessive compulsive disorder treated in adolescence. *Journal of the American Academy of Child and Adolescent Psychiatry, 34,* 1441-1450.

Borduin, C. M., Mann, B. J., Cone, L. T., & Henggeler, S. W. (1995). *Family therapy and beyond: A multisystemic approach to treating the behavior problems of children and adolescents.* Pacific Grove, CA: Brooks/Cole.

Borowsky, I. W., Ireland, M., & Resnick, M. D. (2001). Adolescent suicide attempts: Risks and protectors. *Pediatrics, 107,* 485-502.

Bowlby, J. (1988). *A secure base.* New York: Basic Books.

Bowring, M. A., & Kovacs, M. (1992). Difficulties in diagnosing manic disorders among children and adolescents. *Journal of the American Academy of Child and Adolescent Psychiatry, 31,* 611-614.

Brantley, D. C., & Webster, R. E. (1993). Use of an independent group contingency management system in a regular classroom setting. *Psychology in the Schools, 30,* 60-66.

Brestan, E. V., & Eyberg, S. M. (1998). Effective psychosocial treatments of conduct disordered children and adolescents: 29 years, 82 studies and 5,272 kids. *Journal of Clinical Child Psychology, 27,* 180-189.

Bruch, H. (1991). The sleeping beauty: Escape from change. In S. I. Greenspan & G. H. Pollock (Eds.), *The course of life: Vol. 4. Adolescence.* Madison, CT: International Universities Press.

Cantwell, D. P. (1996). Attention deficit disorder: A review of the past 10 years. *Journal of the American Academy of Child and Adolescent Psychiatry, 35,* 978-987.

Carlberg, C., & Kavale, K. (1980). The efficacy of special versus regular class placement for exceptional children: A meta-analysis. *The Journal of Special Education, 14,* 295-308.

Carlson, G. A. (1983). Bipolar affective disorders in childhood and adolescence. In D. P. Cantwell & G. A. Carlson (Eds.), *Affective disorders in childhood and adolescence* (pp. 61-84). New York: S. P. Medial Science Books.

Carrasco, J. L., Diaz-Marsa, M., Hollander, E., Cesar, J., & Saiz-Ruiz, J. (2000). Decreased platelet monamine oxidase activity in female bulimia nervosa. *European Journal of Neuropsychopharmacology, 10,* 113-117.

Cassidy, J., & Mohr, J. J. (2001). Unresolved fear, trauma and psychopathology: Theory, research and clinical considerations related to disorganized attachment across the life span. *Clinical Psychology Science Practice, 8,* 275-298.

Cautela, J. R., & Groden, J. (1978). Relaxation: A comprehensive manual for adults, children, and children with special needs. Champaign, IL: Research Review.

Center for Effective Collaboration and Practice. (2000). *Students with emotional disturbance.* Retrieved March 24, 2002, from http://cecp.air.org/resources/20th/eligchar.htm

Chamberlain, P., & Reid, J. (1991). Using a specialized foster care community treatment model for children and adolescents leaving the state mental hospital. *Journal of Community Psychology, 19,* 266-276.

Chamberlain, P., & Reid, J. (1998). Comparison of two community alternatives to incarceration for chronic juvenile offenders. *Journal of Consulting and Clinical Psychology, 66,* 624-633.

Chiron, C., Jambaque, I., & Nabbout, R. (1997). The right brain hemisphere is dominant in human infants. *Brain, 120,* 1057-1065.

Christian, B. (1983). A practical reinforcement hierarchy for classroom behavior modification. *Psychology in the Schools, 20,* 83-84.

Cicchetti, D., & Rogosch, F. A. (1997). The role of self-organization in the promotion of resilience in maltreated children. *Developmental Psychopathology, 9,* 797-815.

Cicchetti, D., & Toth, S. L. (1998). The development of depression in children and adolescents. *American Psychologist, 53,* 221-241.

Clark, D. B., & Baker, B. L. (1983). Predicting outcome in parent training. *Journal of Consulting and Clinical Psychology, 51,* 309-311.

Clark, L. (1985). *SOS! Help for parents.* Bowling Green, KY: Parents Press.

Cogan, M. B. (1996). Diagnosis and treatment of bipolar disorder in children and adolescents. *Psychiatric Times, 13*(5). Retrieved September 28, 2002, from http://www.mhsource.com/pt/p960531.html

Cole, D. A., Truglio, R., & Peeke, L. (1997). Relation between symptoms of anxiety and depression in children: A multitrait-multimethod-multigroup assessment. *Journal of Consulting and Clinical Psychology, 65,* 110-119.

Compass, B. E., Connor, J. K., & Hinden, B. R. (1998). New perspectives on depression during adolescence. In R. Jessor (Ed.), *New perspectives on adolescent risk behavior.* Cambridge, UK: Cambridge University Press.

Cornwall, E., Spence, S. H., & Schotte, D. (1997). The effectiveness of emotive imagery in the treatment of darkness phobia in children. *Behavior Change, 13,* 223-229.

Costello, E. J., Angold, A. A., Burns, B. J., Stangl, D. K., Tweed, D. L., Erkanli, A., & Worthman, C. M. (1996). The Great Smoky Mountains study of youth. Goals, design, methods, and, the prevalence of *DSM-III-R* disorders. *Archives of General Psychiatry, 53,* 1129-1136.

Crick, N. R., & Grotpeter, J. K. (1995). Relational aggression, gender and social psychological adjustment. *Child Development, 66,* 710-722.

Crick, N. R., Casas, J. F., & Mosher, M. (1997). Relational and overt aggression in preschool. *Developmental Psychology, 33,* 579-588.

Darveaux, D. X. (1984). The Good Behavior Game Plus Merit: Controlling disruptive behavior and improving student motivation. *School Psychology Review, 13,* 510-514.

Decina P., Kestenbaum, C. J., & Farber, S. (1983). Clinical and psychological assessment of children of bipolar probands. *American Journal of Psychiatry, 140,* 548-553.

DeKlyen, M. (1996). Disruptive behavior disorder and intergenerational attachment patterns: A comparison of clinic-referred and normally functioning preschoolers and their mothers. *Journal of Consulting and Clinical Psychology, 64,* 357-365.

Diller, L. H. (1996). The run on Ritalin: Attention deficit disorder and stimulant treatment in the 1990s. *Hastings Center Report, 26,* 12-18.

Dow, S. P, Sonies, B. C., Scheib, D., Moss, S. E., & Leonard, H. L. (1995). Practical guidelines for the assessment and treatment of selective mutism. *Journal of the American Academy of Child and Adolescent Psychiatry, 34,* 836-846.

Drummit, E. S., Klein, R. G., Tancer, N. K., Asche, B., Martin, J., & Fairbanks, J. A. (1997). Systematic assessment of 50 children with selective mutism. *Journal of the American Academy of Child and Adolescent Psychiatry, 36,* 653-660.

Duncan, B. B., Forness, S. R., & Harsough, C. (1995). Students identified as seriously emotionally disturbed in day treatment: Cognitive, psychiatric and special education characteristics. *Behavioral Disorders, 20,* 238-252.

Durlak, J. A. (1998). Common risk and protective factors in successful prevention programs. *American Journal of Orthopsychiatry, 68,* 512-520.

Dwyer, K. P., & Stanhope, V. (1997). IDEA "97": Synopsis and recommendations. *NASP Communique, 16*(1) [Handout supplement]. Washington, DC: National Association of School Psychologists.

Egeland, J. (2000) Prodromal symptoms present a decade before diagnosis of bipolar disorder. *Journal of the American Academy of Child and Adolescent Psychiatry, 39,* 1245-1252.

Embregts, P. J. C. (2000). Effectiveness of video feedback and self-management on inappropriate social behavior of youth with mild mental retardation. *Research in Developmental Disabilities, 21,* 409-423.

Emslie, G. J., Rush, A. J., & Weinberg, W. A. (1997). A double-blind, randomized, placebo-controlled trial of fluoxetine in children and adolescents with depression. *Archives of General Psychiatry, 54,* 1031-1037.

Erickson, M. F., Sroufe, L. A., & Egeland, B. (1985). The relationship between quality of attachment and behavior problems in preschool in a high-risk sample. In I. Betherton & E. Waters (Eds.), Growing points of attachment theory and research. *Monographs of the Society for Research in Child Development, 50*(1-2 Series No. 209), 147-166.

Farmer, T. W., & Rodkin, A. C. (1996). Antisocial and prosocial correlates of classroom social position: The social network centrality perspective. *Social Development, 5,* 174-178.

Field, T., Fox, N., Pickens, J., & Nawrocki, T. (1995). Relative right frontal EEG activation in 3- to 6-month-old infants of depressed mothers. *Developmental Psychology, 31,* 358-363.

Firestone, P., Kelly, M. J., & Fike, S. (1980). Are fathers necessary in parent training groups? *Journal of Clinical Child Psychology, 9,* 44-47.

Forehand, R., & McMahon, R. (1981). Helping the noncompliant child: A clinician's guide to parent training. New York: Guilford.

Forman, S. G. (1993). *Coping skills interventions for children and adolescents.* San Francisco: Jossey-Bass.

Frazier, J. A., Meyer, M. C., & Biederman, J. (1999). Risperidone treatment for juvenile bipolar disorder: A retrospective chart review. *Journal of the American Academy of Child and Adolescent Psychiatry, 38,* 960-965.

Frick, P. J. (2001). Effective interventions for children and adolescents with conduct disorder. *Canadian Journal of Psychiatry, 46,* 597-608.

Frick, P. J., Lahey, B. B., Loeber, R., Tannenbaum, L., Van Horn, Y., Christ, M. A., Hart, E. L., & Hanson, K. (1993). Oppositional defiant disorder and conduct disorder: A meta-analytic review of factor analyses and cross-validation in a clinic sample. *Clinical Psychology Review, 13,* 319-340.

Fung, D. S. (2002, February). Web-based CBT for selective mutism [Letter to the editor]. *Journal of the American Academy of Child and Adolescent Psychiatry.*

Gabel, S. (1997). Oppositional defiant disorder. In J. D. Noshpitz (Ed.), *Child and adolescent psychiatry* (Vol. 2, pp. 351-359). New York: John Wiley.

Garcia-Sanchez, C., Estevez-Gonzalez, A., Suarez-Romero, E., & Junque, C. (1997). Right hemisphere dysfunction in subjects with attention-deficit disorder with and without hyperactivity. *Journal of Child Neurology, 12,* 107-115.

Geist, R., Davis, R., & Heinman, M. (1998). Binge/purge symptoms and comorbidity in adolescents with eating disorders. *Canadian Journal of Psychiatry, 43,* 507-512.

Geller, B. (1996). The high prevalence of bipolar parents among prepubertal mood-disordered children necessitates appropriate questions to establish bipolarity. *Current Opinions in Psychiatry, 9,* 239-240.

Geller, B., & Luby, J. (1997). Child and adolescent bipolar disorder: A review of the past 10 years. *Journal of the American Academy of Child and Adolescent Psychiatry, 36,* 1168-1176.

Geller, B., Cooper, T. B., Sun, K., Zimerman, B., Frazier, J., Williams, M., & Heath, J. (1998). Double-blind and placebo-controlled study of lithium for adolescent bipolar disorder with secondary substance dependency. *Journal of the American Academy of Child and Adolescent Psychiatry, 37,* 171-178.

Geller, B., Fox, L. W., & Clark, K. A. (1994). Rate and predictors of prepubertal bipolarity during follow-up of 6- to 12-year-old depressed children. *Journal of the American Academy of Child and Adolescent Psychiatry, 33,* 461-468.

Geller, B., Sun, K., Zimerman, B., Luby, J., Frazier, J., & Williams, M. (1995). Complex and rapid-cycling in bipolar children and adolescents: A preliminary study. *Journal of Affective Disorders, 34,* 259-268.

Geller, D. A., Hogg, S., Heiligenstein, J., Ricardi, R., Tamura, R., Kluszynski, S., & Jacobson, J. G. (2001). Fluoxetine treatment of obsessive-compulsive disorder in children and adolescents: A placebo-controlled clinical trial. *Journal of the American Academy of Child and Adolescent Psychiatry, 40,* 773-779.

Gibbs, J. T., & Huang, L. N. (2001). Framework for the psychological assessment and treatment of minority youth. In J. T. Gibbs & L. N. Huang (Eds.), *Children of color* (pp. 112-142). San Francisco: Jossey-Bass.

Gibbs, J. T., & Huang, L. N. (Eds.). (2001). *Children of color.* San Francisco: Jossey-Bass.

Gillberg, C. (1989). Asperger's syndrome in 23 Swedish children. *Developmental Medicine and Child Neurology, 81,* 520-531.

Gonzalez, P. (1991). *A comparison of state policy of the federal definition and a proposed definition of "serious emotional disturbance."* Washington, DC: National Association of State Directors of Special Education.

Gottlieb, J., Alter, M., & Gottlieb, B. W. (1991). Mainstreaming mentally retarded children. In J. L. Matson & J. A. Mulick (Eds.), *Handbook of mental retardation* (pp. 63-73). New York: Pergamon.

Gould, M. S., Fisher, P., Parides, M., Flory, M., & Shaffer, D. (1996). Psychosocial risk factors of child and adolescent completed suicide. *Archives of General Psychiatry, 53,* 1155-1162.

Graziano, A. M., & Mooney, K. C. (1980). Family self-control instruction for children's nighttime fear reduction. *Journal of Consulting and Clinical Psychology, 48,* 206-213.

Graziano, A. M., & Mooney, K. C. (1982). Behavioral treatment of "Nightfears" in children: Maintenance of improvement at 2½ to 3 year follow-up. *Journal of Consulting and Clinical Psychology, 50,* 598-599.

Greenhill, L. (1998). Attention-deficit/hyperactivity disorder. In B. T. Walsh (Ed.), *Child psychopharmacology* (pp. 91-109). Washington, DC: American Psychiatric Association.

Greenhill, L. L., & Setterberg, S. (1993). Pharmacotherapy of disorders of adolescents. *Psychiatry in North America, 16,* 793-814.

Griest, D., Wells, K. C., & McMahon, R. J. (1980). An examination of differences between nonclinic and behavior problem clinic referred children and their mothers. *Journal of Abnormal Psychology, 89,* 497-500.

Gross-Tsur, V., Shalev, R. S., Manor, O., & Amir, N. (1995). Developmental right hemisphere syndrome: Clinical spectrum of the nonverbal learning disability. *Journal of Learning Disabilities, 28,* 80-86.

Hacker, A. (1992). Two nations: Black & white, separate, hostile, unequal. New York: Scribner.

Hancock, L. N. (1996, March 18). Mother's little helper. *Newsweek,* pp. 51-56.

Handen, B. L. (1998). Mental retardation. In E. J. Mash & L. G. Terdal (Eds.), *Treatment of childhood disorders.* New York: Guilford.

Harnadek, M. C. S., & Rourke, B. P. (1994). Principal identifying features of the syndrome of nonverbal learning disabilities in children. *Journal of Learning Disabilities, 27,* 144-153.

Harris, S. L. (1983). Families of the developmentally disabled: A guide to behavioral intervention. New York: Pergamon.

Henderson, K. (2001, March). *An overview of ADA, IDEA and Section 504: Update 2001.* The Eric Clearinghouse on Disabilities and Gifted Education. Retrieved March 21, 2002, from http://www.ldonline.org/ld_indepth/legal_legislative/update_504_2001.html

Henggeler, S. W., Schoenwald, S. K., Borduin, C. M., Rowland, M. D., & Cunningham, R. B. (1998). *Multisystemic treatment of antisocial behavior in children and adolescents.* New York: Guilford.

Herzog, D. B., Keller, M. B., Sacks, N. R., Yeh, C. J., & Lavori, P. W. (1992). Psychiatric comorbidity in treatment-seeking anorexics and bulimics. *Journal of the American Academy of Child and Adolescent Psychiatry, 31,* 810-818.

Hinshaw, S. P., & Erhardt, D. (1991). Attention-deficit hyperactivity disorder. In P. Kendall (Ed.), *Child and adolescent therapy: Cognitive-behavioral procedures* (pp. 98-128). New York: Guilford.

Hocutt, A. M. (1996). Effectiveness of special education: Is placement the critical factor? *The Future of Children, 6,* 77-102.

Holland, R., Moretti, M. M., Verlaan, V., & Peterson, S. (1993). Attachment and conduct disorder: The response program. *Canadian Journal of Psychiatry, 38,* 420-431.

Hops, H. (1992). Parental depression and child behavior problems: Implications for behavioral family intervention. *Behavior Change, 9,* 126-138.

Horner, R. H., & Day, H. M. (1991). The effects of response efficiency on functionally equivalent competing behaviors. *Journal of Applied Behavior Analysis, 24,* 719-732.

Huang, L. N., & Ying, Y. W. (2001). Chinese American children and adolescents. In J. T. Gibbs, N. L. Huang, et al. (Eds.), *Children of color.* San Francisco: Jossey-Bass.

Humphrey, L. L. (1989). Observed family interactions among subtypes of eating disorders using structural analysis of social behavior. *Journal of Consulting and Clinical Psychology, 57,* 206-214.

IDEA practices. (1999). Retrieved March 20, 2002, from www.ideapractices.org

Jacobs, J. (1971). *Adolescent suicide.* New York: John Wiley.

Jensen, M. (1988). An unexpected effect: Restitution maintains object throwing. *Education and Treatment of Children, 2,* 252-256.

Jimerson, D. C., Herzog, D. B., & Brotman, A. W. (1993). Pharmacologic approaches in the treatment of eating disorders. *Harvard Review of Psychiatry, 1,* 82-93.

Joyce, R. R. (1983). Age of onset in bipolar affective disorder and misdiagnosis as schizophrenia. *Psychology of Medicine, 14,* 145-149.

Kagan, J., & Snidman, N. (1991). Temperamental factors in human development. *American Psychologist, 46,* 856-862.

Kane, M., & Kendall, P. C. (1989). Anxiety disorders in children: A multiple baseline evaluation of a cognitive-behavioral treatment. *Behavior Therapy, 20,* 499-508.

Kaslow, N. J., & Thompson, M. P. (1998). Applying the criteria for empirically supported treatments to studies of psychosocial interventions for child and adolescent depression. *Journal of Clinical Child Psychology, 27,* 146-155.

Kaufman, A. S., & Lichtenberger, E. O. (2000). *Essentials of WISC-III and WPPSI-R assessment.* New York: John Wiley.

Kavale, K., Forness, S., & MacMillan, D. L. (1998). The politics of learning disabilities: A rejoinder. *Learning Disability Quarterly, 21,* 306-317.

Kazdin, A. E. (1994). *Behavior modification in applied settings* (5th ed.). Pacific Grove, CA: Brooks/Cole.

Kazdin, A. E. (1996). Problem solving and parent management in treating aggressive and antisocial behavior. In E. S. Hibbs & P. S. Jensen (Eds.), *Psychosocial treatments for child and adolescent disorders: Empirically based strategies for clinical practice* (pp. 377-408). Washington, DC: American Psychological Association.

Kazdin, A. E., & Weisz, J. R. (1998). Identifying and developing empirically supported child and adolescent treatments. *Journal of Consulting Clinical Psychologist, 66,* 19-36.

Kazdin, A. E., Esveldt-Dawson, K., French, N. H., & Unis, A. S. (1987). Problem-solving skills training and relationship therapy in treatment of antisocial child behavior. *Journal of Consulting and Clinical Psychology, 55,* 76-85.

Kazdin, A. E., Rodgers, A., & Colbus, D. (1986). The Hopelessness Scale for Children: Psychometric characteristics and concurrent validity. *Journal of Consulting and Clinical Psychology, 54,* 241-245.

Kazdin, A. E., Siegel, T. C., & Bass, D. (1992). Cognitive problem-solving skills training and parent management training in the treatment of antisocial behavior in children. *Journal of Consulting and Clinical Psychology, 60*, 733-747.

Kehle, T., Hintze, J. M., & DuPaul, G. J. (1997). Selective mutism. In G. Bear, K. Minke, & A. Thomas (Eds.), *Children's needs II. Development, problems and alternatives* (pp. 329-386). Bethesda, MD: NASP.

Keller, M. B., Ryan, N. D., & Strober, M. (2001). Efficacy of paroxetine in the treatment of adolescent major depression: A randomized, controlled trial. *Journal of the American Academy of Child and Adolescent Psychiatry, 40*, 762-772

Kendall, P. C. (1988). *Stop and think workbook* (2nd ed.). Ardmore, PA: Workbook.

Kendall, P. C. (1994). Treating anxiety disorders in children: Results of a randomized clinical trial. *Journal of Consulting and Clinical Psychology, 64*, 724-730.

Kendall, P. C., & Treadwell, K. R. H. (1996). Cognitive behavioral treatment for childhood anxiety disorders. In E. D. Hibbs & P. S. Jensen (Eds.), *Psychosocial treatments for child and adolescent disorders: Empirically-based strategies for clinical practice*. Washington, DC: American Psychological Association.

Kendall, P. C., Chansky, T. E., Kane, M. T., Kim, R. S., Kortlander, E., Ronan, K. R., Sessa, F. M., & Siqueland, L. (1992). *Anxiety disorders in youth: Cognitive-behavioral interventions*. Needham Heights, MA: Allyn & Bacon.

Kershaw, P., & Sonuga-Barke, E. (1998). Emotional and behavioral difficulties: Is this a useful category? The implications of clustering and comorbidity, the relevance of a taxonomic approach. *Educational and Child Psychology, 15*, 45-55.

King, R. A., Leonard, H., & March, J. (1998). Practice parameters for the assessment and treatment of children and adolescents with obsessive-compulsive disorder. *Journal of the American Academy of Child and Adolescent Psychiatry, 37*, 27-45.

Klin, A., Sparrow, S. S., Marans, W. D., et al. (2001). Assessment issues in children and adolescents with Asperger syndrome. In A. Klin, F. R. Volkman, & S. S. Sparrow (Eds.), *Asperger syndrome*. New York: Guilford.

Klin, A., Sparrow, S. S., Volkmar, F. R., Cicchetti, D. V., & Rourke, B. P. (1995). Asperger syndrome. In B. P. Rourke (Ed.), *Syndrome of nonverbal learning disabilities: Neurodevelopmental manifestations*. New York: Guilford.

Koegel, R. L., Schreibman, L., Britten, K., Burke, J., & O'Neill, R. (1982). A comparison of parent training to direct child treatment. In R. L. Koegel, A. Rincover, & A. L. Ege (Eds.), *Educating and understanding autistic children* (pp. 260-279). San Diego, CA: College-Hill Press.

Koehler-Troy, C., Strober, M., & Malenbaum, R. (1986). Methylphenidate-induced mania in a prepubertal child. *Journal of Clinical Psychiatry, 47*, 278-279.

Kovacs, M. (1992). *Children's Depression Inventory manual*. Toronto: Multi-Health Systems.

Kovacs, M., & Devlin, B. (1998). Internalizing disorders in childhood. *Journal of Child Psychology and Psychiatry and Allied Disciplines, 39*, 47-63.

Kovacs, M., Devlin, B., Pollock, M., Richards, C., & Mukerji, P. (1997). A controlled family history study of childhood-onset depressive disorder. *Archives of General Psychiatry, 54*, 613-632.

Kovacs, M., Obrosky, D. S., Gastonis, C., & Richards, C. (1997). First-episode major depressive and dysthymic disorder in childhood: Clinical and sociodemographic factors in recovery. *Journal of the American Academy of Child and Adolescent Psychiatry, 36,* 777-784.

Kratochwill, T. R., Elliott, S. N., & Rotto, P. C. (1990). Best practices in behavioral consultation. In A. Thomas & J. Grimes (Eds.), *Best practices in school psychology–II* (pp. 147-170). Silver Spring, MD: National Association of School Psychologists.

Kronenberger, W. G., & Meyer, R. G. (2001). *The child clinician's handbook* (2nd ed.). Boston: Allyn & Bacon.

Kutcher, S. (1993). Bipolar disorder in an adolescent cohort. *Paper presented at the Annual Meeting of the American Academy of Child and Adolescent Psychiatry*, San Antonio.

Lalli, J. S., Kates, K., & Casey, S. D. (1999). Response covariation: The relationship between correct academic responding and problem behavior. *Behavior Modification, 23,* 339-357.

Larson, J., & Lochman, J. E. (2002). Helping school children cope with anger: A cognitive-behavioral intervention. New York: Guilford.

Last, C. G., Perrin, S., Jersen, M., & Kazdin, A. E. (1992). *DSM III-R* anxiety disorders in children: Sociodemographic and clinical characteristics. *Journal of the American Academy of Child and Adolescent Psychiatry, 31,* 1070-1075.

Lazarus, A. A., & Abramowitz, A. (1962). The use of "emotive imagery" in the treatment of children's phobias. *Journal of Mental Science, 108,* 191-195.

LeCroy, C. W. (1994). Social skills training. In C. W. LeCroy (Ed.), *Handbook of child and adolescent treatment manuals.* New York: Lexington Books.

Leitenberg, H., & Callahan, E. J. (1973). Reinforced practice and reduction of different kinds of fears in adults and children. *Behavior Research and Therapy, 11,* 19-30.

Leonard, H. L., Swedo, S. E., & Rappaport, J. L. (1991). Diagnosis and treatment of obsessive compulsive disorder in children and adolescents. In M. T. Pato & J. Zohar (Eds.), *Current treatments of obsessive compulsive disorder* (pp. 87-102). Washington, DC: APA Press.

Leonard, H. L., Swedo, S. E., Lenane, M. C., Rettew, D. C., Hamburger, S. D., & Bartko, J. J. (1993). A 2- to 7-year follow-up study of 54 obsessive-compulsive children and adolescents. *Archives of General Psychiatry, 50,* 429-439.

Lesser-Katz, M. (1988). The treatment of elective mutism as stranger reaction. *Psychotherapy, 25,* 305-313.

Leutwyler, K. (1996). Paying attention: The controversy over ADHD and the drug Ritalin is obscuring a real look at the disorder and its underpinnings. *Scientific American, 272*(2), 12-13.

Lewandowski, L. M., Gebing, T. A., Anthony, J. L., & O'Brien, W. H. (1997). Meta-analysis of cognitive behavioral treatment studies for bulimia. *Clinical Psychology Review, 17,* 703-718.

Lewinsohn, P. M., Clarke, G. N., Hops, H., & Andrews, J. (1990). Cognitive-behavioral treatment for depressed adolescents. *Behavior Therapy, 21,* 385-401.

Lewinsohn, P. M., Clarke, G. N., Rhode, P., Hops, H., & Seeley, J. (1996). A course in coping: A cognitive-behavioral approach to the treatment of adolescent depression. In D. Hibbs & P. S. Jensen (Eds.), *Psychosocial treatments for child and adolescent disorders: Empirically based strategies for clinical practice* (pp. 1109-135). Washington, DC: American Psychiatric Association.

Lewinsohn, P. M., Hops, H., & Roberts, R. E. (1993). Adolescent psychopathology: Prevalence and incidence of depression and other *DSM III-R* disorders in high school students. *Journal of Abnormal Psychology, 102,* 133-144.

Lewinsohn, P. M., Rogdem, P., & Seeley, J. R. (1998). Major depressive disorder in older adolescents. Prevalence, risk factors, and clinical implications. *Clinical Psychology Review, 18,* 765-794.

Lilenfeld, L. R., Kay, W. H., & Greenco, C. G. (1998). A controlled family study of anorexia nervosa and bulimia nervosa: Psychiatric disorders in first-degree relatives and effects of proband comorbidity. *Archives of General Psychiatry, 32,* 1031-1038.

Lipsey, M. W., & Wilson, D. B. (1993). The efficacy of psychological, educational and behavioral treatment: Confirmation from meta-analysis. *American Psychologist, 48,* 1181-1209.

Lish, J. D., Dime-Meenan, S., Whybrow, P., Price, R., & Hirschfeld, R. M. (1994). The National Depressive and Manic-Depressive Association (DMDA) survey of bipolar members. *Journal of Affective Disorders, 31,* 281-294.

Little, L. M., & Kelley, M. L. (1989). The efficacy of response cost procedures for reducing children's noncompliance to parental instructions. *Behavior Therapy, 20,* 525-534.

Lochman, J. E., & Wells, K. C. (1996). A social cognitive intervention with aggressive children: Prevention effects and contextual implementation issues. In R. D. Peters & R. J. McMahon (Eds.), *Preventing childhood disorders, substance abuse and delinquency* (pp. 111-143). Thousand Oaks, CA: Sage.

Lochman, J. E., Burch, P. R., Curry, J. F., & Lampron, L. B. (1984). Treatment and generalization effects of cognitive-behavioral and goal-setting interventions with aggressive boys. *Journal of Consulting and Clinical Psychology, 52,* 915-916.

Lochman, J. E., Lampron, L. B., Gemmer, T. C., & Harris, S. R. (1987). Teacher consultation and cognitive-behavioral intervention with aggressive boys. *Psychology in the Schools, 26,* 915-916.

Lochman, J. E., Lampron, L. B., Gemmer, T. C., & Harris, S. R. (1989). Teacher consultation and cognitive behavioral interventions with aggressive boys. *Psychology in the Schools, 26,* 179-188.

Luthar, S. S. (1993). Annotation: Methodological and conceptual issues in research on childhood resilience. *Journal of Child Psychology and Psychiatry, 34,* 441-453.

Lynch, E. W., & Hanson, M. J. (1998). *Developing cross-cultural competence* (2nd ed.). Baltimore, MD: Brooks.

Lyons-Ruth, K., & Jacobvitz, D. (1999). Attachment disorganization: Unresolved loss, relational violence and lapses in behavioral and attentional strategies. In J. Cassidy & P. R. Shaver (Eds.), *Handbook of attachment: Theory, research, and clinical applications* (pp. 520-554). New York: Guilford.

MacMillan, D. L., & Forness, S. R. (1998). The role of IQ in special education placement decisions: Primary and determinative or peripheral and inconsequential. *Remedial and Special Education, 19,* 239-253.

MacMillan, D. L., & Reschly, D. J. (1998). Over-representation of minority students: The case for greater specificity or reconsideration of the variables examined. *Journal of Special Education, 19,* 239-253.

MacMillan, D. L., Gresham, F. M., & Bocian, K. M. (1998). Current plight of borderline students: Where do they belong? *Education and Training in Mental Retardation and Developmental Disabilities, 33,* 83-95.

MacMillan, R. C. (1998). A longitudinal study of the cost effectiveness of educating students with emotional or behavioral disorders in a public school setting. *Behavioral Disorders, 25,* 65-75.

Mahler, M. S., Pine, F., & Bergman, A. (1975). *The psychological birth of the human infant.* New York: Basic Books.

Main, M. (1990). Cross-cultural studies of attachment organization: Recent studies, changing methodologies, and the concept of conditional strategies. *Human Development, 33,* 48-61.

Main, M., & Hesse, E. (1990). Parents' unresolved traumatic experiences are related to infant disorganized attachment status: Is frightened and/or frightening parental behavior the linking mechanism? In M. T. Greensberg, D. Cicchetti, & E. M. Cummings (Eds.), *Attachment in the preschool years: Theory, research, and intervention* (pp. 161-182). Chicago: University of Chicago Press.

Main, M., & Solomon, J. (1986). Discovery of an insecure-disorganized/disoriented attachment pattern: Procedures, findings and implications for the classification of behavior. In T. B. Brazelton & M. Yogman (Eds.), *Affective development in infancy* (pp. 95-124). Norwood, NJ: Ablex.

Malphurs, J. E., Field, T. M., Larraine, C., Pickens, J., Lelaez-Nogueras, M., Yando, R., & Bendell, D. (1996). Altering withdrawn and intrusive interaction behaviors of depressed mothers. *Infant Mental Health Journal, 17,* 152-160.

March, J. S., & Mulle, K. (1998). *OCD in children and adolescents: A cognitive-behavioral treatment manual.* New York: Guilford.

March, J. S., Mulle, K., & Herbel, B. (1994). Behavioral psychotherapy for children and adolescents with obsessive-compulsive disorder: An open trial of a new protocol-driven treatment package. *Journal of the American Academy of Child and Adolescent Psychiatry, 33,* 333-341.

Marriage, K. J., Gordon, V., & Brand, L. (1995). A social skills group for boys with Asperger's syndrome. *Australian and New Zealand Journal of Psychiatry, 29,* 58-62.

McInerney, M., Kane, M., & Pelavin, S. (1992). *Services to children with serious emotional disturbance.* Washington, DC: Pelavin Associates.

McMahon, R. J., & Slough, N. M. (1996). Family-based intervention in the FAST Track Program. In R. deV. Peters & R. J. McMahon (Eds.), *Preventing childhood disorders, substance abuse, and delinquency.* Thousand Oaks, CA: Sage.

McPhail, C. H., & Chamove, A S. (1989). Relaxation reduces disruption in mentally handicapped adults. *Journal of Mental Deficiency Research, 33,* 399-406.

Mendlowitz, S., Manassis, K., Bradley, S., Scapiliato, D., Miezitis, S., & Shaw, B. F. (1999). Cognitive-behavioral group treatments in childhood anxiety disorders. *Journal of the American Academy of Child and Adolescent Psychiatry, 38,* 1223-1229.

Minuchin, S., Rosman, B. L., & Baker, L. (1978). *Psychosomatic families: Anorexia nervosa in context.* Cambridge, MA: Harvard University Press.

Mitchell, J., McCauley, E., & Burke, P. M. (1988). Phenomenology of depression in children and adolescents. *Journal of the American Academy of Child and Adolescent Psychiatry, 27,* 12-20.

Monroe, S. M., Rohde, P., & Seeley, J. R. (1999). Life events and depression in adolescence: Relationship loss as a prospective risk factor for first onset of major depressive disorder. *Journal of Abnormal Psychology, 108,* 606-614.

Montgomery, D. (1990). *Children with learning difficulties.* New York: Nicholas Publishing.

Mortweet, S. (1997). The academic and social effects of a class-wide peer tutoring for students with educable mental retardation and their typical peers in an inclusive classroom (Doctoral dissertation, University of Kansas, 1997). *Dissertation Abstracts International: Section B: The Sciences & Engineering, 58,* 1515.

Murphy, M. L, & Pichichero, M.E. (2002). Prospective identification and treatment of children with pediatric autoimmune neuropsychiatric disorder associated with Group A streptococcal infection (PANDAS). *Archives of Pediatric and Adolescent Medicine, 156,* 356-361.

Nabasoku, D., & Smith, P. K. (1993). Sociometric status and social behavior of children with and without language difficulties. *Journal of Child Psychology and Psychiatry and Allied Disciplines, 34,* 1435-1448.

National Joint Committee on Learning Disabilities. (1987). Learning disabilities: Issues on definition. *Journal of Learning Disabilities, 20,* 107-108.

Neuman, P. A., & Halvorson, P. A. (1983). *Anorexia nervosa and bulimia: A handbook for counselors and therapists.* New York: Van Nostrand-Reinhold.

Neziroglu, F., Yaryra-Tobias, J., Walz, J., & McKay, D. (2000). The effect of fluvoxamine and behavior therapy on children and adolescents with obsessive-compulsive disorder. *Journal of the American Academy of Child and Adolescent Psychiatry, 10,* 295-306.

Neziroglu, F., Yaryura-Tobias, J. A., Walz, J., & McKay, D. (2000). The effects of fluvoxamine and behavior therapy on children and adolescents with obsessive-compulsive disorder. *Journal of Child & Adolescent Psychopharmacology, 10,* 295-306.

O'Shea, L., & O'Shea, D. (1988). Using Repeated Reading. *Teaching Exceptional Children, 1,* 26-30.

Ollendick, T. H., & King, N. J. (1994). Diagnosis, assessment and treatment of internalizing problems in children: The role of longitudinal data. *Journal of Consulting and Clinical Psychology, 62,* 919-927.

Ollendick, T. H., & King, N. J. (1998). Empirically supported treatments for children with phobic and anxiety disorders: Current status. *Journal of Clinical Child Psychology, 27,* 156-167.

Olmstead, M. P., Kaplan, A. S., & Rockert, W. (1994). Rate and prediction of relapse in bulimia nervosa. *American Journal of Psychiatry, 151,* 738-743

Oswald, D. P., Coutinho, M. J., Best, A. M., & Nguyen, N. (2001). The impact of socio-demographic characteristics on the identification rates of minority students as mentally retarded. *Mental Retardation, 39,* 351-367.

Papolos, D., & Papolos, J. (2000). School: A child's world beyond home: Hypothetical baseline information and draft IEP for a bipolar student. In D. Papolos & J. Papolos, *The bipolar child* (pp. 280-284). New York: Broadway Books.

Pasternack, R. H. (2002, March). *The demise of IQ testing for children with learning disabilities.* Distinguished Lecture presented to National Association of School Psychologists Annual convention, Chicago. Retrieved March 24, 2002, from Louisiana State University Health Sciences Center Web site: http://www.hdc.lsuhsc.edu

Patterson, G. R., & Gullion, M. E. (1968). *Living with children: New methods for parents and teachers.* Champaign, IL: Research Press.

Patterson, G. R., Reid, J. B., & Dishion, T. J. (1992). *Antisocial boys.* Eugene, OR: Castalia.

Patton, J. R., Beirne-Smith, M., & Payne, J. S. (1990). *Mental retardation.* New York: Macmillan.

Pelham, W. E., Jr., Wheeler, T., & Chronis, A. (1998). Empirically supported psychosocial treatments for attention deficit hyperactivity disorder. *Journal of Clinical Child Psychology, 27,* 190-205.

Peterson, A. C., Compas, B., Brooks-Gunn, J., Ey, S., & Grant, K. E. (1993). Depression in adolescence. *American Psychologist, 48*(2), 155-168.

Peterson, B. S., Leckman, J. F., Arnsten, A., Anderson, G. M., Staib, L. H., Gore, J. C., Bronen, R. A., Malison, R., Scahill, L., & Cohen, D. J. (1998). Neuroanatomical circuitry. In J. F. Leckman, D. J. Cohen, et al. (Eds.), *Tourette's syndrome—Tics, obsessions, compulsions: Developmental psychopathology and clinical care.* New York: John Wiley.

Phares, V., Compas, B. E., & Howell, D. C. (1989). Perspectives on child behavior problems: Comparisons of children's self reports with parent and teacher reports. *Psychological Assessment, 1,* 68-71.

Polloway, E. A., Patten, J. R., Smith, J. D., & Roderique, T. W. (1991). Issues in program design for elementary students with mild retardation: Emphasis on curriculum development. *Education and Training in Mental Retardation, 26,* 144-150.

Proctor, M. A., & Morgan, D. (1991). Effectiveness of a response cost raffle procedure on the disruptive classroom behavior of adolescents with behavior problems. *School Psychology Review, 20,* 97-109.

Rapoport, J. L., & Ismond, D. R. (1996). *DSM-IV training guide for diagnosis of childhood disorders.* New York: Brunner/Mazel.

Rapport, M. D., Murphy, H. A., & Bailey, J. S. (1982). Ritalin vs. response cost in the control of hyperactive children: A within-subject comparison. *Journal of Applied Behavior Analysis, 15,* 205-216.

Rathvon, N. (1999). Effective school interventions: Strategies for enhancing academic achievement and social competence. New York: Guilford.

Rebert, W. M., Stanton, A. L., & Schwarz, R. M. (1991). Influence of personality attributes and daily moods on bulimic eating patterns. *Addictive Behaviors, 16*, 497-505.

Rey, J. M. (1993). Oppositional defiant disorder. *American Journal of Psychiatry, 150*, 1769-1777.

Reynolds, C. J., Salend, S. J., & Beahan, C. L. (1989). Motivating secondary school students: Bringing in the reinforcements. *Academic Therapy, 25*, 81-90.

Reynolds, C. J., Salend, S. J., & Beahan, C. L. (1992). Reinforcer preferences of secondary school students with disabilities. *International Journal of Disability, Development and Education, 39*, 77-86.

Reynolds, C. R., & Kamphaus, R. W. (1992). *BASC: Behavior Assessment System for Children manual.* Circle Pines, MN: American Guidance Service.

Richters, K., & Weintraub, S. (1990). Beyond diathesis: Toward an understanding of high-risk environments. In J. Rolf, A. Masten, D. Cicchetti, K. Nuechterlein, & S. Weintraub (Eds.), *Risk and protective factors in the development of psychopathology* (pp. 67-96). New York: Cambridge University Press.

Riddle, M. A., Scahill, L., King, R. A., Hardin, M. T., Anderson, G. M., & Ort, S. I. (1992). Double-blind, crossover trial of fluoxetine and placebo in children and adolescents with obsessive-compulsive disorder. *Journal of the American Academy of Child and Adolescent Psychiatry, 31*, 1062-1069.

Riddle, M. A., Subramaniam, G., & Walkup, J. T. (1998). Efficacy of psychiatric medications in children and adolescents: A review of controlled studies. *Psychiatric Clinics of North America: Annual of Drug Therapy, 5*, 269-285.

Robison, L. M., Sclar, D. A., Skaer, T. L., & Galin, R. S. (1999). National trends in the prevalence of attention-deficit/hyperactivity disorder and the prescribing of methylphenidate among school children: 1990-1995. *Clinical Pediatrics, 38*(4), 209-217.

Rodin, J., Striegel-Moore, R. H., & Silberstein, L. R. (1990). Vulnerability and resilience in the age of eating disorders. Risk and protective factors for bulimia nervosa. In J. Rolf, A. S. Masten, D. Cicchetti, K. H. Nuechterlein, & S. Weintraub (Eds.), *Risk and protective factors in the development of psychopathology* (pp. 361-383). Cambridge, MA: Cambridge University Press.

Rogers, S. J. (1998). Empirically supported comprehensive treatments for young children with autism. *Journal of Clinical Child Psychology, 27*, 168-179.

Rohde, P., Lewinsohn, P. M., & Seeley, J. R. (1991). Comorbidity of unipolar depression: II. Comorbidity with other mental disorders in adolescents and adults. *Journal of Abnormal Psychology, 100*, 214-222.

Rohde, P., Lewinsohn, P. M., & Seeley, J. R. (1994). Are adolescents changed by an episode of major depression? *Journal of the American Academy of Child and Adolescent Psychiatry, 33*, 1289-1298.

Rosenbaum, J., & Kienke, A. (2001, May). Program and abstracts of the 154th Annual Meeting of the American Psychiatric Association, New Orleans.

Rosenblatt, J. A., & Furlong, M. J. (1998). Outcomes in a system of care for youth with emotional and behavioral disorders: An examination of differential change across clinical profile. *Journal of Child and Family Studies, 7*, 1217-1232.

Rourke, B. P. (1989). *Nonverbal learning disabilities: The syndrome and the model.* New York: Guilford.

Rourke, B. P. (1993). Arithmetic disabilities, specified and otherwise: A neuropsychological perspective. *Journal of Learning Disabilities, 26,* 214-226.

Rourke, B. P. (1995). Treatment program for the child with NLD. In B. P. Rourke (Ed.), *Syndrome of nonverbal learning disabilities: Neurodevelopmental manifestations.* New York: Guilford.

Rourke, B. P., Young, G. C., & Leenaars, A. A. (1989). A childhood learning disability that predisposes those afflicted to adolescent and adult depression and suicide risk. *Journal of Learning Disabilities, 22,* 169-175.

Rourke, B. P., Young, G. P., Strang, J. D., & Russell, D. L. (1986). Adult outcomes of childhood central processing deficiencies. In I. Grant & K. M. Adams (Eds.), *Neuropsychological assessment of neuropsychiatric disorders* (pp. 244-267). New York: Oxford University Press.

Rutherford, R. B., Jr., & Nelson, C. M. (1988). Generalization of treatment effects. In J. C. Witt, S. N. Elliott, & F. M. Gresham (Eds.), *Handbook of behavior therapy in education.* New York: Plenum.

Rutter, M. (1987). Psychosocial resilience and protective mechanisms. *American Journal of Orthopsychiatry, 57,* 316-330.

Rutter, M. (1990). Psychosocial resilience and protective mechanisms. In J. Rolf, A. Masten, D. Cicchetti, K. Nuechterlein, & S. Weintraub (Eds.), *Risk and protective factors in the development of psychopathology* (pp. 181-214). New York: Cambridge University Press.

Ryan, N. D., Puig-Antich, J., & Ambrosini, P. (1987). The clinical picture of major depression in children and adolescents. *Archives of General Psychiatry, 44,* 854-861.

Sabine, W. (2001). Obsessive compulsive disorder. In W. Lyddon & J. V. Jones, Jr. (Eds.), *Empirically supported cognitive therapies: Current and future applications* (pp. 118-133). New York: Springer.

Sackeim, H. A., & Decina, P. (1983). Lateralized neuropsychological abnormalities in children of bipolar probands. In P. Flor-Henry & J. Gruzelier (Eds.), *Laterality and psychopathology.* New York: Elsevier Science.

Sattler, J. (2002). *Assessment of children: Behavioral and clinical applications* (4th ed.). San Diego, CA: Jerome M. Sattler.

Schreier, H. (2001). Socially awkward children: Neurocognitive contributions. *Psychiatric Times, 17*(9). Retrieved March 30, 2003, from http://www.mhsource.com/pt/srchild.html

Shaffer, D., & Craft, L. (1999). Methods of adolescent suicide prevention. *Journal of Clinical Psychiatry, 60,* 70-74.

Shaffer, D., Garland, A., & Bacon, K. (1989). Prevention issues in youth suicide. In D. Shaffer, I. Philips, & N. Enzer (Eds.), Prevention of mental disorders, alcohol and drug abuse in children and adolescents (*OSAP Prevention Monograph, 2,* pp. 373-412). Rockville, MD: Alcohol, Drug Abuse and Mental Health Administration.

Shaffer, D., Garland, A., Vieland, V., Underwood, M., & Busner, C. (1991). The impact of curriculum-based suicide prevention programs for teenagers. *Journal of the American Academy of Child and Adolescent Psychiatry, 30,* 588-596.

Shaffer, D., Gould, M. S., Fisher, P., Trautment, P., Moreau, D., Kleinman, M., & Flory, M. (1996). Psychiatric diagnosis in child and adolescent suicide. *Archives of General Psychiatry, 53,* 339-348.

Shaw, S. F., Cullen, J. P., McGuire, J. M., & Brinckerhoff, L. C. (1995). Operationalizing a definition of learning disabilities. *Journal of Learning Disabilities, 26,* 586-597.

Sluckin, A., Foreman, N., & Herbert, M. (1991). Behavioral treatment programs and selectivity of speaking at follow-up in a sample of 25 selective mutes. *Psychologist, 26,* 132-137.

Smith Myles, B., Jones Bock, S., & Simpson, R. L. *Asperger Syndrome Diagnostic Scale (ASDS): Examiner's manual.* Austin, TX: Pro-ed.

Solantaus-Simula, T. (2002). Children's responses to low parental mood: Balancing between active empathy, overinvolvement, indifference, and avoidance. *Journal of American Academy of Child and Adolescent Psychiatry, 41,* 278-286.

Solnick, J. V., Rincover, A., & Peterson, C. R. (1977). Some determinants of the reinforcing and punishing effects of timeout. *Journal of Applied Behavior Analysis, 10,* 415-424.

Spaccarelli, S., Cotler, S., & Penman, D. (1992). Problem-solving skills training as a supplement to behavioral parent training. *Cognitive Therapy and Research, 16,* 1-18.

Spangler, G., & Grossmann, K. (1999). Individual and physiological correlates of attachment disorganization in infancy. In J. Solomon & C. George (Eds.), *Attachment disorganization* (pp. 95-126). New York: Guilford.

Spencer, T., Wilens, T., Biderman, J., Faraone, S. V., Ablon, J. S., & Lapey, K. (1995). A double-blind, crossover comparison of methylphenidate and placebo in adults with childhood-onset attention deficit hyperactivity disorder. *Archives of General Psychiatry, 52,* 434-443.

Stark, K. D., Reynolds, W. M., & Kaslow, N. J. (1987). A comparison of the relative efficacy of self-control therapy and a behavioral problem-solving therapy for depression in children. *Journal of Abnormal Child Psychology, 15,* 91-113.

Stark, K. D., Rouse, L., & Livingston, R. (1991). Treatment of depression during childhood and adolescence: Cognitive-behavioral procedures for the individual and family. In P. Kendall (Ed.), *Child and adolescent therapy* (pp. 165-206). New York: Guilford.

Steinhauer, P. D. (1996). The diagnosis, prevention and management of attachment disorders in children. *P.R.I.S.M.E., 6,* 604-617. (Original in French)

Steinhauer, P. D. (1998). *Separation and attachment—Treatment issues.* Paper presented to The Children's Aid Society of the County of Perth, Stratford, Ontario.

Stokes, T. F., & Baer, D. M. (1977). An implicit technology of generalization. *Journal of Applied Behavior Analysis, 10,* 349-368.

Strang, J. D., & Casey, J. E. (1994). The psychological impact of learning disabilities: A developmental neurological perspective. In L. F. Koziol & E. E. Scott (Eds.), *The neuropsychology of mental disorders: A practical guide* (pp 171-186). Springfield, IL: Charles C Thomas.

Strober, M. (1992). Bipolar disorders: Natural history, genetic studies and follow-up. In M. Shafii & S. L. Shafii (Eds.), *Clinical guide to depression in children and adolescents* (pp. 251-268). Washington, DC: American Psychiatric Press.

Strober, M., Lampert, C., & Burrough, J. (1990). Relapse following discontinuation of lithium maintenance therapy in adolescents with bipolar I illness: A naturalistic study. *American Journal of Psychiatry, 147,* 457-461.

Szatmari, P. (1991). Asperger's syndrome: Diagnosis, treatment and outcome. *Journal of the Psychiatric Clinics of North America, 14,* 81-93.

Taylor, A. (1986, April). *Loneliness, goal orientation and sociometric status: Mildly retarded children's adaptation to the mainstream classroom.* Paper presented at the annual meeting of the American Educational Research Association, San Francisco.

The MTA Cooperative Group. (1999) A 14-month randomized clinical trial of treatment strategies for attention-deficit/hyperactivity disorder. The MTA Cooperative Group. Multimodal Treatment Study of children with ADHD. *Archives of General Psychiatry, 11,* 1073-1086.

Thieneman, M., Martin, J., Creggar, B., Thompson, H., & Dyer-Friedman, J. (2001). Manual-driven group cognitive-behavioral therapy for adolescents with obsessive-compulsive disorder: A pilot study. *Journal of the American Academy of Child & Adolescent Psychiatry, 40,* 1254-1260.

Thompson, S. (1997). Nonverbal learning disorders revisited in 1997. Retrieved September 17, 2002, from http://www.nldline.com/nld.htm

Tueth, M. J., Murphy, T. K., & Evans, D. L. (1998). Special considerations: Use of lithium in children, adolescents and elderly populations. *Journal of Clinical Psychiatry, 59,* 66-73.

Turton, M. D., O'Shea, D., Gunn, I., Beak, S. A., et al. (1996, January 4). A role for glucagon-like peptide-1 in the central regulation of feeding. *Nature, 379,* 69-72.

U.S. Bureau of the Census. (1996). *Statistical abstract of the United States, 1996* (116th ed.). Washington, DC: U.S. Department of Commerce.

Valleni-Basile, L. A., Garrison, C. Z., Jackson, K. L., Waller, J. L., McKeown, R. E., & Addy, C. L. (1994). Frequency of obsessive-compulsive disorder in a community sample of young adolescents. *Journal of the American Academy of Child and Adolescent Psychiatry, 33,* 782-791.

Volkmar, F. R., Cohen, D. J., & Hoshino, Y. (1988). Phenomenology and classification of the childhood psychoses. *Psychological Medicine, 18,* 191-201.

Walrath, C., Nickerson, K., Crowel, R., & Leaf, P. (1998). Serving children with serious emotional disturbance in a system of care. Do mental health and non–mental health agency referrals look the same? *Journal of Emotional and Behavioral Disorders, 6,* 205-213.

Walters, E. E., & Kendler, K. S. (1995). Anorexia nervosa and anorexia-like syndromes in a population based female twin sample. *American Journal of Psychiatry, 152,* 64-71.

Waters, T., Barrett, P. M., & March, J. S. (2001). Cognitive-behavioral family treatment of childhood obsessive-compulsive disorder: Preliminary findings. *American Journal of Psychotherapy, 55,* 372-387.

Webster-Stratton, C. (1984). Randomized trial of two parent-training programs for families with conduct-disordered children. *Journal of Consulting and Clinical Psychology, 52,* 666-678.

Webster-Stratton, C. (1994). Advancing videotape parent training: A comparison study. *Journal of Consulting and Clinical Psychology, 62,* 583-593.

Weist, M. D., Ollendick, T. H., & Finney, J. W. (1991). Toward the empirical validation of treatment targets in children. *Clinical Psychology Review, 2,* 515-538.

Weller, E. (2000, May). *Bipolar children and adolescents: Controversies in diagnosis and treatment.* Paper presented to the American Psychiatric Association 153rd Annual Meeting, Chicago.

Weller, E. B., Weller, R. A., & Fristad, M. A. (1995). Bipolar diagnosis in children: Misdiagnosis, underdiagnosis and future directions. *Journal of the American Academy of Child and Adolescent Psychiatry, 34,* 709-714.

Wells, V. E., Deykin, E. Y., & Kierman, G. L. (1985). Risk factors for depression in adolescence. *Psychiatric Development, 3,* 83-108.

Werner, E. E., & Smith, R. S. (1992). *Overcoming the odds: High risk children from birth to adulthood.* Ithaca, NY: Cornell University Press.

Werry, J. S., & Wollersheim, J. P. (1991). Behavior therapy with children and adolescents: A twenty year overview. In S. Chess & M. E. Hertzig (Eds.), *Annual progress in child psychiatry and child development, 1990* (pp. 413-447). New York: Brunner/Mazel.

Wielkiewicz, R. M. (1995). *Behavior management in the schools* (2nd ed.). Boston: Allyn & Bacon.

Wilens, T. E. (2001). ADHD and alcohol or drug abuse. Program and abstracts of the 154th annual meeting of the American Psychiatric Association, New Orleans.

Williams, K. (1995). Understanding the student with Asperger syndrome: Guidelines for teachers. *Focus on Autistic Behavior, 10,* 9-16.

Wilmshurst, L. (2002). Treatment programs for youth with emotional and behavioral disorders: An outcome study of two alternate approaches. *Mental Health Services Research, 4*(2), 85-96.

Wolpe, J. (1958). *Psychotherapy by reciprocal inhibition.* Stanford, CA: Stanford University Press.

Wolraich, M. L., Hannah, I. N., Pinnock, T. Y., Baumgaerrel A., Brown, J. (1996). Comparison of diagnostic criteria for attention-deficit hyperactivity disorder in a county-wide sample. *Journal of American Academy of Child and Adolescent Psychiatry, 35,* 319-324.

World Health Organization. (1992). *International classification of diseases and related health problems* (10th ed.). Geneva, Switzerland: Author.

Ysseldyke, J. E., Thurlow, M. L., Christenson, S. L., & Muyskens, P. (1991). Classroom and home learning differences between students labeled as educable mentally retarded and their peers. *Education and Training in Mental Retardation, 26,* 3-17.

Index